# HOPE &
# SOLIDARITY

# HOPE & SOLIDARITY

*Jon Sobrino's Challenge
to Christian Theology*

*Edited by*
Stephen J. Pope

ORBIS BOOKS
Maryknoll, New York

Founded in 1970, Orbis Books endeavors to publish works that enlighten the mind, nourish the spirit, and challenge the conscience. The publishing arm of the Mary-knoll Fathers and Brothers, Orbis seeks to explore the global dimensions of the Christian faith and mission, to invite dialogue with diverse cultures and religious traditions, and to serve the cause of reconciliation and peace. The books published reflect the views of their authors and do not represent the official position of the Maryknoll Society. To learn more about Maryknoll and Orbis Books, please visit our website at www.maryknoll.org.

Copyright © 2008 by Stephen J. Pope.

Published by Orbis Books, Maryknoll, NY 10545-0308.

All rights reserved.

No part of this publication may be reproduced or transmitted in any form or by any means, electronic or mechanical, including photocopying, recording, or any information storage or retrieval system, without prior permission in writing from the publisher.

Queries regarding rights and permissions should be addressed to: Orbis Books, P.O. Box 308, Maryknoll, NY 10545-0308.

Manufactured in the United States of America.

*Library of Congress Cataloging-in-Publication Data*

Hope and solidarity : Jon Sobrino's challenge to Christian theology /
    edited by Stephen J. Pope.
        p. cm.
    Includes index.
    ISBN-13: 978-1-57075-765-5
    1. Sobrino, Jon. 2. Jesus Christ—Person and offices. 3. Liberation
theology. I. Pope, Stephen J., 1955-
    BT203.H66 2008
    230'.2092—dc22
                                                    2008000232

*To the memory of Pedro Arrupe, S.J.,*
*and to the work of those who continue*
*to be inspired by his vision of the church*
*as a community of men and women for others.*

# Contents

# Preface

STEPHEN J. POPE

This book originates where two episodes intersect. The first involves the notorious massacre of six Jesuits, their housekeeper, and her daughter at the University of Central America by members of the Salvadoran military on the night of November 16, 1989.[1] Jon Sobrino is the surviving member of this Jesuit community, and he would not have been spared had he not been engaged in pastoral duties in Asia at the time. After having moved from his native Spain to serve the people of El Salvador, Sobrino's direct engagement with the poor led him to undergo a powerful commitment to human rights and solidarity. All of his subsequent theological reflection is moved by the conviction that genuine Christian faith involves following Jesus of Nazareth in his bringing "good news" to the poor, the marginalized, and the oppressed.

The second episode, on November 26, 2006, ten days and seventeen years after the assassinations in San Salvador, was the release by the prefect of the Vatican Congregation for the Doctrine of the Faith, Cardinal William Levada, of a "Notification on the Works of Father Jon Sobrino, S.J."[2] The Notification mentions two of Sobrino's books by name: *Jesucristo liberador: Lectura histórico-teológica de Jesús de Nazareth* (Madrid: Trotta, 1991) and *La fe en Jesucristo: Ensayo desde las víctimas* (Madrid: Trotta, 1999).[3] The focal point lies at the center of Christian faith, the identity of Jesus Christ.

The Notification raises issues that are substantive as well as methodological, especially regarding the relevance of Christology to the struggle for social justice. It praises Sobrino's "preoccupation" with the poor and oppressed as "admirable," but it worries that he gives too much authority to the "church of the poor" and not enough respect to the apostolic faith transmitted through the Catholic tradition. The Notification is also concerned that Sobrino's use of Scripture tends to downplay the divinity of Jesus, that his language suggests the presence of two subjects in Christ (the Son and Jesus) rather than one, that he draws too sharp a distinction between Jesus and the kingdom of God, that "by depicting Jesus as a believer like ourselves," he compromises the "filial and messianic consciousness of Jesus," and that Sobrino says that Jesus was not conscious of his own death as bearing salvific significance.

The Notification in fact functions in a fruitful way to raise significant questions that the authors of this collection undertake to address in focused ways. This volume was produced in the attempt to take seriously both the concerns of the Congregation for the Doctrine of the Faith and the theological insight offered by Sobrino to the church. It strives to examine selected issues in Sobrino's writings with an eye on some of the Notification's concerns but with a stronger focus on the significance of Sobrino's theology for the life of the church in the twenty-first century. The life of the church includes its identity as people of God, communion, and sacrament, and its mission to serve as a beacon of faith, peace, and justice in the world. The chapters of this volume thus begin with an examination of the principles underlying Sobrino's approach to the discipline of theology, then examine major themes in Christology and ecclesiology; the book concludes with a discussion of topics pertaining to moral theology.

The authors of the chapters of this book were chosen because of their scholarly competence, theological depth, and clarity of writing style. The volume includes contributions from writers from Latin America as well as North America, from moral theologians as well as systematic theologians (and one biblical scholar), and from members of the laity as well as Jesuits (and one Franciscan). To describe the authors of a book on liberation theology as "centrists" might be taken as either insulting or disingenuous, depending on one's political perspective, but all of the contributors to this volume are known to write in balanced, fair, and responsible ways and to understand the centrality of social justice for Christian faith. In accord with the commitment of the authors of this volume, and with Sobrino, the proceeds from this volume will be donated to a scholarship fund for students from El Ocotillo, a rural village in the province of Morazan, in the eastern highlands of El Salvador.

All of the chapters of this book are published for the first time in this volume, with the exception of William Loewe's expanded version of an article that appeared in *Commonweal* magazine. Special gratitude for finding merit in this project goes to Robert Ellsberg, the publisher of Orbis Books. Special thanks for the financial support are due to the office of Dr. Kevin Bedell, vice provost for research of Boston College, and to Kevin Burke, S.J., the academic dean of the Jesuit School of Theology at Berkeley in California.

The authors dedicate this volume to the memory of the late father general of the Society of Jesus, Pedro Arrupe, S.J. Arrupe was an inspiration to Sobrino and many of his fellow Jesuits throughout the world; his work, moreover, has also had a lasting impression on many lay Catholics, Christian activists, and people of other faith traditions who encountered Arrupe. From the Basque country in Spain to Hiroshima to Rome, he communicated a powerful commitment to justice and peace based on a deep Catholic and Ignatian spirituality. He shared a vision of the church as a community in which intensity of faith, piety, and religious devotion would be matched by dedication to people who struggle to survive amidst incredible hardship and immense misery. Arrupe saw himself as blessed to be given a vocation to the priesthood and to the Society of Jesus, but he also experienced suffering at the hands of the church to which he dedicated his life. His commitment to justice and social concern would not have become a lasting legacy were it not for his personal exemplification of the virtues of courageous perseverance, prayerful faith, and patient love of the church. These are traits that we all need to cultivate if we are to help play even a small role in building the kind of church envisioned by Arrupe: a faith community inspiring "men and women for others."

## Notes

1. See Martha Doggett, *Death Foretold: The Jesuit Murders in El Salvador* (Washington, D.C.: Georgetown University Press, 1993).

2. The text of the Notification can be found below on pages 255-66. Also available at http://www.vatican.va/roman_curia/congregations/cfaith/documents/rc_con_cfaith_doc_20061126_notification-sobrino_en.html.

3. These books have been translated into English, respectively, as *Jesus the Liberator: A Historical-Theological Reading of Jesus of Nazareth*, trans. Paul Burns and Francis McDonagh (Maryknoll, N.Y.: Orbis Books, 1993), and *Christ the Liberator: A View from the Victims*, trans. Paul Burns (Maryknoll, N.Y.: Orbis Books, 2001).

# PART I

*Theology*

# 1

# Theology and Solidarity

*Learning from Sobrino's Method*

DEAN BRACKLEY, S.J.

From the beginning, liberation theology emphasized that theological reflection presupposes a practical commitment that locates the theologian in the world of the victims of injustice. While liberation theologians have never claimed to have a monopoly on truth or an automatic advantage over other forms of theology, they have claimed that this commitment and location afford a privileged perspective for understanding both the truths of the faith and reality in the light of faith. Jon Sobrino has developed this thesis in especially rich ways. Before examining how he understands the role that solidarity plays in theology, let me first offer some preliminary reflections.

## A Matter of Perspective

Today, it is rarely necessary to emphasize that everyone's understanding, and therefore everyone's discourse, reflects a limited perspective depending, in part, on location. Particular perspectives involve both benefits and costs. While one perspective may reveal aspects of reality unavailable from other angles, complementary perspectives can and should enrich particular, limited perspectives.

When narrow perspectives widen, we have high drama. The Scriptures provide good examples. In Mark 7:24-30 and parallels, Jesus himself is challenged to broaden his horizon. The faith of the Syrophoenician woman apparently surprises him. He refers to pagans like her as "dogs," and, although it is impossible at this distance to gauge the force of this remark, it clearly reflects the prejudice of his Jewish contemporaries who supposed faith to be scarce among Gentiles and who assumed the world beyond Israel to be one of religious darkness and moral perversion.

While Jesus was socialized into a particular culture like every other human being, he shows himself capable of overcoming the local prejudices this entailed. The most striking thing about this story is the way he lets this Gentile woman help him do that. If Jesus' worldview was necessarily limited, if he needed to learn from other perspectives, how much more do we need this, we who cling, even culpably, to our interested view of things!

The limitations of location are evident in contemporary theology. When John Paul II composed his 1991 encyclical *Centesimus annus,* his chief points of reference were Pope Leo XIII's *Rerum novarum,* and the then-recent collapse of communist regimes in Eastern Europe. This perspective was understandable and in many ways appropriate for reflecting on the previous hundred years of Catholic social teaching and the moral drama of modern industrial societies. Within this framework, the pope rehearsed the errors of the socialist order that was crumbling at the time and the ideology behind it. He pointed out how many of the evils of the market economy have attenuated, at least in North Atlantic countries. He went on to affirm the virtues of the market economy, the legitimacy of the business enterprise and of profit; at the same time, he warned against turning any of these into an absolute. These warnings were accompanied by the following observation, which appears halfway through the encyclical:

> The fact is that many people, perhaps the majority today, do not have the means which would enable them to take their place in an effective and humanly dignified way within a productive system in which work is truly central. . . . [T]hese people crowd the cities of the Third World where they are often without cultural roots, and where they are exposed to situations of violent uncertainty, without the possibility of becoming integrated. . . .
>
> Many other people, while not completely marginalized, live in situations in which the struggle for a bare minimum is uppermost. These are situations in which the rules of the earliest period of capitalism still flourish in conditions of "ruthlessness" in no way inferior to the darkest moments of the first phase of industrialization. In other cases the land is still the central element in the economic process, but those who cultivate it are excluded from ownership and are reduced to a state of quasi-servitude.
>
> Unfortunately, the great majority of people in the Third World still live in such conditions. (*Centesimus annus* 33)

The great majority of people in the Third World live in inhuman conditions within the present system, and this means, perhaps, the majority of humanity.

When we read this in Central America, we can't help but wonder: If the majority of people lives in subhuman conditions, marginalized from productive economic life, why not begin the encyclical with them? How would the encyclical have developed had it begun with what is now paragraph 33 and went on from there to evaluate the mechanisms of the world economy in light of this majority reality? Perhaps this would have led to a clearer recognition that the prosperity that accompanies the reformed capitalism of the affluent North actually requires the "ruthless" capitalism that reigns in the impoverished South. That might in turn have led to a more critical appraisal of the real existing market economy, such as we find in some other encyclicals.

It's a matter of perspective. For liberation theology, trampled human dignity is the place from which to understand better both the human condition and the word of God. Certainly the pope expresses concern for trampled human dignity throughout the encyclical. When read in Latin America, however, it becomes evident that the European perspective is not universal. It needs a corrective complement.

## Entering the World of the Poor

Liberation theologians have this in common with neoconservatives: they have been mugged by reality—not by corporate culture and realpolitik, however, but by the reality of the victims. That has made all the difference. From the perspective of the poor, the world looks different; and, from that perspective, when one reads the Bible or studies doctrinal formulations, one sees things one would not otherwise see.

More than a matter of conceptual change, this perspective involves a practical change that transforms the person and opens her horizons. What do I mean? Most theologians in Latin America are of middle-class origin. While theological reflection surely goes on in poor communities, few professional theologians come from there. They have had access to the kind of education that is denied to the poor, and they have resources to think and teach and write which are unavailable to the poor. When they speak of commitment to the poor as necessary for sound theological reflection in an unjust world, they are usually bearing witness to a process they themselves have undergone.[1] They have had to enter into the world of the destitute and learn. This is a humbling, exhilarating—frequently a wrenching and disorienting—experience, as anyone knows, theologian or not, who has made the journey. It is worth pausing to examine why this is so and what the experience entails.

Everyone's cultural formation, location, experience, and past choices circumscribe his knowing. That includes members of my own middle-class "tribe," which easily mistakes its own perspective for what is "normal," since that perspective dominates public discourse. This does not make us bad. This is what most minorities do, especially privileged minorities. Nor do we have a monopoly on limited perspectives.

Besides the conscious concepts and customs all of us have inherited, unconscious assumptions underlie our thinking. These are the anthropological, cosmological and moral myths and presuppositions that make up the horizon of each one's world, the "grid" through which we interpret and evaluate data. Such assumptions are necessary for knowing. Yet, besides disclosing truth, they also cover it up, thanks to biases and blind spots inherited from our family, social class, race, age group, sex, religion, and nation. As a result, important problems escape our notice and some questions fail to arise. To that extent, discovering truth depends on unmasking the unconscious ignorance, falsehoods, and half-truths that stand between us and reality. We all need cognitive liberation; and we need ongoing discipline, a kind of cognitive hygiene, to keep error at bay and continue to advance in knowledge. Without this discipline, our reflection on the big questions, including our theology, will lack rigor, no matter how many footnotes we produce to back it up.

As a solution to limited experience and bias, most modern thinkers who have thought deeply about this prescribe more pure reason and conscious awareness. But, as necessary as these are, they do not seem to be sufficient. Cognitive hygiene involves more than changing old ideas for new. Why? We cling to our basic assumptions, and we do so because we have a stake in them. They are rooted in habits of the heart that were formed in childhood interaction, habits that are now part of our identity. To question my basic assumptions, then, is to challenge who I am and to shake the foundations of my world. The "conscientization" process involves untangling and ordering our loves. Cognitive liberation requires nothing less than personal transformation, or conversion.

This is what happens when we enter the world of the poor and engage that reality honestly. Letting the poor crash through our defenses usually provokes a wholesome crisis that leaves us shaken and disoriented. If we stay with the poor—listening, observing, interacting—our horizon opens. Our worldview gets reconfigured. What is really important (life itself and love) moves from the margins toward the center of the canvass, displacing what is less important. In general, things turn out to be worse than we thought. Injustice—sin—is more destructive and widespread, more systematic and intractable than we realized. The poor suffer more cruelly. Nor are they a different, distant species. When we see our reflection in their eyes, they can become our friends. When their children die before their time, then that is no longer just tragic; it is outrageous. With time it dawns on us how the vast majority of all people who have ever lived could not, and today still cannot, take life for granted. They have struggled day in and day out to stay alive and to build family and community.

What we learn is hardly all bad news, however. While the truth of poverty and injustice makes a painful entry, the faith, contagious hope, and solidarity that accompany this evil are consoling and uplifting—so much so that life is worth celebrating, almost anytime. This great drama—the struggle of good and evil, grace and sin, the dying and the rising—gradually becomes the integrating factor that reconfigures our world.

In short, as we enter the world of the poor, that reality enters into us and shapes us. We grope our way and discover, much as little children do. Besides facts, we grasp meaning and sift values. This is the prime analogue of knowing—not the subject bumping into objects but the *com-penetration* of knower and known. This is how we get to know persons, new neighborhoods, and work situations. Other kinds of knowing, however valuable, including the knowledge gained by empirical-scientific methods, are derivative.

Engaging the poor expands the horizon within which we interpret not only the world around us but Christian faith itself. As we see the world through new eyes, we hear God's word with new ears. Some truths of the faith (discipleship, reign of God) move closer to the center; others shift toward the edge.

The new perspective "from below" is neither infallible nor always superior. Rather than an impossible universal viewpoint, it makes possible a *more* universal viewpoint from which to overcome bias and better appreciate other viewpoints. From that standpoint, it becomes clear that the dominant perspective needs radical correction—precisely from below. Sobrino spells out for us what this means for theology.

## Sobrino's Theology for a Suffering World

As Sobrino will tell you in conversation, he did not first think through what method to use and then do theology. He elaborated theology and then explained the method he was using. His rich reflections on the role of solidarity in theology are especially worth examining here because some key texts are unavailable in English and because the Vatican has recently questioned his "methodological presuppositions," linking them to what it considers doctrinal errors.[2][3]

### *The Crucified People, the Principal Sign of Our Times*

The decades following World War II ushered in vast changes around the world; including the decolonization of dozens of countries; political transformations; widespread industrialization, labor organizing, and urbanization; the mainstreaming of human-rights language; more frequent travel and powerful new means of mass communications that penetrated rural areas. Because of these changes, the magnitude of world poverty and the aspirations of poor people for freedom captured the attention of more people than ever before. From its very beginnings, liberation theology affirmed that this "irruption of the poor" (G. Gutiérrez), above all in their suffering—"massive, cruel, unjust, structural and enduring"—and their hope, was the fundamental fact of our times.[3]

According to Sobrino, from the standpoint of faith, this is the principal "sign of the times." He distinguishes two senses in which Vatican II's *Gaudium et spes* speaks of such signs. In *Gaudium et spes* 4, the expression refers to novel realities to which the church must respond, or which it must take into account, in order to fulfill its mission—phenomena such as secularism, atheism, nuclear arms, concern for freedom, peace, and justice, and so on. However, *Gaudium et spes* 11 refers to "authentic signs of God's presence and purpose in the happenings, needs, and desires" of people. These are "sacramental" signs that manifest God's active presence and will in history. If this is so, says Sobrino, then the question becomes unavoidable: Where is God especially active today in a way that manifests God's purpose? It would be irresponsible for theology to avoid this question, although it routinely does. By limiting itself to reflecting on the truths of the faith in the abstract and developing their virtualities deductively, theology falls into an implicit "deism." It ignores God's self-communication in history today, degenerating into abstractions that ultimately distort that communication. Not that God communicates a radically new message in our time. Rather, God reminds us of forgotten or undeveloped truths and communicates old truths in new ways that produce life today. It is precisely by attending to such signs, writes Sobrino, that we can best safeguard what God has revealed, develop its virtualities, and recover what has been forgotten.[4]

The Catholic bishops at their historic conference in Medellín in 1968 responded to the irruption of the poor. The suffering of the poor cries to heaven, they wrote; the aspiration for emancipation is a "sign of the Spirit"; and Christians discern God's presence in efforts in favor of liberation.[5] Sobrino is especially impressed by how his colleague Ignacio Ellacuría expressed this: The principal sign of the times today is the "crucified people." They are "the historical continuation of the suffering servant of Yahweh."[6]

The ultimate reason for affirming the irruption of the poor as the most important fact today is pretheological. It is simply the most reasonable conclusion to draw from the cruelty and universality of their suffering. At the same time, it expresses the lived ecclesial faith that inspires liberation theology.[7] This affirmation has been confirmed a posteriori as a datum of the "sense of the faithful," especially the poor, but also of many members of the hierarchy and in official documents. It is further verified by vital new forms of Christian life and theology among the poor and by growth in a faith, hope, and generous love that have suffered persecution and martyrdom and borne abundant fruit. Of course, Scripture confirms this option when it describes God acting on behalf of the poor in the foundational events of salvation history, from the exodus to Jesus' life, death, and resurrection and Matthew's last judgment. In the history of salvation, God's presence in poverty and suffering is "a hidden, disfigured, crucified and scandalous presence; but it is also a salvific presence."[8]

According to Sobrino, reflection on this paramount sign of the times—the crucified people—and reflection on the response to this sign accounts for the real "novelty and creativity" of liberation theology.[9]


### The Location and Sources of Theology

If the crucified people is the principal sign of the times, then not all places for doing theology are equal. The most fruitful place for that is "the world of the poor," although a theologian might work at many possible physical sites, such as a university, a seminary, a diocesan office, a parish or somewhere else.[10] The world of the poor is theology's *Sitz im Leben—und im Tode*. The poor are its life-and-death location. To understand Christ, says Sobrino, we must hearken to the question of the gospel hymn, "Were you there when they crucified my Lord?"[11]

If that is so, then what is the relationship between this location and the *loci theologici*, which are the traditional sources of theological reflection and argument? (The Dominican theologian Melchior Cano of Salamanca developed the concept of *locus theologicus* in the sixteenth century, when the challenge of the Reformation made the sources of doctrine a contentious issue.[12]) What is the relationship between the present reality of the poor, which orients liberation theology, and the past revelation of God expressed in Scripture and the other traditional sources of doctrine? In its March 2007 Notification, the Vatican's Congregation for the Doctrine of the Faith (CDF) criticized how Sobrino answers this question in his two recent works of Christology.[13]

Sobrino argues that, although the location of theology and the traditional sources are conceptually distinct, the former is a source of theological knowledge in its own way, as well as a vital help for understanding traditional sources and their contemporary relevance. It even enjoys a certain primacy, insofar as it is the most important among "theological places" for determining the horizon of reflection and thereby shaping the theologian's thinking. On this point the CDF Notification parts company with Sobrino, affirming the priority of Scripture and the great tradition of which the church community is bearer.

Sobrino adduces several arguments in support of this methodological primacy, arguments that the CDF surely judged to be insufficient. For Sobrino, the world of the poor, and hence the proper place of theology, includes the church of the poor and its living faith. By this Sobrino means simply the church whose members are primarily poor, as in Central America, and whose leaders walk with them, a church that strives to follow Christ in the face of unjust suffering. The situation of this church, and above all its faith, throws a bright light on the truth of the gospel. This light alters no articles of the creed. "We are now talking about the light rather than the subject matter," writes Sobrino. "The light is not what we see, but what makes it possible to see," a light that is unavailable elsewhere. Like Isaiah's suffering servant, the crucified people brings light to the nations. Finally, Sobrino reminds us that the social world itself, which conditions theological reflection, is God's own creation; and theological reflection on that reality seeks to understand what is happening to that creation and what God is doing and saying there.[14]

What about the Christian message comes to light "from below"? For one thing, writes Sobrino, God's partiality for the poor. This in turn illuminates the message as a whole, including, paradoxically, its universality. From the standpoint of the weak, we can better understand the incarnation as God's merciful solidarity with frail humanity as a whole. We can understand how the gospel is good news for the poor and, because it is, appreciate better how it is good news for everyone. Salvation means deliverance from oppression and misery, even though it is not limited to that. When we understand how sin and idolatry cause the death of the poor, we better understand their universal deadly reach. We can more easily grasp why the powerful persecuted and killed Jesus, just as they kill people like him today. When we understand how he died, as Oscar Romero died, for announcing good news to the poor, we can better understand what it means to say that he died for everyone, including me. And, just as he was the first victim of injustice to be raised from death, his victory shows God's will to give life to all such victims; and that means hope of eternal life for all.[15]

Finally, Sobrino believes that from this perspective it becomes possible to configure the truths of the faith as a whole in a more coherent way.[16]

### Theology as "Intellectus Amoris"

Just as theology in modern times has had to face up to the challenge of historical criticism, today it must face up to massive unjust suffering. Honesty in the face of this reality—a constant theme for Sobrino—is a prerequisite for authentic human existence, for Christian life, and for theology. As we saw earlier, it is impossible to engage this reality as a mere spectator. Far more than a change of location, that engagement involves a change of mind and heart, in a word, conversion. The poor themselves help overcome our natural tendency to avoid suffering, especially suffering that challenges and even accuses. They help us avoid the sin—the willful prejudice and consequent distortion—to which theology, like any other activity, is liable.[17]

In this way, liberation theology expands on what a number of twentieth-century theologians, from Rudolf Bultmann to Karl Rahner, call the necessary pre-understanding (*Vorverständnis*) for grasping revelation. These theologians affirm that to hear and understand God's word it is necessary to be a subject constitutively open to receive that word and hence open to a novel future. To this, liberation theology adds that it is necessary to be receptive to the reality of the poor, disposed to respond and able to view reality from their standpoint.[18]

The appropriate response to that reality is compassionate love. This conclusion, too, is basically human and pretheological, but one that, again, revelation abundantly confirms. This is obviously valid for theologians, whose response (praxis) may take many forms. Their theology will be part of that response, so that mercy, and not only a passion for truth, will inform theology. "Mercy must pervade the theological task."[19] More than simply *intellectus fidei*, theology should be *intellectus amoris*.

Sobrino specifies two ways in which liberation theology links theory and praxis. First, we best understand reality, including sin and salvation in history, when we engage it practically; and that, in turn, helps us understand Scripture and doctrine. Second, theological reflection ought to inspire, illumine, and orient praxis and not limit itself to advancing theological knowledge for its own sake. As Ellacuría put it, theology is the ideological moment of ecclesial and historical praxis. "The finality of liberation theology," writes Sobrino, "is the liberation of a suffering world and its transformation into the reign of God." The ultimate reason for this practical orientation is the two pretheological options: the irruption of the poor as the major fact of our times and mercy as the most appropriate response.[20]

Theology should, therefore, be *intellectus amoris* and *amor quaerens intellectum*. In the face of massive injustice, it is *intellectus justitiae* and *intellectus liberationis*. Sobrino believes that this is the most important novelty which liberation theology has produced,[21] and his explanation is penetrating and challenging. Since Augustine's time, he reminds us, theology has been characterized as *intellectus fidei*. This is fitting as far as it goes, for understanding what we believe is a permanently necessary task. It is by no means evident, however, that theology should be only this or even principally this, as it has been since Augustine. For the essence of Christianity is the *real* self-communication of God to the world and our acceptance of that gift in love. In Christianity, love—God's love and our response—takes precedence over knowledge, even knowledge of the truths of the faith. Theology seeks to understand and express what we believe about God and what we hope from God. But the fundamental truth is God's love. Theology must seek to understand that love above all, especially what God is doing today and how God wants us to love in return.[22]

Since faith-hope-love summarizes the appropriate response to God's self-communication, theology is best understood as *intellectus fidei et spei et amoris*.[23] It is at once faith and hope and love seeking understanding. But the greatest of these is love (1 Corinthians 13). While theology is motivated by both faith and hope, it is above all love that must inspire it. Just as love permeates both faith and hope, theology as *intellectus amoris* in no way undermines theology as *intellectus fidei* or *intellectus spei*. Rather, says Sobrino, it strengthens theology's potential to articulate the truth and the promise of revelation. The traditional primacy accorded to theology as *intellectus fidei* and its frequent reduction to that function smack more of Hellenistic *theoria* than Judeo-Christian theology. Limiting theology to clarifying the meaning of the truths of the faith has historically removed it from its biblical origins, undermining both the understanding and the practice of the faith.

Theology as *intellectus amoris* is, finally, mystagogy. It guides the faithful more deeply into the mystery of God, and "it offers the way of love as the primary way of *mystagogy*."[24]

### A Methodological Priority

In practice, liberation theology accords a certain methodological priority over authoritative texts to the reality of the poor, as we have seen. This does not mean that it ranks "reality" as an authority superior to Scripture. The priority is methodological. Sobrino explains:

> in using texts [liberation theology] accords greater priority to what they illuminate about reality than to what they formulated as doctrine. And it gives logical priority . . . to present reality over past reality, even granting that it has been in the past, in the Christ event, where the maximum revelation of God has been given in a definitive and irrevocable way.[25]

It is necessary to expound texts and to make Scripture relevant for today, and liberation theologians do that. They understand their more proper task, however, as discerning how God is acting in an unjust world and how human beings are, or should be, responding in collaboration with God. They try to answer questions such as, Where is God's reign manifest today? What idols oppose it? How should the church respond to injustice? While Sobrino knows that this way of proceeding entails risks, he is convinced that it is necessary and has proven fruitful. To avoid pitfalls, he says, it is necessary to emphasize that the true God is manifest today as Jesus manifested God long ago and that God calls human beings to respond as Jesus did long ago.[26]

In reality, all theology entails risks. Years ago Juan Luis Segundo pointed out the danger of trying to do theology principally by deduction from authoritative texts.[27] He recalled the gospel story about the man with the withered hand. The Pharisees spy on Jesus to see if he will cure on the Sabbath. Jesus calls the crippled man forward to stand before them all and then poses the question sharply: "Is it lawful to do good or to do harm on the Sabbath, to save life or to kill?" Jesus and the Pharisees have different perspectives and different theological methods. The Pharisees' starting point is the Torah. We might fancifully imagine them checking the index of their scroll for the entries "Sabbath" and "cure," in response to Jesus' challenge. His starting point is the man himself with his crippled hand. He has the man stand before them. Starting from there, one can understand the will of the Father, which is life in abundance, especially where life is threatened or truncated, as here. From this point of departure, one can understand the meaning of the Torah and its precepts. The Sabbath exists for people like this man, and not vice versa. Starting from elsewhere, the Pharisees fail to grasp what the Torah, and God, requires. Their direct appeal to the text falsifies God's will and seeks to justify their own lack of compassion. No wonder "Jesus looked at them with anger"!

Sobrino compares our situation to what people faced in biblical times, before all the texts were written or canonized. For those who heard Jesus, for example, the ultimate theological challenge was to respond to him. Since he was the principal sign of the times, responding to him was crucial to understanding the Torah, the prophets, and God's will. Sobrino cautions that the comparison with our times is imperfect, since, when we reflect on God's presence in history today, we already know about the definitive word revealed in Jesus and the church's authoritative interpretations.[28]

## Conclusion

As the poor have erupted in recent decades, Christians have responded. Liberation theology is part of that response. Today, the irruption continues in new forms and under different conditions. While times have changed, the poor are more numerous than ever; and, although some countries have emerged from misery, the gap between rich and poor has grown exponentially.[29]

In both Scripture and common speech, "the poor" can take on different nuances. Nonetheless, the poor remain the victims of economic, political, and social marginalization. At the same time, we can now see better than before how our social relations and institutions marginalize women and ethnic minorities. These same patriarchal institutions have produced an ecological crisis that cries out for action and theological reflection. Today, we incorporate these additional dimensions into the principal sign of our times. To paraphrase Sobrino, that is the most reasonable (pretheological) conclusion to draw from honestly confronting reality. At the same time, it springs from faith.

The victims remain the proper place for theology. Whether or not we label it "liberation theology," it should arise from solidarity with them. While poor countries remain a privileged location for this in general terms, it is possible and necessary to do theology elsewhere in solidarity with the poor. Of course, the social context of affluence presents difficulties and challenges. It inevitably shapes one's thinking. In some ways, this is as it should be, since theologians in wealthy regions must address their own context. However, they will find dialogue with their counterparts in poor regions a necessary complement and corrective. Of course, like everyone else, these counterparts, too, need corrective enrichment. Finally, today we also recognize our need to benefit from dialogue with non-Christian religious traditions.

We are indebted to Sobrino for articulating how theology in solidarity seeks to understand God's action and word in history today. This is necessary for understanding past revelation, by rescuing what has been forgotten and developing what remains latent. This theology as *intellectus amoris* is indispensible for presenting the Christian message as real good news for the crucified peoples of our time, and therefore for all of us and even a suffering planet.

## Notes

1. See the personal accounts of Jon Sobrino, "Introduction: Awakening from the Sleep of Inhumanity," in idem, *The Principle of Mercy: Taking the Crucified People from the Cross* (Maryknoll, N.Y.: Orbis Books, 1994), 1-11; and Gustavo Gutiérrez, "Metodología y espiritualidad," in *Acortar distancias: hijas e hijos de Domingo hacen teología juntos,* ed. Dominican Sisters International (Salamanca: Editorial San Estaban, 2005), 54-60.

2. Congregation for the Doctrine of the Faith, "Notification Concerning the Works of Fr. Jon Sobrino, S.J.: *Jesucristo liberador: Lectura histórico-teológica de Jesús de Nazareth* (Madrid: Trotta, 1991) and *La fe en Jesucristo: Ensayo desde las víctimas* (San Salvador, 1999)," nos. 2-3. The Notification's criticism of the methodology of Sobrino's Christology refers directly to the second chapter of his *Jesus the Liberator: A Historical-Theological Reading of Jesus of Nazareth,* trans. Paul Burns and Francis McDonagh (Maryknoll, N.Y.: Orbis Books, 1993). Sobrino takes up the question of method systematically in two other essays as well: "Los 'signos de los tiempos' en la teología de la liberación," in José M.ª Lera, ed., *Fides quae per caritatem operatur: Homenaje a Juan Alfaro, S.J., en su 75 cumpleaños* (Bilbao: Universidad de Deusto/Mensajero, 1989), 249-69; idem, "Teología en un mundo sufriente. La teología de la liberación como 'intellectus amoris,'" in idem, *El principio-misericordia: Bajar de la cruz a los pueblos crucificados* (Santander: Sal Terrae, 1992), chapter 3 (47-80). This second article originally appeared in the *Revista Latinoamericana de Teología* 15 (Sept.-Dec. 1988): 243-66. A shorter treatment of many themes of these essays can be found in his "Theology in a Suffering World: Theology as *Intellectus Amoris,*" in idem, *The Principle of Mercy,* 27-46. Unless otherwise indicated, all subsequent references are to works by Sobrino.

3. "Teología en un mundo sufriente," 49.

4. "Signos de los tiempos," 250-54; *Jesus the Liberator,* 25-26.

5. Cf. "Signos de los tiempos," 254-55, and the Medellín documents, "Justice," 1; "Introduction to the Final Documents," 4 and 5.

6. I. Ellacuría, "Discernir los signos de los tiempos," *Diakonía* 17 (1981): 58, cited in *Jesus the Liberator,* 26. See I. Ellacuría, "The Crucified People," in *Mysterium Liberationis: Fundamental Concepts of Liberation Theology,* ed. I. Ellacuría and J. Sobrino (Maryknoll, N.Y.: Orbis Books, 1993), 580-603.

7. "Signos de los tiempos," 256; "Teología en un mundo sufriente," 51-54.

8. "Signos de los tiempos," 256-59; final quotation from 258-59; cf. "Teología en un mundo sufriente," 51-54.

9. "Signos de los tiempos," 260.

10. Ibid., 260-63, quotation from 261.

11. *Jesus the Liberator,* 28.

12. In the subsequent history of post-tridentine Catholic theology, these sources (authorities) were hierarchized, related, and interpreted in different ways. The literature is abundant. See José M.ª Rovira Belloso, *Introducción a la teología* (Madrid: BAC, 1996), chapter 4.

13. The Notification (nos. 2-3) criticizes the following theses: that the poor are the normative location for Christology and give it "its fundamental direction"; that the church of the poor is Christology's proper ecclesial setting; that the social setting of the poor is "the most crucial for the faith, the most crucial in shaping the thought pattern of Christology" (*Jesus*

*the Liberator*, 28, 30-31). The Notification charges that this leads Sobrino to downplay Christological dogmas.

14. See *Jesus the Liberator*, 27-33, quotation on 33.

15. Ibid., 24, 32-33; "Teología en un mundo sufriente," 60-62, 75-76.

16. Sobrino organizes the fundamental truths of the faith around the concept "reign of God"; see his "Central Position of the Reign of God in Liberation Theology," in *Mysterium Liberationis*, 350-88.

17. "Teología en un mundo sufriente," 63-65.

18. "Signos de los tiempos," 264-65; "Teología en un mundo sufriente," 57.

19. "Teología en un mundo sufriente," 67.

20. See ibid., 68-70, quotation on 69. See also I. Ellacuría, "La teología como momento ideológico de la praxis eclesial," *Estudios Eclesiásticos* 207 (1978): 457-76.

21. "Teología en un mundo sufriente," 49, 71.

22. Ibid., 72-73.

23. J. Moltmann suggested that theology could be *intellectus spei* and *spes quaerens intellectum* in his *Theology of Hope: On the Ground and the Implications of a Christian Eschatology*, trans. James W. Leitch (New York: Harper & Row, 1974).

24. "Teología en un mundo sufriente," 73-78, quotation on 78.

25. "Signos de los tiempos," 265.

26. Ibid., 266.

27. J. L. Segundo, *La liberación de la teología* (Buenos Aires/Mexico City: Ediciones Carlos Lohlé, 1975), 90-92. More recently, idem, "La opción por los pobres como clave hermenéutica para entender el Evangelio," *Sal Terrae* 74, no. 6 (June 1986): 473-82.

28. "Signos de los tiempos," 265-66.

29. See Manuel Castells, *The Information Age*, vol. 3: *The End of Millennium*, 2d ed. (Oxford: Blackwell, 2000), chapter 2.

# 2

# Theology in the Light of Human Suffering
## A Note on "Taking the Crucified Down from the Cross"

PAUL G. CROWLEY, S.J.

The writings of Jon Sobrino on suffering are so extensive, the theme so pervasively represented in virtually all of his works, that it is difficult to know where to start delineating a "theology of suffering" in his works. Sobrino himself does not identify any one part of his work as a "theology of suffering" per se. Still, there are certain fundamental motifs that recur throughout his writings and that lend to them a coherence and consistency that allow us to take the measure of his contribution to theological reflection on suffering. This project is probably best undertaken in retrospect, as we survey Sobrino's vast corpus, and as we reflect with gratitude on all that this great theologian has given us to consider on the topic of suffering. I will demonstrate here that the attempt to articulate Sobrino's "theology of suffering" will take us directly into his theology of the cross and resurrection—his theology of the paschal mystery—for this is where his fundamental reflections on suffering are to be found.

At the outset it should be said that Jon Sobrino's contribution to a theology of suffering is not so much a theology *about* suffering as it is a theology written *from* suffering, the contexts of suffering that have shaped his life and career in El Salvador for the past several decades. The suffering that motivates his theology is not hidden: It is the suffering that comes upon the impoverished and politically vulnerable by powers beyond themselves, crushing down on them with the force of an affliction.[1] It is, furthermore, the suffering of injustice, which compounds even the ordinary sufferings of life. His concern is for the suffering of whole peoples, those whom he will call the "crucified people," a term we will examine further. It is crucial to understand, therefore, that while he is certainly not uninterested in the personal sufferings of individual human

I am grateful to Dean Brackley, S.J., for helpful orientations into this material, and to Tom Powers, S.J., for theological and editorial consultation.

beings, he sees even these sufferings in the social context of the wider sufferings of peoples in historically conflicted and oppressive situations.

The purpose of his theological reflections on such suffering is not only to understand this suffering but to unmask its causes, and thereby to have theology work toward not only the ameliorization of suffering but also its removal. As a theology of liberation, Sobrino's theological reflection on suffering is therefore written for the sake of freedom from suffering. Following the pattern of his Jesuit companion and intellectual collaborator, Ignacio Ellacuría, Sobrino would have us take the "crucified people" down from their crosses of suffering. He would interrupt these crucifixions, because these crucifixions are themselves expressions of the unjust suffering, suffering caused by the sins of oppressive power. And, crucial to our considerations here, it is important to remember that every part of Sobrino's theology stands in relation to the drama of human suffering to which he has been an integral witness in his years in El Salvador—through civil war and the transformation of the church there into a theater of martyrdom, to earthquake and the exposure of even deeper structures of injustice. This is no armchair theology.

As a point of departure for understanding Sobrino's approach to suffering, and to his theologizing about it, one could not do better than begin with the essay written in the wake of the Salvadoran earthquake of 2001, contained in the collection *Where Is God?*[2] One might think that a natural disaster, such as an earthquake, might elicit from a theologian a classical treatment of suffering, much as the Lisbon earthquake of 1755 resulted in a flood of writing on theodicy, which considered how such catastrophic human suffering could be reconciled with a God both good and omnipotent. While Sobrino is certainly not uninterested in the serious questions of theodicy, and does treat of it, his fundamental question is a different one and could be formulated this way: Why is it that the poor suffer so disproportionately, even in a natural disaster? Sobrino proceeds to demonstrate how even a natural disaster serves to unmask the underlying structures of social and economic injustice because the poor are caught up in a physical embodiment of the oppression that marks their lives all along, robbed of land and now without a roof, literally clinging to cliffsides, and disproportionately buried in the rubble. The earthquake therefore becomes a summons to undo the unjust structures whose raw framework is exposed by natural disaster. The "crucified people" suffer not only directly by virtue of political, economic, social and military oppression, and from the forces of empire and market globalization but also indirectly through the effects of this warping of their lives. They are not only impoverished, but disproportionately vulnerable. They can disappear as if their lives were of no significance whatsoever. And, of course, we see this again and again in natural disasters around the globe.

For Sobrino, what this must elicit is a response, a revulsion against suffering, not in and of itself, but because so much of it is caused by human factors that render it avoidable. A "theology of suffering" would therefore involve a protest against suffering: a prophetic "no" that serves as a summons to bring an end to suffering. In theological terms: The suffering of the cross must be brought to an end. And this is to be accomplished by the liberating power of God's love, which is the power of the resurrection. Sobrino's theology of suffering is framed, then, within the paschal mystery, where the resurrection in relation to the cross becomes a heuristic for the saving work of God, which is reflected in the work of liberation undertaken by people of faith. And that work of liberation is described as taking the "crucified people" down from their crosses. This is at once an image of mercy, hence an interruption and alleviation of suffering, and a deposition, which attends to the suffering even beyond their deaths and cares for their memory, as we see depicted in the images of the disciples taking Jesus down from his cross. But Sobrino intends something more by the use of this image: a remaking of our image of the cross through a remaking of the people who suffer needlessly and at the hands of injustice. It is not suffering itself that is at issue: It is the suffering that issues from injustice. And the image of taking people down from their crosses is intended to address this fundamental fact. It is to join in God's emphatic "no" to such suffering, definitively revealed in the bodily resurrection of Jesus from the dead.

I wish to consider Sobrino's approach to suffering in three stages. First, I will examine Ellacuría's metaphor of the "crucified people." I will then show how Sobrino develops this metaphor in his own work, particularly in his theology of the paschal mystery. Finally, I will suggest that the praxis of resurrection gives concrete form to the summons to remove the suffering poor from their crosses. The whole of Sobrino's theological treatment of suffering, I will argue, can only be seen within the framework of the paschal mystery, both cross and resurrection. Eschewing a theodicy removed from Christology, Sobrino's theology *from* suffering is an integral moment of his Christology and leads to a central insight into suffering: that the power of God's love wants to bring it to an end.

## Sobrino's Indebtedness to Ellacuría

Sobrino's personal indebtedness to Ellacuría's theology is expressed in many places in his theological corpus. It is an indebtedness that arose from their shared Jesuit mission and lives in El Salvador and their colleagueship at the Universidad Centroamericana up until the time of Ellacuría's murder in 1989, along with his Jesuit companions, their housekeeper, and her daughter. His personal admiration for "Ellacu" was expressed shortly after the 1989 assassinations in *Companions of Jesus: The Jesuit Martyrs of El Salvador*, a book he wrote while in residence at Santa Clara immediately after the killings at the university. But the most poignant and telling source of this relationship is to be found in his essay "Ignacio Ellacuría, the Human Being and the Christian: 'Taking the Crucified People Down from the Cross.'"[3]

The most immediately pertinent connection between Ellacuría's thought and Sobrino's theology is to be found in Sobrino's description of the starting point of Ellacuría's own life work: a strong sense of the reality of the people whom he served, "service *from the place of* others." This laid the foundation for a compassion that was not in the least sentimental but was nevertheless real and felt: "Ellacuría was moved to the depths by the sight of a people prostrate, oppressed, deceived, ridiculed—in the forceful terms he always used. He reacted to this, not just by way of lament. Indeed, he never made peace with the pain it implies. . . . "[4] And, further: "The suffering of victims has deep roots, and it is these roots that must be pulled out (no small thing), and replaced by others that produce life and fraternity." The meaning of his whole life, then, was "the struggle to reverse a history of inhumanity."[5] For this reason, Sobrino tells us "his perception of the tragedy of reality: death, the terrible pain of the victims of the world," and that truly this "world is sin, radical negativity, a radical negation of the will of God, and the highest manifestation of the rejection of God." Yet this world is also "the historical appearance of the servant of Yahweh as suffering servant and the appearance of Christ crucified."[6] From the sin of the world emerges the Crucified One from whom salvation comes. It is in this light, then, that Ellacuría would speak of the "crucified peoples" who are strung up unjustly on their crosses of suffering, but from whom, as Christ crucified today, salvation would ultimately also derive. And this would occur through the liberating power of God's love realized in part through a liberating praxis of the gospel.

Ellacuría himself was quite aware of the dramatic punch and even scandalous effect of the image of a crucified people. But it is the scandal of the cross itself, and "we must recover that scandal and madness if we do not want to vitiate the history-making truth of the passion of Jesus."[7] What he wishes to keep alive with this image is the eschatological dimension of the "reign of God," which Jesus proclaimed. The reign of God is actually initiated in the whole of the life, death, and resurrection of Jesus, the whole of the paschal mystery. Thus, the reign begins to be realized within and not apart from history, but finds its ultimate fulfillment in the future of God disclosed by the resurrection of Jesus. Due to its eschatological character, the initiation of the reign of God has not brought a final end to the "reign of sin" within history itself, even though history is already redeemed. "It is precisely the reign of sin that continues to crucify most of humankind and that obliges us to make real in history the death of Jesus as the actualized passover of the Reign of God."[8] That is, the suffering of Jesus on the cross continues in history today, and it is we who live now who are called on to respond to the suffering of this cross, to become agents of liberation from suffering, as did the Father in the Passover that was newly realized on the cross of Jesus' death.

Relying on the thought of the German Protestant theologian Wolfhart Pannenberg, Ellacuría holds that the not-yet-fully-realized eschatology of the reign of God in history indicates a certain tension between the crucifixion and the resurrection. The resurrection marks the beginning of a new life for the human race, but it points back to the crucifixion, which is a constant reminder that the reign "is not possible as a community of human beings in perfect peace and total justice, without a radical change of the natural conditions that are present in human life. . . . "[9] The enduring power of the resurrection points to the enduring power of sin, which, within history, persists as a fact of human life that is expressed in the unjust suffering of whole peoples. The crucifixion continues in history, just as the power of the resurrection continues to work its effect, and, in God's future, will bring an end to the suffering and death that are the crucifixion of whole peoples.

The crucifixion of Jesus continues, therefore, in the crucifixion of the poor. For Ellacuría, the crucified people are "that collective body" who owe their suffering "to the way society is organized and maintained by a minority that exercises its dominion through a series of factors, which taken together and given their concrete impact with history must be regarded as sin."[10] At the same time there are "subsystems of crucifixion" that include not only the oppressed poor, but those who oppress them, directly or indirectly. The latter, too, suffer, albeit in a different way, from the diminishment of humanity caused by the sinfulness in which they are enmeshed, leading to a flight from themselves in a drive to dominate the vulnerable or to pursue a life that excludes the horizon of the world's impoverished.[11] This includes, of course, the privileged few of the developed world for whom the vast majority of humanity, all of them poor and who make possible through their labors the wealth of the rich, is almost completely invisible. Yet, God will work salvation and establish the reign definitively through the crucified people, who stand in history today as the realization of the Suffering Servant of Isaiah, who bore Israel's offenses and thus saved Israel.[12] Like the Suffering Servant, the image of "the crucified people has a twofold thrust: it is the victim of the sin of the world, and it is also bearer of the world's salvation."[13]

This focus on the crucifixion of the crucified people leads us to a focus on the enduring sin of the world. The power of God over sin and death, revealed in the resurrection of Jesus, must also be treated. "Salvation does not come through the mere fact of crucifixion and death; only a people that lives because it has risen from the Death inflicted on it can save the world."[14] This is where Sobrino takes up the mantle of Ellacuría, for in the notion of taking the crucified people down from their crosses, he is in fact suggesting a praxis of resurrection faith, a way that the power of the resurrection over sin and death in history can be effected and the reign of God established in history.

### The "Crucified People" in Sobrino's Christology

The themes sketched above are found in many places in Sobrino's work. Perhaps the most succinct summary is in his essay "The Crucified Peoples: Yahweh's Suffering Servant Today," an essay written in memory of Ellacuría and in anticipation of 1992, the four-hundredth anniversary of the arrival of the Spanish in the Americas.[15] In this essay, Sobrino describes the "horrifying fact" of the crucified people in the inhuman poverty and misery in which they live, the marginalization of the poorest of the poor (especially indigenous peoples), and the crucifixion by impoverishment and disease that leads to actual death for so many. And, like Ellacuría, Sobrino sees the crucified people as the contemporary embodiment of the Suffering Servant, and as bearers of salvation.

Now, it is at this point that Sobrino introduces a creative tension into the working out of salvation in history. For, it is imperative that "we" bring the crucified people down from the cross. The tragedy that has been visited on them must be brought to an end. This is the requirement of an "anthropodicy by which human beings can be justified."[16] Although he does not develop this idea, the reference is significant. If the question for theology after Auschwitz was how to justify God, a question strictly speaking of theodicy, the question for the tragedy of Latin America is how to justify the human beings who have been the cause of so much tragedy. The only way the perpetrators can be seen as justified (from a human standpoint) is if they are converted to a new vision for humanity and themselves begin to take the crucified down from their crosses, thus working for their integral liberation rather than the continuing oppression that has resulted in suffering and death. To take people down from their crosses is to engage in the praxis of resurrection. This degree of conversion would seem to be rare, but not impossible. Sobrino frequently cites the conversion of Archbishop Oscar Romero himself from a position of upholder of the status quo to a prophetic leader of the crucified people and a stalwart defender of their dignity and rights.

And here enters the creative tension. For, as in the case of Romero, the ones who will show the way to conversion are the crucified peoples themselves. They themselves offer the insight into and grounding for a praxis of resurrection. Without wishing to romanticize the oppressed poor, Sobrino nevertheless suggests that they offer Western civilization a set of values (openness, cooperation, simplicity), a sense of hope, a capacity for love, a readiness to forgive, a demonstrated solidarity, and a testament to faith as church that the powerful and privileged have much to learn from.[17] All of this comes from his lived experience with poor people in El Salvador. So he concludes: "It is paradoxical, but it is true. The crucified peoples offer light and salvation."[18] This does not mean that the poor do not sin or that they are not themselves in need of personal conversion. But Sobrino wants to emphasize that they are, nevertheless, instruments of salvation, perhaps in spite of themselves, precisely because of their impoverishment and weakness.

These two parts of Sobrino's approach to the crucified people—taking them down from the cross and seeing in them the source of salvation—are in fact a reflection of a deeper structure in his theology from suffering: the pattern established in the life and ministry of Jesus. Both dimensions of this picture are reflected in his theology of the paschal mystery contained in his Christology. Indeed, we find these themes expressed very early on in his 1982 work on Christology, *Jesus in Latin America*.[19] Here we find the familiar motifs of the crucified people and of their embodiment in history as the Suffering Servant of Yahweh. Rather than focus on taking them down from the crosses of suffering, however, Sobrino here focuses on how the crucified people follow as disciples in the pattern of Jesus and thus begift the larger church with an example to follow. They are in a sense, then, sources of salvation to the degree that they resemble Jesus as the living incarnation of Christ. They are enactors of Jesus' message by virtue of who they are, unmasking the false political and economic gods that oppress them.[20] "A crucified people resembles Jesus by the mere fact of what it is and is loved preferentially by God because of what it is. . . . The reality of the act of faith in Christ comes about in this reproducing of his features, in this becoming daughters and sons in the Son."[21] At this stage, then, the suffering of the crucified people is salvific to the degree that it is an entrée into a lived discipleship of Jesus, which includes the enactment of the saving, liberating work of Jesus.

While the discipleship of the crucified people will remain the key to Sobrino's theological understanding of a Christian praxis of liberation, there is a marked shift in his later Christology to a focus on the death of Jesus, and a correlation between the crucifixion of Jesus and the sufferings of the people of Latin America, and more generally of the poor of the world. In *Jesus the Liberator*, the first of his two-volume Christology, he entitles the third part "The Cross of Jesus," and pays specific attention to why Jesus was killed. Here he addresses fundamental historical questions relating to why Jesus was tried and executed by the Roman authorities. This is followed by a theological reflection on the meaning of the cross, focusing on why Jesus *died*—the meaning of his suffering and death. In this theological excursus, Sobrino emphasizes that the revelatory power of the cross as a sign of God's saving work depends on its scandalizing effect. Echoing Ellacuría here, he holds that if we "dull the edge of the scandal of the cross," we risk reducing its role in salvation to a part of a calculus, an explanation that is merely "logical or even necessary."[22] The fact remains, of course, that the cross signals a salvation that comes from suffering. Here Sobrino, following Ellacuría, relates the suffering of Jesus on the cross to the suffering of the Servant in Isaiah. "Jesus is innocent, the sufferings he bears are those that others ought to bear and by bearing them he becomes salvation for others."[23] This suffering and the death that follows are not in themselves and alone the cause of salvation. Rather, the whole of Jesus' life was not accidental to his mission and destiny. It was the expression of his love, love that was pleasing to God and that reached its culmination in his suffering and death. "The cross, as a historically necessary component of love, is part of its historical fullness, and what God was pleased by was this fullness of love."[24] And this is related to the incarnation itself, in that it is the enfleshment of love drawing near to humanity within a world of sin that necessitates such suffering love. The cross is thus a product of an authentic incarnation of God into sin-ridden human reality.[25] The saving love of Jesus is therefore a wholly credible love, a love without limits, even though, within history, its effects are yet to be fully played out.

Sobrino's next move in this Christology is to inquire into what the cross reveals to us about God, precisely as a suffering or "crucified" God. Sobrino is sensitive to criticisms that in his earlier work he focused too much on the cross and not enough on the resurrection. Yet, he says, we risk losing the scandal of the cross if we forget that its meaning is revealed within "the real crucified world" of martyrs. Of course, he has in mind not only his Jesuit brothers and Archbishop Romero, but all those who lost their lives in El Salvador during the civil war because of their witness to faith.[26] "Woe to human beings and believers if they forget the crucifixion!"[27] And here he explicitly invokes the memory of his own brothers martyred at the University of Central America.

In the shadow of this lived reality, which so deeply shades his theology, he focuses in this section on what cannot be avoided about the cross without diminishing its significance: that Jesus, the innocent one, made to be sin by the powers that prosecuted him, felt abandoned by God. The sense of abandonment expressed by Jesus himself on the cross (Psalm 22) raises fundamental challenges to our most cherished ideas about God as loving and present to us in our own sufferings. The "profound isolation" of Jesus, in turn, marked a "theological discontinuity" between Jesus' entire life of absolute closeness to God and now this nightmare of infinite distance: In his greatest hour of need, Jesus finds only the silence of God. This, in turn, reveals to us something about suffering itself, which "remains the supreme enigma for human reason."[28] Drawing on Johannes Metz, Dorothee Soelle, and others, Sobrino confronts the harsh reality of suffering and its defiance of any final meaning in itself, a fact made more forceful when we are considering the suffering of innocent people or people whose suffering is caused by nothing they have called upon themselves.

What, then, do we make of the silence of God? Sobrino arrives at a position that is neither apologetic (God is in no way involved) nor accomodationist (God somehow bore the sufferings of the cross). Rather, squarely facing the silence of God, Sobrino suggests that "God suffered on Jesus' cross and on those of this world's victims by being their non-active and silent witness."[29] For if God allowed himself to become incarnate in the sinfulness of human reality and history, then he also submitted to the limitations of that condition. The silence of God is in some sense an indication of the "weakness" of God precisely because God has entered into solidarity with the suffering victims of history, those who have no voice, who are themselves reduced to a silence in their suffering. But because this is a silence that issues from solidarity—God's solidarity with the suffering— then it does not signal a resignation to suffering, but rather a profound divine sharing in the bearing of injustice. This divine sharing, and not any extrinsic program, theological or political, is the deepest foundation of a praxis of liberation. "In Latin America it is a tangible fact that God's suffering has also been an idea that has encouraged liberation rather than resignation."[30] The suffering silence of God, mirrored in the silence of Jesus himself as he went to the cross, is a powerful unmasking of the "illegitimate interests" that caused such suffering in the first place. This solidarity of the "lesser God," the God of solidarity with the powerless, is in fact a kind of protest against the crucifixions of the world even as God silently bears the pain of such crucifixions.

And here we enter into phase three of this treatment of the cross in Sobrino's Christology, the move from the cross of Jesus and God's solidarity with Jesus precisely in his silence to a consideration of the continuation of the crucifixion in the "collective crosses of whole peoples," in the historical catastrophes of the crucified people of the world. Here he defines what he means by the term "crucified people." First, there is the factual data of poverty and death, the suffering that comes from massive deprivation of the assets of culture because of poverty, disease, war, and natural catastrophe. Second, there is the suffering and death caused by unjust social and economic structures, imposed by "powers" that dominate the poor and weak. Third, there is the theological-religious reality of such suffering, that the very human beings who do so suffer are the suffering Body of Christ in history.[31] The sufferings of these peoples, not only in Central America, but throughout the world, and especially where people are subjected to historical catastrophe caused by human beings, are the "new name for Golgotha today and their peoples are the Suffering Servant."[32]

There can be no doubt that Sobrino's theology from suffering emanates from a first-hand experience of what he has witnessed, and if we are to speak of his theology *of* suffering, we cannot do so apart from a theology of the paschal mystery—a full understanding of the significance of the death and resurrection of Jesus.

## Suffering and the Praxis of Resurrection

The second volume of Sobrino's Christology, originally entitled in Spanish *La fe en Jesucristo: Ensayo desde las víctimas* ("Faith in Jesus Christ: An Essay from the Victims"), was published in English as *Christ the Liberator: A View from the Victims.*[33] Here, in the first third of the book, is Sobrino's long-awaited treatment of the resurrection—his response to those critics who complained of too heavy an earlier emphasis on the cross and the sufferings of the crucified people. Here, too, his prism is the "victims" of history, a term he uses in preference to "the poor." The "poor" are the "impoverished"—a term used to emphasize that poverty is the result of conditions forced on people. To be poor is not a natural state. As such, the impoverished are victims. These victims of history especially include those who are economically poor, because this poverty is caused by an inequality that issues from the indifference of the rich and by institutionalized hypocrisy at many levels. Because of this, Sobrino will hold that poverty "is the most lasting form of violence and the violence that is committed with the greatest impunity."[34] It is from the viewpoint and experience of the victims, therefore, that Sobrino will undertake an interpretation of the resurrection—of its relation to the sufferings of the cross and to the ongoing saving work of Christ in the world.

It is, first, important to note that the resurrection is an eschatological action of God. It is the revelation of the supreme power of God's love over suffering and death, but it is a revelation that occurs within the limitations of time and history. This means that suffering and death remain with us even as this power is being worked out within history. And this means that the victims of history are still suffering. And so they present a reality that must figure into our understanding of the resurrection. Still, the resurrection is also the source of hope for Christians, the pledge that God's future is our own, and that it is life, not death, that God definitively and victoriously establishes. If the resurrection is the final cause of our hope, then how do we bring the horizon of the suffering victims of the world into relationship with the horizon of hope that is the resurrection?

Sobrino's survey of Scripture in this work is the beginning of an answer to this question. In ancient Israel, resurrection stood in opposition to "the tragedy of ending in *sheol*," which was tantamount to "ceasing to be in communion with Yahweh."[35] For Israel, therefore, the promise of resurrection was the promise that the silence of God would not be eternal, that God would once again speak to Israel and be in communion with God's beloved people, and within history. They would be established as a people, secure in their own land. But resurrection also bespoke of a hope of communion with God beyond death. The fidelity of God to Israel resulted in Israel's faith in God's eternal fidelity—the "lordship of Yahweh" beyond history in a way that overcame the finality of death itself. And this triumph over death established God's "eschatological triumph over injustice" not only beyond death but also in the eschatological present. Here Sobrino notes that resurrection in the Hebraic imagination is never that of an individual but of a whole people.[36] The resurrection of the dead, therefore, is the salvation of a whole people, a salvation that begins within history and comes to fulfillment in God's future.

And this has a definite effect on the victims of history, those who suffer but live in hope. This hope of the victims, which is more than hope for a mere survival, is nevertheless a "hope against hope" because of the darkness of suffering that enshrouds them. And, it must be added, not every Christian is a victim of history in precisely the way the impoverished of the world are. The hope of the victims cannot somehow be a hope that is other than the hope of all Christians for eternal life. The question arises, then, as to how hope for *my* resurrection has anything to do with the hope of the victims for resurrection from what is already a living death, which is a living scandal. Sobrino's answer is religiously compelling: "the Christian courage to hope in one's own resurrection depends on the courage to hope for the overcoming of the historical scandal of injustice. In theologal[37] language the question is whether God can do justice to the victims produced by human beings."[38] The power of the resurrection as an eschatological event is, therefore, going to be tied to the way the resurrection is worked out in history, through the agency of the living Body of Christ, the whole church. It will depend, then, in part on the degree to which those who are not victims can participate in God's loving response to the victims of history, how they can undertake a praxis of resurrection. This

> means that we have, in Ignacio Ellacuría's words, to "take the situation on ourselves," in this case the situation of the victims, but it is also true that "the situation takes us on itself" and that it offers us not only sin and the obligation to eradicate it but also grace and the courage to hope.[39]

And this is possible, Sobrino tells us, because "The victims offer us their hope." We have already seen why he finds "light and salvation" in the crucified people.

It is here that the loop begun in the work of Ellacuría, which so strongly influenced Sobrino, is closed. The ways Christians live within the power of the resurrection through what he calls "the praxis of raising the crucified" is the beginning of the realization of our hope. The pattern was set by the apostles, who are described in the Gospels and in the Acts of the Apostles as witnesses to the resurrection—witnesses entrusted with a mission. The resurrection event is not exhausted by the accounts of the appearances of Jesus and the empty tomb; it is fully realized in the apostolate of the witnesses who are commissioned by the gift of the Spirit to carry out the work of the risen Christ. "From this it follows that the apostolate—a praxis—is a hermeneutical principle for understanding the resurrection and that without it the resurrection cannot be understood as an eschatological event that essentially inspires praxis."[40] Praxis is the expression of the hope that motivates the witnesses to history who are also witnesses to the resurrection of Jesus.

How can we bring to fruition this praxis in relation to the suffering of the crucified people? We can do so, first, by proclaiming the resurrection through "putting oneself at the service of the resurrection" by working "in the service of eschatological ideals: justice, peace, solidarity, the life of the weak, community, dignity, celebration, and so on."[41] These are "partial resurrections" that help the eschatological reality of the resurrection itself to be realized in history. Further, this means undertaking courses of action that will bring about social, political, and economic transformation of the structures that have caused so much suffering and created victims. In this kind of work, the resurrection coincides with the establishment of the kingdom, itself an eschatological vision of God's triumph, and the reversal of the programs of death and disintegration that led to the crucifixion in the first place. "And this is also what Ignacio Ellacuría meant when he . . . used the expression 'taking the crucified people down from the cross' as a formulation of Christian mission."[42] Taking the crucified down from the cross is, therefore, an expression of resurrection praxis. It is the most hope-filled activity, positively oriented toward life, that a Christian can imagine. It is the most radical expression of hope in the saving power of God made manifest in the suffering of the cross and vindicated in the bodily resurrection of Jesus, his having been raised from the dead.

## Sobrino's Theology of Suffering in Relation to Other Voices

As I indicated at the outset, Sobrino has given us not so much a theology *of* suffering as he has a theology arising *from* suffering and searching for a response to it inspired by the central mystery of Christian faith: the death and resurrection of Jesus Christ. We have also seen how his powerful image of taking the crucified down from their crosses is motivated both by his own historical experience as a Jesuit companion in El Salvador and also by an understanding of the praxis of the resurrection. This is an enormous contribution to our understanding of the meaning of the Christian message: God's self-communication of his saving power to us in Jesus Christ, realized in history.

Precisely because an understanding of the praxis of the resurrection is such a theological accomplishment, it would behoove us to imagine how the central insights of this theology could find a wider theater of application by entering into conversation with thinking that neither begins within the same historical reality nor is mediated by similar theological categories. For if suffering is universal, if "crucified peoples" are to be found all over the globe, then the language of the "praxis" of resurrection, especially when understood as taking the victims down from their crosses, could well be served by engagement in wider dialogues. I can touch only on three such potential conversations here, but each would, I think, draw Sobrino's thought into wider circles of engagement, understanding, and application.

The first encounter is with the work of Matthias Beier, whose work on psychoanalysis and exegesis explores the origins of a religious typology that could sanction violence, and the visiting of violence upon the innocent. His *A Violent God-Image: An Introduction to the Work of Eugen Drewermann*[43] offers, I think, one valuable contribution to the problematic with which a theology of liberation is concerned: how the oppressors can do what they do even while being

Christians. Beier pushes his investigation through an analysis of war and interprets the cross as a redemption from the violent God-image that has given sanction to the pursuit of war and other ways of creating victims in history. If the praxis of resurrection includes the work of conversion, even of the powerful, then this kind of investigation would be helpful to a liberation methodology.

A second possible encounter with Sobrino's theology would be the work of Elaine Scarey. In *The Body in Pain*[44] she explores the ways human beings, and precisely their bodies, are "unmade" through the pain of torture and war. Certainly, this is timely for the period of war in which the United States now stands convicted of having caused so much unmaking of human lives. While not a theological work, her insights into how the power of oppression actually works to create victims is illuminating and extends the analysis to a broad field of human experience. The second half of the book examines how bodies and lives can be made again, reconstituted, as it were, through appeal to the structures of belief as realized in the materiality of history and concrete circumstance. This work has clear resonances with Sobrino's "resurrection praxis" and could lend further insight into the meaning of taking the crucified down from their crosses. It could help especially to relate this powerful metaphor to concerns in the developed world to bring an end to the machinery of war that contributes to dehumanization and poverty wherever it is waged. Sobrino can attest to that from his experience in El Salvador alone, where the war was fueled by resources from the powerful North. But we are seeing similar and even more disconcerting patterns around the world, with other powers repeating the tragic patterns of empires of the past.

In a similar vein, William T. Cavanagh's *Torture and Eucharist*[45] explores the experience of the church in Chile under the Pinochet regime, and sees the use of torture and the epidemic of "disappearances" as in some sense an ecclesiological problem. He then turns to the gradual conversion of the church into what he calls a "disappearing" church, which, through its eucharistic life, helps to reconstitute the tortured and disappeared Body of Christ in Chile. There would be rich possibilities here as well for interaction with Sobrino's notion of a "resurrection praxis" and the recovery of a prophetic voice in the church that would announce the good news in such a way as to expose the power of oppression for what it is and to work for a new order. In an "anti-prophetic"[46] age, as Sobrino calls it, a resurrection within the church itself of such vitality of spirit is ardently to be hoped for.

Any of these suggested encounters—and there are numerous others to imagine—would be fruitful if only because Sobrino's contribution to theologizing about suffering, within the framework of a Christology, constitutes such a massive gift to those who are concerned with it. They are concerned because human beings are actually suffering in today's world from the paroxysms of inhumanity, barbarity, envy, and greed—the very forces that sent Jesus to the cross. If there were no other reason to thank Jon Sobrino for his theology from suffering, it might be this: that the horizon of the suffering victims is the horizon of his theology, and because of that, for all who take this horizon seriously, there is no possibility of a merely abstract theology of suffering. This is a theology written from witnessing the suffering of the victims, the crucified *and risen* peoples of the world. What is at stake in this theology, therefore, is an understanding of suffering that is rooted in the death and resurrection of Jesus, *and* a lived praxis of the cross and the resurrection.

Sobrino's theology will always thus pose a disturbing challenge to those who would wish to keep at arms length from theology the problem of the suffering caused by injustice, and what we are to do about it in the name of the gospel. But Christian faith and the exigencies of history will not allow us to escape these questions or our responsibilities as baptized people with breath and life. Following Sobrino's lead, we are all called on at this moment in history to learn what it means to enter into solidarity with the victims of history and help take the crucified down from their crosses.

## Notes

1. The reference to "affliction" is from Simone Weil (*malheur*). See Weil, "The Love of God and Affliction," in *Waiting for God*, trans. Emma Craufurd (New York: Harper & Row, 1951). For an explanation of the term, see Paul Crowley, *Unwanted Wisdom: Suffering, the Cross, and Hope* (New York: Continuum, 2005), 35-37.

2. *Where Is God? Earthquake, Terrorism, Barbarism and Hope*, trans. Margaret Wilde (Maryknoll, N.Y.: Orbis Books, 2004).

3. See Kevin F. Burke and Robert Lassalle-Klein, eds., *Love That Produces Hope: The Thought of Ignacio Ellacuría* (Collegeville, Minn.: Liturgical Press, 2006), 1-67. The essay is translated by Robert Lassalle-Klein. For a thorough treatment of Ellacuría's theology, see Kevin F. Burke, *The Ground beneath the Cross: The Theology of Ignacio Ellacuría* (Washington, D.C.: Georgetown University Press, 2000).

4. "Ignacio Ellacuría," in *Love That Produces Hope*, 5.

5. Ibid., 6.

6. Ibid., 7.

7. Ignacio Ellacuría, "The Crucified People," in *Mysterium Liberationis: Fundamental Concepts of Liberation Theology*, ed. Ignacio Ellacuría and Jon Sobrino; trans. Phillip Berryman and Robert R. Barr (Maryknoll, N.Y.: Orbis Books, 1993), 582.

8. Ibid., 584.

9. Ibid., 585.

10. Ibid., 590.

11. Ibid., 591-92.

12. Ibid., 599-602.

13. Ibid., 603.

14. Ibid.

15. In *The Principle of Mercy: Taking the Crucified People from the Cross* (Maryknoll, N.Y.: Orbis Books, 1994), 49-57.

16. Ibid., 53.

17. Ibid., 55-56.

18. Ibid., 56.

19. Eng. trans., Maryknoll, N.Y.: Orbis Books, 1987.

20. Ibid., 162-63.

21. Ibid., 163.

22. *Christ the Liberator: A Historical-Theological Reading of Jesus of Nazareth*, trans. Paul Burns and Francis McDonagh (Maryknoll, N.Y.: Orbis Books, 1994), 221.

23. Ibid., 226.

24. Ibid., 228.

25. Ibid., 229.

26. See Jon Sobrino, "The Spirituality of Persecution and Martyrdom," in idem, *Spirituality of Liberation* (Maryknoll, N.Y.: Orbis Books, 1989), 87-88, where Sobrino provides a list of the martyrs, and includes, beyond that list, "Many other pastoral ministers and lay missionaries, delegates and ministers of the Word, catechists and sacristans, Caritas workers and human rights groups; many Protestant brothers and sisters, pastors and ministers, deacons and preachers; countless campesinos and Amerindians, workers and students, teachers and journalists, nurses, doctors, and intellectuals; persecuted and murdered for the reign of God."

27. Ibid., 235.

28. Ibid., 240.

29. Ibid., 244.

30. Ibid., 246.

31. Ibid., 254-55.

32. Ibid., 256. There follow here in the remaining pages of this remarkable book what may be some of the most trenchant yet lyrical passages ever written in the annals of liberation theology.

33. Trans. Paul Burns (Maryknoll, N.Y.: Orbis Books, 2001).

34. Ibid., 4-5. Sobrino was a witness to that of which he speaks in the form of massacres of innocent poor people, for example, at El Mozote—a form of violence that has been replicated numerous times around the world since the civil war in El Salvador came to an end. Consider Rwanda, Bosnia, and Darfur.

35. Ibid., 37.

36. Ibid., 39.

37. "Theological" here is in contrast to a question that arises from and pertains to the human side of the equation. Here, the question is turned on God.

38. Ibid., 44.

39. Ibid., 45.

40. Ibid., 47.

41. Ibid., 49.

42. Ibid., 48.

43. (New York: Continuum, 2004).

44. (New York: Oxford University Press, 1985).

45. (Oxford: Blackwell, 1998).

46. *Where Is God?* xxx.

# 3

# Visions and Revisions

*The Hermeneutical Implications of the Option for the Poor*

## WILLIAM O'NEILL, S.J.

The historian Alexander Kinglake once proposed that any church promising salvation bear the inscription "Important, if true."[1] So too, perhaps, for the Congregation for the Doctrine of the Faith (CDF)'s "Notification on the Works of Father Jon Sobrino, S.J."[2] Surely, the importance of the CDF's criticism of "grave deficiencies both in terms of methodology and content" depends on its truth-claims—or more precisely, on the hermeneutical strategies employed in their redemption.[3] For at issue, I argue in part 1 of this essay, is less the truth/validity (propositional content) of doctrine than its faithful/valid interpretation— Sobrino's interpretation of doctrine and the CDF's interpretation of Sobrino.

In part 2, I argue that the nub of the controversy rests in the hermeneutical implications of the "option for the poor" in Sobrino's ecclesiology. For the critical solidarity enjoined by the church's social doctrine entails not only social-ethical critique, that is, ethical *locus* of the "world of the poor," but a distinctive *locus theologicus* of interpreting doctrine, that is, the "church of the poor." Finally, in part 3, I consider the implications of the foregoing criticism for interpreting the Notification itself; in particular, the effective displacement of the church of the poor as the "object" of magisterial critique.

## A Question of Hermeneutics?

The introduction to the Notification observes that the CDF "does not intend to judge the subjective intentions of the Author," but seeks, rather, to "offer the faithful a secure criterion, founded upon the doctrine of the church, by which to judge the affirmations" contained in Sobrino's *oeuvre* [1]. Affirmations deemed "erroneous or dangerous" include, *inter alia*, Sobrino's methodological presuppositions; and his treatment of the divinity of Christ, the incarnation, the relationship of Jesus and the Kingdom; Jesus' self-consciousness; and the salvific value of his death [1]. Now, while modern hermeneutics is chary of

31

referring uncritically to the author's "subjective intentions" (*mens auctoris*)[4]; it is notable that Sobrino never disputes these central creedal dogmas. On the contrary, Sobrino writes as a theologian devoted, in the Ignatian tradition, to "thinking with the Church" (*sentire cum ecclesia*).[5] Neither does the CDF deny that Sobrino "considers the theological fonts 'normative'" [2]. The gravamen of the CDF's critique rests not in Sobrino's denial of the cognitive content of christological dogma but rather in his "erroneous or dangerous" interpretations.

The prefatory "Explanatory Note" on the Notification ascribes the source of these errors to the "primary methodological deficiencies" of Sobrino's "affirmation that the 'Church of the poor' is *the* ecclesial 'setting' of Christology and offers its fundamental orientation."[6] The "methodological errors" of adopting such an interpretative perspective, says the CDF, "give rise to conclusions which do not conform to the doctrine of the Church" in the aforementioned "key areas."[7] But to question Sobrino's hermeneutical locus is to raise the question of hermeneutics itself—not only of the epistemic status of the "church of the poor" in Sobrino's ecclesiology but, a fortiori, of CDF's own reading of Sobrino.

### A Hermeneutical Excursus on the "Principle of Charity"

How, then, are we to interpret potentially problematic interpretations? Writing on theological inculturation, the former general of the Society of Jesus, Pedro Arrupe, extends St. Ignatius's "presupposition" in the Spiritual Exercises to interpretation generally. In Arrupe's words, the "*Presupposition* of the Exercises demands a basic disposition at the outset of the retreat which is of immense value . . . to be ready to 'save the proposition of the neighbor' (22). This is where authentic dialogue begins."[8] Such a reading foreshadows the philosopher Donald Davidson's "principle of charity" in interpreting problematic texts. Indeed, we may say that interpreting the text's validity claims entails an extensive application of the principle of charity, whereby the reader assumes the (potential) truth of the author's claims against the backdrop of his/her "patterns of belief" and interprets the sense or meaning of her claim accordingly.[9]

Such a practical attitude of sympathetic identification implies that we hold "belief constant as far as possible while solving for meaning."[10] Davidson argues that "a belief is identified by its location in a pattern of beliefs; it is this pattern that determines the subject matter of the belief, what the belief is about. Before some object in, or aspect of, the world can become part of the subject matter of a belief (true or false) there must be endless true beliefs about the subject matter."[11] A hermeneutics of charity, then, seeks to preserve validity (truth), for example, of a particular doctrine, by respecting the web of belief comprising "ecclesial faith."[12] Interpreting ("solving for meaning") against the backdrop of such faith, we may ask what it would *mean* for a contested interpretation to be valid or true, for example, Sobrino's interpretation of the "church of the poor." Sobrino's own prolegomenon is instructive: "the preliminary task of theology" in and for the church "is to find its place in the reality of this suffering world." Significantly, the place (or *locus*) is not reified:

> This does not mean primarily finding a concrete *ubi* within a world that happens to be suffering, but rather finding a place within the very suffering of this world. Stated graphically, the place of theology is the suffering of the world, and to stand in its place means to stand within the actual suffering that racks this world. The place of theology, then, is much more a *quid* than an *ubi*.[13]

Now, on this reading, the "church of the poor," I shall argue in part 2, is not distinct, or separate from "the *apostolic faith* which the Church has transmitted through all generations."[14] Rather, the principle of charity reveals the ecclesial "option for the poor" to be (a) an authentic interpretation of "ecclesial faith"; and as embodied in "the "church of the poor," (b) a *locus theologicus* of interpreting "ecclesial faith."

### Hermeneutical Implications of the Option for the Poor

The ecclesial "option for the poor" emerges in the second CELAM conference in Medellín, and the third in Puebla—an affirmation extended to the universal church in John Paul II's *Sollicitudo rei socialis* (nos. 42-43). In Sobrino's words, the "response to the suffering of the poor is an ethical demand, but it is also a practice that is salvific for those who enter into solidarity with the poor."[15] Sobrino thus speaks of "God's partiality to victims in virtue of their sheer fact of their being victims, the active defense mounted by God in their behalf, and the liberative divine design in their regard."[16]

And yet this very partiality remains a *crux interpretum* with respect to both its "ethical demand" and "salvific practice." While affirming doctrinal validity of the option for the poor, the Notification (citing the CDF's 1986 *Libertatis conscientia*) insists that "the Church cannot express this option by means of reductive sociological and ideological categories which would make this preference a partisan choice of conflict."[17] The Notification likewise looks to the earlier instruction *Libertatis nuntius* (1984).[18] There, the authentic teaching of CELAM at Puebla is contrasted with a "temptation to reduce the gospel to an earthly gospel": "Concepts uncritically borrowed from Marxist ideology and recourse to theses of a biblical hermeneutic marked by rationalism are at the basis of the new interpretation which is corrupting whatever was authentic in the general initial commitment on behalf of the poor."

While neither Instruction explicitly refers to Sobrino's interpretation, then Cardinal Joseph Ratzinger's remarks on "Liberation Theology" (1984) are particularly critical of Sobrino's adoption of a "Marxist hermeneutics," that is, "the interpretation of the poor in the sense of Marxist, dialectical history and the interpretation of the choice of a party in terms of class struggle." Such a reductive "fusion between God and history" is finally inimical to the church's social doctrine and its emphasis on universal human dignity and human rights.[19] In the words of *Libertatis nuntius*, issued several months later, "the very nature of ethics is radically called into question because of the borrowing of these theses from Marxism. In fact, it is the transcendent character of the distinction between good and evil, the principle of morality, which is implicitly denied in the perspective of the class struggle."[20]

### The World of the Poor

Clearly, such is not the teaching of CELAM. The bishops have not adopted a Marxist hermeneutics of suspicion; but neither, I believe, has Sobrino. As we saw, for Sobrino, ethical "partiality to victims" is divinely sanctioned: "Theology finds its place in a suffering world insofar as such a world is a mediation of truth and absoluteness of God. The determination of the suffering world as the place of theology is an option prior to theology, an option required of all believers and all persons."[21] Indeed, a hermeneutics of charity reveals Sobrino's interpretation to be neither ethically nor theologically reductive.

Ethically, the ecclesial "option for the poor" represents what Sobrino, following Ignacio Ellacuría, describes as the "historicization" of human dignity and rights.[22] In a world of vast poverty and uncivil strife, the "rights of the poor"[23] become, in effect, "the prime analogate of the human right."[24] Far, then, from succumbing to "reductive sociological and ideological categories,"[25] Sobrino's interpretation underscores the *concrete* universality[26] of "the ethical demand" arising, in the words of *Libertatis nuntius,* from "the dignity of the human person, created 'in the image and likeness of 'God' (Gen. 1:26-27)"—a dignity "ridiculed and scorned in the midst of a variety of different oppressions: cultural, political, racial, social, and economic, often in conjunction with one another."[27]

As I have argued in greater detail elsewhere, our very moral entitlement to *equal* respect or consideration justifies *preferential* treatment for those whose basic rights are most imperiled—in Albert Camus' phrase, our taking "the victim's side."[28] For if equal consideration does not imply identical treatment, so we may distinguish legitimately between indiscriminate regard for moral persons and discriminate response to their differing situations.[29] The church's social doctrine expresses such a discriminate response in the graduated moral urgency of differing human rights, that is, the lexical priority of agents' basic rights over other, less exigent claims, for example, property rights, and in the differing material conditions presumed for realizing the same human rights, for example, the greater nutritional needs of pregnant women.[30]

So it is, the fitting historicization of rights—what we might call a postliberal conception—enjoins a primordial responsibility for victims, a moral solidarity with the "world of the poor." Such solidarity, moreover, exercises a hermeneutic function in its own right. For, foremost among the lexically prior "rights of the poor" is the right to effective social participation.[31] Those historically consigned to the margins of history must find their voice—in Sobrino's words, the "irruption of the poor" in history.[32] For if, in society's basic structure, we are all equally worthy of being represented, then the claims of those denied such recognition, often through systemic suppression of their basic rights, become (and remain) morally imperious.[33] (Significantly, precisely by adopting "the concept of the poor in the Synoptics," liberation theology, says Sobrino, "distances itself from Marxism which did not include the poor in this sense as agents of history.")[34]

Seeing the victims' point of view, that is, their epistemic or hermeneutical privilege, emerges then as a touchstone of the legitimacy of our prevailing institutional arrangements; only thus—in "passing over to the victim's side" (Luke 10:34)—can we offer an equitable assessment of our legal enactments, juridical decisions, economic policies, and so forth. The epistemic or hermeneutical privilege of the poor rests, then, not in canonizing a "partisan" or "sectarian" point of view, but rather in revealing the partiality of such illusory or coerced consensus, for example, the systematic distortions of the "variety of different oppressions" to which *Libertatis nuntius* refers.

Ethically, we may conclude, Sobrino's option for the poor is fittingly partial, yet not reductively partisan. Indeed, it is precisely the "rights of the poor," including, a fortiori, their right to effective participation, that demystify prevailing structural inequities, unmasking rather than engendering violence. Yet if, ethically, Sobrino cannot be accused of rejecting "the social doctrine of the church . . . with disdain," neither can he be condemned for emptying the "option for the poor" of its "theological reality."[35] On the contrary, Sobrino stands at the very forefront of those seeking to elaborate a distinctive *theology* of human rights. For Sobrino, theology becomes an *intellectus amoris*, which is historically specified "when confronted with a suffering people (love as justice)."[36]

Sobrino thus concludes, the "practice of love and justice is not only something that theology must foster," ethical practice itself becomes "a mystagogical reality that gives access to the mystery of God. The *intellectus amoris (justitiae)* can function as a mystagogy for the *intellectus fidei*."[37] And so it is, Sobrino speaks of "the *divine* element in the struggle for human rights."[38] The blood of the poor, writes Sobrino, quoting Archbishop Romero, "touches the very heart of God." Resisting a purely secularist, liberal reduction of rights rhetoric, Sobrino writes that the defense of the rights of the poor, "must be effectuated in the spirit of Jesus, in the spirit of the Beatitudes, with a pervading consciousness of the gratuity of both the gift and the task."[39]

## The Church of the Poor

The "struggle for human rights," says Sobrino, "is divine. And this is important . . . for the church." Far from abdicating the church's teaching on human rights, Sobrino insists that the struggle is an essential "mode of expressing the very faith of the church. It is important, and essential, for the very identity of the church, and for its historical relevance." But just so, "for the human rights struggle to be genuinely ecclesial, it must never lose sight of its theological roots."[40]

In the course of his writings, Sobrino often invokes the parable of the Good Samaritan, most notably in interpreting "the Samaritan Church and the principle of mercy."[41] And as Pope Benedict XVI has eloquently written, the church's ethical demands are expressed in Jesus' response to the lawyer's question, "Who is my neighbor?" (Luke 10:29).[42] In Luke's story of the Good Samaritan, impartial regard for my neighbor's rights justifies preferential attention for my neighbor in distress. Luke's narrative reveals the boundless, universal scope of love precisely in demanding a moral solidarity with those who suffer—my "neighbor, the masses."[43] And yet, there is a surplus of religious meaning not exhausted by rights talk. For if our postliberal account of rights demands that we "take the victim's side," so the solidarity enjoined by the "principle of mercy" demands that we take the victim's side *as* our own. As John Donahue observes, "Luke subtly alters the thrust of the parable," for Jesus does not so much answer the lawyer's question as "describe what it means to be a neighbor which then becomes the substance of [his] counterquestion. . . ."[44]

The lawyer's response, "the one who treated him with mercy" (Luke 10:37) is richly ironic, since it is the despised schismatic who teaches the lawyer the meaning of the law.[45] And so, with salvific irony, Jesus bids him, "Go, and do likewise!" Jesus answers the lawyer's first question, "What must I do to inherit eternal life?" in reversing the second. For the command to "love the Lord your God, with all your heart, and with all your soul, and with all your strength, and with all your mind; and your neighbor as yourself" (Luke 10:27) is fulfilled not in this or that particular deed of mercy,[46] but rather in one's becoming neighbor to the stranger (Luke 10:36). And, as modern-day martyrs such as Ellacuría attest, this is the work of love, of mercy.

"What I must do to *live*" (my *metanoia*) is, then, to "turn" to the world of the poor, of the half-dead stranger—in the martyred Archbishop Romero's words, "becoming incarnate in their world, . . . proclaiming the good news to them," even to the point of "sharing their fate."[47] For Christians, the disciple is, in Christ, always already in communion with the suffering "other." "To be a Christian," says Gustavo Gutiérrez, "is to draw near, to make oneself a neighbor, not the one I encounter in my journey but the one in whose journey I place myself."[48] And it is thus that "defense of the life of the poor" becomes "mystagogy, or initiation into the very mystery of God."[49] In Sobrino's words, "It is the

victim lying along the side of the road who de-centers the church and is transformed into the 'other' (and radically 'other') in the eyes of the church. It is the
re-action of mercy that verified whether the church has de-centered itself, and
to what extent it has done so."[50]

What, then, shall we say of the "place" of such mystagogy, "the Samaritan
church"? In applying the principle of charity, we saw, we hold belief constant
against the backdrop of ecclesial faith and solve for meaning, that is, we ask
what it would mean for a belief to be valid or true *for us*—the implied reader.
A hermeneutics of charity, we saw, illumines the ethical meaning of "taking the
victims' side" and the theological meaning of "taking it as our own" (in accordance with "the principle of mercy").[51] But, as in Luke's parable, to prove the
latter true, that is, "to go and do likewise" (Luke 10:37), renders mercy (compassion) itself a way of seeing or interpreting. And thus, for Sobrino, the principle of mercy figures among the "normative fonts" implicitly invoked in
interpreting ecclesial faith. For taking the victims' side as our own determines,
in part, what it means *for us* to verify or vindicate an interpretation of doctrine:
the Samaritan church becomes itself a *locus theologicus*.[52]

Far from adopting a reductive hermeneutics of suspicion, Sobrino specifies
the principle of charity by the principle of mercy, that is, the *intellectus amoris*,
historically determined "when confronted with a suffering people."[53] In effect,
Sobrino presumes the truth of kerygmatic proclamation and interprets particular doctrines, for example, the salvific import of Jesus' resurrection, from the
perspective of a suffering people:[54] the *quid* of ecclesial solidarity, not the *ubi*
of "partisan praxis."[55] To be sure, no single interpretation of "the suffering and
passion of the world" suffices; neither does the principle of mercy bequeath us
a simple decision-procedure.[56] Even among liberation theologians, certain
*quaestiones* remain *disputatae*. The claim is rather that doctrinal interpretation
will be "proven true" inasmuch as it is "effectuated in the spirit of Jesus, in the
spirit of the Beatitudes." How, that is, is the "gospel to the poor" fulfilled "today,"
in our hearing (Luke 4:21)?[57] In Sobrino's words, "In this way, the community
of perspectives required by hermeneutics is achieved in the continuance of
Jesus' practice, which is necessary, though by no means sufficient, to understand the historical Jesus who initiated it."[58]

## The Limits of Suspicion

To understand, writes Paul Ricoeur, is "not to project oneself into the text but
to expose oneself to it; it is to receive a self enlarged by the appropriation of the
proposed worlds which interpretation unfolds."[59] I argued above that appro-
priating the proposed "world of the poor" in Sobrino's text permits us to understand the Samaritan church as a *locus theologicus*. Such a locus becomes, *ab
ovo*, a place from which we interpret doctrine—and only at the limits of such

interpretation, where the principle of charity is systematically distorted by ideology does a "demystifying and reductive hermeneutics" of suspicion succeed to a hermeneutics of charity.[60] The epistemic privilege of the poor, as we saw, reveals such distortions, for example, systemic rights violations, which may go so deep as to remain unrecognized.[61]

For Sobrino, following Ellacuría, for instance, the legal protection of property rights in prevailing regimes may well become "a mask to conceal the fundamental violation of the most basic human rights," so that every "possible ethical defense of human rights crumbles at its base."[62] In the face of systematic bias or distortion, for example, practical or "social Docetism,"[63] "[o]nly the consistent affirmation of the right to life, including the right of freedom, can be the crucial test of what the real understanding of human rights is, as opposed to its self-interested mystification."[64] Here, then, in a demystifying hermeneutics, one seeks not so much to *preserve* the "proposition of the neighbor" as to *explain* it—a gambit warranted by systematic bias in communication. But a hermeneutics of suspicion is not, as *Libertatis nuntius* assumes, Sobrino's starting place; it derives rather from the universal claims of respect and recognition underwritten by the church's social doctrine and, implicitly, by the hermeneutics of charity itself.

One wonders, though, if the CDF has not effectively reversed the hermeneutical flow. For rather than seeking to preserve validity, the Notification seizes on ostensible contradictions, that is, that "on some occasions the erroneous propositions are situated within the context of other expressions which would seem to contradict them" [1]. Perhaps most significant, though, is the strong reading of the "church of the poor." For Sobrino, as indeed for Luke, the poor are, in the first place, materially poor—those who suffer the systemic deprivation of basic human rights. In Donahue's words, "The 'poor' in the Bible are almost without exception *powerless* people who experience economic and social deprivation. In both Isaiah and the Psalms the poor are often victims of the injustice of the rich and powerful."[65]

Now, the "hope against hope" of such victims, we saw, comprised the locus of Sobrino's ecclesial faith.[66] Yet in the very first paragraph of the Notification's Explanatory Note, poverty is redescribed in epistemic rather than material terms: "the first poverty among people is not to know Christ."[67] Here, the locus of the poor becomes, in effect, those who do not know Christ, or whose knowledge is appropriately contrasted with "the experience of the Church herself."[68] But such an implicit antinomy, opposing the "church of the poor" to "the apostolic faith transmitted through the church for all generations," represents a misplaced concreteness [2]: the *quid* of the church's experience—in which mercy becomes itself a way of seeing—projected as the *ubi* of "partisan praxis."

Whence such a reductive reading of the Samaritan church in terms of utopian "particularism or sectarianism"? [69] Here too, perhaps, the issue is less the truth of Sobrino's interpretation than the interpretation of truth, that is, the methodological/hermeneutical premises underlying dogmatic affirmations. For the CDF, it seems, recur to a distinctively modern methodological construal of dogma. As Bernard Lonergan observed, "the theologians at the end of the seventeenth century" introduced a novel interpretation of dogmatic theology:

> It is true that the word "dogmatic" had been previously applied to theology. But then it was used to denote a distinction from moral, or ethical, or historical theology. Now it was employed in a new sense, in opposition to scholastic theology. It replaced the inquiry of the *quaestio* by the pedagogy of the thesis. It demoted the quest of faith for understanding to a desirable, but secondary, and indeed, optional goal. It gave basic and central significance to the certitudes of faith, their presuppositions, and their consequences.[70]

Arrayed against the suspicions of the Enlightenment, the new dogmatic theology, says Lonergan, "owed its mode of proof to Melchior Cano and, as that theologian was also a bishop and inquisitor, so the new dogmatic theology not only proved its theses, but also was supported by the teaching authority and the sanctions of the Church."[71] And yet, as Lonergan concludes, a "quite different foundation" emerges, "when theology turns from deductivism to an empirical approach, from the static to the dynamic, from the abstract to the concrete, from the universal to the historical totality of particulars, from invariable rules to intelligent adjustment and adaptation."[72]

Is it surprising, then, that from the perspective of the former, Sobrino's "postmodern" methodological turn to the concrete, historical (historicized) locus of the church of the poor should meet with suspicion? For the "pedagogy of the thesis" opposes the universal, historically invariable rules of doctrine to the concrete, "historicized" totality of particulars, for example, the locus of the church of the poor. But if, with Sobrino, one understands historicization precisely as the concrete modality of universal validity, the opposition proves illusory. What remains in dispute is the *pedagogy* of the thesis, so that Sobrino's "intelligent adjustment and adaptation" need not, after all, signify "methodological error."

## Conclusion

"Only starting from ecclesial faith, in communion with the Magisterium, can the theologian acquire a deeper understanding of the Word of God contained in Scripture and transmitted by the living Tradition of the Church" [9]. A hermeneutics of charity, I've argued, affirms the primacy of ecclesial faith, from which emerge the proper, charismatic roles of theologian and magisterium. Communion is thus at once a source of wisdom, unfolding insight, and of doctrinal development—"a font of authentic newness and light for people of good will" [9]. So too, communion, as John Paul II reminds us, is the perfection of the ethical virtue of solidarity with the poor and oppressed.[73] And is this not, finally, a summons to prophetic humility for theologians and members of the CDF alike?

## Notes

1. See Geoffrey Madan, *Notebooks*, ed. J. A. Gere and John Sparrow (Oxford: Oxford University Press, 1981), 11.

2. Congregation for the Doctrine of the Faith, "Notification on the Works of Father Jon Sobrino, S.J." (November 26, 2006). Available at http://www.vatican.va/roman curia congregations/cfaith/documents/rc. All citations in brackets in the text refer to the English translation (see below pp. 255-66).

3. Congregation for the Doctrine of the Faith, "Explanatory Note on the Notification on the Works of Father Jon Sobrino, S.J." (November 26, 2006). Available at http://www. vatican.va/roman curia congregations/cfaith/documents/rc, 1.

4. See Hans-Georg Gadamer, *Truth and Method*, 2d rev. ed., trans. Joel Weinsheimer and Donald Marshall (New York: Crossroad, 1991), 270.

5. In his *Profiles in Liberation: 36 Portraits of Third World Theologians*, Deane William Ferm writes that Sobrino's theology is notable precisely for his fidelity to the magisterium: "Jon Sobrino is a firm believer in the dogmas of the Catholic church. . . . He acknowledges, 'the irreplaceable role of the christological dogmas of the church for liberation theology' (*Jesus in Latin America*, 19), and insists that 'there is no reduction of the total truth about Jesus Christ in the christology of liberation, either in intent or in fact' (ibid., 53). An authentic Christology, he believes, can be developed only 'within the framework of the trinitarian reality of God' (*Christology at the Crossroads*, xxiv)" (*Profiles in Liberation: 36 Portraits of Third World Theologians* [Mystic, Conn.: Twenty-Third Publications, 1988], 184-88, at 185).

6. CDF, "Explanatory Note," 3 (emphasis in original).

7. Ibid.

8. Pedro Arrupe, S.J., "Two Letters of Father Arrupe on Inculturation," in *Other Apostolates Today: Selected Letters and Addresses III*, ed. Jerome Aixala, S.J. (St. Louis: Institute of Jesuit Sources, 1981), 170-84, at 175.

9. See Donald Davidson, "Thought and Talk," in *Inquiries into Truth and Interpretation* (Oxford: Clarendon, 1984), 155-70, at 168. For a critical application of the principle, see Steven Lukes, "Relativism in Its Place," in *Rationality and Relativism*, ed. Martin Hollis and Steven Lukes (Cambridge, Mass.: MIT Press, 1982), 261-305.

10. Donald Davidson, "Radical Interpretation," in *Inquiries into Truth and Interpretation*, 137. The principle functions, in Hans-Georg Gadamer's terms, as a pre-judice or fore-structure of understanding (*Vorverständnis*).

11. For Davidson, we are justified in invoking the principle of charity because "disagreement and agreement alike are intelligible only against a background of massive agreement" ("Thought and Talk," 168).

12. Davidson, "Radical Interpretation," 137.

13. Jon Sobrino, *The Principle of Mercy: Taking the Crucified People from the Cross* (Maryknoll, N.Y.: Orbis Books, 1994), 31-32.

14. CDF, "Explanatory Note," 3 (emphasis in original).

15. Jon Sobrino, "Bearing with One Another in Faith," in *Theology of Christian Solidarity*, ed. Jon Sobrino and Juan Hernández Pico, trans. Phillip Berryman (Maryknoll, N.Y.: Orbis Books, 1994), 10-11.

16. Sobrino, *The Principle of Mercy*, 17.

17. See Congregation for the Doctrine of the Faith, "Instruction on Christian Freedom and Liberation" (March 22, 1986) in *Liberation Theology: A Documentary History*, ed. Alfred T. Hennelly (Maryknoll, N.Y.: Orbis Books, 1990), 461-97.

18. See Congregation for the Doctrine of the Faith, "Instruction on Certain Aspects of the 'Theology of Liberation'" (August 6, 1984), in *Liberation Theology: A Documentary History*, 393-414.

19. Joseph Cardinal Ratzinger, "Liberation Theology," in *Liberation Theology: A Documentary History*, 367-74, at 373, 372.

20. Congregation for the Doctrine of the Faith, "Instruction on Certain Aspects of the 'Theology of Liberation,'" 404.

21. Sobrino, *The Principle of Mercy*, 30.

22. For exemplary interpretations of "historicization" in the writings of Ellacuría and Sobrino, see Robert Lassalle-Klein, "Ignacio Ellacuría's Debt to Xavier Zubiri: Critical Principles for a Latin American Philosophy and Theology of Liberation," in *Love That Produces Hope: The Thought of Ignacio Ellacuría*, ed. Kevin F. Burke, S.J., and Robert Lassalle-Klein (Collegeville, Minn.: Liturgical Press, 2006), 88-127; and Kevin F. Burke, "Christian Salvation and the Disposition of Transcendence: Ignacio Ellacuría's Soteriology," in *Love That Produces Hope*, 169-86.

23. See Gustavo Gutiérrez, *The Power of the Poor in History*, trans. Robert R. Barr (Maryknoll, N.Y.: Orbis Books, 1983), 87-88; see likewise Jon Sobrino, *Spirituality of Liberation: Toward Political Holiness*, trans. Robert R. Barr (Maryknoll, N.Y.: Orbis Books, 1988), 103-14.

24. Sobrino, *Spirituality of Liberation*, 107.

25. CDF, "Instruction on Christian Freedom and Liberation," 483, cited in "Explanatory Note," 1.

26. Sobrino writes, "In these poor, a concrete universal irrupts upon us with the power to make us see the totality . . ." (*Spirituality of Liberation*, 55).

27. CDF, "Instruction on Certain Aspects of the 'Theology of Liberation,'" 394.

28. Albert Camus, *The Plague* (New York: Alfred A. Knopf, 1960), 230. In the present context, the term "victim" is an evaluative moral description referring to those suffering deprivation of their basic rights; as such, it is reducible neither to class membership nor to a particular psychological state. I have developed this analysis in "No Amnesty for Sorrow: The Privilege of the Poor in Christian Social Ethics," *Theological Studies* 55, no. 4 (December 1994): 638-56.

29. See Gene Outka, *Agape* (New Haven: Yale University, 1972), 20. Cf. Ronald Dworkin, *Taking Rights Seriously* (Cambridge: Harvard University, 1978), 227.

30. See Jean Drèze and Amartya Sen, *Hunger and Public Action* (Oxford: Clarendon, 1989), 37-42.

31. See Henry Shue, *Basic Rights: Subsistence, Affluence, and U.S. Foreign Policy* (Princeton, N.J.: Princeton University Press, 1980), 71.

32. Sobrino, *The Principle of Mercy*, 32; cf. Sobrino, *Spirituality of Liberation*, 53-58; Gustavo Gutiérrez, *We Drink from Our Own Wells: The Spiritual Journey of a People*, trans. Matthew J. O'Connell (Maryknoll, N.Y.: Orbis Books, 1984), 19-32.

33. John Rawls, "Fairness as Goodness," *Philosophical Review* 84 (1975): 536-54, at 539.

34. Jon Sobrino, *Jesus the Liberator: A Historical-Theological Reading of Jesus of Nazareth*, trans. Paul Burns and Francis McDonagh (Maryknoll, N.Y.: Orbis Books, 1993), 127.

35. Congregation for the Doctrine of the Faith, "Instruction on Certain Aspects of the 'Theology of Liberation,'" 407, 405.

36. Sobrino, *The Principle of Mercy*, 36.

37. Ibid., 42-43.

38. Sobrino, *Spirituality of Liberation*, 113.

39. Ibid., 112.

40. Ibid., 114.

41. Sobrino, *The Principle of Mercy*, 15-26.

42. See Benedict XVI, *Deus caritas est*, no. 15. Available at the Vatican Web site.

43. M. D. Chenu, "Les masses pauvres," in G. Cottier et al., *Eglise et pauvreté* (Paris: Cerf, 1965), 169-76, at 169. Wolfgang Schrage, *The Ethics of the New Testament*, trans. David Green (Philadelphia: Fortress, 1988), 78, 81.

44. John Donahue, "Who Is My Enemy? The Parable of the Good Samaritan and the Love of Enemies," in *The Love of Enemy and Non-Retaliation in the New Testament*, ed. Willard M. Swartley (Louisville: Westminster John Knox, 1992), 144.

45. The lawyer's response, "'The one who showed him mercy (Luke 10:37),'" says Donahue, alludes to the prophetic tradition of Hosea 6:6 and Micah 7:8, whose authority was not recognized by Samaritans. Not only, then, "is the Samaritan a neighbor but he acts according to those scriptures which the lawyer himself recognizes as authoritative" ("Who Is My Enemy?" 145).

46. See Karl Rahner, "The 'Commandment' of Love in Relation to the Other Commandments," in *Theological Investigations* 5, trans. Karl H. Kruger (New York: Seabury, 1966), 439-59, at 453; cf. "The Theology of Freedom," in *Theological Investigations* 6, trans. Karl and Boniface Kruger (New York: Seabury, 1974), 178-96; and Rahner's observation that "freedom is not simply the capacity to do this or that but (formally) a self-disposing into finality" ("Reflections on the Unity of the Love of Neighbour and the Love of God," in *Theological Investigations* 6, 231-49, at 240).

47. Oscar Romero, "The Political Dimension of the Faith from the Perspective of the Option for the Poor," in *Liberation Theology: A Documentary History*, 292-303, at 298.

48. Gustavo Gutiérrez, "Toward a Theology of Liberation" (July 1968), trans. Alfred T. Hennelly, in *Liberation Theology: A Documentary History* 62-76, at 74.

49. Sobrino, *Spirituality of Liberation*, 113.

50. Sobrino, *The Principle of Mercy*, 22.

51. See Jon Sobrino, *Christ the Liberator*, trans. Paul Burns (Maryknoll, N.Y.: Orbis Books, 2001), 45.

52. Sobrino writes that the option for the poor "is an all-embracing option to grasp the whole view, but to see it consciously from one position. This does not mean reducing the whole to one of its parts, but we hope—and in this sense the option is also a 'wager'—that from the point of view of the poor we will see more and see more clearly than from any other position" (*Jesus the Liberator*, 33; cf. *Christ the Liberator*, 18).

53. See *Jesus the Liberator*, 33-34.

54. See Jon Sobrino, *Christ the Liberator*, 17-53. "Having hope for victims is the first demand Jesus' resurrection makes of us, but so is taking an active part in that hope. Being capable of making their hope ours, being ready to work for it, even if this makes us victims, is an irreplaceable hermeneutical principle. . . . Those who love the victims, who feel total compassion for them, who are ready to give themselves to them and share their fate—such can see hope for themselves too in Jesus' resurrection" (*Christ the Liberator*, 44-45).

55. CDF, "Instruction on Certain Aspects of the 'Theology of Liberation,'" 404.

56. See Walter Benjamin, *The Origin of German Tragic Drama*, trans. John Osborne (London: Verso, 1998), 166.

57. In his commentary on the pericope, Robert Karris observes that the word "today," in Luke's Greek, refers not to "the historical then of Jesus' time," but rather "to the present today of the time of fulfillment." See Robert J. Karris, "The Gospel According to Luke," in *The New Jerome Biblical Commentary*, ed. Raymond Brown, Joseph Fitzmyer, and Roland Murphy (Englewood Cliffs, N.J.: Prentice Hall, 1990), 690.

58. Sobrino, *Jesus the Liberator*, 51.

59. Paul Ricoeur, "Hermeneutics and the Critique of Ideology," in *Paul Ricoeur: Hermeneutics and the Human Sciences*, ed. and trans. John B. Thompson (Cambridge: Cambridge University Press, 1981), 94.

60. Paul Ricoeur, "A Response by Paul Ricoeur," in *Paul Ricoeur*, 34.

61. For this reason, it is at best ambiguous to say that Sobrino's "preoccupation for the poor and oppressed, particularly in Latin America . . . *certainly is shared by the whole Church*" (emphasis added). Were this the case, the CDF could hardly proceed to chastize Christians who "remain indifferent to the grave problems of human misery and injustice" (CDF, "Explanatory Note," 1).

62. Ignacio Ellacuría, "Human Rights in a Divided Society," in *Human Rights in the Americas: The Struggle for Consensus,* ed. A. Hennelly and J. Langan (Washington, D.C.: Georgetown University Press, 1982), 58-59.

63. Sobrino, *Christ the Liberator*, 287. See Sobrino's illuminating interpretation of "countering recurrent Docetism" by progressing "beyond the '*vere* homo' and to see in Jesus Christ the 'homo *verus*'" (290).

64. Ellacuría, "Human Rights in a Divided Society," 58-59.

65. John Donahue, "The Bible and Catholic Social Teaching: Will This Engagement Lead to Marriage?" in *Modern Catholic Social Teaching: Commentaries and Interpretations,* ed. Kenneth R. Himes (Washington, D.C.: Georgetown University Press, 2004), 9-40, at 22.

66. Sobrino, *Christ the Liberator*, 43.

67. CDF, "Explanatory Note," 1. Cf. Benedict XVI, "Message of His Holiness Benedict XVI for Lent 2006. Available at httpf://www.vatican.va/holy_father/benedict_xvi/messages/lent/documents, 2.

68. CDF, "Explanatory Note," 3.

69. Ibid., 1.

70. Bernard Lonergan, "Theology in Its New Context," in *A Second Collection: Papers by Bernard J. F. Lonergan, S.J.,* ed. William F. J. Ryan, S.J., and Bernard J. Tyrrell, S.J. (London: Darton, Longman, & Todd, 1974), 55-67, at 57.

71. Ibid.

72. Ibid., 63-64.

73. See *Sollicitudo rei socialis*, no. 40.

# 4

# On Not "Abandoning the Historical World to Its Wretchedness"

*A Prophetic Voice Serving an Incarnational Vision*

### Stephen J. Pope

The church is said to be facing a "crisis," or, indeed, a number of crises. African theologian Peter Kanyandago regards the most important challenge confronting the church in Africa to be the lack of "interface between what people are living and experiencing, and the Christian message as conveyed mainly through the western and cultural influence that has strongly marked African Christianity." Kanyandago describes this separation as a form of "schizophrenia."[1] His lament partially concerns inculturation in Africa, but it also pertains to the perceived distance of the everyday experience of ordinary Christians from the church's official liturgical life, institutional structures, and teachings.

Spanish Jesuit José González Faus relates the "crisis in credibility" to both a "crisis of sacraments" that do not bear adequate "signifying power"[2] for the faithful and to a crisis of religious authority separated from the vital spiritual experience of ordinary Christians. James F. Keenan, S.J., points to a related problem when he describes "the gulf between the teachings the leadership expresses and the needs and faith that the people of God hold."[3]

These scholars raise a variety of questions concerning what can be broadly called the "crisis of credibility" facing the contemporary church. It is important to note that this crisis is due to inadequacies on the part of the laity as well as the clergy—weak levels of commitment, lack of vision, improper training, failure of communication, and so forth. Misunderstanding, half-heartedness, and hypocrisy have, of course, compromised the church since the time Jesus called the first disciples. Yet González Faus maintains that the church's growing "crisis of credibility" is owing to the fact that instead of "moving in the direction of the gospel," the institution is "moving in the opposite direction."[4]

This chapter will advance the twofold thesis that Sobrino's work is best understood as a prophetic response to the church as it moves "in the wrong direction," and that this prophetic enterprise reflects his deeper underlying incarnational vision of the Christian life. It argues, in other words, that he addresses the church's failure to "move in the direction of the gospel" because he believes that God has given the church a sacramental mission of facilitating the reception of grace in the world and promoting the coming of the kingdom of God. Sobrino is more interested in addressing the suffering of the poor than building up the church's credibility, but the difficulties with the latter are substantially connected to its failures sufficiently to address the former.

Sobrino's theology appears to some readers to negate or at least to compromise some important components of Christian doctrine. He is suspected of affirming Jesus but not Christ, emphasizing the crucifixion but not the resurrection, embracing the church of the poor but not all of God's people, and denouncing social sin but not personal sin. This chapter will argue, though, that what might appear to be one-sided negations actually function to overcome false dichotomies based on abstract and one-sided distortions of the Christian faith. Some of these abstractions that lead to imbalance are christological: Christ without Jesus, resurrection without crucifixion; some of these abstractions are ecclesial: preaching without action, worship and liturgy without conversion, church without the world, hierarchy without the people; some are anthropological: soul without the body, intellect without affections, feelings, and emotions, theory without praxis, persons without community; some are ethical: power without responsibility, possession and belief without action and discipleship, charity without justice, reconciliation without honesty and truth.

This chapter will argue that Sobrino's work intends to retrieve the second of these pairs without sacrificing the first; in fact, it is precisely by properly recovering and properly valuing the latter that we can authentically appreciate the former. Sobrino resists abstract affirmations and false oppositions in order to promote a more properly balanced Christian theology and in order to promote greater integrity in the lives of Christians. This synthetic vision offers a way of working to close the "gap" between belief and life decried by Kanyandago, González Faus, and Keenan. Sobrino's theological synthesis is at once traditional and innovative: it is traditional in the centrality it accords divine love, but it is innovative in the way priority of the poor organizes the elements of the synthesis.

This chapter's central claim is that Sobrino's prophetic voice serves his incarnational vision. To do this it proceeds in the following three steps: first, it considers the prophetic dimension of Sobrino's work; second, it examines the incarnational vision underlying his prophetic voice; and then, third, it discusses, in an illustrative rather than comprehensive way, the synthetic implications of Sobrino's incarnational vision for our understanding of some of the central elements in the Christian faith: God, Christ, the church, and the Christian moral life.

## The Prophetic Voice

Christians praise solidarity, universal human rights, and economic development, Sobrino complains, while all the time "ignoring the basic fact that a sharp division exists between those who have and those who do not—a gap which is ever growing."[5] We praise mercy but refuse to let it shape our attitudes, and we pursue the "civilization of wealth"[6] and disdain the "civilization of poverty" associated with the kingdom of God.

There is no doubt that Sobrino regards the gospel as profoundly countercultural.[7] Christians must cease having faith in idols and instead begin to resist them.[8] The inclusive message of the gospel opposes the exclusiveness of globalization, the peace of Christ stands against institutionalized violence, and the righteousness rooted in the truth of God contradicts the "institutional lie" that supports "structural injustice."[9] The parable of Lazarus and the rich man (Luke 16:19-31) sheds light on the contradiction between human decency and the massive underdevelopment of the world of the poor. Just as the rich man is oblivious to Lazarus's suffering, so the wealthy see neither the suffering of the poor nor the deep injustice of massive global inequalities, where so few have so much and so many have almost nothing. It is "obscene," writes Sobrino, that we do not feel shame in allowing widespread deprivation to exist alongside incredible opulence.[10] The poor offer the possibility of correcting this inequity, and they have a "humanizing potential" because "they offer community against individualism, service against selfishness, simplicity against opulence, creativity against an imposed copycat culture, openness to transcendence against bleak positivism and crass pragmatism."[11]

The church too often focuses almost exclusively on doctrinal teachings, liturgical practices, and canonical regulations without regard to their human implications for the poor.[12] Ecclesiastical triumphalism of some forms of traditionalist Catholicism presents one set of obstacles to noticing the poor, but even progressive theology developed in universities can leave theologians in a oblivious and complacent "sleep of egocentrism and selfishness."[13]

Isolation encourages the clergy to regard the poor as "objects" of charity rather than as intelligent subjects of their own lives from whom the church might learn.[14] The church's "activities tend to be more charitable than liberating: the Church acts in support of the weak, but it does not enter into confrontation with the oppressors."[15] Church authorities often cooperate with established powers involved, either directly or indirectly, in the exploitation of the poor.[16] This cooperation is fueled by the church's preoccupation with its own institutional security and status, and with an agenda focused on concerns such as "combating the sects, maintaining the number of members and their religiosity (even an alienating religiosity), its obsessive faithfulness to the magisterium, and a long list of other concerns. . . ."[17] The prophetic voice must confront injustice as well as unmask ideologies and denounce idols wherever they exist. This agenda inevitably leads to conflict with reigning powers, whether political and economic or ecclesial.

Some sociologists of religion describe this gap in terms of an inevitable divide between the prophetic and priestly "ideal types" of religious authority. Max Weber and Ernst Troeltsch found the priestly role tending to adapt, soften, or even eliminate the energetic and creative inspiration of those moved by a prophetic inspiration.[18] "Charismatic" individuals initiate creative movements that over time are subjected to historical and social forces that lead to their "routinization."

Yale theologian H. Richard Niebuhr held that "prophetism" represents "the dynamic element in Christianity" that is "poured into the social life" of communities. Eventually "white-hot convictions" inevitably "cool off into crystallized codes, solidified institutions, petrified creeds."[19] Niebuhr maintained that reducing "prophetic ethics" to a "code" enabled Judaism to be transmitted to future generations and that entrusting its interpretation to a professional class facilitated its enforcement in daily conduct. The process of "crystallization" brings consolidation, stability, and conservation of important values, but it also has the negative effect of decreasing the movement's responsiveness to new developments and, more importantly, to undermine its spontaneity, creativity, and "inner vitality."[20] Niebuhr worried that "by limitation and loss of symbolic reference, and by the substitution of the static for the dynamic, institutions deny what they wish to affirm and become the antithesis to their own thesis. The antithesis is never complete; something is always conserved, but much is lost and repudiated."[21]

Seen through this lens, the gap between the church's professed beliefs and actual practices is more than simply the age-old problem of religious hypocrisy; it is, rather, symptomatic of a familiar sociological process of what he called institutional "petrification." Prophets discern crises that constitute an opening to the resurgence of religious dynamism, but priests insist on maintaining the established institution, including its ensconced power structure, religious doctrines, and legal codes.

The Weberian and Niebuhrian analyses of ideal types can be very useful for comparative purposes. The prophet is characteristically critical, dissatisfied, disruptive, and, sometimes, utopian.[22] Highly critical of accommodation and suspicious of betrayal and hypocrisy, the prophet opposes any hint of identifying God with a merely human institution. The priest, on the other hand, is affirming, sensitive to the presence of the holy in the midst of the world, sees the community and its institutions as mediators of God's goodness, and calls attention to harmony, loyalty, fulfillment of the divine plan or will.[23] Applied to the New Testament, this paradigm makes it clear that Jesus is a prophetic figure whose demise was engineered, as Luke puts it, by the chief priests, the elders, and the leaders of the people (see, e.g., Luke 22:2, 66). Jesus understood himself as following in the inspired line of the Hebrew prophets and John the Baptist.[24]

While the sociological perspective can be useful, it can be misused, especially by those given to fitting complex figures into overly simple categories. Generalizations about "prophets," for example, should not ignore the complexity of the role of biblical prophets, for example, the existence of court prophets and institutionalized prophetic guilds.[25] The sociological perspective also underestimates the complexity and variance of prophetic roles in different biblical contexts, for example, the fact that the Deuteronomistic perspective regarded prophets as preservers of the Mosaic law.[26] It also fails to account for, or explains away, the scriptural description of Jesus as "priest, prophet, and king." Finally, it does not acknowledge the emergence of early Christian leaders, notably Paul and Peter, who play both prophetic and priestly roles. Weber and his followers have been criticized for failing to see the ongoing charisma maintained in some communities and their institutions.[27]

We misunderstand Sobrino if we reduce him to a prophet who simply denounces the ecclesiastical or political-economic powers. His prophetic indictments are a function of his dual theological identity as "prophet" and "priest." As "prophet," Sobrino calls our attention to the places and times in which God is absent, or his will violated (the "anti-kingdom," in Sobrino's language). As "priest," he calls attention to the places and times in which God is present (the kingdom). Both perspectives enable us better to work for an expansion of God's presence in our own lives and communities. According to Sobrino, the "priest" is called to the essentially sacramental task of "rendering the goodness of God present" in the life of the church and of "helping human beings respond to and correspond to God."[28] This service is exercised in distinct but related ways by clergy and laity (who are marked by the "common priesthood of the baptized"[29]), but also and most importantly by the whole church, which serves in an evangelical way when its action contributes to the "communication and concretization of good news."[30]

It is especially important to note, in contrast to the Weberian typology, that Sobrino is not suggesting that the priestly dimension of the gospel necessarily compromises prophetic indignation. On the contrary, the more profound the sense of priestly service, the more heightened the sense of outrage at injustice. Far from encouraging a "softer prophetic denunciation," Sobrino holds, the "formality of priestly service" requires "an even more powerful denunciation and condemnation of those who stand against and act against . . . the profoundest reality of God."[31] Instead of priestly opposition to prophetic inspiration, the former, at least in its most authentic expression, generates and intensifies the latter.[32] Sobrino's paradigm of the priesthood is, of course, Archbishop Romero.[33]

## The Incarnational Vision

As noted already, Sobrino's writings consistently attempt to close the distance between the faith preached by the church and the lives of Christians. This gap is actually composed of a variety of distorted relations between commitments that ought to be held together but often, in the concrete world, are not. They operate on a variety of levels, both practical and theoretical.

This hermeneutical lens helps us to understand the fundamentally Catholic and Jesuit spirit of Sobrino's project.[34] His incarnational theology seeks to be attentive to the ways in which we encounter grace in the real world in which we live, and how this presence of grace affects the whole person rather than simply the soul, and the whole community and not just individuals within it. "In gospel terms," Sobrino writes, "the structure of Jesus' life is a structure of incarnation, of becoming real flesh in real history."[35] The incarnation as the meaning of the whole of Jesus' life is expressed in the cross, where Jesus "draws near" the human experience of those who suffer in a world pervaded by injustice.

Thus, according to Sobrino, "real incarnation in a world of sin is what leads to the cross, and the cross is the product of a real incarnation."[36] The cross should thus be regarded "as a consequence of God's original choice, incarnation, a radical drawing near for love and in love, wherever it leads, without escaping from history or manipulating it from outside."[37] The culminating expression of the incarnation is God's acceptance of human suffering on the cross.[38] "God-with-us" implies "God-like-us,"[39] even unto suffering, humiliation, and death.

Divine acceptance of human suffering teaches and encourages disciples to accept suffering as an element of fidelity to the kingdom of God. Martyrs thus contribute to the expression of the kingdom in a particularly dramatic way. The "most complete way of bearing witness to the God of love, mercy, and justice is to make God present through loving activity in history, through works of mercy and justice."[40] This incarnational vision generates a sacramental sense of all of creation as a mediation of divine grace, but liberation theology highlights the way in which *action in solidarity*—as distinct from the beauty communicated in art and music, liturgy and literature—manifests the presence of God. Sobrino thus praises the Jesuit martyrs of the University of Central America in the following way: "They were not conventionally 'pious' types, repeating 'Lord, Lord' in the temple, but they were people who went out in the streets to do God's will."[41]

Understood in this context, the prophetic voice supports rather than undermines this incarnational vision. The agenda articulated in Sobrino's preface to *The Principle of Mercy* seems to motivate all of his major writings: "This, then, is our hope in publishing this book: To help the First World halt its slide down the slippery slope of misunderstanding, dissimulation, and oppression of the 'crucified peoples.' We should like to help the First World look these people straight in the eyes and decide to take them down from their cross."[42] Sobrino's prophetic voice denounces all the ways in which the "developed" world, including the churches, ignore, or are complicit in, the misery of the poor. His incarnational vision encourages us to see that genuinely encountering the poor also constitutes an encounter with the divine.

Sobrino's prophetic voice speaks from an underlying incarnational vision of God's relation to the world and of our relation to God in the world. Divine love leads God to enter into the human condition to become one of us. The "sacramental" implication of this incarnational vision views this world as bearer of divine grace, a place where God communicates to us through the particular context and events of everyday life. Commenting autobiographically, Sobrino notes that his own "final awakening" came not from reading Rahner and Moltmann—wise and scholarly theologians from whom Sobrino has learned much—but from directly encountering the truly poor "face-to-face," and in such a way as to see the "good news" with "new eyes."[43]

The incarnational vision also emphasizes the human grace-empowered capacity to cooperate with God in a world created to be the context for the mediation of divine grace. Sobrino takes this vision from Scripture and the Christian tradition, his Jesuit commitment to "finding God in all things," and the teachings of the Second Vatican Council, particularly the Pastoral Constitution *Gaudium et spes*. It also reflects his appropriation of the commitment undertaken by the Latin American bishops at the CELAM meetings at Medellín in 1968 and Puebla in 1979, the work of Monsignor Oscar Romero, Ignacio Ellacuría and the other Jesuits at the University of Central America, and the inspiration of the people involved in the base Christian communities of El Salvador.

This theological vision supports Sobrino's theological tendency to work with a "both/and" rather than an "either/or" response to truth claims. This synthetic and analogical mode of reflection calls for a differentiation that can help us identify the incarnational theology that underlies Sobrino's prophetic statements. His intent is to overcome unnecessary and counterproductive oppositions as well as to provide a synthetic theological perspective based on a proper ranking of Christian priorities.


### Synthesis: Moving beyond Oppositions

Sobrino has consistently attempted to overcome false dichotomies and distortions of the gospel. He opposes abstract affirmations that omit some aspect of Christian faith. One can trace abstractions that lead to imbalanced and lopsided theology in four essential spheres of theological reflection: (1) theological: divine love without solidarity, divine mercy without justice; (2) christological:

Christ without Jesus, resurrection without crucifixion; (3) ecclesiological: preaching without action, worship and liturgy without conversion, church without the world, hierarchy without the people; and (4) ethical: power without responsibility, profession without discipleship, charity without justice, reconciliation without truth. We will now illustrate how Sobrino attempts to overcome unhelpful distortions in each of these spheres of theology.

### God

Sobrino believes that El Salvador (and, of course, similar places of deprivation and oppression) helps us think more appropriately about God and God's relation to humanity. He writes in light of his own pastoral experience that "the goodness and the mystery of God . . . have become sharply real to me in El Salvador."[44] The goodness of God's love is mysterious in that God not only loves the "victims of this world" but even identifies with them and their suffering. This is a God, Sobrino announces, "who not only favors the victimized but is at the mercy of their torturers."[45] God suffers in, and through, and with the victims. The fact that "God on the cross is as impotent as the victims themselves" indicates the extent to which God exists in "solidarity with those victims."[46]

The overriding theological issue for Christians concerns whether we can view the world in light of God's love for the "crucified creation."[47] This perspective encourages us to identify our worship of false gods, who wrongly but powerfully elicit human allegiance and who always claim victims as the price of obedience to them. "If there is one single deep conviction I have acquired in El Salvador, it is that such idols are real," he confesses.[48] God asks not only that believers debunk such false gods but also that we struggle against them. Thus, the key question for Sobrino is not whether we are believers, but rather in which divinity we believe and against which enemies we fight.

Sobrino is clear that, in his theology, God is for the poor but not for the poor *alone*. In other words, the universality of divine love is expressed in a special care for those who suffer the most in this world. Moreover, the extensiveness and depth of divine love are revealed in that God embraces those the world deems most "unworthy" of love.

This radically inclusive divine love that suffers with the victims of injustice gives rise to hope, not other-worldly resignation. Referring to the devastating earthquakes in El Salvador of January and February 2001, Sobrino writes, "God is hidden in the earthquake and 'suffers' in silence with the victims. But hope does not die, and in hope God remains mysteriously present."[49] God suffers with all victims in the suffering of Christ on the cross. On the cross, "God shows his love by being close to the victims, being in solidarity with them, completely and forever."[50]

## *Jesus Christ*

Sobrino wants to understand that Christ is a "sublime abstraction" when he is detached from Jesus of Nazareth. The docetic Christology that characterizes much of traditional Latin American Catholic piety embraces Christ as love or as "almighty Lord." These images of the powerful Christ "ignore and reject Jesus, whose power is service and whose place is below, in the power of truth and love."[51] Sobrino also complains of "christological deism." As Dean Brackley points out in chapter 1 of this volume, Sobrino observes that when theology falls into "limiting itself to reflecting on the truths of the faith in the abstract and developing their virtualities deductively, theology falls into an implicit 'deism.'"[52] Such functional deism, Brackley writes, effectively "ignores God's self-communication in history today, degenerating into abstractions that ultimately distort that communication."[53] These references seem related to a difficulty expressed in Karl Rahner's complaint that Christians often function with a kind of latent christological monophysitism—a divine Christ stripped of the humanity of Jesus. Docetic Christology ignores the teachings, life, and passion, death and resurrection of Jesus and therefore presents an obstacle to understanding the true meaning of the gospel.

Sobrino also identifies two other forms of reductionism that function to neutralize Jesus' message: Christ the "reconciler" abandons Jesus' prophetic judgment when it presents "a Jesus who proclaimed beatitudes for the poor (who, moreover, were usually not taken to be real poor people) and no curses on the rich, a Jesus who loves everyone, but without specifying the different forms this love takes, defending the poor and issuing a radical call on their oppressors to be converted."[54] Sobrino's point is similar to that made by H. Richard Niebuhr against the liberal Protestantism of his day: "A God without wrath brought men without sin into a kingdom without judgment through the ministrations of a Christ without a cross."[55] Sobrino's version would read: "A God without hatred of injustice brought people without responsibility for injustice into a heaven without concern for this world through the ministrations of a Christ without a cross bearing historical significance."

To correct this flawed and imbalanced approach to Christ, Sobrino insists that we return to Jesus of Nazareth. He describes this approach to Christology as "new" for the Latin American context, but it is, in fact, "conservative" in the best sense of the word: it attempts to conserve what is valuable, and indeed essential, to the tradition. As Sobrino observes of his method, "this 'new' way of seeing means only that we are returning to the 'older' way, thinking of Jesus' cross as the ultimate witness to God's love, particularly for victims and against their oppressors."[56]

"Faith in Christ means," Sobrino writes, "first and foremost, *following Jesus*."[57] Following Jesus properly means recognizing that he was "*for* some, the oppressed, and *against* others, the oppressors."[58] This should not be taken to suggest that Jesus is against the oppressed *simpliciter,* or as human beings as such. Sobrino explains that the "principle of impartiality" holds that Christ brings salvation equally to all people.[59] But he does oppose the powerful to the extent that they act as agents of oppression. Jesus struggled against oppression in all its effects and in its causes, so he resisted oppressors for their own sakes as well as for the sake of their victims. The same is true of Isaiah's claim that God will slay the wicked (Isa 11:4) or Jesus' claim that a person cannot be a disciple without hating his mother and father, wife and children (Luke 14:26-27).

Finally, Sobrino also criticizes the reduction of Christ to his role as Son in trinitarian relations. While perfectly appropriate, this trinitarian relation has sometimes improperly functioned to supplant Jesus' historical reality. It must be criticized if and when "it leads us to ignore Jesus' constitutive historical relatedness to the Kingdom of God and the God of the Kingdom."[60]

Sobrino thus calls for correcting this imbalance by supplementing "Jesus' transcendent Trinitarian relatedness" with his "historical relatedness."[61] A correction focusing on Jesus' relation to the coming of the kingdom of God helps to avoid a "personalist reduction of the faith" that "leads to an abandoning of the historical world to its wretchedness."[62] Loving Christ means loving the world as Jesus loved it, which for Sobrino means preparing it for the in-breaking of the kingdom of God. This preparation demands the denunciation of injustice, not its passive acceptance. We cannot love Christ "alone" but rather in and through loving our brothers and sisters here and now.[63] Reconciliation between God and humanity, and therefore between human beings themselves, is neither a purely spiritual activity nor a completely eschatological event. True reconciliation is not amnesia about the past or obtuse inattention to present forms of conflict, but rather promotion of genuine unity by identifying and overcoming the causes of oppression.[64]

Sobrino credits the bishops at Medellín for recovering a more adequate image of Jesus and for rejoining Christianity and Jesus, and thereby for providing a "safeguard" against "creeping neo-Christendom."[65] The heart of Sobrino's project is to recover Jesus Christ in his complete meaning against all forms of docetism that deny Jesus' humanity. Christ is traditionally said to be present, in different ways, in the liturgy, in Scripture, and in pastors, but Medellín also recognized that Christ is also distinctively present in "those who are poorest and weakest."[66]

Sobrino finds two key implications of this claim in the 1979 CELAM meeting at Puebla. First, the bishops understood that Christ's mission is primarily directed to the poor simply because they are poor, "whatever may be the moral or personal situation in which they find themselves."[67] This includes the conviction that Christ does not love the poor only when they are virtuous or on the basis of their faith or because they are "poor in spirit." God loves the poor because they are in need.

Second, the bishops described the poor as "a sort of sacrament of the presence of Christ."[68] Victims have an "evangelizing potential" or "prophetic potential" for challenging the church to deeper conversion. Sobrino adds to these first two claims a third, that some poor people manifest special virtues that have been cultivated in their impoverished circumstances. Poor people function effectively to "evangelize" when they "incarnate in their lives the evangelical values of solidarity, service, simplicity, and openness to accepting the gift of God."[69]

The first claim pertains to divine love, the second concerns the moral significance of victims (regardless of their moral state), and the third points to the special goodness manifested in the lives of some poor people. Each of these affirmations can be distinguished from the other two, but Sobrino joins all three in a mutually complementary set of claims about the centrality of the poor for the church's quest to grow in understanding of and in fidelity to Christ.

### Church

Sobrino takes a strongly prophetic stance toward the church: "the church must be converted and become the church of the poor."[70] Ecclesial conversion is the path to overcoming the "ecclesial docetism" that "distances itself from 'real' reality and chooses the sphere of reality in which it wants to be Church: the religious, the doctrinal, the liturgical, the canonical."[71] The option for the poor puts a converted church in contact with the reality of the poor. Sobrino goes so far as to say that "perhaps the greatest contribution of Monsignor Romero was to go beyond Docetism and build a 'real' Church."[72] In this context, Sobrino cites Romero's startling statement, "I am glad, brethren, that the Church is persecuted because of its preferential option for the poor and for trying to incarnate itself in the interest of the poor."[73] Romero goes on to say, perhaps even more starkly, "It would be sad if in a country where people are being murdered so horribly, there were not also priests among the victims. They are the witness of a church incarnated in the problems of the people."[74]

This reality of the church "incarnated" in the people is closely related to the way in which Christ is "incarnated" in the "crucified peoples." Sobrino cites Ellacuría in this regard: "This crucified people is the historical continuation of the suffering servant of Yahweh,"[75] and also Romero's statement to survivors of a massacre, "You are the image of the pierced God."[76] The fact that the poor are a "sign of the times" means that history and God's presence must be interpreted in light of their reality.

Sobrino is quite clear that the church bears the primary responsibility for preserving, transmitting, and providing the authoritative interpretation of Scripture.[77] The church, of course, is not primarily an institution, but a graced community attempting to put her faith, hope, and charity into concrete practice. To the extent that she does so, the church "becomes a sacrament in relation to Christ and ultimately becomes his body in history."[78]

Christology is ecclesial in two senses: because individuals believe within the Christian community and because, as Sobrino puts it, "we carry one another in faith, give our own faith and receive it, so that, formally, it is the community that believes in Christ."[79] We receive and communicate faith within the community in "pilgrimage." The church as the "people of God" in history must be engaged in the process of "rethinking its faith throughout history, [and with] learning to learn."[80] The church's "secondary ecclesiality" concerns its institutional life, but its "primary ecclesiality" deals with its existence as a community of faith that is the Body of Christ in history.

The institutional church, Sobrino points out, is not always sufficiently attentive to the image of Jesus as liberator. Catholic Christology sometimes functions in ways not dissimilar to the otherworldly image of Christ promoted by "spiritualistic movements and sects."[81] We forget that Jesus was concerned not simply with a "transcendental" salvation but with one that relates to human history—"on earth as it is in heaven." Unfortunately within the church, it is too often the case that "Compassion is tolerated, even praised, as long as it does not turn into a struggle for justice."[82] The church continues to exhort the faithful to do their part in a spirit of charity to alleviate the suffering of the poor,[83] but it does not insist that this commitment is obligatory rather than supererogatory.

The appropriate ecclesial setting for Latin American Christology is the "church of the poor."[84] The faith of the poor is directed to "liberating activity, discipleship of Jesus, which resembles Jesus in his option for the poor, in his condemnations and in his historical destiny."[85]

The church of the poor plays a variety of roles. First, it plays an important cognitive role in that it helps the church to understand the reality of the world as it really exists and not as it is imagined in the minds of those whose wealth leaves them aloof from it. It helps to challenge our blindness, mendacity, and self-deception.[86]

Second, it plays a critically important moral role when it helps us to become more responsible agents. Greater knowledge of self and other "humanizes" us when it leads us to engage in liberating praxis, particularly as inspired by love, courage, and justice.[87]

Third, the poor who deal with poverty as Christians offer a salutary model of discipleship. The church as a whole can learn about the nature of true discipleship by attending to the ways in which poor Christians are engaged in "being and acting like Jesus," including their victimization and their deeply communal faith.[88] The church constitutes an inclusive and complementary community. The church can only function as a community of mutual learning and teaching that is borne by "a mutual carrying of one another in faith"[89] to the extent to which she forms a community of solidarity in service of which the institutional church devotes its resources for the sake of the poor.[90] Solidarity thus enables the poor to teach the whole community what it means to follow Christ in a time of oppression.

Finally, the church of the poor helps the institution to overcome a dualistic tendency to separate the church from the world. Sobrino credits the bishops of Medellín for providing the ecclesial basis for ending "the secular dualism" that posits a division between "the temporal and the eternal, between the secular and the religious, between the world and God, between history and the church."[91]

Christ becomes present to the church, and the church becomes the Body of Christ in history when the poor manifest liberating hope and action. Christ can be present to various cultures in many different modes, but the suffering of the poor of Latin America makes crucifixion the dominant mode of Christ's presence there today. The image of crucifixion helps us to see the presence of Christ in history and encourages us to act in its light. Christians who have made an option for the poor, whose "thinking is done from the world of the poor and is done to liberate them," are best positioned to understand who Christ is and what belief in him entails in the way of practical commitment.[92]

### The Christian Moral Life

In the preface to *The Principle of Mercy*, Sobrino acknowledges "the fundamental problem of our world: ignorance, dissimulation, and torpor in the presence of a most cruel inhumanity."[93] The challenge to the church concerns both the need for greater knowledge—how to understand more adequately the world in which we live—and the need for greater integrity—how to overcome the contradiction between professed faith and concrete action.

Sobrino's agenda carries both cognitive and moral implications for the Christian moral life. First, the cognitive implication identifies our need to see the world differently in order more adequately to understand it. When we in the developed world do not know about the suffering of the poor in the developing world it is often, Sobrino observes, "because we do not want to know," and perhaps because we do not want to think about how we are beneficiaries of a destructive international socioeconomic system.[94] Indeed, not only are we beneficiaries, Sobrino adds, "Western human beings have to a great extent produced an inhuman world."[95]

Christians need to learn how to "let suffering speak" and to let it affect our understanding, imagination, reflection, and action. Praxis informed by participation in the lives and suffering of the poor leads to concrete action that shows mercy to victims, overcomes injustice, repairs the harm done to innocent people, and works for reconciliation among enemies.[96]

Apathy and ignorance, "selfishness and aloofness"[97] leave us out of touch with reality. Social location can either promote or undermine our ability to understand ourselves and the world in which we live. "Unless we allow ourselves to feel suffering and react with compassion, we lose something fundamental: that, I believe, is the great crisis of our time."[98] The major upheavals and threats to our world are based in this failure to understand and to live as human beings. Inhumanity lies behind terrorism, war, the nuclear threat, the ecological devastation of the planet, and "the exclusion from life of a large part of humanity."[99] "Immunization" from how most of the human race struggles to survive renders us unable to understand the world and incapable of experiencing compassion for the poor.

Sobrino advocates epistemological realism, in the sense that he believes the human mind can come to a greater understanding of reality if allowed to act on the natural desire for knowledge. He follows Ellacuría's argument that the formal structure of understanding consists of facing three dimensions of reality: the noetic, the ethical, and the practical. The act of "facing real things," Ellacuría held, includes "getting a grip on reality," "taking on the burden of reality," and "taking responsibility for reality."[100] The Christian life functions properly to the extent that one's knowledge of Christ is informed by these three kinds of actions, intellectual, ethical, and practical knowledge. The Christian moral life is not just a matter of applying teachings or rules to concrete cases but much more a process of following Christ where Christ is to be found—in and with the poor—and then choosing to live, to think, and to make practical moral decisions in accord with this discipleship.

Moreover, the moral challenge lies in living a life based on mercy. The notion of love is central to Christian ethics: God first loved us, so we ought to love one another. Liberation theology highlights God's primary concern for the most needy, oppressed, and marginalized. This concern leads Sobrino to construe *agape* as issuing in mercy. The suffering of victims leads him to maintain that "effective mercy comes before all else, and must permeate all human and Christian activity, and also theology."[101] "Effective mercy" can be distinguished from sentimentality or passive sympathy that "feels another's pain" but does not act to remedy it or attack its causes. The "principle of mercy" displayed in the parable of the Good Samaritan involves "making someone else's pain our own and allowing that pain to move us to respond."[102]

The moral primacy of mercy in the Christian moral life has implications for Sobrino's approach to the discipline of Christian theology. His definition of theology as *intellectus amoris*, the understanding of love, is not intended to replace the traditional definition of theology as *intellectus fidei*, the understanding of faith, but as distinct and complementary to it.[103] Sobrino makes this harmony explicit when he suggests that the situation of the poor makes it imperative to describe theology as *intellectus misericordiae, iustititiae, liberationis*, an understanding of mercy, justice, and liberation.[104] The Western ideals of equality and freedom must similarly be connected to justice and solidarity if they are to be more than merely formal ideals that ignore the plight of the poor.[105]

Effective mercy moves us to work for justice, which he describes as "the name love acquires when it comes to entire majorities of people unjustly oppressed."[106] Justice is exercised in one's own personal life, in one's thinking, judging, and acting in relation to friends and associates, but also in relation to one's place in society, in one's professional roles, one's relation to fellow citizens, and so on. Justice concerns not only concrete acts but also public policies and laws that can provide alternatives to structural injustice.

Instead of being opposed to each other, mercy and justice are interdependent and mutually reinforcing. Mercy is primary but its necessary effect is the commitment to justice. Moreover, the struggle for justice and love "enables hope and faith to be made concrete and to take on Christian form."[107] Rather than opposing liberation to reconciliation, commitment to the former is the authentic condition for the latter: true reconciliation takes place only in conditions of shared solidarity.[108] Sentimental love and sham justice can lead only to illusory reconciliation.

## Conclusion

Sobrino's theological synthesis is ultimately rooted in God, and specifically in God's universal love. The incarnational vision underlying his theology is characteristically Catholic. The distinctiveness of Sobrino's vision concerns the way in which distinct theological themes are related to one another in an incarnational unity. This vision assigns a new kind of priority to God's mercy for the "least" as an expression of God's universal love.[109] It bears repeating that this priority is not "new" in the sense that it was invented by liberation theologians, who in fact maintain that it is at the heart of the gospel but in the sense that it presents a new organizing principle within which systematic and moral theology proceed: to rethink Christian faith and action in light of the suffering of the poor. As Sobrino puts it, "its thinking is done from the world of the poor and is done to liberate them."[110] Theology is done not primarily as faith seeking understanding, but as mercy seeking understanding.[111]

If the incarnation represents God's will to be human, then the cross reflects God's will not only to be "God-with-others" but also to be "God-at-the-mercy-of-others," to embrace and experience what it is to be subjected to persecution, torture, and death at the hands of oppressors. "This decentering of God in favor of human beings, poor, weak, and victimized, is the fundamental thesis of the Christian religion,"[112] Sobrino writes. The same language of "decentering" is invoked when he argues in *Witnesses to the Kingdom* that Christians, "truly love and serve the church when, within it, we decenter it in favor of the kingdom of God, when we make the church a sacrament of something greater than itself, when it becomes a sign of God's kingdom and wholly devoted to the poor of this world, for whom the kingdom of God exists."[113]

The prophet knows that to be rightly related to God is to do justice to the oppressed: "To know God is to do justice for the oppressed, as Jeremiah says (22:15-16)."[114] The priest sees and announces God's presence in and with the poor: "To find God means finding the poor, and to serve God means serving the poor, as Jesus says at the end of his life, in Matthew 25."[115] This discovery has the power to overcome the "true dividing line" in the world today, which is not between different religions but rather between "mercy to the weak (which to believers is the essence of God) and indifference to, oppression of the weak (selfishness)."[116] Sobrino thus speaks in a prophetic voice from an incarnational vision that provides a way to start closing the gap between faith and life, and the prophet and priest, through love for the poor.

## Notes

1. Peter Kanyandago, "African Churches and the Crisis of Christianity," in *Christianity in Crisis?*, ed. Jon Sobrino and Felix Wilfrid; *Concilium* 2005, no. 3 (London: SCM Press, 2005), 7.

2. José Ignacio González Faus, "A Crisis of Credibility in Christianity," in *Christianity in Crisis?*, ed. Sobrino and Wilfrid, 41.

3. James F. Keenan, "Notes on Moral Theology: Crises and Other Developments," *Theological Studies* (forthcoming, 2008).

4. González Faus, "A Crisis of Credibility," in *Christianity in Crisis?* 43.

5. Jon Sobrino, *The Principle of Mercy: Taking the Crucified People from the Cross* (Maryknoll, N.Y.: Orbis Books, 1992), 8.

6. Jon Sobrino, *Where Is God? Earthquakes, Terrorism, Barbarity, and Hope*, trans. Margaret Wilde (Maryknoll, N.Y.: Orbis Books, 2006), xx.

7. Ibid., 103.

8. *Principle of Mercy*, 9.

9. *Where Is God?*, 33, 41.

10. Ibid., 60-61.

11. Jon Sobrino, *Jesus the Liberator*, trans. Paul Burns and Francis McDonagh (Maryknoll, N.Y.: Orbis Books, 1993), 263.

12. *Where Is God?*, 100.

13. *Principle of Mercy*, 3.

14. See ibid., 2.

15. Jon Sobrino, *Witnesses to the Kingdom: The Martyrs of El Salvador and the Crucified Peoples* (Maryknoll, N.Y.: Orbis Books, 2003), 143.

16. See *Where Is God?*, 101.

17. Ibid.

18. See Max Weber, *The Sociology of Religion*, trans. Ephraim Fischoff (Boston: Beacon Press, 1971), chapters 2 and 5; and Ernst Troeltsch, *The Social Teaching of the Christian Churches*, 2 vols., trans. Olive Wyon (Louisville: Westminster John Knox, 1992 [original

1912, original Eng. trans. 1931]). See also Friedrich Nietzsche's discussion of the "priestly ideal" in the third essay of *On the Genealogy of Morals*, trans. D. Smith (New York: Oxford University Press, 1998).

19. H. Richard Niebuhr, *The Kingdom of God in America* (San Francisco: Harper & Row, 1937), 167.

20. Ibid., 168.

21. Ibid.

22. See James M. Gustafson, *Modes of Moral Discourse: Prophetic, Narrative, Ethical, and Policy* (Grand Rapids: Stob Lectures, Calvin College, 1988).

23. See Karl Rahner, "Priest and Poet," in *Theological Investigations* 3 (Baltimore: Helicon Press, 1967), 294-317.

24. See "What Got Jesus Killed?" by Daniel J. Harrington, chapter 6 in this volume.

25. See Joseph Blenkinsopp, *A History of Prophecy in Israel* (Louisville: Westminster John Knox, 1996).

26. See Joseph Blenkinsopp, *Sage, Priest, Prophet: Religious and Intellectual Leadership in Ancient Israel* (Louisville: Westminster John Knox, 1995).

27. For example, see Hermann Strasser and Gunther Schlegl, "Gemeinschaft or Gesellschaft? Two Competing Visions of Modernity in Werner Stark's and Max Weber's Sociology," *Thought* 64 (1989): 51-66; Werner Stark, "A Survey of My Scholarly Work," in *The Sociological Writings of Werner Stark: Bibliography and Selected Annotations*, ed. M. Engel (New York: Fordham University Press, 1975), 2-17.

28. *Principle of Mercy*, 116.

29. Ibid., 118.

30. Ibid., 119.

31. Ibid.

32. See ibid., 119-43.

33. See Sobrino's introduction to Archbishop Oscar Romero, *Voice of the Voiceless: The Four Pastoral Letters and Other Statements,* trans. Michael Walsh (Maryknoll, N.Y.: Orbis Books, 1999).

34. See *Witnesses to the Kingdom*, 69-71; also chapters 1 and 8, 9, and 11.

35. *Principle of Mercy*, 15.

36. *Jesus the Liberator*, 229.

37. Ibid., 244.

38. See ibid, 244.

39. Ibid., 245.

40. Ibid., 269.

41. *Witnesses to the Kingdom*, 67. See "The Christology of Jon Sobrino," by Roberto Goizueta, chapter 7 in this volume, on the interconnection of the gratuitousness of divine love or grace and action in solidarity.

42. *Principle of Mercy*, viii.

43. Ibid., 3, 4.

44. Ibid., 8.

45. Ibid.

46. Ibid., 9.

47. Ibid., 5.

48. Ibid., 9.

49. *Where Is God?*, 137.
50. Ibid. 145.
51. *Jesus the Liberator*, 15.
52. See "Theology and Solidarity," by Dean Brackley, chapter 1 in this volume, page 8.
53. Ibid.
54. *Jesus the Liberator*, 16.
55. *The Kingdom of God in America*, 193.
56. *Jesus the Liberator*, 269.
57. Ibid., 13.
58. Ibid.
59. Ibid., 18.
60. Ibid., 16.
61. Ibid.
62. Ibid.,
63. See ibid., 16-17.
64. On the importance of truth, see *Principle of Mercy*, 94-96; on forgiveness intending reconciliation, see chapter 4 in that volume.
65. See *Where Is God?* 136; *Jesus the Liberator*, 17.
66. See *Jesus the Liberator*, 21, citing no. 196 of Medellín. The issue of docetism comes up frequently in Sobrino's writings, for example, *Witnesses to the Kingdom*, 3, 5.
67. *Jesus the Liberator*, 21, citing no. 1142 of Puebla.
68. Ibid.
69. Ibid., 21, citing Puebla no. 1147.
70. *Witnesses to the Kingdom*, 86.
71. *Where Is God?*, 100.
72. Ibid., 101.
73. Cited in ibid.
74. Ibid.
75. *Jesus the Liberator*, 26, where Sobrino cites Ignacio Ellacuría, "Discernir el 'signo' de los tiempos," *Revista Latinoamericana de Teología* 14 (1988), 58. On the meaning of "crucified peoples," see "Theology in the Light of Human Suffering," by Paul Crowley, chapter 2 in this volume.
76. Ibid., citing J. Sobrino et al., *La voz de los sin voz* (San Salvador, 1980), 208; Eng. trans. *Voice of the Voiceless: The Four Pastoral Letters and Other Statements.*
77. See *Jesus the Liberator*, 28-29.
78. Ibid., 29.
79. Ibid.
80. Ibid.
81. Ibid., 13.
82. *Where Is God?*, 111.
83. Ibid.
84. *Jesus the Liberator*, 30.
85. Ibid., 30.
86. *Principle of Mercy*, 6.
87. *Where Is God?*, 101.
88. *Jesus the Liberator*, 30.

89. Ibid.

90. See *Principle of Mercy*, 10.

91. Sobrino, "Introduction," *Voice of the Voiceless,* 67.

92. *Jesus the Liberator*, 31, 33.

93. *Principle of Mercy*, vii.

94. See ibid., 4.

95. Ibid., 7.

96. *Where Is God?* 121.

97. *Principle of Mercy*, 7.

98. *Where Is God?*, 112.

99. Ibid.

100. Cited in ibid., 34. See also Jon Sobrino, *No Salvation outside the Poor: Prophetic-Utopian Essays* (Maryknoll, N.Y.: Orbis Books, 2008), chapter 1.

101. *Jesus the Liberator*, 34. On the role of mercy in Christian ethics, see also James F. Keenan, S.J., *The Works of Mercy: The Heart of Catholicism,* 2d ed. (Lanham, Md.: Sheed & Ward, 2007).

102. *Principle of Mercy*, 10.

103. *Where Is God?*, 34.

104. Ibid. See also *Principle of Mercy*, viii.

105. Ibid.

106. Ibid., 10.

107. Ibid., 44.

108. On the relation between forgiveness and justice in El Salvador, see Stephen J. Pope, "The Convergence of Forgiveness and Justice: Lessons from El Salvador," *Theological Studies* 64 (December 2003): 812-35.

109. See *The Principle of Mercy*, part 1.

110. *Jesus the Liberator*, 31.

111. *Principle of Mercy*, viii.

112. *Where Is God?*, 134.

113. *Witnesses to the Kingdom*, 88.

114. *Where Is God?*, 134.

115. Ibid.

116., Ibid., 136.

# 5

# The Mystery of God and Compassion for the Poor
## The Spiritual Basis of Theology

### J. Matthew Ashley

When histories of Catholic theology are written, the closing decades of the twentieth century will be remembered for many things; one of them will be the recovery of spirituality as a source and locus of theological work. Beginning around mid-century, a number of theologians, including Hans Urs von Balthasar, Karl Rahner, and Marie-Dominique Chenu, began pressing the point that spirituality was not just a derivative of dogmatic theology but was internal to it, permeating its operation and results. In his essay on the study of St. Thomas Aquinas from the late 1930s, Chenu gave expression to this insistence in a way that had a lasting impact on liberation theologian Gustavo Gutiérrez, who quoted his words almost half a century later:

> The fact is that in the final analysis theological systems are simply the expressions of a spirituality. It is this that gives them their interest and their grandeur.... One does not get to the heart of a system via the logical coherence of its structure or the plausibility of its conclusions. One gets to that heart by grasping it in its origins via that fundamental intuition that serves to guide a spiritual life and provides the intellectual regimen proper to that life.[1]

Reflecting recently on this relationship, Gutiérrez writes simply, "Spirituality gives theology its most profound meaning."[2]

He is not the only liberation theologian to assert this kind of relationship; indeed, according to Jon Sobrino it is generally held by liberation theologians as a group:

> Liberation theology, therefore, has been gradually becoming more and more a spiritual theology too. Spirituality is a dimension that is as original

and necessary for it as is liberation, and the two of them require one another. This is how many of us see things at present. . . . We believe, furthermore, that spirituality is being understood not only as one dimension of theology, but rather as an integrating dimension for the whole of theology.[3]

This "integrating dimension" is found not so much in the analysis and deployment of a particular content as it is in a general disposition with which the whole endeavor of theology is taken up and conducted. Detecting a spirituality's influence on theology will thus be more a matter of considering certain fundamental choices a theologian makes, the way that his or her imagination is shaped, whereby he or she comes to grasp the salvific point of a given complex of doctrines and practices in order then to seek out conceptual tools and argumentative strategies adequate to the ways that these doctrines and practices have made (and must continue to make) Christian faith present and compelling for a given community of believers.[4] Understanding the spirituality out of which a theologian does her or his work, then, makes a necessary (if not in itself sufficient) contribution to an understanding of the final theological system.

In what follows I explore this claim with regard to Sobrino's Christology. First, I provide a brief overview of Sobrino's understanding of spirituality, then of the difference it can and should make for theology.[5] This will set the stage to consider some elements of Sobrino's Christology that are illuminated by considering what spirituality means for him. I briefly take up three cases. I argue, first, that spirituality sheds light on Sobrino's very definition of the task and genre of his work; second, that it illumines his approach to defining Jesus' relationship to God, in particular his choice (highly objectionable for the CDF Notification) not to focus on language of hypostatic union and beatific vision. Third, spirituality will positively illuminate his emphasis on a title for Jesus that is unique to his Christology: Jesus as good news.

## Spirituality Defined

Like many who study spirituality today, Sobrino rejects a view that confines spirituality to one specific region of human nature and existence, particularly to the extent that this regionalization maps a division of the human into "material" and "spiritual" realms. For Sobrino, spirituality is a global, integrating phenomenon in human life. Recapitulating the route by which the term "spirituality" entered into theological discourse in history, he begins with the Pauline notion of "living according to the Spirit," which he renders "living with spirit," or "being human with spirit."[6] What Sobrino emphasizes above all is that spirituality is not a dimension of human experience or a set of practices that removes us from the concrete, historical reality in which we live, but is constituted precisely in the way we relate to reality, confront reality, engage it: "Spirituality is simply the spirit of a subject—an individual or a group—in its relationship with the whole of reality."[7] And again: "This dimension of 'being-human-with-spirit'—that responds to what there is in reality of crisis and promise, and that unifies the different elements of this response to reality so that, when all is said and done, reality is more promise than crisis—is what we call 'spirituality.'"[8]

This focus on "reality" is deliberate and draws on a complex set of background philosophical claims that was elaborated by Sobrino's friend and collaborator, Ignacio Ellacuría. For Ellacuría, engaging reality in a holistic and sustained way is the defining mark of human intelligence. In an essay in which he attempted to lay out philosophical foundations for Latin American theology, Ellacuría argued that "the distinctive function and formal structure of intelligence . . . is not that of comprehending being or grasping meaning; rather, it is that of apprehending and engaging reality."[9] He expands on what apprehending and engaging reality means by laying out a view of intelligence with internally self-referential noetic, ethical, and practical moments. He names the first moment "realizing the weight of reality," which entails "a being in the midst of the reality of things, . . . which, in its active character of existing, is anything but static and thingly. . . ."[10] To know reality is to find a specific place in reality and take up a stance toward and within the unfolding dynamisms of reality at that place. As such it necessarily includes an ethical moment, "shouldering reality's weight," in which human intelligence grasps the demands that reality places on us as that species which self-consciously participates in and carries forward the ongoing history of created being. Finally, human intelligence is short-circuited if it stops short of corresponding to the "active character" of that which it apprehends; in other words, it necessarily includes transformative action that participates in and contributes to the ongoing history of reality—"taking charge of the weight of reality."[11]

Ellacuría's unyielding insistence on "reality" (and not "meaning" or "Being") as the ultimate context and horizon for the realization and comprehension of the most distinctively human features (such as intelligence and free will) means that an account of human self-transcendence—and a fortiori, of "spirituality"—has to do justice to the ways that human beings are always embedded in and involved with reality from beginning to end. Any such account that envisions transcendence as leaving reality behind in its various dimensions—physical, biological, and especially social-historical—is by that fact inadequate. Sobrino embraces this philosophical background, although he works it out in different directions. For Sobrino, then, "being human with spirit" and "confronting reality" are tantamount to the same thing once one understands what "spirit," "human," and "reality" mean. To "have spirit," to live in terms of a transcendent horizon, is precisely to engage reality as a multidimensional field of elements and dynamisms, most fully instantiated and actualized at the level of human history (in other words, as *historical* reality). He describes the most fundamental structures of this engagement of reality in terms of three interrelated features: being *honest* with reality, being *faithful* to reality, and allowing oneself to be *carried by* reality.[12]

To engage reality with honesty and integrity (*honradez con lo real*) means more than being rigorously observant and methodically objective. These are necessary but not sufficient conditions. Sobrino habitually delineates this stance in terms of its opposite, calling on Paul's description of the ungodly in the Letter to the Romans: those who "by their wickedness suppress the truth" (Rom 1:18). Positively, Sobrino describes it as a way of letting reality be what it is, rather than distorting or selectively ignoring reality in the way that least infringes on our interests. We habitually lie about reality in order to avoid the way it challenges and unsettles our interests. "To overcome this proclivity [to lie], we have need of spirit."[13] To fail in this fundamental way of living with spirit, of engaging reality with "*honradez*," has disastrous consequences. Sobrino calls again on Paul:

> Honesty with the real, then, is a matter of great activity and requires spirit. If this basic honesty with the real is not exercised, the consequences for the human being are catastrophic. As Paul says, the heart is darkened (subjectively) and things are no longer (objectively) creatures, sacraments of God, but manipulated realities. And from the root of this fundamental dishonesty follow all those sinful fruits that Paul enumerates, and God's wrath, rather than God's grace, is revealed towards those who are not honest with the real.[14]

In today's world, Sobrino contends, this honesty cannot but become an engagement of reality guided by compassion. This is because letting reality be what it is without the veil of ideology and lies by which we suppress its truth means exposing ourselves to suffering on a massive scale, systematically produced, maintained, covered over, and tolerated. Not to be moved to compassion for those who suffer so needlessly means that one has not yet really confronted oneself with this reality in a human way. "When we respond [to reality] with mercy, we are being honest with reality."[15]

To follow this initial reaction over the long haul, no matter where it leads, is demanding, and can be done only by virtue of a mature spirituality. "We need spirit to maintain our honesty regardless of where it leads."[16] Sobrino calls this "fidelity to the real."[17] The attempt to put compassion into practice, both on the individual level by acts of charity, and with broader social and political structures in view by working for justice, will require hard work and will bring persecution. It will also bring moments of disappointment and bewilderment—when a seemingly well-conceived plan doesn't work, or when reactionary violence wipes away one's work, even one's friends and colleagues (as happened with Sobrino himself). The danger of disillusionment, burn out, and a cynicism that withdraws from active commitment, or itself takes up the means of unrestricted violence, is ever present.[18]

If honesty with the real takes concrete shape in the presence of a suffering world as compassion, then fidelity to the real takes the form of hope. This is not just a subjective feeling but a correspondence with a dynamism inherent to the real itself, and finding that dynamism is part of a mature spirituality. Continuing his use of Paul, Sobrino calls on Rom 8:18-25:

> In Pauline language it is as if creation were suffering birthpangs and crying to be delivered. In reality itself, then, there is something of promise and of unsilenced hope. This is the experience of centuries. Reality itself, in spite of its long history of failure and misery, posits ever and again the hope of fullness.[19]

Ultimately, then, if one is empowered, enspirited, to remain faithful no matter where the initial honesty with reality leads, then one will find that one is being carried by reality.[20] Here Sobrino's language becomes more overtly theological:

> There is a hope-filled, honest, loving current [in reality], which becomes a powerful invitation to us, and once we have entered it, we allow ourselves to be carried along by it. Just as there is an original sin that becomes a structural dimension of reality, so also there is an original grace, which becomes a graced structure of reality. . . . To accept that grace emerging from reality, to allow ourselves to be permeated by this grace, to place our wager on it, is also an act of spirit. To accept that grace is to plunge headlong into reality and allow ourselves to be borne up on the "more" with which reality is pregnant and which is offered to us freely, again and again, despite all.[21]

While the language takes this explicitly theological turn at the end, Sobrino maintains that these three dispositions are constitutive (even if we fail in them) to the apprehension of and engagement with reality that is at the core of what being human is.

> Honesty with the real, fidelity to the real, and allowing ourselves to be carried forward by the real are acts of spirit that, in one form or another, by action or omission, every human being performs. Thus we have called them, all three taken together, fundamental spirituality, because they concern every human being.[22]

They also actualize in a distinctively human way that fundamental relationship to God that is inherent to created being, as definitively ordered toward a full sharing in God's trinitarian life. To this extent, Sobrino refers to "theologal" spirituality. There are strong echoes of Karl Rahner's theology here. On a first level of approximation one may say that just as for Rahner every person is constituted as a "hearer of the word," a recipient of God's self-communication, for Sobrino the medium for this address is reality and the person "hears" this word by being honest with reality, by being faithful to reality, and by allowing oneself to be carried by reality. In this way, "the mystery of God does indeed become present *in* reality. Transcendence becomes present *in* history. In this wise, in responding to reality, explicitly or implicitly we have the experience of God in history."[23]

Sobrino admits that his articulation of this "fundamental, theologal spirituality" has already been carried forward with the God of Jesus in view (in the same way that Rahner admits that in the concrete we can work out the philosophical anthropology in *Hearer of the Word* precisely because God has, in fact, addressed us in history in Jesus Christ). *Christian* spirituality makes the implicit explicit: "Christian spirituality is no more and no less than a living of the fundamental spirituality that we have described, precisely in the concrete manner of Jesus and according to the spirit of Jesus. This is the following of Jesus."[24] Following Jesus means not a literal duplication of Jesus' life, but a creative representation of that life, empowered and guided by the Holy Spirit, attending to the basic elements that structure it: incarnation, mission, death, and resurrection.

The structure of incarnation manifests God's honesty to the real. God responds compassionately to a world stricken with sin and suffering, and takes flesh. That compassion governs the place of the incarnation: among the poor and the victims. We recapitulate that structure to the extent that we are similarly honest and discern what place to take up in reality. In a suffering world this place should be, as it was for Jesus, the place of the poor: thus, the option for the poor is an option in spirituality, a matter of discernment, before it is a theological notion or ethical or pastoral guideline.[25] Mission expresses fidelity to the real. Jesus proclaimed the kingdom of God, in part by denouncing its opposite—the anti-kingdom. He himself "gave spirit," inspiring hope and love by the signs he performed.[26] We are called to do the same in a creative fidelity that responds to new situations under the guidance and power of the Spirit but always in reference back to Jesus of Nazareth.

Jesus was faithful to the real, even at the cost of his life, in fidelity to a God whom he experienced as loving Father but also as unmanipulable mystery. This is the structure of cross, the counter-reaction of the anti-kingdom to a life lived honestly and with fidelity to the real. But finally, Jesus was raised from the dead, which manifests in an ultimate and irrevocable way the hope- and grace-filled current in reality. Finally, then, spirituality entails releasing oneself into that current, living (and acting) as ones already risen into the triumph of God's reign.[27]

The Ignatian overtones of all this are clear, not surprisingly, given Sobrino's own Jesuit identity, and the influence of Ellacuría, who himself wrote extensively on Ignatian spirituality.[28] The *Spiritual Exercises*, Ignatian spirituality's central text, defines a spirituality focused on following Jesus and is at the same time (and because of this) a powerful tool for apprehending, confronting, and responding to reality in the three dimensions that Sobrino lays out. Its stated purpose is ridding ourselves of disordered attachments (which, in Sobrino's terms, prevent us from being honest with the real), and ordering our life more in accordance with God's will in our concrete circumstances (Sobrino: to allow us to live in fidelity to the real and to be carried by the real). Its various mental and spiritual exercises press us first to an honest assessment of the presence of sin in the world and in ourselves ("first week") and then proceed with meditations on incarnation, as God's response, and then on Jesus's manner of carrying out his mission (second week), even to the cross (third week). Taking up the resurrection (fourth week), the *Spiritual Exercises* concludes with the famous "Contemplation to Attain Love," in which Ignatius has us reflect on all the ways that God is present to us in and through reality in order to bring us to a profound sense of gratitude that motivates a radical gift of self in service of God's will for the world. To use Sobrino's terms, the point of the exercise is to make us aware of being carried along in one's life by this grace, a life-sustaining sense that, in its many dimensions, Ignatius sums up with the word "consolation." As Sobrino himself notes, it is this more profound dialectic of loving divine initiative and grateful human response that underwrites the Ignatian understanding of finding God in all things and of relating prayer and action by being "contemplatives in action."[29] What does this mean for the particular action of doing theology?

## Spirituality, Theology, Christology

Sobrino's answer to this question is that spirituality should be a spiritual theology. A spiritual theology is one that not only lays out and attempts to systematize the materials of faith, hope, and love that are given to it from Scripture and tradition, but one that makes it possible in a given situation that they be generated anew. Such a theology takes its starting point from a concrete situation of Christian spirituality (a "theologal spirituality" that is specified as a following of Jesus in a particular situation—with both individual and communal elements inextricably intertwined) and seeks to communicate spirit so that this spirituality might move forward.

Echoing Rahner again, such a theology must be a mystagogy, an invitation to immerse oneself in the unmanipulable and demanding mystery of God, a mystery that still discloses itself (in *reality*) to us as loving Father.[30] Since the *story* of Jesus, his "history," is so crucial to Sobrino's understanding of spirituality, a spiritual theology must have conceptual and argumentative tools for making "history" a primary ontological category. Finally, it must have a trinitarian structure, reflecting spirituality's own such structure: an encounter with Jesus and a response to the call to discipleship that is only possible in the power of the Spirit and that has as its ground an encounter with the Father in history and participates in the unfolding of history in accordance with the Father's will.[31]

This is a tall order, of course, but understanding this exigency for theology can help us understand key features of Sobrino's two-volume work on Christology. A full justification of this claim about the relationship between spirituality and theology in Sobrino's two volumes on Christology exceeds the scope of this essay. All I can do here is to give an initial justification by using it as a heuristic device, which I will do with three issues: his definition of the genre of his work; his (controversial) approach to talking about Jesus' divinity; and his formal inclusion of a christological title not often found in academic christologies: "good news."

### Christology as "Open Parable"

At the beginning and the end of the second volume of his Christology Sobrino talks about his conception of the overall shape and goal of his Christology, its genre. He declines to define his project simply in academic terms as "a conceptual analysis of the reality of Jesus Christ," even though the two volumes and six-hundred-plus pages have more than their share of conceptual analysis. It is, he tells us, more an "open parable," which confronts us with the historical reality of Jesus and invites us, indeed, challenges us, to take a stance—but not just toward Jesus.[32] In a clear reflection of his claim that spirituality at root involves confronting reality as a whole, he tells us that Christology involves more than just reflection on Jesus Christ. Rather, the faith in Jesus that Christology reflects upon involves "taking up a stance before reality as a whole."[33] This "taking a stance before reality as a whole," then, marks the connection to Christian spirituality at the very point at which Sobrino defines his task.

### Jesus' Relationship to God

Sobrino maintains the irrevocable normativity of the councils, particularly in the formal character of their statements, but he argues that we can and should flesh out that formal structure "from the perspective of the victims of history." This brought the harshest critique from the Notification, which objects that while Sobrino holds the "theological fonts" (by which it means the early ecumenical councils in particular) to be normative, "the lack of due attention that he pays to them gives rise to concrete problems in his theology."[34] Concretely, it objects to Sobrino's exploration of alternative language to articulate the unique relationship that Jesus enjoys to the Father, however scriptural that language might be (for example, Sobrino draws liberally on the Letter to the Hebrews). In opposition to this kind of exploration, the Notification maintains that only terminology repeating or centering on the concepts of "hypostatic union" and even "beatific vision" can adequately articulate the uniqueness of Jesus' relationship to God and role in salvation.

These are extremely complex issues, and here my intention is only to point to one fruitful avenue for understanding what is at stake: contextualizing Sobrino's theology in terms of the underlying spirituality, which suggests in turn asking what spirituality underlies the objection! We have seen that for Sobrino the heart of the Christian spiritual life is the following of Jesus, which, to repeat, has a trinitarian structure and has its orientation toward the transcendent, its element of union with God, by virtue of the way it "confronts reality" in the threefold way laid out earlier. I suggest that the key here is the way that "union with God" is conceived, since we can expect that this conceiving will have an impact not just on how one configures Christian spirituality, for which union with God is the paradigmatic finality, but also how one will think about the more primordial instantiation of this union in the relationship between Jesus and God.

Starting from the former we recall that Sobrino understands "union with God" along the lines of the Ignatian ideal of contemplation in action. By following Jesus we make God present in history, which entails finding and experiencing God already there in history (this is particularly evident in the third dimension of spirituality, "being carried by reality," which corresponds to the structure of "resurrection"). If one considers this emphasis on transcendence *in* history, on human action in history as the locus at which union with God is realized, uniquely and definitively in Jesus and derivatively in us, by the power of the Spirit that enables us to follow him, it is no surprise that Sobrino will attempt to move beyond (without necessarily denying) language such as "beatific vision" or even "union of natures." The language of beatific vision, in particular, tends to privilege contemplation over action as the locus of union with God, and the language of nature emphasizes who Jesus is as the point at which to identify his affinity to God but neglects what Jesus does—in history and to transform history—which is at least as important.

To turn the problematic in the other direction: might not the overly rigid emphasis on language of "nature" and "beatific vision" reflect for its part a reading of the conciliar tradition that is too exclusively influenced by spiritualities (largely Neoplatonic) that one-sidedly privilege contemplation over action, Mary's part over Martha's? This has been an ongoing debate in Christian spirituality ever since it adopted the Greek terminology of *theoria* and *praxis*. Here, as in the past, this debate has emerged into theology, narrowly construed. It would be helpful to recognize that the debate over Sobrino's theology is a part of this long debate in the history of Christian spirituality. In so doing one could construe Sobrino's contribution in this way: as a theological exploration that operates on the wager that the conciliar traditions can be a productive inter-locutor not just for the Greek, Neoplatonic spiritualities (in the context of which they arose) but also for that constellation of modern spiritualities that empha-size "contemplation in action," which are surely an enduring and important achievement of the Christian tradition. Seeing Sobrino in this light can also help us understand why it is so important for him that spiritual theology be related to an adequate theology and philosophy of history. This is important because it can give this relatively novel theological language about Jesus and his relationship to God the kind of "ontological density" that the traditional conciliar languages gained by virtue of the powerful, but ahistorical, meta-physics of the Greek philosophical traditions.[35]

### Jesus as Good News

In the second division of *Christ the Liberator*, Sobrino explores the various Christologies that emerged in the New Testament period by attending to some of the titles given to Jesus. Most of them are well known and traditional—High Priest, Messiah, Lord, Son of God, and so forth. But one in particular, the one with which he closes his analysis of christological titles, is not well known: Jesus as *Eu-Aggellion*; Jesus as "Good News." Connected with this title is a dimen-sion of "correct faith" that complements both "ortho-doxy" and "ortho-praxis": "orthopathy," a striking neologism in Sobrino's recent work. What drives this innovation? I suggest, again, that the underlying spirituality can shed light here.

Sobrino gives clear indication that this title marks the point at which spir-ituality comes closest to breaking through as a specific content, insofar as he claims that giving an account of the good news found in Jesus "is the most basic way of relating Christology and spirituality."[36] Sobrino assigns this as a "title" in its own right because in his view it is crucial to maintain not only that what Jesus proclaimed and initiated (the kingdom of God) is good news, and not only that what happened to Jesus as a result (cross and resurrection) is good news, but to maintain explicitly and formally in one's Christology that the *man-ner* in which Jesus did all this, the "spirit" he brought to carrying out his mis-sion, is itself good news. Jesus, Sobrino asserts, was not only good at mediating salvation, but he was a *good* mediator; he attracted people by his honesty, mercy, fidelity, his freedom to love, his propensity and ability to celebrate, which invited others into that celebration. If Christology did not attend explicitly and formally to this, it would fail to do justice to its subject matter, in part because it would fail to highlight the ways in which those who successfully follow Jesus (saints and martyrs) share in this particular feature, and that this sharing is part of what is involved in being conformed to Christ.

"Orthopathy" is the way we correspond to this dimension, and it is, despite its neological character, recognizably at home in the history of Christian spirituality. Sobrino works it out this way: We respond to the good news of Jesus' mission by ourselves participating in it: *orthopraxis*. We respond to the good news of what happened to Jesus on the cross and in the resurrection by correctly naming it, and, thus correctly naming Jesus and Jesus' God: *orthodoxy*. Finally, we respond to the good news that is found in the way that Jesus carried out his work by allowing ourselves to be attracted to it, taken up by it, affected by it. This is *orthopathy*: "the correct way of letting ourselves be affected by the reality of Christ."[37] It would not be too much to say that, defined in these terms, "orthopathy" is the particular concern of all Christian spirituality, and particularly of those strands that focus on the inherent attractiveness of the person of Jesus.[38] Its inclusion in his Christology is an integral part of Sobrino's strategy to frame a spiritual theology, as he himself defines it.

## Conclusions

I have argued that there is, in fact, a "fundamental intuition" at work in Sobrino's Christology, a spirituality. I suggested that on at least some of the issues named in the Notification we can understand what is at stake by considering this spirituality, which leads Sobrino to take his bearings on the normative sources of Scripture and tradition in novel ways. I took primarily a "formal" path to sketch this spirituality, using his own formal definitions of it as a "fundamental theologal spirituality" and as following Jesus. Such a presentation can and should be complemented by a more substantive account. The spirituality that illumines Sobrino's theology shines through at many other points, but perhaps nowhere so clearly as in his essays on Romero and Ellacuría and the other martyrs of El Salvador.[39] One could also analyze it as very much an Ignatian spirituality, as I have intimated above.

Of course, to say that a theology is inspired and formed by a particular spirituality does not in itself justify the particular approach a theology chooses and the conclusions it draws. It does, however, aid in understanding the theology better, and it opens up lines of dialogue with other theologies that are shaped by different spiritualities (provided, of course, that they recognize this fact as well). We need to ask whether it is, in fact, the case that this spirituality is present and vital to the church, on which issue, it seems to me, the list of holy men and women and martyrs in Latin America gives eloquent answer, and whether or not it deserves to be taken seriously and given theological voice. Just as we need to preserve and nourish genetic diversity in our biosphere and cultural diversity among the earth's peoples, so too do we need to preserve and nourish the diversity of spiritualities that are expressions, in so many different ways, of the one Spirit. That this task has been taken up in the past, and that it has often reached down to the very foundations of theological discourse, has been demonstrated by historians like M.-D. Chenu, with whom I began, and Jean LeClercq.[40] Sobrino's work should be understood and evaluated in the same vein.

## Notes

1. From M.-D. Chenu, *Une Ecole de Théologie: Le Saulchoir* (Paris: Cerf, 1985). Cited in Gustavo Gutiérrez, *We Drink from Our Own Wells: The Spiritual Journey of a People* (Maryknoll, N.Y.: Orbis Books, 1984), 147 n. 2.

2. Gustavo Gutiérrez, "Memory and Prophecy," in *The Option for the Poor in Christian Theology*, ed. Daniel Groody (Notre Dame, Ind.: University of Notre Dame Press, 2007), 33.

3. Jon Sobrino, "Spirituality and Theology," in *Spirituality of Liberation: Toward Political Holiness*, trans. Robert R. Barr (Maryknoll, N.Y.: Orbis Books, 1988), 46. This is my translation, from "Espiritualidad y Teología," in *Liberación con espíritu: Apuntes para una nueva espiritualidad* (San Salvador: UCA Editores, 1985), 63.

4. On the importance of imagination in theology, see Roger Haight, S.J., *Dynamics of Theology* (Mahwah, N.J.: Paulist Press, 1990), *inter alia*, 24f., 76f., 207.

5. Sobrino treats spirituality in a wide variety of contexts and essays. I focus on the essays in *Spirituality of Liberation*, providing my own translations where necessary, as well as a summary essay, "Spirituality and the Following of Jesus," in *Mysterium Liberationis: Fundamental Concepts of Liberation Theology*, ed. Jon Sobrino and Ignacio Ellacuría (Maryknoll, N.Y.: Orbis Books, 1994), 677-701. When necessary I provide my own translations from "Espiritualidad y Seguimiento de Jesus," in *Mysterium Liberationis: Conceptos fundamentales de la teología de la liberación* (San Salvador: UCA Editores, 1993), 449-76.

6. "Spirituality and Theology," 46;"Spirituality and the Following of Jesus," 677f.

7. "Presuppositions and Foundations of Spirituality," in *Spirituality of Liberation: Toward Political Holiness*, trans. Robert R. Barr (Maryknoll, N.Y.: Orbis Books, 1988), 13.

8. "Spirituality and the Following of Jesus," 677f. (my translation, see "Espiritualidad y Seguimiento de Jesus," 449f.).

9. Ignacio Ellacuría, "Hacia una fundamentación del método teológico Latino-americano," in *Liberación y Cuativerio: Debates en Torno al Método de la Teología en American Latina*, ed. Enrique Ruíz Maldonado (Mexico City, 1975), 625.

10. Ibid., 626.

11. The idioms quoted here operate with cognates of the Spanish *cargo* and *cargar* that are virtually untranslatable into English. I follow Kevin Burke's translation and analysis in *The Ground Beneath the Cross: The Theology of Ignacio Ellacuría* (Washington, D.C.: Georgetown University Press, 2000), 100-108. What should be borne in mind is that Ellacuría chooses these expressions in order to underline the indissoluble unity-in-difference of these three moments.

12. *Spirituality of Liberation*, 14-20; "Spirituality and the Following of Jesus," 681-85.

13. "Spirituality and the Following of Jesus," 681.

14. Ibid., 681, translation slightly emended (cf. "Espiritualidad y Seguimiento de Jesus," 454).

15. Ibid., 683.

16. Ibid., 684.

17. Ibid., 683-85; cf. *Spirituality of Liberation*, 17-19.

18. Ibid., 690-93; cf. *Spirituality of Liberation*, 84-86, 96-100.

19. Ibid., 684.

20. Ibid., 685 (the Spanish verb here is *llevar*, which can be translated "to take," "to lead or guide," or "to carry").

21. Ibid.

22. Ibid., 685f.

23. Ibid., 686.

24. Ibid.

25. For more on this understanding of "place" and its importance, see Jon Sobrino, *The Principle of Mercy: Taking the Crucified People from the Cross* (Maryknoll, N.Y.: Orbis Books, 1994), 30-32.

26. This is described at length in *Jesus the Liberator: A Historical-Theological Reading of Jesus of Nazareth,* trans. Paul Burns and Francis McDonagh (Maryknoll, N.Y.: Orbis Books, 1993), 67-102.

27. See "Spirituality and the Following of Jesus," 696f. See also his further elaboration of this theme in the second volume of his Christology: *Christ the Liberator: A View from the Victims*, trans. Paul Burns (Maryknoll, N.Y.: Orbis Books, 2001), 74-78.

28. On Ellacuría's appropriation and use of Ignatian spirituality, see J. Matthew Ashley, "Ignacio Ellacuría and the *Spiritual Exercises* of Ignatius Loyola," *Theological Studies* 61 (2000): 16-39; and idem, "Contemplation in the Action of Justice: Ignacio Ellacuría and Ignatian Spirituality," in *Love That Produces Hope: The Thought of Ignacio Ellacuría,* ed. Kevin F. Burke, Robert Lassalle-Klein (Collegeville, Minn.: Liturgical Press, 2006), 144-65.

29. See *Spirituality of Liberation*, 68. As Sobrino avers, this way of posing the issue also reflects the influence of Gustavo Gutiérrez's seminal work, *We Drink from Our Own Wells*.

30. Ibid., 71f.

31. Ibid., 72-79 (on the trinitarian character of spirituality, see pp. 50-52).

32. *Christ the Liberator*, 3.

33. Ibid., 2. This is my translation of "tomar postura ante *la totalidad* de la realidad." See the Spanish original, *La Fe en Jesucristo: Ensayo desde las víctimas* (Madrid: Trotta, 1999), 13.

34. Congregation for the Doctrine of the Faith, "Notification on the Works of Father Jon Sobrino, S.J.," no. 3.

35. This transformation of horizons—from natural-cosmic (the ancient world) or individual-subjective (modernity) to social-historical—was perhaps *the* principle goal of Ignacio Ellacuría's philosophical labors.

36. *Christ the Liberator*, 213.

37. Ibid., 210.

38. One thinks here of figures such as Origen, Bernard of Clairvaux, Francis of Assisi, and Ignatius of Loyola (but of course, not just them), for whom the beauty and goodness of Jesus can and should intoxicate the soul and inflect all of our thinking, feeling, and acting.

39. One could profitably consult *Witnesses to the Kingdom: The Martyrs of El Salvador and the Crucified Peoples* (Maryknoll, N.Y.: Orbis Books, 2003). On Ellacuría in particular, see Sobrino, "Ignacio Ellacuría, the Human Being and the Christian: 'Taking the Crucified People Down from the Cross,'" in *The Love That Produces Hope*, 1-67.

40. For LeClercq, see *The Love of Learning and the Desire for God* (New York: Fordham University Press, 1982).

# PART II

*Jesus Christ and Christology*

# 6

# What Got Jesus Killed?
## Sobrino's Historical-Theological Reading of Scripture

DANIEL J. HARRINGTON, S.J.

In the last thirty years hundreds of books on Jesus have been published. The more serious historical studies have often been lumped together under the title "the third quest of the historical Jesus." But as John P. Meier has suggested, the project is better named "the quest of the historian's Jesus," since the goal is to determine what can be said with high probability about Jesus of Nazareth by using the tools of modern historical research.[1]

The first quest took place for the most part in the nineteenth century and was described brilliantly and analyzed critically by Albert Schweitzer.[2] The second quest occurred in the 1950s and 1960s mainly among students of Rudolf Bultmann, who in reaction to their teacher's skepticism about recovering the historical Jesus contended that through the use of various authenticating criteria applied to the sayings of Jesus we could at least grasp the existential self-consciousness of Jesus. The first two quests took place almost exclusively among German Protestant professors.

The third quest has been much more ecumenical and international. One strand of the third quest, represented by the Jesus Seminar, has concentrated on the sayings of Jesus and has tended to play down the Jewish context and identity of Jesus.[3] Another strand has focused more on the deeds of Jesus and has stressed Jesus' context within Judaism.[4]

The methodology used by representatives of the third quest is historical criticism, which seeks to understand Jesus (or any other figure) in his own historical setting and (where possible) to get behind the literary sources in order to recover with high probability what Jesus said or did. This version of historical criticism is ideologically neutral, and has been declared "indispensable" by no less an authority than the Pontifical Biblical Commission.[5]

However, there is a version of historical criticism that is not so neutral. As described in classic form by Ernst Troeltsch,[6] the narrower version of historical criticism operates on three principles: (1) analogy—the past is much the same as the present, and vice versa; (2) cause and effect—historical events must be explained by historical causes, without recourse to supernatural interventions; and (3) probability—historians can arrive at best probable explanations, not certainty. These principles are in obvious tension with the Gospels, which are the only substantial sources that we possess regarding Jesus of Nazareth. Those who follow these principles rigidly must dismiss, ignore, or explain away Jesus' virginal conception, miracles, and resurrection.

The name of Jon Sobrino seldom appears in discussions of the third quest of the historical Jesus. He is neither a historian nor a biblical exegete. Nor does he claim to be such. Nevertheless, I hope to show that with reference to his treatment of the death of Jesus in his *Jesus the Liberator*,[7] Sobrino has made an important methodological contribution toward developing a more adequate hermeneutical approach for dealing with the Jesus of the Gospels. The key to his contribution comes in the words "historical-theological" in the subtitle of his work. My point is that while the narrow version of historical criticism is an inadequate tool, the historical-theological approach illustrated by Sobrino is a more adequate and fruitful way of treating the ancient sources about Jesus.

### The Problem

In response to publications associated with the third quest of the historical Jesus, I have taught several times a seminar entitled "Jesus and Hermeneutics." The goal is to try to understand what is going on in the new books about Jesus and what we can learn about Jesus and about historical and theological methodology in the process.

The course begins with the writings of biblical scholars who identify themselves mainly as historians: Gerd Theissen, John P. Meier, Burton L. Mack, E. P. Sanders, Ben Witherington, and N. T. Wright. Then there is an interlude devoted to the hermeneutical theories of E. D. Hirsch, Hans-Georg Gadamer, and Paul Ricoeur. Finally we move to interpretations of Jesus from various ideological and theological perspectives: Elisabeth Schüssler Fiorenza (feminism), Sobrino (liberation theology), Geza Vermes (Judaism), John Howard Yoder (pacifism and nonviolence), Edward Schillebeeckx (historical and classical Catholic theology), and so forth. Sobrino has been included as a representative of Latin American liberation theology, and the selections from his *Jesus the Liberator* concern why Jesus was killed and why he died. The two chapters correspond to the historical reasons for Jesus' death and how it was interpreted by early Christians and by the church throughout the centuries.

Here I want to focus on Sobrino's treatment on the reasons for Jesus' death, or what got Jesus killed.[8] Many third questers find this a difficult topic. For example, Burton L. Mack, an early member of the Jesus Seminar, suggests that the best source for understanding Jesus is the earliest (wisdom) stratum of the Sayings Source Q, the collection of sayings used independently by Matthew and Luke. The Jesus of this stratum is a wisdom teacher who sounded and looked like a Cynic philosopher. What he said and did may have been mildly annoying to some, but they were hardly the kinds of things that got Jesus (or anyone else) killed.

On the other hand, E. P. Sanders in his study of Jesus within Judaism gives particular attention to the episode customarily called "the cleansing of the temple" (Mark 11:15-19) and interprets it as a prophetic demonstration that aroused the fears and anxieties of the temple officials and their Roman masters. Sanders doubts that they regarded Jesus as a really serious political threat, since although they eventually had Jesus executed they did nothing to his followers. One gets the impression that Jesus was another failed visionary and that his death in Sanders's view was merely a tragic mistake, the result of misunderstanding Jesus the apocalyptic visionary for a political revolutionary.

The more times I have taught "Jesus and Hermeneutics," the more convinced I have become that Jon Sobrino's "historical-theological" reading of Jesus of Nazareth offers important methodological contributions to both the historical and the theological study of Jesus and his death. Sobrino makes no claim to be a biblical scholar, nor does he regard himself as being on the cutting edge of academic theology. Nevertheless, he can and does hope to make a distinctive contribution to Jesus research by doing theology among the "crucified people" of Latin America. From that vantage point he is convinced that he can see things in the ancient texts of the New Testament that tenured professors in the great universities of Europe and North America may fail to see.

For Sobrino, a "historical-theological" reading of Jesus of Nazareth does not mean the history of theology. Rather, it involves taking seriously the historical data about Jesus and trying to do theology on the basis of and in the light of these data. How he deals with the death of Jesus historically will illustrate, I hope, both the inadequacy of historical criticism narrowly defined and the positive value of his own historical-theological approach.

## Sobrino on Why Jesus Was Killed

The question why Jesus was killed is basically a historical question. Why Jesus died is a theological question. But in order to answer the first question, one must approach it not only as a historian but also as a theologian. Sobrino deals with both questions but in separate chapters.

What got Jesus killed, according to Sobrino, was the fact that he was a radical threat to the religious and political powers of his time. He insists that Jesus' death was not a mistake, tragic or otherwise. Rather, it was "the consequence of his life and this in turn was the consequence of his particular incarnation—in an anti-Kingdom which brings death—to defend its victims."[9]

The standpoint from which Sobrino proposes to understand Jesus' death is that of the crucified people of the Third World, that is, the context in which Sobrino has lived and worked for many years. Whereas the setting for the work of many recent Jesus questers has been "after Auschwitz," he describes his own setting as "in Auschwitz." The implication is that the conditions under which many people in Latin America live is analogous to the conditions in which Jesus lived and died in first-century Palestine. It is the "crucified people" that can best understand what got Jesus killed.

According to Sobrino, Jesus had to be killed because he got in the way of the political and religious powers. He traces the offense that Jesus gave to the struggle between "the gods"—between the humanly constructed gods of the Romans (and of some Jewish leaders) and the God revealed in the Scriptures of Israel and in Jesus (who called him "Father").

Both the Synoptic Gospels and John's Gospel portray Jesus as the victim of hostility and persecution from the beginning to the end of his public career. While the opponents represent a wide range of groups and movements—Pharisees, chief priests, scribes, Herodians, and Sadducees, as well as the Roman officials, they all had some kind of religious or political power. The "crowds" are the common people. They are generally well disposed or neutral toward Jesus, though in the end their leaders manipulate them to call for the crucifixion of Jesus. The four Gospels are united in presenting Jesus as the victim of persecution and in suggesting that his death was not merely a tragic mistake but rather the logical consequence of who Jesus was and the circumstances in which he lived and worked.

Did Jesus know beforehand that he was going to suffer and die in Jerusalem? Biblical scholars suggest that the three passion predictions (Mark 8:31; 9:31; 10:33-34) in their present forms may reflect the events described later in the passion narratives. In other words, they sound like *vaticina ex eventu,* that is, predictions drawn from events that had already happened. That may be so. But the question remains, Did Jesus himself expect to suffer and die in Jerusalem?

Here Sobrino wisely points to the fate of John the Baptist. Jesus knew John, accepted his baptism, was mentored by him to some extent, and in many ways carried on his ministry. He surely knew that John had been executed under Herod Antipas, the ruler in Galilee. Whether one accepts Mark's account that John was killed for criticizing Herod's marriages (as in Mark 6:14-29), or Josephus's claim that Herod Antipas feared John as a political rival for the people's affections (*Jewish Antiquities* 18.116-19), makes no real difference. Jesus was surely familiar with the possible consequences of speaking the truth to power from the case of John the Baptist. Moreover, he was surely also cognizant of the long line of contemporary Jewish religious figures who had suffered fates like that of John the Baptist. And, of course, he knew well that it was the destiny of prophets to suffer rejection and persecution (Mark 6:4 parr.). The fact that Jesus the prophet of God's kingdom went up to Jerusalem, Sobrino observes, was "the measure of his faithfulness to God."[10] He did so out of fidelity to the cause of the kingdom of God, out of confidence in the one whom he called "Father," and out of loyalty to his prophetic calling.

At the root of Jesus' resolve to go to Jerusalem, according to Sobrino, was his understanding of his life as service on behalf of others, even to the point of sacrificial service. This is the link between the historical Jesus and the Christ of faith, between Jesus of Nazareth and the early church's interpretations of him (Christology). It is expressed clearly in Mark 10:45: "the Son of Man came not to be served but to serve, and to give his life as a ransom for many." It is alluded to in the saying over the cup at the Last Supper: "This is my blood of the covenant which is poured out for many" (Mark 14:24). The allusions to Jeremiah (the new covenant, see Jer 31:31-34) and the Suffering Servant (Isaiah 53) in the so-called words of institution reflect Jesus' self-consciousness as a prophet in the line of suffering prophets.

There has been much scholarly debate among legal, historical, and biblical scholars over the character of the "trials" of Jesus before the Jewish council known as the Sanhedrin and the Roman governor, Pontius Pilate. Whatever their precise legal status may have been, the New Testament accounts suggest that the major charges against Jesus involved his threat to destroy the Jerusalem temple and the popular claims that Jesus was the Messiah.

Although Mark rejects the temple charge as false (14:59), Jesus' "cleansing" of the temple on entering the city (Mark 11:15-19) and his prophecy of the temple's destruction (13:2) indicate that there was some substance to the charge made at the trial before the Sanhedrin (14:58). The temple action and saying not only fit with Jesus' preaching about God's kingdom (and not the temple) as the focus of Judaism but also posed a threat to the temple officials (chief priests, elders, Sadducees, and so on) and all those who made their living off the pilgrims coming to the temple (providers of lodging and food, construction workers, the purveyors of animals and other material for sacrifices, and so on). Sobrino notes that it is reasonable to conclude that at the "religious" trial Jesus was accused of wanting to destroy the temple not only because he criticized certain aspects of it but also because he offered an alternative (the kingdom of God) that implied that the temple would no longer be the core of the political, social, and economic life of the Jewish people.

In treating the "political" trial before Pilate, Sobrino takes as his starting point Luke's summary of charges in 23:2: "We found this man perverting our nation, forbidding them to pay taxes to the emperor, and saying that he himself is the Messiah, a king." While this may well be a Lukan formulation, it is very likely an accurate summary of what got Jesus in trouble with the Jewish and Roman authorities. In this way the Jewish religious officials portrayed Jesus as a political threat to the Roman empire in general and to Pilate as prefect of Judea in particular. The charge that Jesus made himself "the Messiah, a king" would have been especially incendiary in this context. And the Roman policy for dealing with such "messianic" figures was swift and brutal execution.

While the Evangelists present Pilate as hesitant to execute Jesus, he finally does sentence Jesus to die and directs that the inscription on the cross should read "The King of the Jews" (Mark 15:26). This title, which was the Roman translation of "Messiah," served as a warning to other would-be Messiahs who might be tempted to lead an uprising against the Roman occupiers and their emperor.

Sobrino interprets the encounter between Jesus and Pilate as "a confrontation between two 'mediators' . . . representing two 'mediations,' the Kingdom of God and the Roman empire (the *pax romana*)."[11] He sees the trial before Pilate as a contest or choice between the God of Jesus and Pilate's god (the emperor and the state gods who maintained the *pax romana*). Sobrino concludes that Jesus was killed "because of his kind of life, because of what he said and what he did."[12] In other words, the teachings and actions of Jesus provide the point of continuity with the early church's interpretations of his death and with the experiences of the "crucified people" throughout the centuries and in our own time.

## Sobrino in Hermeneutical Perspective

Sobrino does not claim to be a historical critic in the narrow sense, such as E. P. Sanders might describe himself.[13] He does claim to be offering a "historical-theological reading of Jesus of Nazareth." The criteria by which his work may best be judged come from philosophical hermeneutics and from Gadamer, Hirsch, and Ricoeur rather than from Troeltsch. Here I want to examine his interpretation of what got Jesus killed in the light of some basic concepts in hermeneutical theory: preunderstanding, fusion of horizons, verification, and appropriation. These concepts in turn may better illumine Sobrino's methodology in *Jesus the Liberator* and in particular his chapter on the death of Jesus.

### Preunderstanding

Every interpreter brings to the biblical text (or any other text) a set of preunderstandings or prejudices. The challenge is to discern what are true or salutary prejudices and what are false or distorting prejudices.[14] Sobrino's prejudices regarding the Bible include the assumption that it is a classic and even sacred text. That is, it transcends the original circumstances of its production (a classic text) and can be an occasion for encountering God (a sacred text, the word of God).

Moreover, the interpreter needs to be aware of the tradition in which he or she stands. In most of these matters Sobrino is not unusual or exceptional. He is from Spain, was educated both in Spain and in the United States and Germany, and has lived and worked in El Salvador for many years. He is a Catholic, a priest, a Jesuit, and a professor of theology. He has written many books and articles on a variety of theological topics. What sets him apart from most theologians is his conviction that the strong analogies between first-century Palestine and late-twentieth-century El Salvador have enabled him to see aspects of the New Testament that other interpreters in other circumstances may miss.

All analogies limp. But some limp more than others. Indian and African exegetes and theologians have often argued that they have more intellectual and emotional kinship with the biblical authors than those who bring to the biblical texts the philosophical baggage of the European Enlightenment. Latin American liberation theologians make a similar case with regard to the sociopolitical conditions in which they live and the cultural assumptions that shape their societies (stratified social classes, patriarchy, hierarchy, honor and shame, and so forth). They observe that the Word became flesh (John 1:14) in this kind of society. Not that this is an ideal world that should be preserved. Rather, it was the world that Jesus challenged and that eventually had him killed. If we want to understand his death, we must try to understand the horizon in which it occurred.

### Fusion of Horizons

A horizon is the range of vision that includes everything that can be seen from a particular vantage point. Understanding takes place in the fusion of horizons between the text and the interpreter. Interpretation involves the sharing of common meaning so that there is an interplay or dialogue between the text and the interpreter.[15]

Sobrino comes to the Gospel passion narratives as a well-educated Catholic theologian. What makes his approach different from others is his personal and pastoral experiences of life among the poor of El Salvador. He was close to Archbishop Oscar Romero, who was murdered while saying Mass in a hospital chapel in 1980. Several of his Jesuit colleagues at the University of Central America in San Salvador were brutally executed by an army gang in 1989.

Sobrino knows firsthand what it means to suffer in an oppressive society. Thus, he is better positioned than most of us to enter into the horizon of Jesus' passion and death, and to explain to the rest of us what got Jesus killed. He has earned a serious hearing, and that is what his work has generally received over the years. In the process his work has become the occasion by which the "crucified people" of Latin America and people all over the world have come to understand and appreciate better Jesus' life, death, and resurrection. He writes neither as a biblical exegete nor as a historian nor as a classic dogmatic theologian. Rather, he deliberately presents a "historical-theological" reading of Jesus of Nazareth. He tries to take seriously and bring together the horizons of first-century Palestine and late-twentieth-century life in Latin America.

## Verification

In hermeneutics the interpreter's goal is to show that one reading is more probable than others and preferable to them. The process of verification is always a matter of weighing relative probabilities. The hermeneutical theorist, E. D. Hirsch, offers four criteria for establishing an interpretation as the most probable: legitimacy, correspondence, generic appropriateness, and coherence.[16]

To satisfy the criterion of legitimacy, the reading must be permissible in the context in which the text was composed. The events described in the Gospel passion narratives took place in first-century Palestine, in a time and place where there was much political turmoil among the local population and vigorous repression on the part of the Roman officials and their local allies. Richard A. Horsley has aptly described this situation as a "spiral of violence" in which oppression led to uprisings, which in turn led to further repression, which issued in full-scale rebellion and the ultimate destruction of Jerusalem in A.D. 70.[17] Mark's Gospel, which is regarded as the earliest Gospel, was very likely composed in Rome around A.D. 70, when the local Christian community there had undergone persecution and martyrdom under Nero and expected more to come. In both the Judean and the Roman contexts the perception that Jesus and the early Christians were somehow dangerous to the sociopolitical and religious status quo along the lines suggested by Sobrino would certainly have been legitimate.

According to the criterion of correspondence, the reading must account for each linguistic component in the text. Sobrino's major source is Mark 14–15, with some elements (especially the trial before Pilate) taken from John 18–19. Of course, both Mark and John wrote from the perspective of Easter. They and their first readers knew that Jesus' story did not end on Good Friday but rather continued (and continues) through Jesus' resurrection from the dead. Sobrino too comes to the events described in the Gospel passion narratives with full knowledge about how Jesus' story came out. Nevertheless, if we try initially (as he does) to approach the Gospel passion narratives as to some extent historical sources and to read them while bracketing temporarily the Evangelists' more obvious post-Easter theological interpretations, then Sobrino's account of what got Jesus killed fits well with the picture of Jesus as the prophet of God's kingdom who made himself inconvenient to both the Jewish and the Roman authorities in his time and place. Indeed, the ways in which Jesus is presented in the passion narratives has made him the archetype of the rejected prophet throughout the centuries. The Gospels do not describe Jesus' death as simply a tragic misunderstanding or a mistake. Rather, the Evangelists describe Jesus as someone who was very much "in the way" of the political and religious authorities and whose death was the natural outcome of who Jesus was and what he stood for. Sobrino's reading of the Gospels is surely more plausible than those of Mack and Sanders in this regard.

According to the criterion of generic appropriateness, the interpretation must fit with the literary genre of the text. To most people in antiquity, the Gospels would have looked like biographies. However, ancient biographers were not as interested in chronological details and brute facts as they were in the moral significance and exemplary value (positive or negative) of their subjects. All the Evangelists emphasize that from the beginning of his public ministry (and even from his infancy according to Matthew) Jesus was the object of hostility and plotting from various groups. In this matter there is no reason to doubt their historical accuracy. Without such growing enmity it is impossible to understand the passion narratives. Moreover, the Evangelists portray Jesus as the prophet of God's kingdom and as fundamentally a religious teacher. Just as it is impossible to understand the ministry of Martin Luther King Jr. without attending to its biblical foundations, so Sobrino correctly emphasizes that it was Jesus' religious message about God's kingdom that especially got him into trouble and eventually put to death. It appears that Sobrino's historical-theological reading of Jesus of Nazareth is appropriate to the genre of the Gospels that are the primary sources for his interpretation of Jesus' passion and death.

When examined in the light of Hirsch's criteria for verification, it appears that Sobrino's historical-theological interpretation of what got Jesus killed is legitimate and permissible in its original historical setting, accounts for the data presented in the primary sources, and is appropriate to how the Evangelists told their stories of Jesus. His historical-theological reading of Jesus is certainly more coherent with regard to the sources and more plausible with regard to history than the narrow historical-critical readings are.

### Appropriation

The hermeneutical theorists whose insights I am using to explain and assess Sobrino's interpretation of Jesus' death insist that the reading of a classic text should have a real effect on the reader.[18] To express this point, they use different terms: significance (Hirsch), fusion of horizons and effective history (Gadamer), and appropriation (Ricoeur). In some circles this element is called actualization.[19] While Hirsch regards significance as a separate step beyond determining the most probable meaning of a text, both Gadamer and Ricoeur consider it as an integral part of the interpretive process itself.

Sobrino's concluding meditation on the death of Jesus and the crucified people provides an excellent example of biblical actualization and appropriation.[20] In it he shows that this process is integral to the Bible itself and is carried on in the life of the church throughout the centuries and today.

Sobrino first reaches back to the description of the Suffering Servant in Isaiah 53 as a model of both the passion of Jesus and the passion of the crucified people of Latin America. The Servant seeks to establish right and justice, is chosen by God for salvation, bears the sin of the world, is a light to the nations, and brings salvation. Next he makes connections between the Servant, Jesus, the Body of Christ, and the crucified people. He defines martyrdom as not only dying for Jesus but also dying like Jesus and for the cause of Jesus. The martyrs bear witness to the God of the kingdom proclaimed by Jesus. They include Archbishop Oscar Romero, his own Jesuit and lay colleagues, the many Christians who struggle politically and religiously, and the innocent and anonymous victims of murder.

Here Sobrino's methodology is more hermeneutical and homiletical than in other chapters in *Jesus the Liberator*. But such an actualization is an integral part of his historical-theological reading of Jesus. The story of Jesus had already begun in the figure of the Servant of the Lord in the sixth century B.C. And it continues in martyrs like Oscar Romero and Martin Luther King, as well as in the less obvious sufferings and deaths of the anonymous crucified people. In his meditation Sobrino illustrates the biblical dynamic of appropriation and actualization that is present in the Bible itself and that provides the impetus and inspiration for preachers, theologians, and all of God's people who constitute the Body of Christ.

## Conclusion

Sobrino's treatment of what got Jesus killed is a good illustration of his "historical-theological" methodology in approaching Jesus. He is neither a historical critic in the narrow sense nor a dogmatic or systematic theologian in the classical sense. Rather, he tries to take seriously the data of Scripture and at the same time to respond to the dynamism within the biblical sources that pushes us forward beyond establishing historical details into theological reflection. In doing so he finds analogies and models in the Scriptures for people in the context in which he has taught and worked. On the other hand, he discovers in his own present-day context a vantage point from which to read and interpret both the Jesus of history and the Scriptures more appropriately. He also challenges those of us who live in other contexts to read the Gospels in fresh ways and to recognize the crucified people among us in our world and in our own neighborhoods.

## Notes

1. John P. Meier, *A Marginal Jew: Rethinking the Historical Jesus. Volume One: The Roots of the Problem and the Person* (New York: Doubleday, 1991), 25.

2. Albert Schweitzer, *The Quest of the Historical Jesus: First Complete Edition* (Minneapolis: Fortress, 2001).

3. For example, Burton L. Mack, *The Lost Gospel: The Book of Q & Christian Origins* (San Francisco: HarperCollins, 1993); and Robert W. Funk, *Honest to Jesus: Jesus for a New Millennium* (San Francisco: HarperSanFrancisco, 1996).

4. For example, E. P. Sanders, *Jesus and Judaism* (Philadelphia: Fortress, 1985); and N. T. Wright, *Jesus and the Victory of God* (Minneapolis: Fortress, 1996).

5. See the Pontifical Biblical Commission's 1993 document "The Interpretation of the Bible in the Church," in *The Scripture Documents: An Anthology of Official Catholic Documents,* ed. Dean P. Béchard (Collegeville, Minn.: Liturgical Press, 2002), 249.

6. Ernst Troeltsch, *Der Historismus und seine Probleme* (Tübingen: Mohr, 1922). See also Robert Morgan and Michael Pye, eds., *Ernst Troeltsch: Writings on Theology and Religion* (London: Duckworth, 1977).

7. Jon Sobrino, *Jesus the Liberator: A Historical-Theological Reading of Jesus of Nazareth,* trans. Paul Burns and Francis McDonagh (Maryknoll, N.Y.: Orbis Books, 1993), 195-211.

8. John P. Meier criticized Sobrino's claims as simplistic and naïve ("The Bible as a Source for Theology," *Catholic Theological Society of America Proceedings* 43 [1988]: 1-14). However, everyone writes from somewhere, and that "somewhere" influences the product. Sobrino is more forthcoming and creative about this than are most authors of recent books about Jesus.

9. Sobrino, *Jesus the Liberator,* 210.

10. Ibid., 201.

11. Ibid., 209.

12. Ibid.

13. Sanders, *Jesus and Judaism,* 319-27.

14. Hans-Georg Gadamer, *Truth and Method* (New York: Seabury, 1975), 235-45.

15. Ibid., 269-74.

16. E. D. Hirsch, *Validity in Interpretation* (New Haven/London: Yale University Press, 1967), 236.

17. Richard A. Horsley, *Jesus and the Spiral of Violence: Popular Jewish Resistance in Roman Palestine* (San Francisco: Harper & Row, 1987). Horsley's approach to Jesus' death seems so political as to obscure the religious dimensions of Jesus' actions and teachings.

18. Gadamer, *Truth and Method,* 267-69; Hirsch, *Validity in Interpretation,* 211; and Paul Ricoeur, *Hermeneutics and the Human Sciences* (Cambridge: Cambridge University Press, 1981), 131-44, 182-93.

19. See the Pontifical Biblical Commission's 1993 document "The Interpretation of the Bible in the Church," in *The Scripture Documents,* ed. Béchard, 303-6.

20. Sobrino, *Jesus the Liberator,* 254-71.

# 7

# The Christology of Jon Sobrino

Roberto S. Goizueta

It was a *shock*. I was in Thailand giving a course precisely on christology, speaking about whole peoples who are crucified.

> —Jon Sobrino recounting the moment when he learned of the assassination of his Jesuit companions, their housekeeper, and her daughter on November 16, 1989.[1]

During the fifty years of his ministry in El Salvador, Jon Sobrino has been among the most prolific scholars in the church, writing on topics that span the breadth of the theological disciplines. Yet at the very heart of this extraordinary scholarly corpus stand his numerous, systematic, and profound reflections on the person of Jesus Christ. There is little doubt that, for this Jesuit pastor-theologian, all theology is—or ought to be—Christocentric from beginning to end. Sobrino's christological thought emerges as a *cantus firmus* that runs through his life and work. The principal challenge facing anyone attempting an exposition and analysis of Sobrino's Christology is not only that of dissecting his explicit reflections on the topic but also, and perhaps more importantly, of understanding how these can be interpreted, or "heard," only within the context of his entire work and, especially, his profound faith and commitment to Christian discipleship.

Our approach will be primarily methodological and thematic, highlighting the central themes of Sobrino's thought on the topic while attempting to demonstrate how these themes arise from his theological methodology. We will begin with an analysis of this method, focusing on the relationship between Christology and praxis. This method will then yield insights into the nature of Christ's person and mission, particularly what it means to proclaim that Jesus Christ is "the Way, the Truth, and the Life." For it is this assertion—not only as profession but especially as lived commitment—that is at the very heart of Sobrino's Christology and constitutes the core of his vocation as Christian and theologian. When rooted in the praxis of following Jesus, the proclamation of the Good News of Jesus Christ is revealed as inextricably linked to its enactment in history. To profess the truth of Christ is to walk with Christ. (It is no coincidence that, as a Jesuit, Sobrino belongs to the *Compañia de Jesús,* the Company of Jesus, those who accompany Jesus.)

## Praxic Christology: Following Jesus

For Sobrino, the starting point of theology is "the faith that God has made a self-bestowal on us by grace."[2] Consequently, Christology "cannot presume to verify the truth of Christ by what we think we already know in advance, but must maintain an openness to receiving from Jesus definitions of the divine and the human."[3] Christology begins as receptivity to God's self-gift in Jesus Christ: "To have genuine love for our sisters and brothers, we must have an experience of the God who loved us first. . . . 'it all started with God.'"[4] Like all theological reflection, Christology begins in silence; Sobrino quotes Gustavo Gutiérrez's observation that "speaking about God (theo-logy) comes from the silence of prayer and commitment. . . . To put it in a nutshell, our methodology is our spirituality."[5] For Sobrino, any approach to Christology "has to be rigorously intellectual—even doctrinal, some would add—but its deepest essence lies in being something 'spiritual'; in that it should help persons and communities to meet Christ, to follow the cause of Jesus, to live as new men and women and to conform this world to the heart of God."[6]

Sobrino's insistence that "the believer's faith does not create its object" but is, instead, a response to that object's own self-revelation is crucial for understanding the Jesuit's theology and Christology.[7] "The true theologian," writes Sobrino quoting Leonardo Boff, "can speak only from Jesus, that is, moved by his reality experienced in faith and love."[8] Without a due appreciation of the centrality of such assertions to Sobrino's theological enterprise, one will misinterpret his work. This is particularly important in Sobrino's case precisely because such assertions seem to contradict regnant, influential stereotypes of liberation theology. Indeed, while arguing for the spiritual ground of theology, Sobrino himself notes, with tongue in cheek, that such arguments "might even seem disconcerting on the lips of a liberation theologian."[9]

Sobrino's spirituality is thus deeply Christocentric; it is predicated on and derived from an ongoing encounter with Christ. Yet such an encounter has concrete historical contours; to encounter Christ—or, more specifically, to be encountered by Christ—presupposes that we be present there where Christ is himself present, where Christ himself has said he will be present. If *theologically* the starting point for Christology is the reality and truth of Jesus Christ as the one who loved us first, *phenomenologically* the starting point is this "place," this "locus" where we are encountered by and receive his love and grace. And the one who reveals this privileged locus is Christ himself. Consequently, christological reflection cannot be undertaken apart from reflection on the Jesus of history as he is revealed in the Sacred Scriptures and in tradition. For here we discover not only *who* Christ is but also *where* he is and, thus, where we must place ourselves—literally and concretely—if we are to encounter and come to know that Christ. In other words, Sobrino's Christology is "from above" insofar as it asserts the reality, truth, and priority of God's self-revelation in the person of Jesus Christ, but it is "from below" insofar as it asserts that the *credibility* of God's self-revelation in Christ—precisely as the revelation of "the Truth, the Way, and the Life"—depends on its actually being received and lived as such (otherwise it's not revelation at all but illusion). If, as theologians from Paul to Pope Benedict have consistently argued, it is the saint who embodies, witnesses to, and thus makes credible the claims of the Christian faith, it is ultimately Jesus Christ who, in his life, death, and resurrection, fully and definitively embodies and makes credible those claims. This is what Sobrino means when he avers that the starting point of Christology must be the historical Jesus, for in the person of the Nazarene God's self-revelation is made credible and, thus, capable of being received. By virtue of "his life, his mission and his fate," we can indeed proclaim "that this Jesus is more than Jesus, that he is *the* Christ."[10]

## The Historical Jesus

The very term "the historical Jesus" has for decades, indeed centuries, been fraught with contention. One need not be a theologian or biblical scholar to remember the debates that, not long ago, revolved around the Jesus Seminar and the front-page declarations concerning the historicity, or lack thereof, of Jesus' actions and sayings as depicted in the Gospels. At last count, there have been three "Quests for the Historical Jesus." The possibility and even desirability of attempting a retrieval of the Jesus of history, the Jesus "behind" the scriptural texts, continue to be debated today and will be debated long into the future.

So when Sobrino states in *Jesus the Liberator* that "I have chosen as my starting point . . . what is usually called the 'historical Jesus'" he is aware that he is wading into roiling waters. "The *real* starting point," he writes, "is always, in one way, overall faith in Christ, but the *methodological* starting point continues to be the historical Jesus."[11] Sobrino insists that retrieving the historical Jesus is an imperative for Christology precisely in order to safeguard Jesus' divinity.[12] That is, if Christology is to avoid reducing Jesus Christ to any merely human projection, it must insist on the historical particularity of Jesus as the one who, because he is the definitive incarnation of the Absolute Other, subverts all such reductionism. It is precisely the concrete historical particularity of Jesus' life, mission, and fate that reveals the transcendent (and therefore scandalous!) character of God. "Thus, paradoxical though it may appear," suggests Sobrino, "the highest christological affirmation about Christ may subtly become an alibi for not recognizing—and following—Jesus."[13] Conversely, a Christology that appears to be "low" because of its emphasis on the historical particularity of

Jesus may in fact be preserving the character of God as mystery, as transcendent, more surely than putatively "high" Christologies that, in fact, end up reducing Christ to our own human constructs, whether theoretical, existential, or political. The historical Christ, in other words, is a necessary safeguard against constructing "Christs" in our own image.

To cite but one example: an awareness of the connection between Jesus' actions, the sociohistorical context in which he undertook those actions, and his ultimate fate at Calvary can deepen our appreciation of the cross as the scandalous revelation of an incomprehensible, literally in-conceivable God, a God who chooses to be revealed not on a throne but on a cross, not in the person of a royal monarch but in the person of a condemned criminal. Such an awareness of the scandalous character of the historical Jesus safeguards the necessarily "receptive" (rather than "constructive") character of Christian faith, and therefore the sovereignty of God, in that it strips us of all our preconceptions of who God is, what God is like, and where God is to be encountered. Standing before the Jesus whose scandalous actions led to his crucifixion, we can no longer claim to know the meaning of love and justice; we dare not ascribe these terms to Jesus but must allow his own life, mission, and fate to define them for us: "Christ died to make it clear that not everything is permitted."[14] Christ died to make it clear that not every "God" is *the* God, not every "Christ" is *the* Christ.

Before the historical Jesus we can no longer profess that "God is love," since this presupposes that we can define God in terms of our own conception of love. The mystery revealed on the cross demands, rather, that we confess that "love is God"; it is Jesus Christ himself, inseparable from the "historical Jesus," who embodies and defines love. Jesus in all his historical particularity is the one who reveals that God is indeed mystery, God is indeed transcendent. Sobrino starts with Jesus of Nazareth in his historical particularity, then, in order to emphasize Jesus' divinity, he says: "Although it may seem a play on words, everything is decided by the choice to give methodological priority to one of these statements: 'Jesus is Christ,' or 'Christ? He's Jesus.' I believe that the New Testament bluntly says the second."[15] And it's the second that safeguards the identity between Jesus of Nazareth and the Christ of God.

## Jesus and the Kingdom of God

One of the most important aspects of Sobrino's christological thought is his call for an adequate appreciation of the intrinsic relationship between Jesus Christ and the kingdom, or reign of God; without such an appreciation, the social, ethical implications of Christ's life and mission will be lost. This, he suggests, is precisely what has occurred in some contemporary First-World Christologies.

At the core of Jesus' self-understanding was his awareness of his own unique relationship to the Father and to God's reign:

In the Gospels this something central in Jesus' life is expressed by two terms: "Kingdom of God" and "Father." Of both, the first thing to say is that they are authentic words of Jesus. The second is that they are all-embracing, since by "Kingdom of God" Jesus expresses the whole of reality and of what is to be done, and by "Father" Jesus expresses the personal reality that gives final meaning to his life, that in which he rests and what in turn does not allow him to rest. Finally, "Kingdom of God" and "Father" are systematically important realities for theology, giving it a basis on which better to organize and grade Jesus' multiple external activities, to conjecture his inner being and, undoubtedly, to explain his historical fate of dying on the cross.[16]

For Jesus, argues Sobrino, these two are co-implicit terms, since "though distinct and not simply interchangeable, [they] complement one another, and so 'the Kingdom explains God's being *abba* and the Fatherhood of God provides a basis for and explanation of the Kingdom.'"[17] This has crucial implications: the God of Jesus Christ is one who is intrinsically relational, who cannot be known apart from God's relationship to history and to God's people. Even when, as in the wisdom traditions, God appears silent or absent, "it is not the mere absence of God from history, but a silence that makes itself felt."[18]

While the centrality of the kingdom to Jesus' message is evident, however, Jesus never actually defines what the kingdom is; its meaning and content remain vague. Nevertheless, contends Sobrino, that meaning and content can be derived from the Gospel texts in several ways. The first he calls the "notional way": Jesus draws on preexisting notions of the kingdom already familiar to his Jewish audiences:

> So confession of the kingship of Yahweh is basic to Israel and runs right through its history; it is another way of saying that God acts in history and takes Israel's side.... The Kingdom of God has two essential connotations: (1) that God rules in his acts, (2) that it exists in order to transform a bad and unjust historical-social reality into a different good and just one. So the term "reign" of God is actually more appropriate than "kingdom" of God.... So God's "reign" is then the positive action through which God transforms reality and God's "Kingdom" is what comes to pass in this world when God truly reigns: a history, a society, a people transformed according to the will of God.[19]

This reign Jesus declares to be "at hand." Moreover, the coming of God's reign is portrayed as being pure gift and grace, made possible by God's initiative alone. At the same time, our ability to accept this gift "demands a conversion, *metanoia*, which . . . is a task for the listener: the hope the poor must come to feel, the radical change of conduct required of the oppressors, the demands made on all to live a life worthy of the Kingdom."[20] The kingdom of God is thus good news to the victims of injustice, in that they are given new hope of liberation, and to the oppressors, in that they are offered the possibility of conversion. And it is precisely the gratuitous character of the kingdom, as pure gift of God, that makes possible and generates conversion:

> Gratuitousness and action are not opposed then. The coming of the Kingdom of God is something that, on the one hand, can only be asked for, not forced; but on the other, the will of God has to be put into effect now on this earth. What is clear is the absolute loving initiative of God, which is neither forced nor can be forced—this being both unnecessary and impossible—by human actions. Clear too is that this gratuitous love of God's is what generates the need and the possibility of a loving human response. When a sinner is converted, it is God's goodness and mercy that move the sinner to change.[21]

Despite its gratuitous character—or perhaps because of it—the coming of the kingdom is not an immediately irenic experience or reality. Insofar as God's reign involves God in history, where God enters to transform injustice, God's reign involves a confrontation with oppressive "principalities and powers" that in turn elicits their resistance:

> The Kingdom of God appears as good news in the midst of bad things, in the midst of the *anti-Kingdom*, that is. The Kingdom of God will not arrive, so to speak, from a *tabula rasa*, but from and against the anti-Kingdom that is formally and actively opposed to it. The Kingdom of God is, then, a dialectical and conflictual reality, excluding and opposing the anti-Kingdom.[22]

As pure gift that brings about reconciliation and justice, God's reign elicits opposition from those who, by demanding through their actions that history bend to their own will, reject the possibility of a reconciled humanity and, even more fundamentally, reject the possibility that such reconciliation could be a divine gift rather than an exclusively human achievement.

The second way in which we can determine what constitutes the "kingdom of God" is what Sobrino calls "the way of the addressee." While Jesus' offer of salvation is universal, it is extended in a special way to the poor and marginalized. Sobrino makes clear that the privileged position of the poor in God's economy is not sectarian or antagonistic.[23] Quoting Joachim Jeremias, Sobrino argues that, notwithstanding its universal intent and orientation, the "essential feature" of Jesus' offer of salvation is that the "Kingdom belongs *uniquely to the poor.*"[24] The Gospel is "Good News *to the poor.*" This in no way suggests that the poor are morally superior, but that their social situation places them in a priv-ileged position for receiving God's offer of universal mercy and accepting God's reign. Moreover, the situation of poverty itself is not a value—indeed, it is a *dis-value* and an evil. Because "the poor" is a relative, relational term (vis-à-vis "the rich"), what makes poverty and marginalization evil is precisely the fact that these exist alongside wealth and privilege.[25] Poverty includes but goes beyond economic poverty, yet it should not be reductively spiritualized "so that all human beings can be included in the category of poor."[26] Ultimately, the poor are all those persons who cannot take life for granted. And this includes at least two-thirds of the global population.[27]

That the coming kingdom of God is Good News to the poor reflects God's preferential (not exclusive) love for the poor. "As an eschatological reality," explains Sobrino, "the Kingdom of God is universal, and open to all, though not to all in the same way."[28] The offer of salvation is universal insofar as all (whether rich or poor) are invited to accept its universal, gratuitous character. For the poor, this implies acceptance of the liberative hope given expression in God's reign; for the rich, it implies acceptance of the possibility of conversion. So the proclamation of the kingdom is, indirectly, also "good news" for the rich, since it reveals the hope and possibility that the rich can enter into solidarity with the poor, thereby coming to an awareness of the gratuitous character of God's love and reign.

The partial, preferential character of the kingdom is what made—and still makes—it a scandalous image. That the gospel is good news to the poor, that God loves the poor preferentially, that the kingdom is proclaimed to the poor (simply because of their social situation) are all perceived as scandalous by the powerful precisely because these characteristics of Jesus' message all reveal the utter gratuitousness of God's love. The real scandal is not that the poor are pre-ferred but that God can love those persons whom human societies have deemed inherently unlovable and, indeed, sub-human. Only insofar as we, rich or poor, can accept that fact—that God loves and welcomes *all*—can we be open to God's gratuitous, universal love. Therefore, those persons whom human soci-eties have presumed to exclude from God's love are in a privileged position to mediate the scandalous, gratuitous nature of that love. Again, at the very heart of Sobrino's Christology and theology is the insistence that "God loved us first," that Christian faith is ultimately a lived encounter with a universal unmerited love that, as such, is historically mediated in a special way by those persons whom our societies have deemed to be themselves without merit.

The third, and final way Sobrino adduces for defining the Kingdom of God is "the way of the practice of Jesus." That is, Jesus not only proclaims the king-dom; he *enacts* it. Jesus not only proclaims the kingdom; he "practices" the kingdom. Thus, the kingdom of God is a term that not only provides *meaning* but, even more importantly, effects *liberation*; its significance is not only noetic but also practical. Drawing on much recent exegetical scholarship, Sobrino analyzes Jesus' activities as enactments of God's reign. By working miracles, casting out demons, and, especially, by welcoming sinners, the poor, and the outcast, Jesus makes God's reign present and demonstrates its character.

And that character provokes a violent reaction. Another important contribution to Christology is Sobrino's contention that theologians misunderstand Jesus Christ and the kingdom he ushers in if they ignore the kingdom's relationship to the "anti-kingdom." The reign Jesus Christ enacts is such that it elicits violent rejection. By extending hospitality to the outcasts and identifying them with God's reign, Jesus Christ demonstrates the subversive character of that reign vis-à-vis social arrangements that marginalize and exclude the poor. After all, the very notion of "kingdom" implies a particular kind of social organization or social arrangement; God's own social arrangement subverts human social arrangements. The reaction of the "principalities and powers" to the appearance of God's reign in their midst will thus be swift and violent. When the kingdom of God is understood in isolation from this "anti-kingdom," argues Sobrino, the subversive, liberating, and social character of God's reign will necessarily be relativized, if not ignored altogether.

Moreover, when the intrinsic connection between Jesus' hospitality to outcasts and his violent death is ignored, so too will the intrinsic, intimate connection between Jesus Christ (as mediator) and the kingdom of God (what is mediated). The kingdom of God must thus stand at the center of any Christology:

> In this sense we can and must say, according to faith, that the definitive, ultimate and eschatological mediator of the Kingdom of God has *already* appeared: Jesus . . . Christ is *the* mediator. From this standpoint, we can also appreciate Origen's fine definition of Christ as the *autobasileia* of God, the Kingdom of God in person: important words that well describe the finality of the personal mediator of the Kingdom, but dangerous if they equate Christ with the reality of the Kingdom. God's will for creation is not simply, however, that a definitive mediator should appear, but that human beings, God's creatures, should live in a particular manner. . . .[29]

When Christologies ignore the centrality of the kingdom to Christ's identity (precisely as mediator) they will tend toward a realized eschatology that, by not appreciating the "not yet" character of God's reign, will fail to fully appreciate the continuing, persistent power of the anti-kingdom in history. The kingdom that Jesus enacts is one that creates scandal and generates opposition, not because the kingdom is in any way inherently conflictual, but precisely because it is *not*; the powerful elites, the beneficiaries of existing divisions and conflicts, will not abide Jesus Christ's message of liberation and reconciliation.

For Sobrino, then, belief in the God of Jesus Christ implies a rejection of the idols worshipped by those who promote the anti-kingdom. The opposite of belief in Jesus Christ is not unbelief but idolatry. Jesus' proclamation and enactment of God's reign are directly linked, therefore, to his passion and crucifixion. When Jesus offers hospitality to outcasts and identifies that praxis with God's reign he sets in motion a series of events that will eventually culminate on Calvary.

## The Crucified and Risen Christ

A Christology that stresses the intrinsic connection between the mediator (Jesus Christ) and "what is mediated" (the kingdom of God) will likewise stress the intrinsic connection between the violent human rejection of Jesus (crucifixion) and God's ultimate response to that rejection (resurrection). Jesus' life and message, his proclamation and enactment of God's reign, reveal the fact that "God loved us first." This revelation is rejected. And, in the end, God vindicates and justifies the victim of that rejection. If the kingdom of God elicits violent rejection by the anti-kingdom, the crucifixion-resurrection of Christ definitively reverses this dialectic: the anti-kingdom is itself destroyed and its victims vindicated through the crucifixion and resurrection of Jesus Christ.

While an understanding of the "historical Jesus," especially his proclamation and enactment of God's reign, is not sufficient for understanding the crucifixion and resurrection, therefore, the scandalous character of these (including their social implications) demands an appreciation of the connection between the salvation effected through Jesus' cross and resurrection, on the one hand, and the liberation implied in Jesus' praxis of God's reign, on the other: "the very fact of its being scandalous makes the cross an authentic 'revelation' of God."[30] That is: (1) if God is mystery, God's revelation will be unexpected and unanticipated; (2) if revelation is unexpected and unanticipated, it is mediated by those persons and in those places whom society deems the least capable of mediating God's revelation; (3) by definition, this fact is perceived as unthinkable and, indeed, scandalous; and, therefore, (4) the scandalous character of God's revelation in the person of Jesus Christ—and, derivatively, in those to whom belongs God's kingdom—is precisely what safeguards the mystery and transcendence of God. Only a kingdom that is proclaimed to and belongs to the poor and outcast can be the revelation of a transcendent God. Everything else is idolatry. If the powerful do not (at least initially) perceive God's reign as scandalous, it cannot be the reign of a transcendent God but only the reign of an idol. And their conversion is what will reveal to them the connection between scandal and transcendence ("Lord, when did we see you hungry . . . ?").

In the context of God's reign, as this is proclaimed and practiced by Jesus, the resurrection is revealed as God's vindication of the victim crucified on Calvary. If Jesus' resurrection represents the victory of life over death, Sobrino suggests, this fundamental Christian belief cannot be adequately understood apart from its concrete, historical connection to Jesus' own life and death; the one who is raised by God from the dead is the same one who was crucified unjustly, for proclaiming and enacting God's reign. What we call "death," then, cannot be understood apart from its intrinsic connection to injustice: the one crucified was innocent. And what we call "life" cannot be understood apart from its intrinsic connection to justice: the innocent one who was crucified has been vindicated. Though the terms "death" and "life" embrace more than this, they necessarily include and demand the justification of the victim, the vindication of *his* life.[31]

Thus understood, death and life are revealed as inherently relational terms: the cross represents not just the death of an individual but the death of communion, and the resurrection represents not just the raising of an individual but the restoration of communion, now in the form of true justice and reconciliation. If Jesus' death and resurrection bring about our salvation from sin, this necessarily includes the restoration of right relationships. "The danger," warns Sobrino, "is that within this all-embracing salvation the plurality of salvations brought about by Jesus of Nazareth is not made explicit: salvation from any sort of oppression, inner and outer, spiritual and physical, personal and social."[32]

An appreciation of this relational, interpersonal, or social dimension of the cross is essential for understanding the correlation of cross and resurrection, and the social implications of the cross for Christian praxis. On the cross, Jesus experiences the full ravages of our human condition, not only by undergoing death, but by undergoing an unjust, violent death that reaches its climax in the experience of abandonment: "My God, my God, why have you abandoned me?" Intrinsic to Jesus' death on the cross, therefore, is his experience of being abandoned, not only by the friends who had deserted him on the way to Calvary, but even by the Father, the one with whom Jesus had lived in absolute unity to the end. Sobrino rejects attempts to soften this experience of abandonment by, for example, pointing to the hopeful ending of Psalm 22, the beginning of which is echoed in Jesus' words from the cross. The fact remains, observes Sobrino, that these more hopeful lines are not mentioned in the Gospel accounts. More importantly, perhaps, it is precisely in his experience of abandonment by the Father that Jesus assumes—and therefore redeems—our human mortality in its most radical dimensions; he experiences the *physical* death of crucifixion, the *social* death of the innocent victim abandoned by his friends, and the most devastating death of all, the *spiritual* death of the one who feels abandoned by God:

> In conclusion, if the passion narratives describe the gradual desertion of Jesus' disciples, including the betrayal of one and the cowardice of another, so that Jesus' death is presented in historical isolation, the end of Jesus' life in Mark's account ends with the silence of God or, at all events, without the active presence of God the Father. . . . This new form of God's relationship with Jesus, whether it be called abandonment, silence, or simply

distancing or inaction on the part of God, is the most wounding element of Jesus' death.[33]

Sobrino's contention that the experience of God's absence represents a "new form of relationship" is important for understanding the intrinsic connection between the crucifixion and the resurrection. Even in the face of God's silence, Jesus never despairs; he continues to cry out to a God who appears to be absent. Jesus thus refuses to accept abandonment but stubbornly continues to call on God.

From the perspective of the poor, suggests Sobrino, the cross-resurrection dialectic can best be understood through the experience of abandonment-accompaniment. Even if experienced as abandonment, God is present to Jesus on the cross—so intimately that the centurion is compelled to cry out, "Truly, this was God's son." On the cross, Jesus Christ is revealed as truly Emmanuel, "God-with-us," in that God's loving nearness is no longer limited or circumscribed by our own preconceptions but is now revealed in all its scandalous transcendence: "What does Jesus' cross really say? It says that God has irrevocably drawn near to this world, that he is a God 'with us' and a God 'for us.'"[34] That very nearness, however inconceivable, becomes the seedbed of hope and, thus, of resurrection. When God raises Jesus, God thus destroys not only the power of death but also the power of abandonment (inasmuch as the former implies the latter), granting us the assurance of life and God's unwavering loving presence with us; the justice of accompaniment conquers the injustice of abandonment. It is this presence, this nearness that makes Christ credible and gives hope in the face of hopelessness. For the poor, avers Sobrino, what makes the resurrection credible is the experience of Christ's nearness on the cross, in the midst of their own crucifixion:

> On Jesus' cross, in a first moment, God's impotence appeared. Of itself this impotence is not the cause of hope. But it lends credibility to the power of God that will be shown in the resurrection. The reason for this is that God's impotence, God's helplessness, is the expression of God's absolute nearness to the poor, sharing their lot to the end. God was on Jesus' cross. God shared the horrors of history. Therefore God's action in the resurrection is credible, at least for the one who has been crucified. . . . The cross says, in human language, that nothing in history has set limits to God's nearness to human beings. Without that nearness, God's power in the resurrection would remain pure otherness and therefore ambiguous, and for the crucified, historically threatening. But with that nearness, the crucified can really believe that God's power is good news, for it is love.[35]

The truth revealed in Jesus' cross and resurrection, therefore, is no merely general or abstract "truth"; it is a truth made historical, social, and embodied in the person of Jesus Christ himself. "If we believe in Jesus as the Son," writes

Sobrino, "it is because in him the truth and love of the mystery of God have been shown in an unrepeatable form, and been shown in a way that is totally convincing to a crucified people who have no problem in accepting Jesus' unrepeatable relationship with God so that they can confess him to be in truth the Son of God."[36]

The hope Jesus offers is not reducible to other forms of "hope"; Christ's is the foolish, scandalous hope that death and abandonment will not have the last word, that the victims of death and abandonment will themselves find justification. Sobrino insists:

> The resurrection of the one who was crucified is *true* [emphasis in the original]. Let it be foolishness, as it was for the Corinthians. But without this foolishness, because it is true—or without this truth, because it is foolish—the resurrection of Jesus will only be one more symbol of hope in survival after death that human beings have designed in their religions or philosophies. It will not be the Christian symbol of hope.[37]

Likewise, the faith Jesus compels is no merely general or abstract "faith"; it is a faith in the God of Jesus Christ, revealed above all in Jesus' crucifixion-resurrection. Christian truth, hope, and faith are not easily generalizable because they are literally inconceivable without "an experience of the God who first loved us," the God who comes near to us on the cross:

> A vague, undifferentiated faith in God is not enough to generate hope. Not even the admission that God is mighty, or that God has made promises, will do this. Something else besides the generic or abstract attributes of the divinity is necessary in order to generate hope. This distinct element—which, furthermore, is the fundamental characteristic of the Christian God—is something the poor have discovered viscerally, and in reality itself: the nearness of God. God instills hope because God is credible, and God is credible because God delivers up the Son, and that God is crucified—something that to the mind of the nonpoor will always be either a scandal or a pure anthropomorphism—then, paradoxically, their hope becomes real. The poor have no problems with God. The classic question of theodicy—the "problem of God," the atheism of protest—so reasonably posed by the nonpoor, is no problem at all for the poor (who in good logic ought of course to be the ones to pose it).[38]

For the poor, then, the resurrection is not only the assurance of life *after* death; it is, above all, the assurance of life *before* death. Because Jesus lives and accompanies us in our struggles, we ourselves can dare to live, struggle, and hope:

> A resurrection rendered credible by God's nearness on the cross likewise confirms the deepest intuition of the crucified in the present, however this

intuition may be constantly threatened by resignation, skepticism, or cynicism. At bottom, good is more real than evil, although the latter inundates us; grace is more real than sin, although it does not cease its death-dealing. There is more truth in the stubbornness of hope, in ever attempting the new, in ever seeking historical liberations, in refusing to strike any compact with what is limited and sinful in history—although both are omnipresent—than in the seeming wisdom of resignation.[39]

Though the resurrection is God's definitive redemptive act, Jesus' crucifixion already points to the resurrection insofar as, on the cross, God's silent, compassionate presence already affirms the ultimate indestructibility of love in the face of death.

None of this is to suggest that God's redemptive act in Jesus Christ can be reduced to Jesus' nearness on the cross. As we have seen, Sobrino goes to great lengths to safeguard the gratuitous and efficacious character of God's salvific activity in Christ; "to have genuine love for our sisters and brothers, we must have an experience of the God who loved us first. . . . 'it all started with God.'"[40] What makes possible our love of others is the gift of God's own love poured out in our hearts. And God's nearness in the person of Jesus Christ, especially in his crucifixion-resurrection, is what makes that gift credible. This practical experience of God's nearness is the seedbed of Sobrino's Christology.[41]

## Notes

1. Jon Sobrino, quoted in Jesús Ruiz Mantilla, "Jon Sobrino: Radicalmente cristiano," *El País Semanal*, June 17, 2007, p. 15 (my translation).

2. Jon Sobrino, "Systematic Christology: Jesus Christ, the Absolute Mediator of the Reign of God," in *Systematic Theology: Perspectives from Liberation Theology*, ed. Jon Sobrino and Ignacio Ellacuría (Maryknoll, N.Y.: Orbis Books, 1993), 131.

3. Jon Sobrino, *Jesus the Liberator: A Historical-Theological View* (Maryknoll, N.Y.: Orbis Books, 1993), 39.

4. Jon Sobrino, *Spirituality of Liberation: Toward Political Holiness* (Maryknoll, N.Y.: Orbis Books, 1988), 58.

5. Ibid., 70.

6. Sobrino, *Jesus the Liberator*, 7.

7. Sobrino, "Systematic Christology," 131.

8. Sobrino, *Jesus the Liberator*, 5.

9. Sobrino, *Spirituality of Liberation*, 57.

10. Sobrino, *Jesus the Liberator*, 36-37. Sobrino's repeated insistence on Jesus Christ, salvation, and the kingdom of God as *gift* is significant in light of the criticism proffered in the Vatican Notification: "Redemption thus seems reduced [in Sobrino's thought] to the appearance of the *homo verus*, manifested in fidelity unto death. The death of Christ is *exemplum* and not *sacramentum* (gift)" (no. 10).

11. Sobrino, *Jesus the Liberator*, 55.

12. Ibid., 38-39.

13. Ibid., 40.

14. José Miranda, quoted in ibid., 47.

15. Ibid., 40.

16. Ibid., 67.

17. Ibid.

18. Ibid., 69.

19. Ibid., 71; see also n. 10 above.

20. Ibid., 76.

21. Ibid., 77.

22. Ibid., 72.

23. Ibid., 79.

24. Joachim Jeremias, quoted in ibid. (Sobrino's italics).

25. Ibid., 79-80.

26. Ibid., 80.

27. Ibid., 85.

28. Ibid., 82.

29. Ibid., 108. See also Jon Sobrino, *Christ the Liberator: A View from the Victims*, trans. Paul Burns (Maryknoll, N.Y.: Orbis Books, 2001), 334-35. It would be instructive to read these texts, and others in which Sobrino stresses the identity between the kingdom of God and Jesus Christ as the Absolute Mediator who *embodies* and *enacts* the kingdom, in the context of the Vatican Notification (no. 7), which criticizes Sobrino for drawing too sharp a distinction between the kingdom and Jesus.

The Notification, furthermore, suggests that Sobrino affirms "that the possibility of being mediator belongs to Christ from the exercise of his humanity," thereby denying "the fact that his condition as Son of God has relevance for Jesus' mediatory mission" (no. 7). As evidence, the Notification quotes the following sentence from *Christ the Liberator*: "Christ does not, then, derive his possibility of being mediator from anything added to his humanity; it belongs to him by his practice of being human" (*Christ the Liberator*, 135). It is clear from the context of this quote, however, that the comparison Sobrino intends is not between Jesus' humanity and his "condition as Son of God," but between his humanity as such and other *social* roles or titles "added" to his humanity. Appearing in a chapter on the concept of "high priest," the particular sentence in question is followed immediately by the following sentence: "It [i.e., Jesus' possibility of being mediator] does not come to him from a super-human dignity (as religions generally understand priesthood), or from an added *sociological* category" (my emphasis). What need not be added to Jesus' humanity, according to Sobrino, is some special *sociological* function that would set him apart from other "mere" human beings.

30. Sobrino, *Jesus the Liberator*, 227.

31. Sobrino, *Christ the Liberator*, 14-15.

32. Sobrino, *Jesus the Liberator*, 222.

33. Ibid., 239.

34. Ibid., 231.

35. Jon Sobrino, *Jesus in Latin America* (Maryknoll, N.Y.: Orbis Books, 1987), 153.

36. Ibid., 165.

37. Ibid., 158.

38. Sobrino, *Spirituality of Liberation*, 166-167.

39. Sobrino, *Jesus in Latin America*, 153-154.

40. Sobrino, *Spirituality of Liberation*, 58.

41. This is the "seed" of Christian faith that will later be made increasingly explicit and specific in conciliar christological definitions. Yet, as I suggested above, it is this evangelical seed that safeguards the transcendent character of the Christian God against attempts to reduce God to those very definitions. Like any seed, however, the Gospels contain the entirety of the faith, even if not fully elaborated in all its philosophical complexities.

In its critique of Sobrino, on the other hand, the Vatican Notification seems to use two different, conflicting definitions of "seed." Even as a "seed" in Mary's womb, Jesus was already completely formed in his full humanity and divinity: "For hardly was he conceived in the womb of the Mother of God when He began to enjoy the Beatific Vision" (no. 8). This, of course, also follows the understanding that the whole person (all the necessary "genetic material") is already fully present in the conceptus, the human seed, an understanding of the term that is at the heart of the official Catholic position on abortion. I would argue that this is precisely what Sobrino intends when he writes, as the Notification quotes him in no. 4: "The New Testament . . . contains expressions that contain the seed of what will produce confession of the divinity of Christ in the strict sense" (*Christ the Liberator*, 257). In this specific case, however, the Notification interprets the word "seed," as used by Sobrino, to mean incomplete, partial, and *not* whole—though its own assumptions about the nature of human "seeds" would suggest a very different, alternative understanding that would make possible a more positive reading of the Sobrino text.

# 8

# Hermeneutics and Theology
# in Sobrino's Christology

RAFAEL LUCIANI

## Elements in the Horizon and Previous Understanding of Latin American Theological Activity

### Social Setting as an Element That Shapes the Epistemological Setting

The question about the human nature of Christ cannot be addressed generically. Nor can it be restricted to the concepts and notions found in earlier dogmatic formulations.[1] Our social contexts cry out before human conditions that are increasingly undergoing processes of real dehumanization and sustained impoverishment. This concern is framed within what Sobrino refers to as the "major fact," which is the way in which the conditions and the structures of social reality generate sociopolitical and economic processes of massive and sustained impoverishment. They appear as a profound scandal when understood in light of Christian identity on the Latin American continent.[2] This "major fact" is characterized by Sobrino from the point of view of the current reality of the suffering poor,[3] and it is this social setting that will shape the epistemological horizon of his theological work as a whole. Three main elements are derived from this fact, and they constitute the framework for the christological proposal of this well-known Latin American theologian:

(a) Every theology presupposes a horizon from which it turns into something real. This points at the relevance of the social and the theological setting as a horizon that shapes theological activity as a whole.[4] In Latin America, this major fact (reality as it appears in the full scandal of its inequity) is the horizon itself from which theology is practiced. In other words, "the option of seeing the major fact in the suffering poor is like the pre-understanding for theology, both in order to be able to understand the text of the Scriptures and to understand the text of today's reality".[5] Ultimately this is always an option.

(b) History participates in the salvific dimension inherent in its condition as a created reality. This implies that, when characterizing our current reality, it is essential to determine what God is really saving us from.[6] This is especially the case when there are personal and structural conditions that are against the salvific offer—even denying it and hindering it. When faced with the major fact of our reality, God manifests himself by listening to the clamor of the suffering poor. Nevertheless, "He manifests himself as related to a concrete negativity and in order to liberate [us] from that concrete negativity."[7] This revealing action of God turns the *pro nobis* into a *pro pauperis*.

(c) The way in which God acts by means of Christ in history is what is known as "liberation," and it frees us from both personal sin and structural sin. Liberation expresses the concrete way in which God is revealed as saving— by listening to the clamor of the suffering poor and, by means of them, to listen to the clamor of the rest of humankind. It is a particular and specific modality of praxis.[8] "In other words, the relationship between God and the poor is not only circumstantial and passing, in the Exodus, in the prophets, or in Jesus, but it is rather structural. There is a transcendental correlation between the revelation of God and the cry of the poor."[9]

This transcendental correlation between the revelation of God and the cry of the poor is reaffirmed by three ecclesiastic events that determine and inspire the epistemological option of the Christology of Sobrino: the Second Vatican Council (1962-1965), the Second Assembly of the Latin American Episcopate that was held in Medellín (1968) and the Third Assembly of the Latin American Episcopate that was held in Puebla (1979). In the case of the Second Vatican Council, Sobrino values the theology of the signs of the times when accepting its historical-salvific sense as "true signs of the presence or of the plans of God" in this history.[10] These are historical modalities of reality that make up authentic settings of revelation and salvation. This salvific dimension of history, however, is the result of the presence *in actu* of God in this history. In Latin America, this divine presence is understood not in generic terms but in a concrete manner in the figure of Christ himself. What is at stake is determining where and how Christ is present in this historical reality.

In order to answer these questions, Sobrino refers us to the texts of the Assemblies of the Latin American Episcopate. The text of Medellín clearly sheds light on the first question: where God is present, based on the principle of partiality by means of which Christ is present in a special way because of his relations with poverty and with the poor,[11] who cry out for "a change from less human living conditions to more human conditions."[12] This clamor is vital not only for developing the historical framework in its structural and dynamic internal conditions but also for the total fulfillment of the same salvific mission that is commended by Christ.[13] The text of Puebla sheds light on the second question: how God is present in our reality. It answers this question with the well-known preferential option for the poor as the primary focus of the historical action of Jesus and of the liberating revelation of God, by the fact itself that they are poor and that they suffer. In this respect, according to the text of Puebla, "the poor deserve preferential attention, whatever the moral or personal situation they live in."[14]

The option for the poor is ultimately based on the transcendental correlation between the way in which the revealing action of God is evidenced and the primary subjects of that action—the suffering poor—to whom God listens and offers an answer. This is clearly evidenced in the historical praxis of a God who favors justice and opposes the oppression of his people in Egypt. In this context, the exodus became a sign of God's will for the liberation of all humankind.

### A Theology of the Signs of the Times

In Latin American Christology, the social setting or the so-called major fact (historical-pastoral dimension of reality: *Gaudium et spes,* 4) is an authentic sign of the times insofar as it points at the determining horizon of theological activity and the way of understanding reality as a *theo*-logic notion, as the *locus theologicus,* in other words, as the place of revelation of the presence of God (historical-theological dimension of reality: *Gaudium et spes,* 11). Hence, it is not enough to practice Christology by just taking into account the categorical theological settings (*ubi*) that are common (tradition, teaching, and Scripture), but, rather, it should be practiced from the substantial reality itself (*quid*) that determines all these settings and grants them their sense and current status—in other words, from the major fact adopted as the "sign of the times" in its two senses, as set forth in *Gaudium et spes,* 4 and 11. According to Sobrino, "Latin American Christology determines that its setting as a substantial reality is the poor of this world, and this reality is the one that should be present and felt in any categorical setting where it takes place."[15]

In this respect, if we say that currently the sustained impoverishment of the world stands out as the sign that urges and cries out for the salvific presence of God—a liberating presence and a life-giving presence where peace and justice come together—then "the *ubi* should be pervaded by the *quid*. Wherever it is practiced empirically, theology should be affected in-depth by the reality of the poor. The suffering of the poor is precisely what should make us think and ponder. Their hope is what should shape the salvific nature and inclination of every Christian theology. In other words, theology can be practiced in many physical settings, but it has to be practiced based on the reality of the poor,"[16] because, as stated by the Second Vatican Council in *Lumen gentium*:

"the church embraces all those who are afflicted by human weakness and, even more so, it acknowledges in the poor and in those who suffer the image of its poor and suffering Founder and it strives to alleviate their needs, and it is aimed at serving Christ in them."[17]

However, is it possible to say that God is more present in one place than in another? To answer that question, we must look more in depth at the semantics of the terms *ubi* and *quid* as they used by Sobrino in many of his documents. To this end, let us examine the term *ubique,* which is used by Anselm and Thomas Aquinas when speaking about God as someone who is everywhere. In the first place, it is not a matter of a universal or generalizing notion of the presence of God that dilutes God into a transcendent being wholly lacking in reality. It is rather a term that implies a transcendental correlation between the way in which God is in the world and the way in which the world cries out to God in realization of the human vocation. The term *ubique* is made up of two elements that can help us structure theological reflection. On the one hand, it points at a categorical setting or place—*ubi*, a space or physical presence that can change—and, on the other, to a substantial reality—*quid*, the world of the suffering poor, the so-called major fact as an authentic theological place that is acknowledged as the "sign of the times."[18] By no means is God present in the physical and categorical place where he reveals himself, but, rather, he is present in relation to an individual, to a time, to a history. Nevertheless, his presence in a specific place reveals a substantive reality that is no longer tangible for the human being and that acquires an absolute value because it starts to reveal something that pertains inherently to God, to his way of being and of making himself present. This reflection leads us to a conclusion that places Christianity in an authentic drama because the God in whom we believe is the God revealed—the God of life, of justice, of peace and of mercy. The God of the poor is the God who gives life, who exercises justice, who gives comfort, who grants pardon and who fraternizes. The God in whom we believe is the God who humanizes by means of a historical fraternity revealed by way of his filiation.

In this sense, the Christology of Sobrino takes seriously the theological assumption that is implicit in the Second Vatican Council's theology of the "signs of the times," which understands the salvific action of God by acknowledging and interpreting the real events that signal his presence in the midst of our concrete history. We are dealing here with signs that tell about the real way of God's being, even though, indeed, they do not exhaust every aspect of his mystery. In this way, the theology of Sobrino is true to the creaturely condition of history and its revealing nature,[19] which can be brought up to date in each period of time through the events that weave the historic fabric—though always read together with the traditional sources of theology (*locis theologici*) and in the light of the historical praxis of Jesus of Nazareth as it has been conveyed to us by the Gospels.

## Elements in the Horizon and Contents of Sobrino's Christology

### *The Horizon: Victims as the Crucified People Who Bring Salvation*

In applying the principle of the structural isomorphism of situations between the time of Jesus and our times, Sobrino shares the opinion of Leonardo Boff. Hence, he defines it as the common contextual conditions of "oppression and objective dependence that are lived subjectively, as contrary to the historical plan of God."[20] Amidst all these conditions that are still present in other current conflicts—as is the case in the Latin American reality—the cause for the historical Jesus and his practice was revealed. Both realities—the Palestinian of the first century and the Latin American evidenced today—generate conditions of dehumanization that can be witnessed in their own sociopolitical, religious, and economic structures. In this respect, Sobrino is able to put forth a certain structural isomorphism between both situations in view of the fact that they both generate victims.[21]

Based on this scandalous fact, Sobrino takes the reality of the victims to a theological category. To this end, he applies a theological image that is used by Monsignor Romero and by Ignacio Ellacuría: the analogy of the "crucified peoples"[22] as a historical continuation of Yahweh's Suffering Servant.[23] This concept refers to the majorities who live affected by the drama of death that is brought about as a consequence of injustice, cruelty, inequity, and disdain. The "crucified peoples" are the individuals who have no voice and who are denied their very existence.[24] This theological image enables Sobrino to frame the horizon of his Christology in the understanding that hermeneutics should not be limited to posing common horizons of cultural understanding between the present and the past, but rather and mostly, common horizons of reality, which include two aspects: the existence of victims and its historical-salvific nature.[25] The victims are those innocent individuals who suffer daily the burden of an unfair and dehumanizing situation derived from the action of other individuals who produce and justify it. Nevertheless, at the same time, these victims are the bearers of a soteriological dimension because they bring salvation to human beings as a light that unmasks the lies and the dehumanization that exist in the world. The reality of the victims is like a light that cries out to God and urges oppressors to convert themselves so as to keep that situation from continuing.[26] In Latin America, Christology must acknowledge the urgency and need of getting this poor people down from the cross where they suffer as innocent victims.[27] This type of Christology is destined to see the evangelizing potential of the poor as the bearers of the values that humanize us, and they must do so as subjects rather than mere objects of policies designed to assist them.

Upon raising the reality of the victims to a theological category, under the image of the "crucified people," Sobrino applies the hermeneutics of a theology of the "signs of the times," and in this way he sees the reality of the poor of Latin America as the sign of our historical-theological times par excellence.[28] Sobrino explains:

> As related to this conviction, Latin American Christology has in its favor the argument of "reality." Seen from the reality of the continent, if Jesus "died in this way," it is quite likely that he "lived in this way." This is not a logical conclusion, although this conclusion is aimed at showing the internal historical coherence of the evangelical stories of the life of Jesus though seen from our current reality. In other words, the subjective pre-comprehension (*Vorverständnis*) used to address today in this text the evangelical stories, shaped and triggered by the objectiveness of what happens every day, makes the substantial historicity of these stories both plausible and congruent.[29]

Sobrino interprets this situation christologically and not only from the point of view of the social sciences. The poor are the setting where Christ, seen as the poor, is present in history. Their living conditions and their values express the way in which that presence is offered to the world, as the "crucified people" who bring salvation and carry the burden of the sin of the world because they are victims of unfair structural conditions that they do not want for themselves.

### The Main Criterion: The Praxis of the Historical Jesus as a Follow-up— Norma Normans, Non Normata

The reality of the victims is framed within the christological horizon of the historical praxis itself of Jesus of Nazareth as the Suffering Servant. In this respect, every Christology, understood in this way, must have a different method and different questions to those posed by the modern Western world. The methodological problem of the historical Jesus in Sobrino's Christology is not aimed primarily at eliminating the myths of the texts, nor at looking for historical elements that enable us to rebuild the historical figure of Jesus within the context of the first century in Palestine. If the assumption of reality shapes the horizon of theological activities, then the christological method will be derived from the latter. In other words, it will be understood as the determination of the elements that shape the historical practice of Jesus insofar as it appears as a criticism and an urge to transform the reality of the victims.[30] This responds to the fact that the cultural assumption is not based on the question of the lack of meaning suffered by the modern individual when faced with his own existence, or on his fulfillment in the midst of society as a whole. On the contrary, it is based on the lack of sense of the tragedy of reality within which personal life will derive its sense or will have no sense at all. From this point of view, the greatest urgency for faith is not the demythologization of Christ—as was the case in the progressive theologies—but rather the depacification of Christ: so that He does not leave us in peace when faced with the misery of reality and, no doubt, his deidolization: so that in his name reality cannot be oppressed.[31]

In this respect, we can see some influence of the *Theses on Feuerbach,* written by Karl Marx in 1845. In "thesis 11," he points out that "philosophers have simply interpreted in different ways and modalities the world, but what is rather at stake is the need to transform it."

How can a Christology be aimed at the transformation of the world? It can only achieve this transformation from the determination of what is really historical in Jesus of Nazareth as a basic element for Christian discernment and for following Christ. How does Sobrino understand, then, the problem of the historical Jesus? In a general sense, "when we refer to the historical Jesus, we refer to what we understand as the life of Jesus of Nazareth, his words and deeds, his activity and his praxis, his attitude and his spirit, his destiny in the cross (and his destiny of resurrection)."[32] In a more concrete sense, "our thesis is that the most historical element of the historical Jesus is his *practice* and the *spirit* with which he carried it out. When we refer to *practice,* we understand this term as the set of activities carried out by Jesus in order to have an effect on the social reality and to transform it, so as to take it in the specific direction of the kingdom of God. Hence, and in the first place, what is historical is precisely what triggers history."[33] This practice or way of living of Jesus is the main criterion or the *norma normans, non normata* of Christology as set forth by Sobrino, because it is the practice of Jesus himself.[34] In Jesus we recognize a normative nature par excellence for those who follow him; and, consequently, he appears before them as an ultimate, truly personal reality and as the Christ of faith.[35] On account of this fact, it is not a common practice. Rather, it is a practice with spirit, a specific way of living when faced with our own history, with the sense of "honesty with respect to reality, partiality with respect to what is small, a basic mercy and loyalty to the ministry of God."[36] In short, from this christological disposition "there is a better access to the internal life of Jesus (the historicity of his subjectivity) through the external aspects of his practice (his way of doing history), rather than the other way around."[37] This does not mean that there is an absolute continuity between the historical Jesus and the Christ of faith. However, this view does enable Sobrino to set forth a relationship of historical normativity that is based on Jesus' praxis and that reveals the spirit with which he acted, the spirit of God. This can give an ultimate sense to our historical reality.

Nevertheless, when we refer to a specific choice of life—as that of Jesus—we find many elements that make up and shape his practice with spirit. On account of this, "we must ask ourselves which of them is more historical: the one that best introduces the totality of Jesus and better organizes the diverse elements of this totality."[38] This core and shaping element in the life of Jesus of Nazareth is the kingdom of God.[39]

### The Historical-Eschatological Contents of Christology: The Correlation between the Reality of the Kingdom of God and the Practice of Jesus

God reveals his reality when he goes through history in a specific way and in the middle of specific structures and concrete conditions. His salvific action is liberating because it enables the re-creation of better and more human living conditions. These are the minimum conditions of a creaturely justice (protology); it points to a *plus* that is always greater and to its ultimate consummation (eschatology). It is on account of this fact that when God reigns, he makes real the justice that the poor of this world are awaiting. The reality of the revelation of God is what Jesus discovers and reveals so that it shapes his own filial existence when faced with the liberating praxis of the Father in this world.[40] It is important to emphasize, Sobrino writes, that

> Jesus did not only preach of himself and the ultimate for him was not simply "God" but the kingdom of God. The fact that Jesus preached and talked about God as the Father leaves no room for discussion, and this is also true of the fact that this Father was the ultimate personal reference that he had and that he also offered to others. . . . What we now would like to emphasize is that, for Jesus, even "God" is seen as part of a wider totality: "the kingdom of God."[41]

Even more so, this is a God who acts as a good and merciful Father, thus urging all of us to shape and build our existence as children united by the same fraternal spirit of justice.

Jesus takes charge of this reality of God in history from the kingdom where he reigns and, hence, he expresses it through his own praxis when he takes care of the kingdom and makes it possible. In other words, his message turns into a *eu-topia*, which is good and which should dwell in the most important possible place in this world—as is the case of justice, fraternity, and hope, among others. This sets forth an important correlation between the kingdom of God and the practice of Jesus under the modality of a dual unity.[42] In this sense, the historical practice of Jesus is the criterion for ensuring the fulfillment and establishment of the ultimate reality of the kingdom in this world. In other words, it refers to the way in which God reigns, although this could never fully coincide with the kingdom itself nor exhaust its ultimate contents because it belongs to the Father, the God of the kingdom. "In the field of hermeneutics, this means that 'kingdom' is not only a concept 'of sense'—in this case, of hope—but that it is also a 'praxic' concept that implies the need to implement what it entails; in other words, the demand for practice in order to get it started and, upon doing so, it generates a better understanding of what the kingdom is."[43]

The revelation of the reality of God is evidenced in the midst of the specific conditions of history, and it is never neutral. In short, by revealing who God is, it is possible to be in touch with reality and with the presence of the adversary: the "anti-kingdom,[44] and this is the reason why "the coming of the kingdom is in an antagonistic relationship with the anti-kingdom. What one does is opposed to the other. This is a piece of evidence that is overwhelmingly obvious in Latin America: the kingdom is not built from a *tabula rasa* but against the anti-kingdom, and, indeed, we see the actual verification of this fact in persecutions."[45] The practice of Jesus is pervaded by a kind of oppositional dynamics. The possibility that a historical practice can dehumanize and oppose itself to the salvific plan of God is always a possibility to which this world is open. This is why it is absolutely necessary to implement a continuous discernment around the type of spirit that moves it.[46] On the one hand, a practice can be inspired by the fraternal spirit of justice—as is the case with the historical Jesus, who expresses what is desired by the God of the kingdom when he reigns in history. On the other hand, a practice can conform to the spirit of the anti-kingdom, which wants to be established in this world by exercising power and imposing ideologies that are geared to co-opt and shape our social reality according to its own interests and desires. A spirit such as this generates human subjects who are accustomed to dehumanizing structures, even to the point of considering themselves and such unjust conditions as a normal and a necessary fact of the process of life rather than a major and scandalous distortion.[47]

This oppositional dynamic typical of the liberating presence of the kingdom of God reveals both the timely nature of the kingdom that is called to make itself present in this world in order to transform it and its absolute nature, which stands against any historical modality that does not acknowledge it and is even aimed at denying it. Although it is true that liberation theology claims that the kingdom cannot be fully established in history because it always remains, in a certain way, a *u-topía*,[48] it is also true that it regards the kingdom as a reality that can be promoted in society by means of historical mediations. These mediations can be expressed at all levels of reality because they are mostly and above all *eu-topía*. They are that which is good and ultimate and something which we must be ready and willing to accept and welcome as present in the different social, economic, religious, and political situations of this world. Hence, we are facing a historical-eschatological reality. "What liberation theology emphasizes is that the kingdom of God is attested to and takes place in history when history is transformed, because it is all of history that God wants to transform, and it would be a contradiction that it is precisely God who reigns but does not ensure any transformation in history."[49]

The correlation of the kingdom (mediation) and historical practice with the spirit of Jesus (mediator) is realized in intercession, where what is proto-logical and what is eschatological meet with each other. Although it is true that historical practice with the spirit of the mediator (Jesus of Nazareth) refers us to the ultimate mediation of the reality of God (kingdom) and is not under-stood outside its scope, it is also worth emphasizing that this reference always closes the historical gap that exists between the Father and the incarnated Son. In this way, the mediator cannot be identified in an absolute (unequivocal) manner with a mediation that ultimately belongs to God the Father. The basic content of the kingdom that is really manifested in the historical practice of Jesus is related to the establishment of a "fair life" for the poor in this world. Bearing this criterion in mind, Sobrino does not refer to a yearning for the maximum conditions of fulfillment that would only point at the eschatological dimension of the kingdom, but, rather, he mostly refers to the search for the minimum conditions of justice and dignity that can support life with really human possibilities (protological or creaturely dimension of the kingdom) so that there are no longer any more victims.

## Conclusion: Following the Practice with the Spirit of Jesus of Nazareth

Our main attempt in these pages has been to present some of the basic hermeneutical criteria involved in Sobrino's Christology. The specific practice of Jesus becomes the key criterion for all Christians, who, one hopes, pervaded by clear discernment and commitment, sincerely long for the transformation of the circumstances and institutions that make up our reality.

Such a Christology understands its basic content from the reality of the kingdom of God and the dynamics of his kingdom. The action of the kingdom of God, of the good and merciful God, is not neutral but rather dialectical and oppositional. It has as its preferential subjects the poor and the victims of this world because his love is shown in opposition to the historical conditions that deny his kingdom of justice. At the same time, his love appears as a radical demand that cries out for personal conversion and social transformation so that there are no longer any victims in this world. Every dehumanizing reality appears as anti-kingdom and produces victims and more poor. On account of this, the salvation that God offers to all humanity cannot neglect those poor who clamor for liberation and more dignified and fair living conditions so that the God of life "may be all in all" (1 Cor 15:28) and so that his infinite goodness can be trustworthy. Hope will no longer be only an eschatological *utopia* that is both transcendental and desired; on the contrary, it will be the real historical and social *eutopia* that is already being built.

Latin American theology does not refer to the kingdom only as an ultimate reality that is not yet fully present amidst historical tragedy. In a certain way, its presence is already begun in historical mediations that are opposed to socioeconomic, religious, and political situations and conditions that deny it. In other words, it is already present in a world that does not want to recognize the reign of God and the universal goodness of his presence. Can a theology such as this celebrate the victory of life over death? What is the hope that God conveys to us by means of the resurrection of Jesus? We must remember that the resurrected one is the crucified one. We must remember that the response of God when he resurrected Jesus acknowledges the practice and the life of an innocent and suffering servant who has endured the evils of the world but has found in them the always-triumphant love of the God of life.[50] It is an answer that questions the powers of the anti-kingdom and that takes the side of the fair, the crucified.

If God recognizes the life of the innocent one who has died on the cross, then the honest follow-up to the historical practice of Jesus of Nazareth is still being reinterpreted in each age, and it is still striving to keep up with the reality of the kingdom of God in our world. We have been called to follow Jesus of Nazareth because his life revealed God, a good and merciful Father, and because his resurrection not only revealed that God is on the side of the victims[51] but also revealed the nature of God's kingdom as one opposed to injustice and the impoverishment of society.[52] Central to Christianity is following the historical practice of one who has been crucified by the religious and political powers of this world, but who has also been resurrected by his Father, the God of the kingdom. On account of this fact, the practice of Jesus continues to be revelatory for us today. This is the real hope, the *eu-topia*, that will accommodate the space for the "good news" insofar as we become followers of Jesus of Nazareth, through his historical practice, and we confess that he is the Christ of our faith, the Son of God, through his Spirit of fraternal love.

## Notes

1. All translations of texts were done by the author of this essay. "In Latin America, faith in Christ has been maintained for centuries without any special christological discussions. In fact, dogmatic statements have been accepted. These statements emphasize the divinity of Christ more than his real human nature, thus further accentuating his individual and transcendent salvific significance rather than his historical meaning. Popular religiousness interpreted in its own way the deity of Christ as a power facing its impotence and looked for its own ways of recovering its human nature, especially in the suffering Christ" (Jon Sobrino, *Jesús en América Latina: Su significado para la fe y la cristología* [Santander: Sal Terrae, 1982], 17-18).

2. *Puebla: III Conferencia del Episcopado Latinoamericano* (Caracas: Mosen Sol, 1979), 28-30.

3. "Seeing the totality of reality from the vantage point of the suffering poor as the major fact seems to us clearly reasonable in today's world. Rather than being surprised that this is not the case, we could wonder why it is that not all theologies see it in this way. Nevertheless, this determination of the major fact is ultimately an option" (Jon Sobrino, "La teología en mundo sufriente. La teología de la liberación como *Intellectus Amoris*," *Revista Latinoamericana de Teología* 15 [1998]: 249).

4. See Jon Sobrino, *Jesucristo liberador* (Madrid: Trotta, 1991), 51.

5. Jon Sobrino, "La teología en mundo sufriente," 249.

6. In the realm of theology "it is essential to determine what God is saving [us] from. In other words, the salvific formality of the Christian message does not take place in a neutral world or in one that is simply limited but, rather, in a world that is actively deprived of salvation and subject to some type of slavery—the anti-kingdom, which is opposed to the kingdom of God" (Sobrino, "La teología en mundo sufriente," 245-46).

7. Ibid., 248.

8. *Medellín: II Conferencia del Episcopado Latinoamericano* (Bogota: CELAM, 1968), 3.

9. Sobrino, "La teología en mundo sufriente," 248. This correlation is also mentioned on p. 252.

10. *Gaudium et spes*, 11.

11. "Christ our Savior did not only love the poor 'but, rather, being rich became poor,' lived in poverty, focused his mission on announcing liberation to the poor, and founded his church as a sign of that poverty among men" (*Medellín: Pobreza de la Iglesia*, 7).

12. *Medellín: II Conferencia del Episcopado Latinoamericano*.

13. "The poverty of so many brothers cries out for justice, solidarity, testimony, commitment, effort, and betterment for fully complying with the salvific mission entrusted by God" (*Medellín: Pobreza de la Iglesia*, 7).

14. *Puebla*, 1142.

15. Sobrino, *Jesucristo liberador*, 47.

16. Jon Sobrino, "Los signos de los tiempos en la teología de la liberación," in *Fides quae per caritatem operatur: Homenaje a Juan Alfaro SJ en su 75 cumpleaños*, ed. José María Lera (Bilbao: Universidad Deusto—Ediciones Mensajero, 1989), 262.

17. *Lumen gentium*, 8.

18. "The statement that we would like to make in this respect is that the setting of theological activities is the setting where the current signs of the times take place, and that setting is the world of the poor. By saying this we mean that the setting of theology should not be understood primarily as an *ubi* (a categorical place) but rather as a *quid* (a substantial reality). Theological activities must be carried out ultimately in the reality of the world of the poor, whatever their immediate categorical setting" (Sobrino, "Los signos de los tiempos," 261).

19. "The signs of the times are a source of revelation that also give evidence of God not as in the other sources—the Scriptures or tradition—but in historical and social *reality* itself and in accordance with his peculiar idiosyncrasy. . . . Hence, the everyday occurrences and events of men turn into the scope of the manifestation of God in a nonconventional manner" (M. Rubio, "Los signos de los tiempos como hermenéutica del acontecer de Dios en los acontecimientos de los hombres," *Moralia* 49 [1991]: 23).

20. Leonardo Boff, *Jesucristo y la liberación del hombre* (Madrid: Cristiandad, 1981), 25.

21. "In fact, there are currently thousands of peoples who have died a death similar to that of Jesus, and the reasons for their deaths—those put forward by their executioners— are similar to those that were put forward against Jesus" (Sobrino, *Jesucristo liberador*, 89-90).

22. "In Latin America, basic theologization is simply a matter of taking into account the crucified people as the current version of the crucified Christ, the real servant of Yahweh, so that the crucified people and Christ the servant of Yahweh refer to each other and explain each other" (Jon Sobrino, "Los pueblos crucificados, actual siervo sufriente de Yahvé," *Christus* 644 [1991]: 33).

23. Ignacio Ellacuría, "Discernir el 'signo' de los tiempos," *Diakonía* 17 (1981): 58.

24. "With these words, Ellacuría wants to refer to vast majorities. Hence, the language that refers to the people, nations, etc. that are pervaded by death—indeed, not a natural death, but a historical death that takes the shape of crucifixion, murder, active historical deprivation of life, be it fast or slow. He refers to this death as the result of injustice together with cruelty, disdain, and, on the other hand, covering up. I usually add that the crucified people is also denied a voice and even a name, and, hence, they are denied their very existence" (Jon Sobrino, "El pueblo crucificado y la civilización de la pobreza," *Revista Latinoamericana de Teología* 66 [2005]: 212).

25. See Sobrino, "Los pueblos crucificados," 33.

26. Ibid., 34-35.

27. Ibid., 36-37.

28. See Sobrino, *Jesucristo liberador*, 45.

29. Ibid., 90.

30. "In Latin America, it is more urgent to eliminate any manipulation and to rescue Christ from connivance with idols. Demythologization is important because without it Christ appears as dangerously abstract and idealistic. This is not enough, however, if it does lead to his demanipulation. Demythologizing Christ in Latin America does not primarily involve setting forth the argument of his historical truth vis-à-vis rational criticism, even though this argument is also required. What is absolutely necessary . . . the 'depacification'— if I may be excused for this neologism—of Christ: in other words, that Christ does not live reality in peace" (Sobrino, *Jesús en América Latina*, 101).

31. Sobrino, *Jesucristo liberador*, 75.

32. Ibid., 76.

33. Ibid., 77.

34. "We can go back to the practice of Jesus under the assumption that in that practice there is something essential of a *norma normans, non normata* (a ruling rule that is not ruled by any other thing). Precisely what we have to analyze is the fact that it is essential. The assumption is clear, however: we have to go back to the practice of Jesus, *because* it is precisely the practice of Jesus" (ibid., 79).

35. "This way of having access to the historical Jesus is also the most adequate way from the logical point of view of having access to the Christ of the faith . . . an ultimate normativity is being accepted in Jesus, and by way of this, he is being declared as someone who is really ultimate, though implicitly he is already being declared as the Christ, even though later it would be necessary to explicitly state this confession" (ibid., 81).

36. Ibid., 78.

37. Ibid., 80.

38. Ibid., 76.

39. Ibid., 89.

40. See Jon Sobrino, "La centralidad del Reino de Dios anunciado por Jesús," *Revista Latinoamericana de Teología* 68 (2006): 136.

41. Sobrino, *Jesucristo liberador*, 89

42. "Jesus expresses the ultimate in a dual unity or in a unified duality. God is always present in what is ultimate, as is also the case for what is not God. This dual unity, which is the ultimate, is what 'kingdom of God' is formally aimed at expressing and precisely what Jesus announced" (ibid., 97-98).

43. Ibid., 122.

44. "And let us state in passing that in the activities of the kingdom we more clearly know the real existence of its opposite: the anti-kingdom" (ibid., 122).

45. Ibid., 167. As also explained in another document: "the fate of Jesus as the fate of others who preceded him and others who came after shows above all that the kingdom of God is proclaimed and established in the presence of and against a bad reality, the anti-kingdom" (Jon Sobrino, "Misereor Super Turbas," *Christus* 662 [1993]: 37).

46. "In history, there is an excluding and duel-like opposition between the *mediations* of the deity (in the time of Jesus, the kingdom of God, on the one hand, and the *pax romana* and a society around the temple, on the other) and between the *mediators* (Jesus, on the one hand, and the high priest and Pilate on the other). Indeed, this dialectic is evidenced in the way in which God is revealed" (Jon Sobrino, *La fe en Jesucristo. Ensayo desde las víctimas* [Madrid: Trotta, 1999], 131).

47. See Jon Sobrino, "La centralidad del Reino de Dios anunciado por Jesús," 155.

48. "The kingdom of God can never be adequately rendered in history because it is a utopia. Nevertheless, this does not deprive it of its historical nature but moves us to turn to the present by means of historical mediations and to become a reality at all levels of historical reality. The utopia turns into a source of functional ideologies that shape history" (Sobrino, *Jesucristo liberador*, 171).

49. Ibid., 172.

50. Hence, the christological perspective of Sobrino "assumes that the resurrected can be victoriously present when following the crucified, so that this decision to follow him can be pervaded now by the triumph that the resurrection of Jesus entails" (Sobrino, *La fe en Jesucristo*, 28).

51. "The resurrection is presented directly as a fair reaction of God when faced with an unfair action of men. God makes justice for a victim—Jesus, the fair, the innocent. This reveals mostly who is God: the one who liberates victims (as in the Old Testament he reveals himself by liberating an oppressed nation subject to slavery). He also reveals what is the hope of the victims and of those who die in solidarity with them. And he finally reveals that Jesus of Nazareth—and not any other one—in his fulfillment of life, history, and destiny is the manifestation of what is really human and what is really divine and is the Son of God and our eldest brother" (Sobrino, "Misereor Super Turbas," 37).

52. In this way, "the transcendent nature of God will appear not only as something beyond what is created, but also as something that is against what it is created, rendering everything absolute as an idol" (Sobrino, *La fe en Jesucristo*, 131-32).

# 9

# Central Themes in Sobrino's Christology

JORGE COSTADOAT, S.J.

This chapter considers Jon Sobrino's liberation Christology in his two main works: *Jesucristo liberador* and *La fe en Jesucristo*.[1] Sobrino's Christology reflects his soteriological interest, and it is organized with reference to a very particular historical context requiring a specific kind of Christology. Early in the 1990s, he explained that "the context is what continues to require more rather than less liberation, what continues to need a liberation Christology."[2] This requirement remains and becomes even greater as we proceed through the first decade of the new millennium.[3]

Sobrino's Christology strives to convince the reader that, in order to be Christian, it is not sufficient simply to confess faith in Christ, that we must recognize the anger of using his name for ideological purposes and that we need to return to Jesus of Nazareth to reclaim his liberating power. We must not be naïve. All Christologies reflect specific interests, and among these, says Sobrino, we must distinguish between those that correspond to Christ and those that distort him. In his own words,

> Christology can be useful for good things, but it can also be used for bad things, which should not surprise us, since, as it is created by human beings, it is also subject to their sinfulness and manipulation. We must not forget that in history there have been objectively harmful, heretical Christologies which have presented a different Christ, who was actually objectively contrary to Jesus of Nazareth. Let us remember that our Christian continent has endured centuries of inhuman and anti-Christian oppression; Christology apparently took no notice of it and did not offer any prophetic denunciation of it in the name of Jesus Christ.[4]

Latin American Christology has the virtue of being structured soteriologically. Unlike some other Christologies, it is articulated with regard to a salvation that it hopes will begin to appear now in its own history. In the following sections we shall see how the liberation of the poor fundamentally determines its methodology. In order to become historical salvation for the poor, Sobrino's Christology has had to recover Jesus Christ's eschatological character—with his double reference to the kingdom of God and the God of the kingdom—and Jesus Christ's own profound humanity and historicity.

## Methodological Originality

Assuming that the eschatological event has already occurred, that Christ is present in history and his action in this world is already believed in faith, Sobrino's methodology uses current hermeneutical insights to make transcendent salvation understood as an immanent reality among the poor. This theological purpose clearly and honestly sets out where his Christology is "coming from." If the object of all Christology is Jesus Christ, Sobrino fulfills his task by a circular hermeneutic: the texts of revelation that speak of Jesus Christ are understood in the context of Christ becoming present in history and, vice versa, those same texts throw light on where it is possible to find Christ today in history, which then becomes Christology's ideal "setting."

The context of Latin American Christology, its "theological setting" because of Christ's presence in it, are "the poor of this world."[5] This general context unfolds analytically as both the "ecclesial setting" (where the knowledge is kept of who Jesus Christ is) and the social setting of Christology (where the poor, as "signs" of all times, influence the way to approach Jesus Christ). Of course, Sobrino stresses that this theological setting of Latin American Christology, and especially its social setting, represents an epistemological break with traditional Christologies: "Thus, the social setting is the most decisive for faith, the most decisive for shaping christological thinking. It is what requires and facilitates an epistemological break."[6] The following of Christ rooted in this setting enables us to know Christ himself better. In very simple terms, Sobrino states: "We think that Christ can be known better from the standpoint of the poor, and that better-known Christ is the one who, we believe, sends us back to the poor."[7]

Sobrino's Christology is characterized as starting from the study of Jesus of Nazareth and his total dedication to the kingdom (reign) of God. Unlike other Christologies, though, Sobrino's use of history does not lead to the demythologizing of Christ's person and work, but in the face of the senseless tragedy of the lives of the poor, it tries to "unsettle" and "de-idolize" Christ so that he neither soothes us in the face of wretched poverty nor justifies oppression.[8] Unlike liberal theology, Sobrino's Christology draws from faith in Christ's divine person in a way that understands his incarnation as an act of solidarity with the poor. Sobrino's faith trusts a genuinely liberating Christ.

Thus, we understand that, for Sobrino, the historical is not just what can be

a social and world structure that has continued up to our time, which Sobrino calls "an idolatrously theological structure of reality." In history there exists the true God (of life), his mediation (kingdom), and his mediator (Jesus), and there also exist the idols (of death), their mediation (the anti-kingdom), and their mediators (oppressors). The realities of the two are not only distinct, but they are formally opposed to each other. In a world organized according to this historical and eschatological struggle, Jesus reveals an "antagonistic God,"[18] a God who is incompatible with idolatry.

### Recovery of Jesus' Humanity

Faith in Christ in Latin America has proved incapable of changing the lives of the poor, according to Sobrino, because it is centered on a Christ who is more divine than human. This is the Christ preached by the institutional church. In all the alienating images of Christ in Latin America, the transcendent aspect is given more attention than Jesus' actual historical life and humanity. This is true whether that faith focuses on a suffering Christ (who merely encourages resignation), or whether it consists of an "abstract" Christ (the *Love-Christ* or the *Power-Christ,* based on a preconceived notion of love and of power, and not on how Jesus was love or what kind of power he had), or a "reconciling" Christ (which fails to take into account Jesus' prophetic denunciations or his conflicts), or an "Absolutely Absolute" Christ (which has no reference to the kingdom of God or the God of the kingdom).[19] Against these serious distortions of Christ, Sobrino focuses on the emerging figure of "Christ the Liberator," which is derived from Jesus of Nazareth's humanity and historicity.

The adoption of the historical Jesus as the methodological starting point of Sobrino's Christology aims to correct this failure and to prevent the manipulation of Christ. The hermeneutic circularity that Sobrino establishes between the historical Jesus and following Christ for the sake of the poor relies on the human reality of both Jesus and the poor as common denominator and as a reciprocal epistemological principle for understanding praxis, cross, and resurrection, or the totality of the real. Following Christ in a world of poor people requires us to recognize the full humanity of Jesus, crucified and risen, and that, in turn, enables, illuminates, and impels a concrete following of Christ in accordance with Jesus' own example and under the influence of the Spirit.

In his approach to the study of conciliar Christology, Sobrino tries again to recover the "reality"[20] of Jesus' humanity. He recovers it in the dogmatic formulas elaborated by the Greek fathers. But he could not do it without knowing Jesus of Nazareth and his mission. He has spoken about the latter in *Jesucristo liberador (Jesus the Liberator),* and about the former in *La fe en Jesucristo (Christ the Liberator).* Sobrino rescues Christ's humanity in the ancient formulas. For without their history, and in particular Jesus' history, these formulas normally lead to that docetism which has dogged the church to this day.

Sobrino analyzes the conciliar definitions from this viewpoint. At Nicaea the fathers had the "audacity and honesty" to declare the divinity of one who had been crucified. Against Arius, the council achieved a true de-Hellenization of Christianity. The affirmation of the *homoousios* conceived of Christ starting from his transcendental origin (and not from Jesus' life and destiny) and served as a criterion to distinguish the human from the divine and to grant God lordship over the whole of human history. By making God the ultimate foundation of Christ's being, the council did not overcome the essentialism of Greek philosophy. Nevertheless, by making space for Jesus in God, Nicaea implicitly affirmed that God suffers with human beings, in his self-determination to be exposed to them. By the fathers' acceptance of the divinity of a suffering Christ, the council preserved the (scandalous and fortunate) novelty of the New Testament and the indispensable condition of "affinity" for the salvation of suffering humanity.[21]

Sobrino affirms the supreme importance of Christ's suffering humanity inasmuch as it belongs to the Son of God. That is the pivot of Christian salvation. The "reality principle" in Christ is not merely Jesus of Nazareth. Chalcedon maintained that the unity of the divinity and humanity in Christ ultimately depended on his "divine reality" and, therefore, expressed his mystery. The council fathers had the audacity to affirm a unified "totality" in Christ, without intermixing, of transcendence and history: "Thus Chalcedon affirms that Jesus Christ is a single—not double—divine reality—a statement that can be understood in principle—who subsists in two forms of reality, in two natures, human and divine, a relationship it described by the well-known adverbs *inconfuse* (without confusion), *inmutabiliter* (without change), *indivise* (without disunity), *inseparabiliter* (without separation)."[22] The fathers' whole *pathos* respected the holy mystery of Jesus Christ, who paradoxically unites two realities in himself, but they did not explain how. The perspective of the victims opens the way to thinking that in the incarnation, as understood by Chalcedon, God assumes "the little, weak, limited and mortal," and, on the other hand, the human in all its littleness can manifest God, "although it may be as *Deus absconditus.*"[23]

The Chalcedonian expression "in two natures" has, in general terms, safeguarded Christ's humanity. According to the council, in the incarnation, "his humanity continues to be real, even after it has been assumed by the *Logos*"[24]; and vice versa, the human in all its weakness is "capable of being the bearer of God, without ceasing to be human and weak."[25] For in the incarnation the man Jesus continues to be God. He merits a correspondence of faith. The human continues to be human in him, exempt from super-power and super-knowledge. Even given its own possibilities, this humanity is what humanizes and saves. By saying that the union of natures is "without separation," that is "for ever," Chalcedon affirmed by extension that only the human can lead to God. [26]

By the term *prosōpon* or *hypostasis*, Chalcedon affirmed the ultimate divine reality of Christ, and this constitutes the metaphysical in Jesus Christ as divine and human. For the council, "that which is ultimate and incommunicable in the concrete reality of Christ is in the Son and not in his human nature," that is, "what is 'ultimate' in Christ is divine."[27] Christ represents the radicality of the divine initiative to communicate itself humanly to humanity, and also that the human only finds its principle of realization in God. Salvation comes from God in Christ, but as fulfillment of the human. And further, in Christ's unity Sobrino discovers the greatest "unrepeatable and supreme expression of reality," the overcoming of all Manichaeism, Marcionism, and other forms of dualism.[28] By virtue of the unity of the incarnate son, we can hope that the end of history will result in a peaceful recapitulation, an encounter, not a failure to meet.

But like other contemporary christologies, Sobrino warns us of a final difficulty, a language trap. Over fifteen hundred years the word *persona* has undergone such a great change that it has come to express exactly the opposite of what it meant at Chalcedon. Today, it is necessary to recognize a human *persona* in Jesus.[29] The fact that the Latin term *persona* translates *prosōpon* and *hypostasis* and expresses the divine principle in Christ does not mean that in him his divine being annuls his human being, because in conciliar Christology the term *persona* is used in an ontological and not an anthropological sense.

## Salvation as Liberation

Sobrino's Christology has the virtue of being articulated in soteriological terms. The oppression of the poor is the reason that impels him to think of Christ in an eschatological perspective, to deepen his humanity, and above all, to think of salvation as historical liberation. In immediate terms, the reference to the Latin American context gives this Christology an unparalleled historical relevance among other Christologies.

The starting point of Sobrino's Christology is the realization that in Latin America faith in Christ has not been liberating, but on the contrary, it has kept the poor in their misery and sometimes even justified their oppression. Sobrino, however, celebrates the fact that in recent years, under the influence and with the support of Medellín and Puebla, the image of the "liberator Christ," derived from the Gospels, has arisen on the continent. This constitutes the greatest christological fact and an authentic sign of the times, because by recovering the identity of Jesus of Nazareth the Christ of faith has also recovered his historical relevance. The new image of Christ is liberating because it has the "capacity to liberate from the various slaveries that afflict the poor of the continent, to give direction to this liberation and to encourage believers to become active agents of it."[30]

Within this recovery of Christ's humanity, the proclamation of the kingdom of God to the poor has decisive importance. That is the viewpoint from which Sobrino understands eschatological salvation as historical liberation. As the New Testament also speaks of Jesus as "gospel," Sobrino points out that Jesus' personal way of being, "his mercy, honesty, loyalty, and firmness," are "good news" and salvation for human beings.[31] However, the person of Jesus and his kingdom project are not enough. The possibility of anticipating transcendent salvation as immanent liberation ultimately depends on our understanding of Christ's death and resurrection.

Sobrino demands that we recognize that Jesus' cross is the culmination of his life. His total dedication to the proclamation of the kingdom of God for the sake of the poor "can only be understood salvifically."[32] Only the historical perspective makes it possible to understand that the cross, which is always a "scandal" and which no theology can really "explain," is an expression of God's love.[33] What is pleasing to God, releasing his liberating action in the resurrection, is not the cross in itself, but Jesus, his whole life and self-dedication.

Hence, in Jesus' resurrection God's liberating character is manifested—but not because God raised a man from the dead. Of course, Jesus' resurrection is a triumph over death, but more precisely, it is an eschatological action by which God "saves the just man Jesus and does justice to Jesus the victim and with him the fullness of times is inaugurated."[34] Sobrino refers back in his argument to the origin of Israel's faith in the resurrection of the dead, stressing that it arose as an apocalyptic hope for victims of injustice, and that in Jesus' resurrection it becomes reality precisely as a triumph of justice.

Both from the viewpoint of Jesus' history and that of the church's faith expressed in the ecumenical councils of antiquity, the image arises of a God who is essentially related to human history and its savior. If God expressed in Jesus crucified his affinity with the suffering of the victims of history, if the possibility exists in God of suffering with human beings and in fact he has suffered, in the resurrection God expressed his otherness, his being that is distinct from ours, with its capacity to liberate victims from suffering, injustice, and death. The liberator God is the crucified God.

The historical character of eschatological liberation shows that through Jesus, the mediator, and his kingdom, the mediation, God wants to liberate victims from very concrete evils. The principal evil from which Latin America needs liberating is idolatry. Here "the idol by antonomasia which is the origin of all the others, is the unjust, structural, persistent, economic configuration of society served by many other realities: military, political, cultural, judicial and intellectual power, and also often religious power, which share analogically in the reality of the idol."[35] That is the reason why Sobrino's Christology is structured not in terms of the resurrection but of the kingdom of God. Of course, salvation as liberation means goods for the poor, and through them, for all. It will be salvation for all to the extent that the kingdom is translated into minimal living standards for the poor. However, its precise positive content is manifested historically as a dialectical contradiction to injustice and death.

In an impressive theological turn, Sobrino makes the poor themselves share in the overcoming of injustice and death. Liberation operates by virtue of spiritual action in solidarity, but also thanks to the sharing of the poor in Christ's cross. Salvation depends on Christ, and it is the "crucified peoples" who make Christ's crucified body present in history. The crucified peoples incorporate Christ into history: they "fill up in their flesh what is lacking in the passion of Christ."[36] To the extent that they continue God's passion in the world, they are the cause or principle of the world's salvation. Fully aware that this is a scandalous thesis, Sobrino assimilates it to the scandal that should always be provoked by faith in salvation through God's servant, the crucified God.[37] He demands, at least, recognition that these peoples offer the world the possibility of conversion, values, hope, love, forgiveness, solidarity, and faith.[38]

In the historical present, eschatological liberation comes from a following of Christ that is rooted among the world's poor, and its praxis fundamentally consists in "resurrecting the crucified" or "bringing the crucified people down from the cross."[39] In this way and no other, it is possible to access the reality of Christ's resurrection and bear witness to it. The hope raised by the resurrection "leads directly to justice, not simply to survival; its primary beneficiaries are the victims, not simply human beings; the scandal to be overcome is death unjustly inflicted, not simply death as a natural destiny. The hope that needs to be roused today is not just any hope but hope in God's power against the injustice that produces victims."[40] In this way, faith in the resurrection is liberating. It also adds something substantial to the following of Christ: the need to incorporate the cross into the experience of a God who lets himself be affected by human suffering.

## Some Critical Observations on Jon Sobrino's Christology

The criticisms of Sobrino made by the Notification of the Congregation for Doctrine and Faith pertain to two of Sobrino's main works. These criticisms are notable because they either do not apply to his case or they reveal the theological weaknesses of the Congregation's expert who composed them. I will give an example: the accusation against Sobrino for holding that Jesus had faith in God, a claim that could also be made against the major Christologies of the twentieth century.[41]

In this final section I offer just one criticism of Sobrino's Christology. It goes without saying that this criticism accepts the main thrust of Sobrino's work. Others can make other objections that can be left to argue on future occasions. Although accepting his fundamental thesis, I think Sobrino is guilty of some methodological simplifications that should be corrected and, if not, at least taken into account when using the categories developed in his Christology.

Sobrino uses the "from below" of the Antiochene tradition to broaden his methodology: not only do we know Christ starting from Jesus, but we know Jesus Christ starting from the poor. In its turn this knowledge stimulates the liberation of the poor in hermeneutical circularity. To whom does the "poor" refer?

The choice of a perspective in Christology always has a price, whether stated or not, and as Sobrino teaches us, it is not possible not to choose. In his case, however, the perspective is viewed through simplifications of reality that might mobilize the historical salvation of the poor in the short term while in the longer term frustrating it. One simplification is between the categories "oppressed" and "oppressors"; another is that which differentiates between the poor who possess an alienating image of Christ and those who believe in a liberating Christ.

The sharp distinction between oppressed and oppressors indicates the truth of a conflict that also occurs outside the church. Sobrino is neither afraid to enter this conflict nor, in doing so, to side with the oppressed. He not only invokes God's partiality for them, but above all announces the possibility of salvation for the rest of humanity. By incorporating Christ into history, the poor sacramentally mediate his salvation.

However, the identification of historical victims with the Body of Christ is problematic in two ways. In the first place, the category Body of Christ in theology has normally been applied to the church. Sobrino too applies the term to the church,[42] but then with no lack of continuity, no distinction, no sufficient foundation, he also uses it to refer to the peoples of the Third World.[43] Thus, the church's sacramental function as Christ's Body becomes blurred, and even, to some extent, superfluous. The "crucified peoples" appear to take its place. What still needs to be worked out in Sobrino's Christology is that in applying the term to the Third-World victims, both the distinction and the connection is made between the crucified peoples and the church.

Second, by means of the themes of the Suffering Servant and of martyrdom, Sobrino has shown how these peoples are like Christ, but he has not shown how they are unlike him. In short, the identification of the poor with Christ's Body simplifies the reality by concentrating salvation in them and the opposite in their oppressors.

We can also note a second simplification. Here we find a flaw or methodological error: if Sobrino's merit is to derive christological knowledge from the following of Christ, he is not as concrete or as "real" as he claims when he reduces the reality of Latin Americans to the state of being victims. Although, of course, the vast majority of Latin Americans are victims, they are not *only* victims. As believers, it is not possible to dismiss as merely ideological the many different cultural and religious currents in the faith of the victims. As well as being poor and being Christians, Latin Americans have their own culture, and they have welcomed and reproduced their Christian faith within this culture, even though there might be a great deal of ambiguity here. This "highbrow" Christology tries to be "popular," but it breaks with popular religiosity; in general, it is rooted in the Third-World poor, but in particular, in those communities who confess their faith in Christ the liberator, to whom Sobrino offers his services as a theologian.[44]

His second simplification operates silently, but it is not clear that it operates without diminishing popular culture. In its fundamentals Sobrino's christological method is right, but it loses its way when it does not respect the reality of faith in Christ in Latin America. We do not see how, without recognizing the value of popular religiosity, the christological break being advocated will not end in a lamentable ecclesial iconoclasm. Sobrino's method in Christology still needs to formulate the continuity of popular faith in Christ the savior with the necessary discontinuity required to display the image of Jesus Christ the liberator characteristic of the New Testament and the following of Christ.[45] Only by approaching the deepest "reality" of Christ among the poor and the victims, who have many ways of believing and struggling for life, can Christology overcome the alienations that result from ancient and new abstractions.

*Translated by Dinah Livingstone*

## Notes

1. *Jesucristo liberador: Lectura histórico-teológica de Jesús de Nazareth* (Madrid: Trotta, 1991); Eng. trans., *Jesus the Liberator: A Historical-Theological Reading of Jesus of Nazareth,* trans. Paul Burns and Francis McDonagh (Maryknoll, N.Y.: Orbis Press, 1993); and *La fe en Jesucristo: Ensayo desde las víctimas* (Madrid: Trotta, 1999); Eng. trans., *Christ the Liberator: A View from the Victims,* trans. Paul Burns (Maryknoll, N.Y.: Orbis Books, 2001). Translations of quotations from *Jesucristo liberador* and *La fe en Jesucristo* have been made by the translator of this article.

2. *Jesucristo liberador,* 18.

3. See *La fe en Jesucristo,* 15-17.

4. *Jesucristo liberador,* 13.

5. Ibid., 48.

6. Ibid., 52.

7. Ibid., 56.

8. Ibid., 75.

9. Ibid., 77.

10. Ibid., 77.

11. Ibid., 77.

12. Ibid., 32.

13. Ibid., 95.

14. Ibid., 97.

15. Ibid., 145.

16. Ibid., 166.

17. Ibid., 183.

18. Ibid., 249.

19. Ibid., 25-33.

20. The category "reality" has enormous importance in Sobrino's work. In general terms it is opposed to any kind of "docetism," to any affirmation of the divine to the detriment of the human, either in the case of Jesus or of humanity.

21. *La fe en Jesucristo,* 375-76.

22. Ibid., 415-16.

23. Ibid., 416.

24. Ibid., 420.

25. Ibid., 421.

26. Ibid., 422.

27. Ibid., 423.

28. Ibid., 421.

29. Ibid., 401.

30. *Jesucristo liberador,* 27.

31. *La fe en Jesucristo,* 305.

32. *Jesucristo liberador,* 394.

33. *La fe en Jesucristo,* 305.

34. Ibid., 69.

35. *Jesucristo liberador,* 243.

36. Ibid., 322.

37. Ibid., 328, 330, 477.

38. Ibid., 331-32.

39. *La fe en Jesucristo,* 76-79.

40. Ibid., 70.

41. There are many Christologies that hold that Jesus had to have subjective faith in God. When I investigated I counted fifty. Among them, Hans Urs von Balthasar, *La Foi du Christ: Cinq approches christologiques* (Paris, 1968); Karl Rahner, "Considérations dogmatiques sur la psychologie du Christ," *Exégèse et dogmatique* (Paris: DDB, 1966), 185-210; Bernard Sesboüé, "Science et conscience du Jésus prépascal," *Pédagogie du Christ: Eléments de christologie fondamentale* (Paris: Cerf, 1996), 141-75; Peter Hünermann, *Cristología* (Barcelona, 1997); Jacques Guillet, *La foi du Jésus-Christ* (Paris, 1980); and Cardinal Walter Kasper, current president of the Pontifical Council for the Promotion of Christian Unity, *Jesús el Cristo* (Salamanca, 1989).

42. *Jesucristo liberador,* 45, 49, 51; *La fe en Jesucristo,* 241.

43. *Jesucristo liberador,* 321-22.

44. *Jesucristo liberador,* 20; *La fe en Jesucristo,* 19-20.

45. This important suggestion is made by Juan Carlos Scannone in *Evangelización, cultura y teología* (Buenos Aires: Guadelupe, 1990), 237-43.

# 10

# Hope and the Kingdom of God
## Christology and Eschatology
## in Latin American Liberation Theology

### FÉLIX PALAZZI

Latin American theology recognizes an important relationship between the knowledge of its complex reality and its life of faith. It is not aimed at giving a meaning to faith itself but a meaning from the structural reality of the continent where the great question is raised regarding the meaning of Christian faith for so many men and women living in dehumanizing conditions. Inequity is today one of the most worrisome structural elements on the continent. Several million people live at the limit of what is simply provisional. How can one talk about a hopeful future when faced with a sustained growth of poverty? How can one win back the transcendence of the human subject, his or her openness to what is radical and ultimate, if this same human being is faced every day with the struggle to survive?

We are confronting a *crisis of reality* itself. How can we announce the irruption of eschatology within the framework of this history? Latin American theology adopts the viewpoint of a historical eschatology. This chapter will examine the theology of Jon Sobrino and Ignacio Ellacuría, whose writings attempt to revitalize our sense of history—despite the drama and the tragedy of millions—by projecting it to an absolute future in God.

### The Possibility of the Eschatological Approach
### Based in Reality

The theology of liberation has taken up the dialectical explanation of poverty and inequity as a consequence of social, economic, and political conditions of reality itself.[1] At this point in time, eschatology discovers that we have a long way to go before reaching the future promised by God. Accepting the urgency of the *appeal* for personal and structural conversion constitutes a path to working for better living conditions so that the values of the kingdom of God can become evident. The future is not an absolute reality or a reality in itself. On the one hand, it is the projection of this historical present, though, on the other hand, it is the denial of the existing conditions of sin. As Ellacuría put it: "without eschatology there is no radical force to transform and project the present."[2]

This transformation of reality, however, entails a theological dimension. It comes true by listening and praying the word of God. It is not a matter of giving sense to reality per se as an absolute notion but, rather, of contributing with criteria and horizons that help efficiently transform it in order to give way, even if in minute proportions, to the reality of the kingdom of God amidst our historical temporariness. The word teaches us the way in which God is revealed in his desire to liberate his people and to ensure that injustices are overcome. This is the founding experience of the exodus, of the prophets, of the book of Revelation, and of the Gospels. When reading reality from the word of God we desire to discover the meaning of our present in what is ultimate in the development of our own history per se: the presence of the *eschaton*. The latter is revealed in Jesus of Nazareth, the incarnated Son as "the best way to historically make the kingdom of God come true, understanding the kingdom of God as something that starts in history."[3]

In the case of Latin American theology, eschatology is not content to be discovered after a process of reflection on the ultimate sense of reality. On the contrary, it is reality itself under development and crying for the fulfillment of the kingdom of God. In this way, it can find its ultimate and definite nature by fighting off the idols of death that hinder the appearance of truth. These idols exist in subtle political economic and religious forms that dehumanize and deceive peoples, turning them into mere objects that receive handouts instead of treating them as dignified subjects. "This means that the presence of eschatology in history should be historical, and, hence, an epiphanic presence would not suffice if it is expressed in successive tangential presences of the same eternal and immutable nature. Likewise, it would not be enough to have a merely cultural presence where what once happened would take place 'bloodlessly' once and for all. What is required is a presence that really turns into history as God turned into history in Jesus Christ."[4]

## The Experience of Historical Transcendence in the Eschatology of Liberation

Historical transcendence is usually understood as something that is separated from history, something that is beyond or outside history. From historical eschatology we try "to see transcendence as something that transcends *in* and not something that transcends *from* or something that physically pushes to *more* though not taking anything *outside,* as something that is discarded but at the same time is retained."[5] Hence, finding God in history does not mean abandoning what is human. Likewise, finding what is human does not mean abandoning God. The transcendence of God does not exist by necessity but out of the freedom of the love of God that wants human beings to be saved and to live in plenitude. God listens to the clamor of his oppressed people and wants to give them back the life that has been taken from them by their oppressors. God wants to appear as a liberator in the midst of situations of tragedy, lies, and oppression—all of which strive to deny the transcendence of God. The experience of the transcendence of God that is emphasized in the Old and New Testaments is the basis of the perspective of historical eschatology developed by Latin American theology. Let us now analyze some of its most salient elements.

### The Exodus and the Covenant as the Ethical-Eschatological Call

The covenant is the expression of a living God who listens to the clamor of his people and desires their liberation (Exod 3:7-10). It is the sign of a God who loves by releasing because "God can be worshipped only in a situation of freedom, and in turn freedom reaches its plenitude in the prayers to Yahweh, the God of life. This bond is the very core of the experience of any believer."[6] The exodus and the covenant involve an experience of the faith that liberates and that is present as an ethical-eschatological[7] call that urges the transformation of situations of oppression and death and replaces them with situations of justice and life. It is an ethical consideration because it leads us to take an honest position with respect to reality.

However, it is also eschatological because the ethical dynamism that such a social praxis generates tends toward its definitive realization and its ultimate consummation in the future of God. In other words, it has to project in the present what is already reality in God in the future and what God has been revealing in the past through historical liberating actions. Ethics integrates the past and the future in order to give full sense to the present as a period that is destined to proceed toward an always greater "plus," toward God as an absolute *futurum* of people and their history.

The covenant is, at the same time, the revelation of a near and faithful God: "I will take you as my own people, and you shall have me as your God" (Exod 6:7). It is a relational and liberating term. God does not rule over his people to dominate or deceive them. His intention is not to dominate but, rather, to liberate his people by showing them his love. God does not break his covenant. On the contrary, he offers his love freely in the various promises that become a reality throughout the history of the people of Israel. Loyalty is a trait of God who gives and does not ask for anything in return, and history is a consequence of its eschatological realization and not the other way around. Nevertheless, this same covenant starts the construction of dignified living conditions that point to the promised land. In this way, authentic worship will inspire justice, though under conditions of freedom.[8] This is the ethical and eschatological call that questions us in the experience of the covenant. This is a call that has to be heard in history until the time comes for the great banquet of the Lord where we will all sit together and where there will be no more hunger or social division.

## The Kingdom of God as the Hermeneutical Key of the Historical Eschatology

It is precisely in the person of Jesus that transcendence in history is given and self-communicated to us in a historical path by means of a praxis that coincides with the salvific desire of God the Father for the whole of creation. It is what Jesus discovers in his experience of the kingdom of God that will be the key for interpreting and fulfilling historical eschatology because "the ultimate nature of Jesus was admitted with the ultimate nature of life."[9] In other words, the road to discovering the transcendence or the ultimate reality of history lies *in* history itself by means of historical *praxis* in concrete life. Nevertheless, this reality is not absolute and it is not closed to itself, nor is it static. On the contrary, it is enhanced and triggered by a movement of qualitative realization toward its absolute *futurum* where "God may be all in all" (1 Cor 15:28), though it cries out for everything that is now denied and delayed.

Because the kingdom is an ultimate reality—in other words, an eschatological reality—it completely influences history because "kingdom means the total and global liberation of creation, finally purified from everything that oppresses it, transfigured by the full presence of God."[10] Social conditions become an object of transformation as the place of the historical realization of the kingdom of God. It is a radical "already" because of the absolute nature of the salvific will of God for all, and, at the same time, it is a "not yet" because it is still not possible to build it fully because of the reality of evil and the anti-kingdom. Hence, we must take up the responsibility that results from our own historical freedom so as to cooperate with the divine salvific project.

This fraternal demand is made real in the disciples and followers of Jesus Christ when they are "called blessed, happy, because by giving food to the hungry, water to the thirsty, by clothing the naked and visiting those who are in prison—in other words, by means of concrete gestures—they give life and, hence, they announce and they enter the kingdom."[11] Happiness (blessing) is a consequence of building the kingdom. The kingdom is always manifested in the presence of an anti-kingdom—in other words, it is always manifested against the reality that denies it and manifested as a radical hope in every human being that lights his path toward the ultimate promised future.

### Jesus Christ as the Key for Understanding the Ultimate Nature of the Kingdom: Christology and Eschatology Meet

The ultimate nature of history is revealed to us in Christ, and also the way in which we can make it a temporal reality because he is the full irruption of the truth of history itself. Based on this we can set forth three theses under the modality of christological analogies. These theses have inspired the theologies of Ellacuría and Sobrino, and they motivate the eschatological reading of historical reality.[12]

(a)  History is related to eschatology as the historical Jesus is related to the resurrected Christ. In the historical Jesus we begin to see what God wants for the future of all of humanity. In him, we find a practical answer to the needs of his own time, but also we receive a revelation of the final consummation that will be revealed in the *eschaton*. In this way, what is historic—as a tangible reality—must be transformed and transfigured as a result of the values of the kingdom that Jesus lived so that it can have sense not only in its foundations but also in its own dynamism and progress toward an absolute future. In the resurrection of Christ we see an anticipation of the promise for an ultimate reality that will overcome every crisis. Nevertheless, this reality must be built from the temporal dynamism of our reality by way of the concrete options of individuals until God may be all in all. The future of God does not rule out the present. Rather, it places this present in his truth, revealing the evil that has to be halted and the good that has to be enhanced.

(b)  The ultimate significance of history can only be reached from its eschatological fulfillment, just as the historical Jesus can only be understood from the resurrected Christ. The resurrected Christ does not give new meaning to the historical Jesus but rather reveals fully what his truth is and glorifies his meaning in and for history. In the eschatological consummation, history will not be transformed into another history. Indeed, its real truth will be revealed, and this is something that we can only know as a process that takes place in time. Just as the resurrection reveals the meaning of the death of the crucified, so the eschatological consummation discloses the meaning of the life and death of the crucified of our world. Starting from reality as the place of the revelation of transcendence itself, its meaning will be manifested in the experience of the struggle against the anti-kingdom. It is precisely at this point that the provisional dynamism of what is real will be inspired by hope insofar as it yearns for attainment of its ultimate and true reality.

(c) The possibility that history leads to an eschatology is suggested by the fact that in such a history the God whose glory will only be future is already present as an operating principle, as was the case for the historical Jesus, who was resurrected by God the Father. God is not the future of humanity in the chronological and time-related sense. God manifests his divine presence in the present and also as a projection of the future. Human history is aimed at a "plus" that is beyond; it intends a relationship with God as the one who, summing up all things in Christ, glorifies and transfigures history. If history were not already opened to eschatology, it would be useless to speak about a full and authentic realization of humanity because we would not have anything to do except to wait for God to do everything for us. On the contrary, if the eschatological possibility is already present in history, God can only act *with* humanity as a *God with us* (Emmanuel) who offers himself freely. God as love patiently awaits our answer as he works for the transformation of the world. In this perspective, the primacy of what is eschatological is accepted as the ultimate and radical meaning of history, though understood as an eschatology underway *from* history *against the* drama of the victims and moving *toward* its full consummation in the life of God.

## Hope as an Eschatological Perspective When Faced with the Burden of Reality

### In History but against Situations of Death

Hope is the provisional radical dynamism that moves history toward its ultimate reality, toward its truth in God. Nevertheless, all this takes place amid pain and suffering, amid wars and injustices, because contradiction is an essential and typical reality in human history. From the vantage point of the burden of what is real we can ask: How can we live in the middle of a history like this from a really eschatological perspective? Furthermore, how can we live this historical-eschatological hope through faith in Jesus Christ when the burden of what is real makes us victims of sin in history? The answer can only be hope based on the resurrection of Jesus,[13] knowing—as Sobrino insistently reminded us—that the resurrected one is also the crucified one.

Postmodern subjects ask themselves about the meaning of human existence, and some do not seem to find any reason to continue living. Some live the present as a stream of contingent and passing moments utterly lacking in real and transcendent unity. As part of this position, mention is made of an "end of history," not in a chronological but rather in a qualitative sense. In other words, there is no unity that sums up existence and moves it toward a horizon full of faith in a final realization. Others have opted for another vision, where meaning will be found not in this history but in a metahistory, understood as the beyond, in other words, in a stage of life hereafter that is unknown and unattainable at present and with respect to which we have only to wait. History is lived as a resigned waiting rather than as a realistic hope. Its meaning lies in a "plus" that is found in another life. Indeed, because of its weakness and contradiction it is unable to contain a real sense of its own by virtue of the tragedy of its configuration which is manifested every day in diseases, wars, and in the sorrows of several million people who suffer in an unfair manner. Neither of these groups of individuals have utopias for which they can fight. "The death of utopia and of hope is the end of the long march of individualism witnessed in the Western world. In the ancient Christian world, the individual is born in relation to God. The Hellenistic world valued the individual as opposed to the world. Modernity reverses this situation in seeing only the individual-in-the-world without God. Individuals are autonomous and self-sufficient and no longer in need of utopias or hope. They attempt to attain fulfillment within history by means of their own resources."[14]

Within this somewhat bleak context, how can we talk about eschatology, how can we make real the salvation that God desires for every human being? In short, how can we announce the resurrection of Jesus and the hope that this implies in the process of building that history—though within history itself—if we do not believe precisely in history or if we do not want to take up and carry the burden of what is real with the drama of its harshness and temporary nature as an essential part of it? When we speak about hope, we are referring to an encompassing and dynamic reality that exceeds any utopia because it implies an ethical and eschatological movement. In other words, it does not remain in the horizontal dimension of history but rather points at its ultimate and absolute reality. Hope is not simply waiting. It is basically the theological attitude that enables every human being to carry the burden of what is real (in the historical present) and at the same time to anticipate in present experience a greater and more absolute totality that points to a more human future.[15]

The man who has lost the sense of the development of his life can only recover the eschatological and ultimate perspective of his own personal and social existence based on hope. Nevertheless, nowadays—maybe more than ever before—there is an urgent need to announce hope in the middle of a history that seems to deny it through the prevalence of inequity and injustice. It is not hope itself that is in crisis. One form of crisis lies in the contemporary person who is locked in an individualism that closes off truly human relationships and that prefers virtual or technological relations. Another form of crisis can be traced to contemporary social structures that are so mired in human suffering and evil that they make it nearly impossible to believe in a better future.

Yet, as Sobrino reminds us, "hope has to do directly with justice and not simply with survival. Its primary subjects are the victims and not simply human beings. The scandal that it must overcome is the death that is inflicted unfairly and not simply natural death as the normal destiny. The hope that we have to reformulate and rebuild today is not just any hope, but the hope in the power of God against the injustice that gives rise to victims."[16]

Only carrying the burden of what is real in this unique and unrepeatable history allows us to resist the situations that generate victims and the death of the innocent. Only by so doing can we announce hope to a world that is crying out for the kind of future promised by God. History is the path of conversion toward that promised future that renounces the sinful structures of the present. The future comes more forcefully insofar as the present is more transparent and faithful to what will be revealed to us as its truth, to what will be given to us in a full and permanent way. We can describe this ethical and eschatological movement as a theology of hope in the following terms from the thought of Ellacuría, Sobrino, and other Latin American theologians: living *in* history *carrying* the burden of what is real against situations of death and *toward* an absolute future of life.

The resurrection is revealed in this context as the ideal setting for radical hope, the *topia* or the place par excellence where the future is freely revealed to us in all its might and vigor. In the resurrection, life acquires its nature as something real and lasting, while history reveals the possibility of its glorification and consummation. It is an eschatological event that bursts into history as a radical novelty of the power of God to re-create. We cannot forget, however, that the resurrection takes place in history even though it is not a historical event. It takes place in the personal history of one who was crucified, Jesus of Nazareth, though it is the result of the actions of his Father, the God of the kingdom. In that crucified one from Nazareth who has already been resurrected by the Father we find the face of "those who have suffered so much in the history of this earth that they were able to experience the greatest weakness and humiliation . . . they will then share the victory, the strength, and the glory of God who resurrected his Son Jesus and who will also resurrect the poor of the world."[17] This focuses not only on hope for life hereafter, but also on hope opposed to the death of the victims in our world. It is hope "without a center"—as Sobrino says[18]— because hope founded on the resurrection is no longer just about the past but also about present hope for the resurrection of the victims of our world. It is a hope that refuses to accept the scandal of the death of the innocent in our history and that raises its voice with compassion and mercy to protect those who suffer. In other words, it feels the suffering of others, knowing that the last word has not yet been uttered.

### Calls to Build an Eschatological Practice of the Resurrection Today

A historical eschatology that announces hope through faith in the resurrection of the crucified urges believers to follow an ethical and eschatological praxis related to their own lives and decisions. To do so we must take into account three basic elements.[19]

(a)  As Sobrino points out, the historical practice of Jesus is against the anti-kingdom. In other words, it is evidenced in the struggle against the idols of his time. The same applies today. Among these idols we can mention indifference, which is disguised as the clever principle of tolerance that turns a blind eye before the growing number of victims of our world. People who take seriously the burden of reality devote themselves to the marginal and neglected in this world, to the victims of the major political, economic, and religious structures of our times that are opposed to the desire to build a dignified life for all men and women alike.

(b)  The resurrection of Jesus is God's reaction in enacting justice in the case of one who is crucified, a victim, in short, a suffering innocent—as Sobrino reminds us. The resurrection supports all hope to build creatively, though in due time, a praxis that offers justice to the victims of our world. This praxis brings down the victims from the cross and gives them back the dignified lives that they deserve. This implies that our church should not be satisfied with pastoral activity that is based on mere assistance; rather, it should create prophetic activities that have a clear evangelical nature and that are aimed at compassion and mercy for victims. An eschatological praxis of the church must be aimed at its own *kenosis*, or self-emptying, so that it can be really at the service of the poor and those who are most in need throughout society.

(c)  This type of eschatological praxis should urgently bring about the conversion not only of individuals but also of the structures that generate dehumanizing conditions and that only work for the advantage of a few while allowing legitimating ideologies to gain dominance. Eschatological praxis strives to bring back to life the political, economic, religious, and other conditions that have been affected by sin. "Tolerance" has made us lose the significance of the authentically prophetic nature of our faith. Hope that is not prophetic does not anticipate a *eu-topia* or, in other words, the good news that has no place in this world as it is presently structured. For many, hope only concerns a vague *utopia* that is unattainable in our times. Nevertheless, the salvific "now" of God is faced not only with the "not yet" of those who do not see it as "timely" but also with the "certainly not" of those who reject it openly. We must move in genuine hope and with a strong commitment to ratify a "definitely yes" so that "God may be all in all." In this hope, eschatology will be not only a promise but also the presence of the glory of God that issues a radical judgment of "certainly not" against the structures and relationships that lead to victims and sufferers and that deceive oppressed peoples under the disguise of political ideologies.

## Conclusion: The Evangelical Nature of Hope

This hope—as set forth by the historical eschatology of liberation theology—has to be good news, *eu-aggelion*. It emphasizes what is good, ultimate, and positive, and hence will appear in time insofar as we build social situations that make it possible. The project of the kingdom and its values should not be lived as an apologetic reaction against contemporary society—under the modality of either personal or structural sin. The salvific project of God has to be announced as what is good and positive in what is already present, though minimally, in history. It promotes the complete reign of God in this world. It proceeds despite the fact that human freedom is exercised in the rhythm of the eschatological dynamic between a "right now" though "not yet," and, at the same time, between a "certainly not" and a "definitely yes," as we have explained. This process, however, always takes place within the horizon of the promise of a God who wants only life and goodness and not hate and lies. On account of this fact, "liberation theology maintains its evangelical nature and it does not fall into the disillusionment of faith, into the doubt that paralyzes, into talking about God and Christ with resignation. . . . It indeed takes seriously what it states to be its main objective: the kingdom of God. And, upon taking it seriously, it opens its space so that its activities can be shaped by what that kingdom really is,"[20] even more so, by the good news that God conveys when he reigns.

This good news must be incarnated—as the Word was made flesh and lived among us. It is *the* great and good news that is present in our history. In short, the evangelical nature intrinsic to a historical eschatology of liberation must become a reality with the same energy as the historical practice of Jesus of Nazareth: drawn to the reality of the poor and looked down on during his time, respectful toward the vagaries of human freedom, loyal to the project willed by the Father, outspoken against the anti-kingdom and the powers of this world that create victims and that want to restrain the reigning action of a good God, and, in short, *eutopic*, announcing the good news of an absolute future that has already started, though temporarily, amid our dramatic history, as revealed to us in the resurrection of the crucified one, Jesus of Nazareth, the Son of God. The historic eschatology proposed by Ellacuría and Sobrino—among other Latin American theologians—does not forget that the absolute future belongs only to the kingdom of God. Nevertheless, it is aware of the fact that in this history there are still crucified victims in our world. As Sobrino reminds us, "even after the resurrection of Jesus, the cross of history remains as a massive reality [that] prevails as an essential element throughout human history."[21]

## Notes

1. All translations of texts were done by the author. "It understands poverty as the result of the economic organization of society that exploits some and excludes others from the production system" (Leonardo Boff and Clodovis Boff, *Cómo hacer Teología de la Liberación* [Bogotá: Paulinas, 1986], 37).

2. Ignacio Ellacuría,"Escatología e historia," *Revista Latinoamericana de Teología* 32 (1994): 114.

3. Ibid., 116.

4. Ibid., 117.

5. Ignacio Ellacuría, "Historicidad de la salvación cristiana," in *Mysterium Liberationis I: Conceptos fundamentales de teología de la liberación*, ed. Ignacio Ellacuría and Jon Sobrino (Madrid: Trotta, 1990), 328.

6. Gustavo Gutiérrez, *El Dios de la Vida* (Lima: CEP, 1989), 35.

7. We refer to the *ethical-eschatological* binomial as related to the ethical assumption of reality as the basic attitude when doing liberation theology in order to generate a historical praxis that makes the kingdom of God present in our society. To this end, from a historical eschatology, ethics is the practical way that takes history in its eschatological dynamism toward its definite future, insofar as it brings into the present a life that grows in the fulfillment of what is genuinely human and that fights against the idols of history that generate more sin and death. In short, what is ethical-eschatological shapes a historical-divine unit that starts with the conversion of the human heart and wants to walk in the divine truth toward the definite expression of the Lord when "God may be all in all" and only divine life reigns.

8. "The worship that God wants is inseparable from the practice of justice. This union expresses a key aspect in the faith of the God of the covenant. Real fasting is releasing the oppressed, opening the fetters that imprison them" (Gutiérrez, *El Dios de la Vida*, 107).

9. Jon Sobrino, *La fe en Jesucristo. Ensayo desde las víctimas* (Madrid: Trotta, 1999), 159.

10. Boff and Boff, *Cómo hacer Teología de la Liberación*, 64.

11. Gutiérrez, *El Dios de la Vida*, 257.

12. See Ignacio Ellacuría, "Escatología e historia," *Revista Latinoamericana de Teología* 32 (1994): 116-18.

13. "It is precisely in the revelation of history where the concrete fulfillment of this hope is attained and where we can make it come true. It is a history that we live in the spirit of Jesus and in the hope of the resurrected, a history where Jesus Christ—always a future—enables God to be all in all. This future Jesus Christ is made present in historical events that imply a judgment and a decision. Nevertheless, the anti-Christ is also made present as a disfigurement of history that hinders the Second Coming. On account of this, the scheme of conversion or destruction continues to be valid, and the threat of historical destruction should not paralyze the action of the kingdom" (Ellacuría, "Escatología e historia," 128).

14. Joao Battista Libanio, "Esperanza, utopía, resurrección," in *Mysterium Liberationis I,* ed. Ellacuría and Sobrino, 496.

15. "Hope is theological because its direction is God himself. It is also eschatological because it refers to the ultimate and definite that are already present in our historical reality under the sacramental form of the sign and the mediation and that will be revealed and be full beyond death. . . . Hope reveals the structure of what is real as a movement toward this absolute future and not toward the void or the emptiness" (ibid., 499).

16. Sobrino, *La fe en Jesucristo,* 70.

17. Battista Libanio, "Esperanza, utopía, resurrección," 509.

18. Sobrino, *La fe en Jesucristo,* 72.

19. Ibid., 77.

20. Jon Sobrino, "Jesús, teología y Buena Noticia," *Teología y Liberación: Escri-tura y espiritualidad* (Lima: CEP, 1990), 33-34.

21. Sobrino, *La fe en Jesucristo,* 473-74.

# 11

# Interpreting the Notification
*Christological Issues*

## WILLIAM LOEWE

The Notifications criticizing the work of Jesuit theologians Roger Haight in 2004 and Jon Sobrino in 2007 indicate that the Congregation for the Doctrine of the Faith (CDF) had been clearing the desk of business left pending by its previous prefect, the present pope. The two Notifications differ markedly. On point after point, positions the CDF found in Haight's *Jesus Symbol of God* were deemed unambiguously erroneous and contrary to faith, and the Notification concluded with a sanction prohibiting Haight from teaching Catholic theology. Sobrino's work, specifically *Jesus the Liberator*[1] and *Christ the Liberator*,[2] evokes a more nuanced, at some points tentative, and certainly gentler response. Perhaps most significant, the CDF has not imposed a sanction on Sobrino.

Sobrino's theological *oeuvre* is by no means beyond criticism. My own reading of his *Christology at the Crossroads* (1978), which Sobrino wrote when he was fresh from doctoral studies in Germany, faulted what seemed an uncritical adoption of elements of the theologies of Jürgen Moltmann and Wolfhart Pannenberg that I found problematic.[3] I continue to be unpersuaded by Moltmann's arguments in favor of the historicity of Jesus' experience of abandonment by the Father on the cross, a position that coheres nicely with the Protestant soteriological tradition and its thesis of penal substitution. This position has persisted in Sobrino's writings.[4] From another angle, New Testament scholar John P. Meier has criticized the lack of methodological rigor in Sobrino's claims for "the historical Jesus."[5] Sobrino's "historical Jesus" is not what Meier would require, a construct that emerges from the rigorous employment of historical-critical exegetical methods, but rather in fact a figure that comes into focus when one brings a certain perspective to bear on the Synoptic Gospels. In thus construing the "historical Jesus," Sobrino is at one with Joseph Ratzinger in practice if not in outcome.[6] Still, the CDF's critique seems to measure Sobrino not only by the faith of the church but also, at points, from the view-

An earlier version of this article appeared in *Commonweal*, May 18, 2007.

point of one particular, if rich and valuable, theological tradition, namely, scholasticism. The Congregation omits from consideration the historically minded, praxis-oriented rhetorical structure of Sobrino's theology and thus misses the legitimate differences between a project like Sobrino's and the sapiential, metaphysically informed tradition of scholastic theology that the CDF takes as normative.

In opting for this one theological paradigm, the CDF in my view unnecessarily forecloses a longstanding, productive, and still lively conversation among theologians and exegetes on such issues as the faith of Jesus, his human consciousness, and the extent of his human knowledge. It also neglects the relevance—and challenges—of historical-critical biblical exegesis in favor of an approach to Scripture that is redolent of the proof-texting of an earlier age. The Notification begins by attempting to clarify two major points. On the one hand, it judges that Sobrino's books "contain notable discrepancies from the faith of the church." It offers this judgment with some urgency. For the first time the Congregation published along with its Notification an explanatory note laying out its normal mode of operation and the abbreviated procedure invoked in cases of clear error and danger of grave damage. In Sobrino's case it opted for the latter. And so the Notification condemns certain propositions put forth in Sobrino's writing.

On the other hand, however, the Congregation also notes that its condemnations are circumscribed, in two ways. First, it is passing judgment on propositions, not on the author's subjective intentions. Second, it acknowledges that it is judging these propositions even when they appear in the context of other expressions that seem to affirm their opposite. Thus the Congregation seems to be applying Murphy's Law: if something in Sobrino's writings can be read in a sense contrary to the faith, whether or not the author intended that sense or the context warrants it, it will be.

When it comes to specifics, the CDF groups its concerns under six headings, proposing that defects in Sobrino's methodology generate problems regarding Christ's divinity, the incarnation, Jesus' relation to the kingdom of God, Jesus' self-consciousness, and the salvific value of Jesus' death. We can glean from each of these headings the point of authentic Catholic faith the CDF finds at risk in Sobrino's theology—or, in several instances, the point at which Sobrino's Christology differs from the scholastic paradigm.

## Methodology

The CDF affirms that Christology must be founded on the faith of the church and that it must accord normative status to the New Testament and to the teachings of the great councils. Sobrino is faulted on both counts. With regard to the first, writing from Latin America, Sobrino insists the church of the poor should be *the* ecclesial setting of Christology. Not so, rejoins the CDF: the proper ecclesial foundation of theology is constituted by the apostolic faith transmitted through time by the church. Sobrino would privilege a particular experience, namely, that of the poor, over "the experience of the church herself."

We may observe, however, that a setting is one thing, a foundation another. Given this distinction, a passage from an earlier Instruction that the Congregation cites in its explanatory note becomes significant. The Congregation recalls that in an earlier Instruction it had recognized that "a theological reflection developed from a particular experience can constitute a very positive contribution, inasmuch as it makes possible a highlighting of aspects of the Word of God, the richness of which had not yet been fully grasped." If one moves beyond isolated, decontextualized statements to the fuller context of Sobrino's actual work, one may find that, ironically, this passage from *Libertatis conscientia* admirably captures the intent of his project. Sobrino has more than once acknowledged the particularity of the experience that animates his project, the dire poverty and violent oppression so massively evident in Latin America.[7] He envisages liberation theology as a contribution to the faith of the universal church, and he recognizes the validity and necessity of other projects as well.[8] While he insists on the church of the poor as the ecclesial setting of his theology, what is received in that setting as the foundation of his theology is the apostolic faith of the church.

As for the New Testament and the councils, according to the Notification Sobrino fails to pay due heed to what they affirm. Of particular concern to the CDF is his treatment of the councils. While Sobrino acknowledges that the dogmatic formulations of the councils are both useful and normative, he also deems them conditioned by the cultural context from which they emerged. Conditioning is one thing, but the CDF ups the ante when it charges that Sobrino does not "recognize in them any value except in the cultural milieu in which these formulations were developed." The cultural milieu in question is the Hellenistic culture of the Roman Empire and its tradition of philosophic reflection. With its charge the CDF is identifying Sobrino with a position advanced by German liberal Protestant scholars in the nineteenth and early twentieth centuries. For Adolf von Harnack (1851-1930) and others, classic metaphysical dogmas such as Christ's consubstantiality with the Father (Nicaea, 325) and the hypostatic union of his divine and human natures in his one person (Chalcedon, 451) represent outmoded monuments of a past cultural moment with no claim on faith in the present.[9] The CDF demurs: the "Councils do not signify a hellenization of Christianity but rather the contrary." True, but the charge against Sobrino is puzzling. He explicitly affirms the same thing as the Congregation. He does not advocate but rejects Harnack's Hellenization thesis.[10]

The CDF also takes Sobrino to task for characterizing the classic dogmas as not only limited but also dangerous. This may seem odd. It is important to remember, however, that Sobrino's critique of these classic formulations is best understood in the context of his observation of oligarchic military types in Latin America who could dutifully shepherd their families to Sunday Mass and recite the creed, all the while violently repressing any threat to the hegemony that assured their wealth and status. Sobrino's concern is that the emphasis placed on the dogmas that clarify Christ's metaphysical constitution has fostered neglect of the empowering Gospel narratives of Christ's life, death, and resurrection.[11] Surely the standard neoscholastic tract in Christology that dominated seminary education a generation or two ago validates this concern.[12] Dealing with Christ's humanity under the rubric of a complete human nature, it said nothing about the manner of his life or how it issued in his execution. The resurrection, in turn, was relegated to the course in apologetics. Hence Sobrino's concern. In Latin America, taken in isolation from the church of the poor and from the Gospel narratives, the recitation of dogmas about Christ's divine status, person, and natures risks muting the prophetic-critical voice of Christian discipleship.

### Divinity of Jesus Christ, the Son of God Incarnate

For Sobrino the New Testament plants the seed that will produce the confession of Jesus' divinity in the strict sense, but it does not offer a formal definition of Jesus' divinity. The CDF, to the contrary, thinks the New Testament contains more than a seed. The Congregation's concern is that Sobrino's view of the historical development of dogma leaves room for suspicion that that development was not clearly continuous with the New Testament. In this regard, the Congregation contests Sobrino's reading of two New Testament texts (John 1:1 and 20:28), asserting that both plainly affirm Jesus' divinity. Without such unambiguous verbal clarity, the Congregation appears to think, the conviction that Jesus' divinity belonged to the faith of the church from the beginning would be jeopardized.

Regarding the incarnation, the Notification identifies passages in Sobrino's writing that, if read literally, would imply that the Son of God is one person and Jesus another, thus denying the unity of person affirmed by the councils at Ephesus (431) and Chalcedon. At the same time, the Congregation does not insist that Sobrino *should* be read as saying this, nor does his text support such a reading. Rather, the opposite is the case.[13] In a second, related point, the CDF faults Sobrino's presentation of what is known as the *communicatio idiomatum*. According to this ancient rule for christological discourse, because of the unity of Christ's person, human properties can be attributed to the divine; one can say, for example, that the second person of the Trinity suffered. The reverse also holds, so that it is permissible to say that the Son of Mary is the Word through whom all things are created—the point of the *Theotokos* controversy that led to

Nestorius's downfall. According to the Notification, Sobrino violates this logic when he writes that "the limited human is predicated of God, but the unlimited divine is not predicated of Jesus." Perhaps. But the latter phrase might also safeguard against the ancient heresy of docetism, which imagined Jesus as an omnipotent, omniscient divine person merely parading on earth in human form.

### Jesus and the Kingdom of God

The CDF judges Sobrino's views on this topic "peculiar." Although Sobrino affirms that in Jesus "the definitive, ultimate, and eschatological mediator of the Kingdom of God has already appeared," that is not sufficient for the CDF. (For Karl Rahner, one recalls, the acknowledgment of Jesus as eschatological prophet already contained all that the classic christological dogmas affirm.[14]) Why not? First, the inseparability of Jesus and the kingdom is inadequately articulated. Perhaps on this point the CDF is anxiously looking beyond Sobrino to some Asian theologians who, in an interreligious context, subordinate the church to the kingdom.[15] Second, Sobrino is faulted for affirming that Christ's human activity enables him to mediate the kingdom and therefore "excludes the fact that his condition as Son of God has relevance for Jesus' mediatory mission." Sobrino may not state the latter fact, but does his silence amount to denial? Aquinas, of course, likewise taught that it was in his humanity that Christ exercised the role of mediator of salvation.[16] Is the CDF over-reading Sobrino in this regard?

### Jesus' Self-Consciousness

Sobrino appeals to Heb 1:12 in order to attribute a human, if exemplary, faith to Jesus. On the contrary, writes the CDF, Scripture clearly teaches that Jesus enjoyed "an intimate and immediate knowledge of his Father." Jesus' enjoyment of the beatific vision, the Congregation explains, is a necessary consequence of the hypostatic union. In addition to this knowledge of the Father, Jesus' mission also required that he know the Father's plan of salvation. Hence Jesus cannot be said to be a believer like us. His consciousness was filial and messianic.

With this riposte the CDF is wading into a contemporary theological discussion in which not only Sobrino but far less controversial authors such as Gerald O'Collins, S.J., former dean of the Gregorianum, espouse the notion of Jesus' human faith.[17] At issue is the scholastic doctrine of the triple human knowledge attributed to Christ. Medieval theologians taught that from the first moment of his conception Jesus enjoyed both the beatific vision and specially infused knowledge that brought his human faculty of intellect to perfection.

Aquinas's contemporaries denied that Christ acquired ordinary human knowledge in the ordinary human way, over time and by means of natural perception—given those first two kinds of knowledge, this would be superfluous. Only Aquinas posited that Christ also possessed this third kind of knowledge, a position he came to embrace late in his career, and his thought on the matter became standard in scholastic theology. Thus, the doctrine of Christ's threefold human knowledge.

It is noteworthy that, today, Jean-Pierre Torrell, O.P., the leading contemporary exponent of Aquinas's Christology, takes issue with Aquinas's doctrine of Christ's triple human knowledge. For Torrell, by ascribing the beatific vision to Jesus during his lifetime and indeed from the first moment of his conception, Aquinas came close to transgressing the forceful teaching of the Council of Chalcedon that in his humanity, Jesus was "like us in all things except sin." For this and other reasons the scholastic doctrine has been undergoing reinterpretation among some theologians, while others have simply discarded it.[18]

## The Salvific Value of Jesus' Death

Two issues come into play on this topic. First, did Jesus attribute salvific value to his own death, or was that a discernment of the post-Easter community? The Notification introduces the topic cautiously: "In some texts some assertions of Father Sobrino make one think that, for him, Jesus did not attribute a salvific value to his death." Given the forthrightness of the citations from Sobrino it goes on to proffer, the Congregation's caution would seem unnecessary. Sobrino writes, "Let it be said from the outset that Jesus did not interpret his death in terms of salvation, in terms of the soteriological models later developed by the New Testament. . . ." More generally, he continues, "there are absolutely no grounds for thinking that Jesus attributed an absolute transcendent meaning to his own death, as the New Testament did later."[19] Sobrino's position on this first issue, then, is clear. The soteriological interpretation of Jesus' death derives from the post-paschal Christian community, not directly from Jesus himself. Like Edward Schillebeeckx, Sobrino thinks that Jesus went to his death confidently and as a service for others,[20] an effective example of complete fidelity as the key to true humanity.

The CDF finds this unsatisfactory: Sobrino's position deprives the New Testament affirmations of the salvific value of Jesus' death "of any reference to the consciousness of Christ during his earthly life." This may be true, but its problematic status is not self-evident. Sobrino's position can find reputable exegetical support, and of itself, it is but one instance of the kind of development uncovered in a genetic, historical-critical analysis of the faith articulated in the New Testament. Sobrino's position does, however, conflict with the scholastic thesis that Jesus was specially endowed in his humanity with clear knowledge of his redemptive mission on earth. This would open him to the charge leveled by the CDF of allowing a hypothetical reconstruction of the historical Jesus, deemed erroneous by the CDF, to trump the New Testament data.

Walter Kasper once voiced a concern similar to that of the CDF, fearing that "if the interpretation of Jesus' death as an expiatory surrender to God for men could not be supported at all by reference to the life and death of Jesus himself, the core of Christian faith would come dangerously close to mythology and false ideology."[21] In response he mounted a sophisticated, three-pronged argument, appealing to Albert Schweitzer for a link between the coming of the kingdom and the final trials to place Jesus' passion, for Jesus and his followers, in an eschatological perspective. Kasper adds to this the notions, adduced as well by Sobrino, that Jesus considered his death a service for others and that Jesus persisted in faith (itself an idea rejected by the CDF) and obedience even in the loneliness and darkness of that death. All this supplies Kasper with the point of reference to Jesus' life and death that he requires to establish continuity with the core of Christian faith, allowing him to conclude that Jesus enacted an implicit soteriology. The CDF, by contrast, would seem to simply beg the question when it contents itself with a general appeal to the New Testament data. Data, as such, do not speak for themselves.

Distinct from the issue of the origin of soteriology is the question of how Jesus brought about salvation. The CDF finds that Sobrino's account reduces the redemption to moralism, a matter of "good example." Traditional scholastic theology described the salvific efficacy of Christ's passion in terms of merit, satisfaction, ransom, sacrifice, and instrumental efficient causality. Here, the Congregation observes, by concentrating on Jesus' exemplarity, Sobrino fails to reflect the teachings of the Council of Trent, Vatican II, the *Catechism of the Catholic Church*, and John Paul II, all of which affirm one or more of those further modes. The reason for this failure? It lies, the Congregation suggests, in Sobrino's neglect of Jesus' divine identity.

In Sobrino's construal, however, the notion of exemplarity achieves a density and complexity that distinguish it from simple good example and that offer points of contact with the older tradition. "Actio Christi est nostra instructio" served as a commanding axiom of Aquinas's theology of the mysteries of the life of Christ[22] and a major element in his understanding of Christ's mission to reveal the truth about God and humankind. When Sobrino focuses on Jesus' revelation of authentic humanity, the *homo verus*, as itself redemptive,[23] he also stands in the tradition of those fathers for whom *mimesis* of Christ the Pedagogue entailed *methexis*, transformative participation in and restoration of the archetypal image of God.[24] Furthermore, Sobrino discerns God's initiative behind Jesus' exemplary life and death, so that through the gift of that humanity it is God's love that comes to expression.[25] In a similar vein, Sobrino appropriates Rahner's construal of the relation between Jesus' exemplary humanity and his divinity as sacramental, so that Jesus is seen in his humanity as the real symbol of the Word.[26] Finally, when Sobrino writes that what pleased God about the cross was the fullness of love it enacted, he captures the substance of the traditional category of satisfaction without using the term.[27] In all of this, it seems, he clearly transcends mere moralism.

Perhaps at this point one can discern a pattern running through the Notification. The CDF takes its review of Sobrino as an opportunity to reaffirm the faith of the church as expressed in the New Testament and the classical councils, that Jesus Christ is the Son of God incarnate who through his cross fulfilled God's plan for our salvation. At the same time the Congregation propounds an understanding of that faith centered on the dogma of the hypostatic union and articulated in classic scholastic theology. The latter deduced from the hypostatic union Christ's enjoyment of the beatific vision from the first moment of his conception and his possession of special, infused knowledge equipping him for his revelatory and redemptive mission. On this basis it denied the possibility that Christ, simultaneously *comprehensor* and *viator,* was endowed with and exercised the virtue of faith. In Christ's passion, scholastic theology found that the love and obedience with which the Word Incarnate took on suffering and death, the penalties of original sin, rendered his suffering meritorious and superabundantly satisfactory, and so, metaphorically, a ransom and sacrifice. In God's providence Christ's passion was thus constituted the instrumental efficient cause through which God brought about the salvation of humankind from sin. Reading Sobrino from this perspective, the Notification finds Sobrino's account of the development of conciliar dogma and of its relation to the New Testament, his expression of the unity of Christ's person, his wielding of the *communicatio idiomatum,* his construal of the relationship between Jesus and the kingdom he proclaimed, his attribution of faith to Jesus, and his emphasis on the sacramental, revelatory exemplarity of Jesus' life and death problematic.

Sobrino can, however, be read from a different perspective. While scholastic Christology, fundamentally a metaphysically informed reflection on the dogmatic teaching of the Council of Chalcedon, once held the field, the past thirty years have been witnessing the emergence of a different paradigm among Catholic theologians. Christology from this more recent perspective involves more than a systematic understanding of classical conciliar dogma. That task remains, but as one moment within a broader project that seeks to shed the light of faith on a comprehensive genetic and dialectical account of the origin and development of the church's beliefs about Jesus with a view to bringing his revelatory and redemptive significance to bear on the present. Sobrino's work finds its home within this context.

On this account it seems to me that on those issues on which the Congregation pinpoints substantive differences and real oppositions between Sobrino and the positions it espouses, those differences remain within the realm of legitimate theological inquiry and debate, with Sobrino standing well within the mainstream of reputable contemporary theologians on matters such as Jesus' consciousness and faith. Perhaps one may take the Congregation's failure to conclude its Notification with a sanction as acknowledgment that this is the case.

## Notes

1. Jon Sobrino, *Jesus the Liberator: A Historical-Theological View*, trans. Paul Burns and Francis McDonagh (Maryknoll, N.Y.: Orbis Books, 1993).
2. Jon Sobrino, *Christ the Liberator*, trans. Paul Burns (Maryknoll, N.Y.: Orbis Books, 2001).
3. William Loewe, review of Jon Sobrino, *Christology at the Crossroads: A Latin American Approach*, trans. John Drury (Maryknoll, N.Y.: Orbis Books, 1978), *America* 139 (July 19-Aug. 5, 1978): 66-67.
4. Compare *Christology at the Crossroads,* 217-19, with *Jesus the Liberator,* 235-46.
5. John P. Meier, "Jesus among the Theologians II. Sobrino and Segundo," in idem, *The Mission of Christ and His Church: Studies in Christology and Ecclesiology* (Wilmington, Del.: Michael Glazier, 1990), 49-69.
6. The pope focuses the first seven chapters of his recent essay on Jesus of Nazareth largely on the Synoptics. In his account "the Jesus of the Fourth Gospel and the Jesus of the Synoptics is one and the same: the true 'historical Jesus.'" See Benedict XVI, *Jesus of Nazareth: From the Baptism in the Jordan to the Transfiguration*, trans. Adrian J. Walker (New York: Doubleday, 2007), 111. This is, of course, true, but it ought not be taken to preclude questions about the historicity of the Gospel narratives.
7. For example, *Jesus the Liberator,* 22. See also *Christ the Liberator*, 4: "the 'from where' of this book is a *partial, definite, and concerned* viewpoint: the victims of this world."
8. So, for example, Sobrino acknowledges the Christologies "now arising from indigenous and African-American contexts, from gender and ecological concerns, and from interfaith dialogue . . . as both necessary and positive" (*Christ the Liberator*, 2).
9. Adolf von Harnack, *What Is Christianity?* trans. Thomas Bailey Saunders (New York/Evanston: Harper & Row, 1957).
10. Sobrino twice characterizes the Hellenization thesis as "spurious" (*Christ the Liberator*, 173, 223) and grants that Nicaea "worked a real de-Hellenizing" (*Christ the Liberator,* 261; see also 268).
11. *Christ the Liberator,* 242-43.
12. See, for example, the widely used Patres Societatis Iesu Facultatum Theologicarum in Hispania Professores, *Sacrae Theologiae Summa III: De Verbo Incarnato, Mariologia, De Gratia, De Virtutibus* (Madrid: Biblioteca de Autores Cristianos, 1956).
13. *Christ the Liberator,* 300, 321.
14. Karl Rahner, *Foundations of Christian Faith: An Introduction to the Idea of Christianity*, trans. William V. Dych (New York: Seabury, 1978), 250-54, 298-300.
15. See, for example, Michael Amaladoss, *Life in Freedom: Liberation Theologies from Asia* (Maryknoll, N.Y.: Orbis Books, 1997), 141-42.
16. Thomas Aquinas, *Summa theologiae* III.26.2: "Utrum Christus secundum quod homo sit mediator Dei et hominum."
17. Gerald O'Collins, *Christology: A Biblical, Historical, and Systematic Study of Jesus* (New York: Oxford University Press, 1995), 250-68. Sobrino himself cites K. Rahner, H. Urs von Balthasar, and W. Thüsing. See *Jesus the Liberator,* 155 and 291, notes 48, 49, 50.

18. Jean-Pierre Torrell, *Le Christ en ses mystères: la vie et l'oeuvre de Jésus selon saint Thomas d'Aquin* I (Paris, Desclée, 1999), 135-48.

19. *Jesus the Liberator,* 201.

20. Edward Schillebeeckx, *Jesus: An Experiment in Christology,* trans. Hubert Hoskins (New York: Seabury, 1979), 298-312.

21. Walter Kasper, *Jesus the Christ,* trans. V. Green (London: Burns & Oates/New York: Paulist, 1976), 119.

22. Thomas Aquinas, *Summa theologiae* III.40.1. ad 3um.

23. *Christ the Liberator,* 223.

24. On *paideia* as unifying background for patristic soteriological motifs, see Gisbert Greshake, "Der Wandel der Erlösungsvorstellungen in der Theologiegeschichte," in *Erlösung und Emanzipation,* ed. Leo Scheffcyk. Quaestiones Disputatae 61 (Freiberg/Basel: Herder, 1973), 69-89.

25. *Jesus the Liberator,* 230-31.

26. *Christ the Liberator,* 317-21.

27. *Jesus the Liberator, 228.* For Aquinas, love and obedience constitute the formal element in satisfaction, suffering the material element, *Summa theologiae* III.14.1. ad 1um.

# PART III

*The Church and Ecclesiology*

12

# A Church Rooted in Mercy
*Ecclesial Signposts in Sobrino's Theology*

## Thomas M. Kelly

Several churches were destroyed in the earthquake, among them the church of El Carmen, in Santa Tecla where I live. Sorrowfully the people told their parish priest, "Father, we have been left without a church." And the priest, Salvador Carranza, who came to El Salvador from Burgos, Spain, more than forty years ago replied, "We have been left without a church, but not without a Church. We are the Church, and the Church depends on us to keep it alive."[1]

In his book *The True Church and the Poor,* Jon Sobrino identifies his efforts as "not so much an ecclesiology as it is a theological reflection on the very basis of the Church. On this basis an ecclesiology may then be developed."[2] To the best of my knowledge, Sobrino has never written a full-fledged ecclesiology, that is, "a systematic reflection on all that the Church is and ought to be."[3] For this reason, one may select certain themes from his writings, but no formal ecclesiology can be accessed. This does not mean that certain ecclesial themes are inaccessible in his works—in fact, they abound. There are many ways to elucidate what is most important in the ecclesial thought of a theologian. One can use "models" of the church or reflections on ecclesial themes, such as teaching authority, church polity, or church structure. For the purpose of this chapter, none of these methods are entirely satisfactory for they unnecessarily limit an overview of how Sobrino understands the mission of the church.

Because of the lack of a fully developed ecclesiology, as well as the great variety of works written by Sobrino, I have chosen to highlight certain ecclesial themes that appear again and again in his works. These themes are gleaned from works that treat subjects as varied as people, doctrines, and events. Throughout these works, certain ecclesial themes important to Sobrino continually emerge. These are the following: (1) the church must always be contextually "merciful"; (2) the church that is "merciful" practices a certain mutuality by listening to its people and responding to their needs; (3) the church that practices such mercy and mutuality serves the coming of the kingdom of God as well as those for whom the kingdom is primarily intended. One can determine whether these principles are most important for Sobrino's understanding of the church through a brief analysis of their presence in the second pastoral letter of Archbishop Oscar Romero. This letter, which Sobrino authored, was addressed to the church of El Salvador at the beginning of the country's civil war (1980). It will become clear throughout this chapter, that the christological and ministerial experiences of Archbishop Romero are critically important for how Jon Sobrino understands the mission of the church.

### The Church: Mercy in Context

> People begin to talk about liberation where oppression is blatant. Not only this: it is in this setting and not in any other that liberation becomes a theological datum in the strict sense and as such is rediscovered in revelation. "A sign of the times," in the strict sense—which I shall explain later—was what Ellacuría called it.[4]

One's setting is crucial for how revelation is received. It deeply affects what one chooses to emphasize or de-emphasize and how one appropriates what is most important from the Gospels. According to Sobrino, starting points for Christology, including those he would identify as "alienating," emerge from different readings of revelation, "and the fundamental reason for the different readings was the place from which they were made."[5]

For Sobrino, the fact that "God's order of creation" has been "threatened, debased, and repudiated" is a fact that conditions how revelation is received and understood.[6] This realization that certain historical realities ought to shape how we understand revelation is what the Second Vatican Council identified as the "signs of the times." For Sobrino, the phrase "signs of the times" has two meanings, and these meanings are central for "determining the mission of the church." The first meaning is that some signs of the times have a "historical-pastoral" meaning. They are events "which characterize a period."[7] This refers to the particular historical data to which the church must respond if it is to be pastorally effective.[8] The second meaning is "historical-theologal." These signs are "happenings, needs and desires . . . authentic signs of God's presence and purpose."[9] While this second meaning includes historical data like the first, it also includes the need for interpretation; "God's presence or purpose has to be discerned in them."[10] For this reason, the second meaning of "signs of the times" is "its ability to manifest God in the present." This occurred in Latin America, according to Sobrino, through the Latin American Episcopal Conferences at Medellín (1968) and Puebla (1979), which finally reflected the bishops' own contexts in light of revelation.

What emerged was a mission for the church, in a particular context, that mirrored the practice of Jesus. "Before all else, a true church is a church 'like unto Jesus.'"[11] The primary ecclesiological question for Sobrino is: "What is a church that resembles Jesus?"[12] By taking this point of departure for his understanding of church, it is clear that no church exists in and of itself—nor by itself—but only in reference to its founder and its context. Surely few would disagree. What becomes contentious is which aspect of the founder is emphasized and how a church responds to its own particular context. Throughout his theological works, Sobrino emphasizes two aspects of the life and work of Jesus Christ. The first is Christ's incarnation, "becoming real flesh in real history"; the second is his inaugurating the kingdom or "reign" of God. How did God incarnate God's self into "real" history and how did God inaugurate this "Reign" of God? For Sobrino, both occur in relation to the principle of mercy, specifically in how Jesus of Nazareth chose to bear sin against those who were most vulnerable—the sociologically and economically poor.

Sobrino is very careful when using the term "mercy." He does not want it to be confused with a simple response to immediate needs without a confrontation with the structures that produced those needs. For this reason he uses terms in other works such as "prophetic praxis," "messianic praxis," or "practice in spirit."[13] He defines Jesus' "practice" as "the broad sweep of his activities in the service of the Kingdom."[14] In order to argue for a particular mission of the church, one must model one's vision of church on those aspects of the founder one deems most important. Sobrino knows that where this is done integrally relates to how it is done.

While Sobrino could have argued from any Gospel to try to understand the motive or basis for Jesus' actions, he begins his reflection on "mercy" with the Hebrew Scriptures and the beginning of the salvific process. If one takes a step back and looks at the ancient world with its well-developed empires and impressive civilizations, it is noteworthy that God chose to be in relationship with an enslaved people. Surely this choice of people had something to do with God's compassion. Sobrino begins with this movement of God into human history when arguing for which aspect of Jesus' life and ministry to emphasize: "I have witnessed the affliction of my people in Egypt and have heard their cry of complaint against their slave drivers, so I know well what they are suffering. Therefore I have come down to rescue them."[15]

God's listening to the suffering of people in a particular context and God's liberative response to that suffering is an *action,* one that Sobrino wishes to describe with the term "mercy." It ought to be the determining characteristic of the contemporary church. He argues this by highlighting, within the New Testament, those places where the "ideal" person is exemplified by Jesus—the Good Samaritan, the father in the story of the prodigal son, those healing and gathering food on the Sabbath, those exalted in the Beatitudes, the sheep of Matthew 25, and so on. In each and every instance, a person responds to the suffering of others through a humanizing action that has a living urgency. Such a human response is more important than the specifics of proper worship (why the priest and Levite crossed to the other side of the road in the story of the Good Samaritan) or the Law (why work is more important than the Law when people are hungry or sick). Sobrino makes it clear that while "Mercy is not the sole content of Jesus' practice . . . it is mercy that stands at the origin of all that he practices; it is mercy that shapes and molds his entire life, mission and fate."[16]

Because Sobrino's understanding of church emerges directly from his Christology, he argues that the church ought to embody, or incarnate, the mission that Jesus lived out and practiced during his earthly life, particularly the mission of mercy.

> It is this principle of mercy that ought to be operative in Jesus' church. And it is this *pathos* of mercy that ought to "inform" that church—give it its specificity, shape and mold it. In other words, the church, too even *qua* church, should reread the parable of the Good Samaritan and listen to it with the same rapt attention, and the same fear and trembling, with which Jesus' hearers first heard it. The church should be and do many other things, as well. But unless it is steeped—as a church at once Christian and human—in the mercy of the parable of the Good Samaritan, unless the church is the Good Samaritan before all else, all else will be irrelevant— even dangerous, should it succeed in passing for its fundamental principle.[17]

With this theme firmly articulated, the church can now respond to the particular place it finds itself in the "world." Thus, the church's context becomes critical, and the church must be seriously engaged beyond the regulation, oversight, and verification of its own internal life. It must, instead, focus outward on the "wounded one lying in the ditch along the roadside."[18] This outward focus will, in turn, have profound consequences on the internal workings of the church and the mercy it extends to its own broken members.

In all of this it is important that the church neither spiritualize nor universalize this principle of mercy out of any actual relevance. Yes, the church has always encouraged works of mercy, and yes, there is suffering in every community. But some suffering is primary, namely, the dehumanizing poverty that kills the human spirit, body, and communities in two-thirds of the world today. Making an option for those suffering may even put the church at odds with its own "self-interest" narrowly construed. If the church is actually "governed" by the principle of mercy, it will not only treat symptoms but also unmask causes. This may bring persecution down upon it. Mercy without some form of persecution points to "works" of mercy disconnected from one's context. Thus, "mercy" requires not just the constructive work for the kingdom, the messianic voice, but confrontation with the anti-kingdom, the prophetic voice.

It should be evident from this brief presentation of "mercy" and its constitutive role in the mission of the church that some forms of ecclesiality, of being church, are more fundamental than others. Sobrino indicates this when he makes a distinction between primary and secondary ecclesiality. Secondary ecclesiality considers the church as an institution, as a "guardian of the deposit of faith and ultimate guarantor of truth."[19] While this is important, even necessary, for the survival and flourishing of the historical institution, it presupposes something else. Sobrino calls this something else "primary ecclesiality," namely, "the community's act of faith in Christ and the presentation of Christ in history in his dimension as head of a body that is the church."[20] This "discipleship enacted," when "real faith, hope and charity are put into practice" is fundamentally "church."[21] Without primary ecclesiality, secondary ecclesiality would have little reason to preserve the deposit of faith.

The church of El Salvador as it was led by Archbishop Oscar Romero was the epitome of a church governed by mercy. Because of this mercy, it too shared in the primary ecclesiality of parishes throughout El Salvador. Far from being opposed to the institutional church, Sobrino's hope for the church repeatedly draws on Archbishop Romero as a symbol of true ecclesial leadership who based his ministry on mercy and put the institution in service of the kingdom of God. What made such service possible was an ecclesiality of mutuality embodied by Romero. It would not be too strong to say that for Sobrino, Romero and his ministry were a sign of the times in the second (theologal) sense. Romero's ministry certainly embodied the second theme we will consider here—mutuality.

## The Church and Mutuality

> In all sincerity, and with all gratitude, I must acknowledge that Archbishop Romero's life, work, and word—a word spoken from deep within that life and that work—have been my theological light and inspiration. I do not think that, without Archbishop Romero, I could ever have achieved a satisfactory theological formulation of things as basic as the mystery of God, the church of the poor, hope, martyrdom, Christian fellowship, the essence of the Gospel as good news, or even Jesus Christ, whose three years of life and mission, cross and resurrection, have now been illuminated for me by Archbishop Romero's three years as Archbishop.[22]

A second important ecclesial theme in Sobrino's written work is his insistence that the church operate from a posture of humility and openness made manifest in mutuality. This is especially true of its leadership. Perhaps this theme results from a theologian coming of age between Medellín and Puebla, episcopal conferences that were both generally accepted and decisive for the Latin

American church. The tone of humility on the part of the bishops of Latin America and their desired connection to their peoples are obvious in both groundbreaking documents. At the beginning of the Medellín document they write: "We wish to *feel* the problems, *perceive* the demands, *share* the agonies, *discover* the ways and *cooperate* in the solutions."[23] This continues as they explain that they do not possess "technical solutions or infallible remedies" but wish to accompany all those public and political actors who promote the common good. This tone is further evident in the section titled "Commitments of the Latin American Church," where the bishops state their desire to "live a true scriptural poverty expressed in authentic manifestations that may be clear signs for our peoples," "create new structures in the church," and even to "cooperate with other Christian confessions."[24] The documents of Puebla contain similar language, and it is well known from various biographies of Romero that while he initially resisted the conclusions of Medellín, he eventually not only accepted them but lived them to their fullest.

The mutuality that determined the ministry and vision of Romero can be summed up by the fact that he truly listened to the people for whom he had pastoral responsibility. Many in El Salvador today will argue that this listening was essential to his "conversion" following the death of Rutilio Grande in 1977. It was also essential for the development of his own option for the poor, one that for him "was an ecclesiological principle, as well, since he erected this option into the criterion of all of the activity of the church."[25] In this listening and learning, he did no more than be faithful to the teachings of the Second Vatican Council.

> Faith has to be communal because the church is a reality in process. It is essential to the church to be on pilgrimage, a description Vatican II legitimized in the term "people of God," and this pilgrimage includes action of rethinking its faith throughout history, learning to learn.[26]

It is astonishing when one reads the diary of Romero how many groups and individuals he consulted on a daily basis in the course of his work.[27] While this is normal for any archbishop, the fact that *campesinos* (those from the lowest economic strata in El Salvador) had nearly unfettered access to him was highly unusual.[28] Romero routinely met with the poorest members of the church, consulted with them, and, at times, apologized to them. Dean Brackley, a New York Jesuit who went to El Salvador shortly after the death of the six Jesuits, their housekeeper, and her daughter at the University of Central America in 1989, remarks on the style of Romero's ministry:

> As for Romero, at the beginning of his ministry as archbishop, what most impressed many were his frequent appeals for help and advice. Simple poor people treasure the memory of the archbishop explaining a problem for

them and asking their personal opinion. Each week a team of advisors helped Romero prepare his Sunday homily. His pastoral letters involved countless meetings and rewritings. For the fourth letter, and also in preparation for the Puebla Conference, he used a written questionnaire to solicit opinions throughout the archdiocese.[29]

It is possible that Romero learned this art of listening from Rutilio Grande, one of the first priests and Jesuits to be murdered in El Salvador. Wherever it came from, the mutuality that marked Romero's leadership style was necessary for a church mission centered on "mercy" as defined by Sobrino. This mutuality, for Romero, was essential for a church that embraced an option for those most vulnerable, an option that would have been impossible without a relationship to these people. This set Romero apart from many other archbishops, both then and now. "He let himself be loved, and this is the most radical way to span distances and burst boundaries, which always exist between those of high and low estate."[30]

This spanning of distances is important if the institutional church is to penetrate and accompany Christian communities in its jurisdiction. Romero's efforts to encounter and be in relationship with his people abound throughout his diaries. "I also talked with groups from ecclesial base communities and with the sewing academy that is producing much fruit there in San Rafael Cedros."[31] "Among the visits, I had one from some poor workers or peasants from La Unión in the diocese of San Miguel. One of them had marks of the torture to which he had been subjected. . . ."[32] "After Mass I received many visits from people from the villages, who always are anxious to speak even briefly with their bishop."[33] Ultimately the purpose of this interaction was to learn the situation of the people, especially the poor. This was necessary because the church guided by Romero saw itself in service to something greater than itself, namely, the kingdom of God. When one orients the church toward the kingdom, the poor take center stage, and the church is judged "faithful" only insofar as it facilitates the acceptance of this kingdom among both rich and poor.

## The Church and the Kingdom of God

The kingdom of God is at the heart of Sobrino's Christology as well as of his understanding of the mission of the church. A brief overview of the place of the kingdom in his Christology will allow for a better understanding of its relation to the mission of the church. One way he articulates this is through a reflection on Romero's ministry.

In the fourth chapter of *Jesus the Liberator*, Sobrino argues that final reality for Jesus is the unity of two realities, (1) "a God who gives Himself to history" and (2) "a history that comes according to God."[34] This dual unity is how

Jesus understood the kingdom of God and what he preached, but because Jesus never clearly defined what the kingdom of God constitutes, Sobrino tries to access its meaning through three distinct methods of inquiry: the notional way, the way of addressee, and the way of practice. While Western theology in general has used the notional way, and occasionally the way of practice, it has generally not used the way of addressee. A brief look at each method offers a more complete understanding of how Sobrino determines both what the kingdom of God is and what the church's relation to it should be today.

The notional way compares Jesus' notion of the kingdom of God with earlier ideas from his own Hebraic tradition. According to this method, the kingship of God in the Hebrew Scriptures was made manifest in God's capacity to intervene in history. Following the failure of the monarchy, a clearer idea of the "hoped-for reign of God" emerged, a future kingdom of justice for the people of Israel. This kingdom had two essential dimensions, "God rules in his acts," and the kingdom exists "in order to transform a bad and unjust historical-social reality into a different and good one."[35] Thus, "God's reign is the positive action through which God transforms reality and God's 'Kingdom' is what comes to pass in this world when God truly reigns: a history, a society, a people transformed according to the will of God."[36] Because this kingdom exists in order to transform, it arrives in conflict with what went before it—the order of society that existed contrary to God's will. For this reason, the kingdom of God is "a dialectical and conflictual reality, excluding and opposing the anti-Kingdom."[37]

> To sum up, the Kingdom of God is a utopia that answers the age-old hope of a people in the midst of historical calamities; it is, then, what is good and wholly good. But it is also something liberating, since it arrives in the midst of and in opposition to the oppression of the anti-Kingdom.[38]

The way of addressee argues that if "Jesus' proclamation shows a correlation between the Kingdom and his audience, then the latter can tell us something about the former."[39] Thus, for example, the term "good news" is relational—the audience for such a term knows in what way and to what degree it is "good." If the kingdom of God is the "good news" that Jesus proclaimed repeatedly, "its recipients will help fundamentally in clarifying its content."[40] Jesus addressed the poor not exclusively but primarily, and so Sobrino can say with the Latin American bishops at Puebla, "that by the mere fact of being poor, whatever the moral or personal situation in which they find themselves, God defends them, loves them, and they are the first ones to whom Jesus' mission is directed."[41] And though the First World has a tendency to spiritualize the poor to whom Jesus addresses his good news, Sobrino insists on taking the term as it appears in the Gospels, especially the Gospel of Luke. Using the biblical analysis of Joachim Jeremias, Sobrino understands the poor to be divided into two classes in the Synoptics. There are the economic poor, those "bent under the weight of a burden," and the sociological poor, those "whose religious ignorance and moral behavior closed, in the conviction of the time, the gate leading to salvation for them."[42] The first group physically suffers from the burden of living, while the second is denied the human relationships necessary for human dignity. Often these types of poverty go together in human history and it was to these:

> ... Jesus showed undoubted partiality so that what is now called the option for the poor can be said to start with him (though it goes back before him to the prophets, and indeed to God himself): partiality toward the economic poor, as shown in the beatitudes in Luke, and partiality toward the sociological poor, as shown in his standing up for publicans and sinners expressed with even more force, perhaps, than the former, precisely because their alienation on religious grounds was more provocative to him.[43]

According to Sobrino, the Synoptics speak of the poor in the plural, not simply as isolated individuals. Moreover, they speak of the poor "dialectically." That is, the people are poor in relation to someone else and possibly as a result of someone else; they are not poor in and of themselves but due to an "unjust state of oppression."[44]

For all these reasons, the way of addressee can reveal that both economic and sociological poverty are contrary to the will of God. There is a preference for those who materially suffer from oppression, and the kingdom is "good news" only insofar as it brings about their liberation. "Good news" is constituted not merely by words but by actions that result in a changed reality for those who suffer.

The way of practice understands Jesus' practice "in the broad sense of his words and actions—on the basis that what Jesus said and did was in the service of proclaiming the Kingdom of God."[45] In a general sense this method asks why Jesus did anything for the coming of the kingdom and how he did it. It is clear from the New Testament that Jesus is both the proclaimer and initiator of the kingdom. The term "kingdom," therefore, is not only one with an intellectual "meaning"; it also has what Sobrino calls a "praxic" meaning as well. Meaning is discovered by doing.[46] Access to the practice of Jesus is available by looking at his miracles, his actions that cast out devils and welcomed sinners, as well as his words in parables and teachings. The practice of Jesus is characterized by compassion, a sharing in the suffering of those who were oppressed.[47] The miracles and works of mercy did not transform oppressive structures, but they pointed toward their resolution in the mercy of God. "The reality of the suffering of others is what affected Jesus most deeply and made him react with finality from the inmost depths of his being."[48]

This principle that defined the practice of Jesus along with the notional way and the way of addressee culminates with the following claim about the kingdom of God: "The Kingdom of God is coming for the poor and outcast; it is partial, and therefore causes scandal."[49] Those to whom Jesus addresses his message are clear on two aspects of this kingdom: first, they must be merciful to the needy, and second, they must do things for them. And Sobrino adds, "This is the first and last requirement of the Kingdom and everything depends on it, including final salvation."[50] Never missing an opportunity to apply his theology to the "real" world, Sobrino makes it clear that the importance of the kingdom of God should also define the mission of the church.

> And recalling this is still of supreme importance for the work of the church today. The church often carries out "works of mercy," but making pity for the suffering of the world the first and last criterion of its actions, which means not making itself the final criterion, and showing this in readiness to run grave risks in exercising pity, is very unusual. Personally, this is what most impressed me in Archbishop Romero.[51]

Sobrino believes that four principles guided Romero's judgment. These principles initially came out of Medellín, but they were concretely applied to El Salvador. The first principle is: "The church is not the same thing as the kingdom of God; it is the servant of the Kingdom."[52] This is a perfectly legitimate interpretation of Vatican II's *Lumen gentium*.[53] At the same time, there is enough ambiguity in an earlier section of *Lumen gentium* that seems to equate the church with the "kingdom of Christ" and with "the kingdom of heaven on earth" to create real controversy as to the nature of the relationship between church and kingdom of God.[54] Either way, according to Sobrino, Romero believed that to practice real love and justice in the real world would "enable the Kingdom to take concrete shape."[55]

The second principle is "The poor are those for whom the Kingdom is primarily intended."[56] This signifies for Sobrino that when the poor become agents of their own self-realization, they will have a part in building the kingdom; they will cooperate with God's grace to be in right relationship with God and one's neighbor.

The third principle states: "As the servant of the Kingdom, the church ought also to promote the values of the members of the Kingdom, both while the new society is being built up and when it is at length achieved."[57] This is in contrast to a church that makes every decision in terms of the preservation of its position and power in the world while those more vulnerable suffer from its complacence. Sobrino deeply believes that Romero put the suffering of the Salvadoran people first, and as a result brought about the persecution of the church and eventually his own death.

The fourth principle of Romero's judgment was that "For the church in any way to impede or thwart either the Kingdom of God or the members of the Kingdom is sinful."[58] This principle was applied not only to individual decisions but to structural realities as well. If, therefore, the church serves the kingdom, and the kingdom is primarily intended for the poor, the church ought to promote the values of the kingdom and never impede either the coming of the kingdom or its members. The relationship between kingdom and church is quite clear.

The overall trajectory of Sobrino's understanding of church is grounded on the three main ecclesial themes argued in this chapter: contextual mercy, mutuality, and a servant relationship to the kingdom of God. But how could one analyze the accuracy of this thesis? One method is to briefly and thematically analyze the second pastoral letter of Romero, written largely by Sobrino. This is a productive way to look for an application of these general themes based on his understanding of church.

### "The Church, the Body of Christ in History"[59]

A thematic analysis of Romero's second pastoral letter immediately reveals a concern for historical context and how the church will respond to it. Titled "The Church's Mission Today," this early section succinctly outlines topics such as "church and world," "in the world," "at the service of the world," "the unity of history," "the sin of the world," and "the need for conversion."

The beginning of this section is quite theological. Its goal is to situate the church within the world in general and by doing so, respond to the ecclesiological vision of those from within the archdiocese of San Salvador who oppose Romero's ministerial goals. It quickly moves to the particular manifestations of the church concretely active in the real world. Romero and Sobrino were responding to their context. They were writing specifically against what they perceived to be an outdated ecclesiology (still prevalent throughout Latin and North America) that sought to spiritualize the mission of the church. By that I mean there was a strong movement to disconnect the church from the social and political realities of the day. Throughout this section one sees references to *Gaudium et spes* and Medellín, writings from the institutional church that advocated a direct immersion of the church in the suffering of the world.[60] Sobrino maintains, "With these affirmations Medellín put an end to the secular dualism we had subscribed to, the dichotomy between the temporal and the eternal, between secular and the religious, between the world and God, between history and the church."[61] Toward the end of this section, one sees a hint of the ecclesial theme of mutuality as well. While discussing the need for conversion on the part of individuals, the letter also recognizes the church's need for conversion, and this conversion happens by being in relationship with the poor.

> The church has regained the basic attitude for conversion, which is to turn toward "those who are especially lowly, poor, and weak. Like Christ, we

should have pity on the multitudes weighed down with hunger, misery, and ignorance. We want to fix a steady gaze on those who still lack the help they need to achieve a way of life worthy of human beings."[62]

After a general overview of the relationship between the church and the world, the next section, titled "The Church, the Body of Christ in History," attempts to incarnate this ecclesial theme into the Salvadoran context. By advocating the church as the Body of Christ, the letter is able to make a Christocentric appeal to the mission the church ought to pursue. Thus, the letter addresses topics such as the "person of Christ," "Jesus proclaims the kingdom of God especially to the poor," "Jesus calls to conversion," "Jesus denounces sin," and most importantly "the church continues the work of Jesus." What one sees here is the identification of the church with a particular understanding of the ministry of Jesus which it should emulate. *Jesus the Liberator* has been summarized within an archdiocesan pastoral letter on the mission of the church.

The pastoral letter, to this point, has established that (1) the church ought to be deeply immersed and in service to the world and (2) that this mission is supposed to embody the mercy of Jesus and his proclamation of the kingdom of God. The third section focuses on how this becomes manifest specifically in the archdiocese of San Salvador. It does this by responding to three main accusations against itself; "the church preaches hatred and subversion; the church has become Marxist; and the church has overstepped the limits of its mission and is meddling in politics."[63] It is interesting to note that the pastoral letter has already answered these accusations in full, partly by responding to the outdated ecclesiology upon which they are based. But note what this final section reveals. Romero was deeply aware of those who were unhappy with the direction he was moving the Salvadoran church. He wants to reassure them, by explaining to them why he is doing what he is doing, and invite them to join the church in its mission.

The church neither hates the rich nor preaches violent revolution to the poor. It embraces everyone in the universal love taught by Jesus and modeled in his ministry. This love is extended to all but also generates the preferential option for the poor. This option is prophetic, direct, and unsettling for anyone like the rich young man, who chose to walk away after hearing the directive to sell all that he had, give it to the poor, and follow Jesus in his mission. The church has not become Marxist, but it has questioned an economy that requires the armed forces to defend the privileges of a small number of families who controlled the vast majority of wealth in the country. Finally, the church is not fielding candidates for office; it is helping to guide the direction of civil society. For this reason the letter can say with absolute conviction that the church "does not engage in party politics."[64] This does not mean it has nothing to say about social or political life.

Romero's second pastoral letter sought to define the mission of the church in the context of an increasingly violent country. It did so by articulating an understanding of the church with a mission of mercy in a context where it was dangerous to make an option for those who were most vulnerable. It made this option in light of its proclamation of the kingdom of God, a proclamation that mirrors the ministry of Jesus Christ. But make no mistake, this pastoral letter is written for those who disagree with where the church is going, and this church listened to its people, rich and poor alike, and responded to the best of its ability. While the leader of the archdiocese of San Salvador made a concrete option for the poor, the second pastoral letter tried to explain to those who rejected this option why it was necessary. Hence, the result was a theological lesson of the relationship between church and world, the teaching on where the church derives its mission from, and finally, how the church has listened and continues to listen to those who calumniate it and wish to see its ministry fail.

## Conclusion

> ... the basic source of conflict nowadays is God's revivifying will for the Church, expressed by the Vatican Council and by Medellín. Vatican II and Medellín represent a total shift of emphasis, one which Karl Rahner sees as on par with the early Church's decision to go out to the Gentiles. This breakthrough of itself, even before we explore any of its specific formulations, presupposes historical changes of such scope that the different ways in which people have reacted is understandable. These range from outright or veiled refusal to enthusiastic acceptance. For similar reasons, people have understood or implemented the teachings more or less slowly.[65]

It clearly has been difficult for a theologian writing out of a war zone in El Salvador to convince people of the need for the church to engage and live in what Sobrino calls the "real" world. This world is not the one we want; it is the one we inhabit, and part of the liberative process is to see it clearly and respond to it honestly. Ignacio Ellacuría, often quoted by Sobrino, understood this "act of facing things."[66] According to Ellacuría, the foundation of the liberative method included three dimensions—"getting a grip on reality," "taking on the burden of reality," and, finally, "taking responsibility for reality."[67] Sobrino does not think the overall trajectory of the Catholic Church in general, or the Latin American church in particular, has gone in that direction: "The Church has distanced herself from the world," he says with regret, and has become preoccupied with a "very, very spiritualistic Christianity—what you might call Christ without the world."[68] Whether one agrees with this view or not, Sobrino's ideas on the church continue to force the question of whether the church continues to be faithful to the mission of Jesus in service to the kingdom of God.

## Notes

1. Jon Sobrino, *Where Is God? Earthquake, Terrorism, Barbarity and Hope*, trans. Margaret Wilde (Maryknoll, N.Y.: Orbis Books, 2004), 10. I have changed the translation here from "temple" to "church" with a small "c" to reflect what I believe is an intended pun in the original that seems to have been lost in translation.

2. Jon Sobrino, *The True Church and the Poor* (Maryknoll, N.Y.: Orbis Books, 1984), 1.

3. Ibid.

4. Jon Sobrino, *Jesus the Liberator: A Historical-Theological View*, trans. Paul Burns and Francis McDonagh (Maryknoll, N.Y.: Orbis Books, 1993), 24.

5. Ibid.

6. Jon Sobrino and Juan Hernandez Pico, *Theology of Christian Solidarity* (Maryknoll, N.Y.: Orbis Books, 1985), 8.

7. Vatican II, *Gaudium et spes*, #4 (English translation from Vatican Web site).

8. Sobrino, *Jesus the Liberator*, 25.

9. *Gaudium et spes,* #11.

10. Ibid.

11. Jon Sobrino, "The Samaritan Church and the Principle of Mercy," in *The Principle of Mercy: Taking the Crucified People from the Cross* (Maryknoll, N.Y.: Orbis Books, 1994), 15.

12. Sobrino, *The Principle of Mercy*, 15.

13. Sobrino, *Jesus the Liberator*, esp. chapter 6.

14. Ibid., 160.

15. Exodus 3:7-8; Sobrino, *The Principle of Mercy*, 16.

16. Ibid., 19-20.

17. Ibid., 20-21.

18. Ibid., 21.

19. Sobrino, *Jesus the Liberator*, 29.

20. Ibid.

21. Ibid.

22. Jon Sobrino, *Archbishop Romero: Memories and Reflections* (Maryknoll, N.Y.: Orbis Books, 1990), 29.

23. "Second General Conference of Latin American Bishops," in *Liberation Theology: A Documentary History*, ed. Alfred T. Hennelly (Maryknoll, N.Y.: Orbis Books, 1990), 91.

24. Second General Conference of Latin American Bishops, 91.

25. Sobrino, *Archbishop Romero: Memories and Reflections*, 32.

26. Sobrino, *Jesus the Liberator*, 29.

27. See Archbishop Oscar Romero, *A Shepherd's Diary*, trans. Irene B. Hodgson (Cincinnati: St. Anthony Messenger Press, 1986).

28. Campesinos are inhabitants of "campos," or small rural villages, where peasants live and work the land. I have been told by church people in El Salvador that Romero's policy was to be interrupted anytime *campesinos* came to meet with him—including once when he was meeting with the president of Panama.

29. Dean Brackley, S.J., "Rutilio and Romero: Martyrs for Our Time," in *Monsignor*

*Romero: A Bishop for the Third Millennium*, ed. Robert S. Pelton, C.S.C. (Notre Dame, Ind.: University of Notre Dame Press, 2004), 94-95.

30. Sobrino, *Archbishop Romero*, 35.

31. Romero, *A Shepherd's Diary*, entry from Thursday, April 6, 1978, 29.

32. Ibid., entry from Tuesday, October 10, 1978, 87.

33. Ibid., entry from Sunday, February 25, 1979, 161.

34. Sobrino, *Jesus the Liberator*, 70.

35. Ibid., 71.

36. Ibid.

37. Ibid., 72.

38. Ibid.

39. Ibid., 70.

40. Ibid., 79.

41. Ibid., 80; cf. Puebla, 1142.

42. Sobrino is directly quoting J. Jeremias here, *Jesus the Liberator,* 81.

43. Ibid., 81.

44. Ibid., 82.

45. Ibid., 70.

46. Ibid., 87-88.

47. He specifically cites Mark 1:14; Matt 14:14; Matt 20:34; Mark 6:34; Matt 9:36; Luke 7:13; Matt 20:29-30; Luke 15:20; Luke 6:36; and draws on A. Nolan's *Jesus before Christianity* (Maryknoll, N.Y.: Orbis Books, 1978) for this interpretation. This understanding of compassion is similar to what Henri Nouwen, Don McNeill, and Douglas A. Morrison propose in their book *Compassion: A Reflection on the Christian Life* (New York: Random House, 1983), chapters 1-3.

48. Sobrino, *Jesus the Liberator*, 90.

49. Ibid., 100.

50. Ibid., 102.

51. Ibid., 91, the term "pity" would better be translated as "compassion" in the sense already described, as "compassion" better captures what Sobrino intended.

52. All of Romero's principles are drawn from Sobrino, *Archbishop Romero*, 84-85.

53. Vatican II, *Lumen gentium*, for example, #19.

54. *Lumen gentium* #3 states the following: "It was in Him, before the foundation of the world, that the Father chose us and predestined us to become adopted sons, for in Him it pleased the Father to re-establish all things. To carry out the will of the Father, Christ inaugurated the Kingdom of heaven on earth and revealed to us the mystery of that kingdom. By His obedience He brought about redemption. The Church, or, in other words, the kingdom of Christ now present in mystery, grows visibly through the power of God in the world."

55. Sobrino, *Archbishop Romero*, 84.

56. Ibid.

57. Ibid., 84-85.

58. Ibid., 85.

59. Archbishop Oscar Romero, *Voice of the Voiceless: The Four Pastoral Letters and Other Statements*, trans. Michael J. Walsh (Maryknoll, N.Y.: Orbis Books, 2004), 63-84. In a DVD titled *Jesuit Journeys: The Society of Jesus at the Turn of the Millennium*, Sobrino claims

very clearly to have written the second pastoral letter for Archbishop Romero (Wisconsin Province of the Society of Jesus, 2001).

60. It is interesting that all references quoted by this pastoral letter are from documents of Vatican II, papal documents, or from the *Catechism of the Catholic Church*. Romero and Sobrino were careful to argue directly out of church documents.

61. Jon Sobrino, "Introduction," in Romero, *Voice of the Voiceless*, 67.

62. Ibid, 69. Romero is quoting from Vatican II, Message to the World, October 21, 1962, no. 9.

63. Ibid., 76.

64. Ibid., 78.

65. Jon Sobrino, "Conflict Within the Church," *The Way* 26, no. 1 (1986): 33-43, at 36.

66. Sobrino, *Jesus the Liberator*, quoting Ellacuría, 34.

67. Ibid., 34.

68. Jon Sobrino, in "The Passion of Jon Sobrino," by Simon Lister, *The Tablet* (May 8, 1999): 641.

# 13

# The Faith of the Church, the Magisterium, and the Theologian

*Proper and Improper Interpretations*
*of the Notification*

JAMES T. BRETZKE, S.J.

When I entered the Jesuits five years after the Second Vatican Council ended it was our order's practice to send its novices on various apostolic experiences called "experiments." My first experiment was to a nursing home run by a fairly conservative religious order. In those still heady and unsettled days after the close of the council departures from the priesthood and religious life were fairly common, and each time some author who had been a priest or nun left his or her religious order, the sisters in the nursing home would scour the house library to remove all of this now "disgraced" author's work lest we, or the elderly residents, be scandalized or corrupted by the unseen theological viruses that might be lurking in the pages of the volumes which heretofore had been considered as positive examples of theological and/or spiritual reading.

My early novitiate memory resurfaced immediately after the Congregation for the Doctrine of the Faith issued its Notification on the Works of Jon Sobrino, S.J. (henceforth Notification). The cardinal prefect of the Congregation (henceforth CDF), William Levada, was the former archbishop of San Francisco, and I was a member of his Priest's Council elected to represent the higher education apostolates in that archdiocese. So perhaps because of that connection, or because I was chair of the theology department at the University of San Francisco, I found myself fielding increasingly insistent requests from a lay reporter from the official archdiocesan Catholic newspaper to answer a number of questions regarding the influence of Sobrino at USF and the greater San Francisco Bay Area. Several of the reporter's questions seemed to recall the theological paranoia I first encountered in the nursing home staff nearly four decades earlier: "Were any of Sobrino's texts ever used in any of our theology courses at USF?"; "Did we have courses in liberation theology?"; "Had Sobrino ever taught at—or visited—USF?"; "Did any of the faculty in my department know Sobrino, or had they or anyone in the administration ever visited him in El Salvador?" and so on. I suspect the reporter already knew the answer to most of these questions, and so I'm not sure if he wanted to use this information to bash us all; but I believed I surprised him when I responded with a forthright affirmative, and added that this should be the case in any reputable institution of Catholic higher education seeking to serve the church today.

I also quickly rediscovered that theological paranoia exists throughout the spectrum and is hardly a preserve of the more conservative wing of the church. Indeed, voices from the left could be just as strident and poorly grounded in the facts of what had actually transpired regarding Sobrino. When members of the academic community found out about the CDF Notification, their response was equally swift and predictable: "This is a dark day for the church!"; "Now Ratzinger is finally showing his true colors"; "We should start a campaign to support Sobrino against this ecclesial injustice," and so on. It seemed that the preferred translation of the old theological axiom *Roma locuta, causa finita* as either "Rome has spoken, the case is closed" *or* "Rome has spoken, and the cause is lost" depended largely on one's position prior to the issuance of the Notification. Both sides jumped a bit too quickly, in my opinion, to represent this document as a fundamental fight between the forces of truth and right on one side and darkness and evil on the other. But the apocalyptic views as to who actually was playing the parts of the Dark Lord Voldemort and his Death Eaters, and who was crusading as saintly Harry Potter and his besieged Dumbledore's Army differed sharply, depending on one's prior theological allegiances.

There did seem to be a strong additional negative element shared in common by both sides of the spectrum—namely, how little understood was the actual Notification itself and the general processes by which the CDF came to issue its document. As an attempt to address this lack of procedural understanding I initially wrote a brief set of remarks on what the Notification did and did not mean for my reporter friend, which through the laws of physics of cyberspace seemed to quickly achieve a much wider readership than I had ever imagined. What I endeavor to do here is to expand on these earlier points and then finally to turn to summary remarks on the necessarily uneasy tension between professional theologians and officers of church authority. Hopefully, then, the Sobrino Notification can provide both a teaching *and* a learning moment for us all.

## Basic Guidelines for the Interpretation of Church Teaching

*Lumen gentium*, Vatican II's Dogmatic Constitution on the Church, outlines three basic criteria of attending to the character, manner, and frequency that should guide all of the people of God in the pilgrim church in its critical, thoughtful, and respectful response (i.e., the *obsequium religiosum*) to official church teaching.[1] "Character" refers to the actual content of the teaching. Not all truths are created equal and, as Vatican II reminds us, there is a hierarchy of truths necessary for salvation. The character of the teaching and the manner of teaching may also be on different levels, such that we can have a "lower" doctrine on the hierarchy of truths, yet have it proclaimed at a very high level of authority. One example of this practice is Pope Pius XII's proclamation of the Marian doctrine of the Assumption as a defined article of faith. Many of the concerns enunciated in the Notification concern a relatively small number of points found in two books: *Jesucristo liberador: Lectura histórico-teológica de Jesús de Nazareth* (Madrid: 1991), translated into English as *Jesus the Liberator: A Historical-Theological Reading of Jesus of Nazareth*, trans. Paul Burns and Francis McDonagh (Maryknoll, N.Y.: Orbis Books, 1993), and *La fe en Jesucristo: Ensayo desde las víctimas* (Madrid: Trotta, 1999), translated into English as *Christ the Liberator: A View from the Victims*, trans. Paul Burns (Maryknoll, N.Y.: Orbis Books, 2001). Problems raised with regard to Sobrino's theology seemed to fall largely in the areas of methodology, not about outright denial of any truth of the faith.

"Frequency" points not only to the number of times the teaching is repeated, but also how long the teaching has been asserted. It also concerns the kinds of authority later invoked by the church in the process of disseminating the teaching. A proper consideration of the criterion of frequency involves to a certain extent the ecclesiastical culture of how teaching can change and develop. In Rome errors are often "corrected" and/or teaching or policy "changed" not by saying "oops, we were wrong" but either by ceasing to repeat a certain position or by beginning to nuance the older teaching in new ways. Even some teachings that have been "frequently repeated" over a long period of time and asserted with a high level of authority can still be subjected to change. This kind of change is illustrated in the case of Vatican II's 1965 Declaration on Religious Freedom, *Dignitatis humanae*, which in accepting freedom of religion as an inalienable human right reversed the traditional position enunciated by Gregory XVI (*Mirari vos*, 1832) and Pius IX (*Quanta cura*, 1864). It is probably still too early to judge accurately according to the frequency criterion the level of importance to be attached to the Sobrino Notification, but preliminary indications at the time of this writing would suggest that the CDF made its point and resolved to move on to more pressing matters. Pope Benedict XVI has made no comment on this matter, and very few bishops have had much to add either.

"Manner" is admittedly the criterion most difficult for the novice interpreter to puzzle out, and we will look at this in greater depth shortly. At this point, however, we should attend first to the stated audience or recipient of the Notification, as this will give an initial indication of the intended scope of the document's application. Second, one must look at the mode used to deliver the text, and, third, one needs to take into account the putative authority of the promulgator of the text. For example, the Sobrino Notification concludes with this formula:

> *The Supreme Pontiff Benedict XVI, at the Audience granted to the undersigned Cardinal Prefect on October 13, 2006, approved this Notification, adopted in the Ordinary Session of this Congregation, and ordered it to be published.*
>
> *Rome, from the Offices of the Congregation for the Doctrine of the Faith, November 26, 2006, the Feast of Christ, King of the Universe.*

William Cardinal Levada                              Angelo Amato, S.D.B.
*Prefect*                              *Titular Archbishop of Sila, Secretary*

Now it might seem to the average reader that the pope's seemingly explicit approval gives the Notification the force of a papal decree and that the principal authors of the text must have been Cardinal Levada and/or Archbishop Amato. However, in this case the first supposition (that this Notification is a quasi-papal decree) is certainly false, and it is highly unlikely that either Cardinal Levada or Archbishop Amato was the principal drafter of the actual text. This formula is an example of the standard mode of promulgation *in forma communi* (the common or "usual" form). Only in the case of a document that states explicitly *in forma specifica* ("in specific form") that the pope not only "approves" the document but makes it his own could we say that this becomes a papal document.[2]

It is probably not surprising that Roman Catholic magisterial documents are often misunderstood in terms of the triple criteria of character, frequency, and manner, and this misunderstanding often leads quickly to significant misinterpretations of what was actually promulgated. To wrestle with these interpretive difficulties I have formulated guidelines to act as correctives to six basic misinterpretations of official church teachings. First, as we know from basic hermeneutics, no written text exists that is self-evident, self-interpreting, or self-applying. Even the prominently placed large red octagon with the four-letter-word "STOP" at an intersection does not bring all vehicular traffic to a permanent halt. Rather, we stop, look, and proceed when safety allows. Thus, all texts need to be first translated, read, understood, and interpreted before they can be applied. Second, not all texts are created equal. Just as the church is hierarchical, so too some texts are more authoritative than others. Third, while this may not apply in other institutions, with magisterial teachings the "latest" text is not necessarily the weightiest or most authoritative. Fourth, the language used in the text does not necessarily mean the same as in general idiomatic usage. Fifth, each and every magisterial pronouncement (whether of the pope or lower authorities such as offices, cardinals, bishops, priests, and monsignors working in the Vatican) is not infallible. This means that if a statement is not infallible it is fallible. Fallible does not mean "false," but it does mean that the statement or formulation may be partial, incomplete, open to revision and even rejection later on. Sixth, except when referring geographically to the 108-acre neighborhood at the terminus of Rome's Via della Conciliazione, there is no "Vatican." Similarly, the expression "Vatican spokesman" should not be necessarily seen as representative of papal opinion or policy in the same way that we might view the statements of a White House spokesperson as reflecting the Bush administration's official policy on Iraq.

In terms of the hierarchy of authority based solely on manner of promulgation, the range would be from a defined dogma (*de fide definita*)[3] done either by a church council or the pope himself, speaking *ex cathedra* in the "extraordinary magisterium," down to rather mundane and doctrinally inconsequential texts, such as an address by the Holy Father on the occasion of receiving some official guest in the Apostolic Palace. Even when the individual or office promulgating a certain teaching is the same, such as the pope or the CDF, this does not mean that the various teachings themselves enjoy the same weight. There is a considerable range of distinctions here that are too numerous and detailed to present in this limited space, but I want to highlight an important distinction between items we are called to believe (*credenda*) and items we are called to hold or respect (*tenenda*).

A defined article of the faith is considered necessary to be believed (*credenda*) by those who identify themselves as Catholics, such as the two natures of Jesus Christ or the doctrine of the Trinity. Certainly some of the tension implicit in the Notification is a concern voiced by the CDF that there are at least ambiguities in Sobrino's works that might lead one to depart from certain dogmas that are considered to have been defined. Whether this charge is actually true or not I shall leave to others to discuss, as this falls outside the scope of my assigned topic. On the other hand, not everything the magisterium proposes needs to be "believed" in the sense of *credenda*. Other propositions, acts, decisions fall into another category called *tenenda*. For example, some might argue that based on the biblical evidence contained in the Letter of James (see 5:14-16) regarding the anointing of the sick by the elders in the Christian community, the minister of the sacrament of the sick need not be restricted to ordained priests and bishops. While this issue wouldn't seem to be a critical dogma connected with our salvation in Jesus Christ, the official authority of the church has decreed that only ordained priests and bishops are valid ministers of this particular sacrament.[4]

As a member of the Catholic communion I am enjoined to "hold" or abide by this teaching, even if I might privately conclude that a contrary opinion is also possible. But if I am going to live and work within the sacramental and liturgical structures of the Catholic Church then this means I have to respect certain decisions, even if I might think a different decision would be possible or even preferable. It's a bit like obeying posted speed limits on a given road: I might believe that 70 mph would be a "better" limit on I-94 between Madison and Minneapolis, but as a prudent and loyal citizen I will "hold" to the posted 65 mph—at least in the stretch of road where I believe the highway patrol might be present! According to the notion of *tenenda,* the Notification may call upon us to accept the office and function of the CDF. But the Notification does *not* call upon us in the sense of *credenda* to believe as an article of faith necessary for our salvation that the analysis supplied of Sobrino's two books is full, accurate, and complete. It does seem that this basic distinction between something proposed as *credenda* and something else proposed as *tenenda* is missed, or misunderstood, by many, and I believe that this may account for some of the more extreme reactions to the Sobrino Notification on both sides of the theological divide.

### What Exactly Was the Sobrino Notification and Its Meaning for Us?

As I noted above, *Lumen gentium* #25 indicates that we are to look to the character, frequency of repetition, and manner of promulgation as the primary hermeneutical criteria to aid us in our *obsequium religiosum*—which is *not* the theological equivalent of a lobotomy's mindless assent.[5] According to the magisterium's own position stated in virtually the highest possible authority of a conciliar constitution, we can make a faithful response to magisterial teaching only if we have sufficiently attended to these three criteria first. So let us now consider in greater detail these criteria as they relate to this particular Notification.

As I have suggested several times already, I believe it is the criterion of manner that is most difficult for the average reader to accurately decipher. Let us consider this first. Just as there is a hierarchy of authority within the magisterium (e.g., generally speaking, a papal document would rank above a dicasterial document) there is also a hierarchy of authority of the various texts issued by any particular organ of the magisterium, including the CDF. One quick way to look at the various types of documents issued by the CDF is to consult their part of the Holy See's Web site,[6] which gives a profile of the Congregation and organizes its major documents into sections on Doctrinal Documents, Disciplinary Documents, Documents on Sacramental Questions, as well as links to some other publications and speeches given by the last two cardinals prefect of the Congregation, namely William Levada (the former archbishop first of Portland, Oregon, and then of San Francisco, California) and Joseph Ratzinger (now Pope Benedict XVI).[7]

Now one might think that the Sobrino Notification would be found under the category of "Disciplinary Documents," but this is not the case, and this fact helps us see immediately that the professed intention of this particular text is not meant to be "punitive" of either Sobrino or those who might use his works or also espouse this particular strain of liberation theology. In ecclesial jargon the term "disciplinary" usually does not mean punitive, but rather organizing or governing. Thus, there is a "discipline" for the lawful celebration of the sacraments, especially the Eucharist. One has to follow certain rubrics and norms, and while there is some latitude for individual improvisation it is rather limited. Thus, the vast majority of the Disciplinary Documents deal with various rules and regulations, though there are also some decrees that do carry punitive measures (usually called "sanctions" in church parlance), such as the 1983 *Declaratio de associationibus massonicis* discouraging Catholics from belonging to Masonic orders, but none of these sorts of decrees concerns any theologian who has run afoul of the CDF.

So if one wants to find the actual text of the Sobrino Notification one must turn to the section on "Doctrinal Documents."[8] On this part of the CDF Web site one finds a large variety of document types dated from the present back to 1966. There are Responses, Letters, Considerations, Notes, Declarations, Instructions, Observations, Suggestions, Decisions, Formulae, and so on. Trying to give even a brief indication of the relative weight of each of these various document genres would far exceed my allotted space, but suffice it to say that usually there is a certain correspondence between the relative gravity of the "character" of a magisterial teaching and the "manner" in which this teaching is promulgated. Some of these document types also carry different implications for policy and possibly sanctions as well. Clearly a Suggestion is quite different from a Declaration, and the intent behind an Instruction is clearly weightier than the concerns generated by a Notification.

If I were to suggest a more idiomatic English expression for Notification it might be something along the lines of "Proceed with Caution." Certainly the Sobrino Notification does not mean "Avoid at All Costs"! With just a couple of exceptions, virtually all of the Notifications listed on the CDF Web site concern writings—and usually quite specific texts instead of an individual's entire corpus—rather than more general advisories about an individual or a movement. It might be clearest at this point to lay out briefly in outline form just what the Sobrino Notification does and does not mean in terms of the actual genre and particular text utilized by the CDF.

What the Sobrino Notification Doesn't Say or Do:

- No ecclesiastical sanctions or penalties have been applied to Sobrino by the Holy See.
- Sobrino has *not* been excommunicated from the church, and indeed no

disciplinary action at all has been taken or suggested by the CDF. He remains in good standing a Catholic theologian, a priest, and a Jesuit.

- Sobrino has *not* been accused of heresy or schism; he has not had his *missio canonica* as a Catholic theologian revoked.
- The Notification does *not* accuse Sobrino of denying the divinity of Jesus Christ.
- Sobrino has *not* had his theological or priestly activities curtailed. He has not been forbidden to write, publish, teach, or speak as a Catholic theologian, and he continues to enjoy all of his rights and obligations as an ordained Catholic priest (e.g., he can celebrate the sacraments, preside publicly at Catholic liturgies, wear clerical attire, etc.).
- Sobrino has *not* been forced into retirement or a "sabbatical" (as happened some years ago with Leonardo Boff, O.F.M.).
- Sobrino's works have *not* been proscribed or forbidden to be read or used, either privately or publicly. That is, his texts could legitimately remain part of seminary courses in theology.
- Sobrino's personal reputation and/or character have not been called into question by the Notification—indeed, quite the opposite, because the document praises Sobrino for his attention and devotion to the poor.
- Liberation theology is *not* condemned as an unorthodox theological method that would be unacceptable in the Catholic Church. Indeed, Pope John Paul II's statement that liberation theology is "necessary" remains unchallenged by the magisterium.
- A key tenet of liberation theology, namely, God's (and the church's) "preferential option for the poor" has *not* been called into question or criticized by the Notification; indeed the Notification reaffirms the validity of this central tenet of liberation theology—as does so much else of the church's contemporary magisterial teaching in the area of Catholic social thought.
- No one is asked to subscribe to the Notification's analysis of Fr. Sobrino's writings, either in the *credenda* or *tenenda* modalities discussed above. No one is asked to stop using Sobrino's works in any academic setting or to withhold inviting Sobrino to an academic function, including inviting him to take up a teaching position.

What the Sobrino Notification does say or do:

- The Notification clearly calls into question what the CDF holds to be six important areas or aspects of Sobrino's theological method that could be misleading or confusing in understanding "authentic Christian faith." It counsels the faithful to be aware of these areas of concern in reading or using these two books.
- The language employed in the Notification calls these items "imprecisions

and errors," but there is also a certain "imprecision" in the CDF Notification itself since the text does not clearly delineate what it considers to be an imprecision and what it considers to be an outright error in the two Sobrino books considered. *If* the CDF considered the "errors" to have been serious enough, presumably stronger action would have been taken, such as requiring Sobrino to take a special profession of faith, or to condemn outright the "errors" as heresy. The Notification did neither.

- According to the text of the Notification these six areas are "1) the methodological presuppositions on which the Author [Fr. Sobrino] bases his theological reflection; 2) the Divinity of Christ; 3) the Incarnation of the Son of God; 4) the relationship between Jesus Christ and the Kingdom of God; 5) the Self-consciousness of Jesus, and 6) the salvific value of his Death."

- The Notification states that its purpose is to offer its reflections as an aid and guide so that these six aspects of Sobrino's work will not lead people to misinterpret what constitutes some important aspects of the Christian faith (such as the importance of the apostolic tradition and the divinity of Jesus Christ) as well as what would constitute a fuller and more proper theological method (e.g., to focus on the faith of the whole church and not just a part of the church, even if it be a key part such as the poor).

- In other words, the primary stated purpose of the Notification is "to offer the faithful a secure criterion, founded on the doctrine of the church, by which to judge the affirmations contained in these books." Thus, the Notification's own stated intent would be similar to a commentary or study guide to be used in reading and evaluating Sobrino's works.

While it falls to others in this volume to assess the accuracy of the CDF's judgment in the six areas the Notification contains, I think it might be helpful to a better understanding of this particular text to offer some further remarks about the processes employed by the CDF in its work in general, and in the Sobrino Notification in particular.

## Ongoing Tensions in Light of the Notification

Certainly what sets the Sobrino Notification apart from the other four Notifications in the last forty years that still have active links on the CDF Web site is that in this instance the CDF provided for the first time an Explanatory Note on the process itself.[9] Clearly the *Semper idem* ("always the same") motto of a former prefect of the Congregation, Cardinal Ottaviani, has been laid to rest, and I think most will welcome the greater transparency and openness here than was often found in the past. To a certain extent it might be said that the process followed by the CDF resembles an independent review that academic professors would experience in the United States when they go up for tenure and/or promotion. As part of this promotion process their scholarly works are sent out for review to experts whose identities remain confidential (i.e., neither the individual professor nor college review board would know the names of these reviewers). Of course one always hopes for a positive response, but even in academia this is not always the case; and drawing on my own experience of sitting on several of these review committees over the years I know first-hand that there are often quite sharp disagreements among scholars in their assessments of another's work. To some extent this same sharp division of opinion is manifest in the Sobrino case.

Two of the tensions that always exist in processes such as these—whether the CDF investigation or an academic tenure/promotion review process—are the issues of secrecy and transparency. While these terms are related, they are not identical. Transparency I take to refer to an acknowledged objective procedure that is known beforehand by the involved parties. Secrecy can still be part of a transparent objective process. As I mentioned above, in virtually every academic process for tenure and promotion with which I am familiar, an applicant's publications are sent out to a select number of outside reviewers. The applicant can usually suggest some potential reviewers, but the reviewers actually chosen—along with other reviewers not on the applicant's list—remain completely unknown to the applicant (and often also unknown by the committee charged with the evaluation of the candidate's dossier). While the applicant may be uneasy with this process s/he agrees to it because this is the standard and accepted practice for serious evaluation of one's academic work.

While there are certain analogues between the academic and the CDF processes there are quite a number of notable differences that have caused much pain and anguish in the past, and probably will continue to do so in the future. I think the vast majority of theologians, myself certainly included, would be desirous of having a different procedure that would separate out the "review process" from the "judgment/decision process." In the academic process I've outlined above we have this division. The external reviewers know two things in advance: first, that their anonymity will be respected, so they have the freedom to speak in utter frankness without fear of reprisal or ending a friendship; and second, they know that their evaluation is just one part of the final decision-making process and that their review does not in and of itself determine the final outcome. I believe that this process is more desirable because it separates and distributes the various power-and-responsibility dynamics in such a way that it is easier to fulfill the distinct responsibilities without running the risk of serious abuse of power and an excessive degree of subjectivism. While I think such a process could be developed for use in the CDF this has not yet been done, and it does seem that theologians lack the requisite influence to bring such a change about at this point in history.

Given the actual processes in place, however, the CDF seems to have followed its own internal policies, and thus in that sense was in full compliance with its version of what we might call due process, which could be summarized as follows: Sobrino was informed of the ongoing process and his response to the problematic elements outlined was solicited and received. In his response, Father Sobrino indicated some areas of his work that had developed and in which his thinking had modified, and other areas in which his views remained unchanged. Ultimately, the CDF judged Sobrino's response insufficient to address all of its areas of concern, and thus the Notification went forward. Despite using what the CDF called the "expedited format," the process took a considerable amount of time (several years in this case). Finally, as noted above, while the Notification was approved by Pope Benedict XVI *in forma communi* (the common or usual form), the authority of the document itself remains at the level of a CDF document.

Clearly, Sobrino, and many other respected theologians, does not accept the overall validity of the CDF assessment of his work. These would judge his work to be a legitimate, orthodox articulation of the Christian faith and would not accept a claim that Sobrino is denying the Christian faith or using an unorthodox theological method. On the other hand, I think it would be fair to say that others, including other respected theologians, would in fact join the CDF's view that these six areas remain problematic in Sobrino's work. Several other theologians in the history of the church have encountered similar (and sometimes far more serious) problems, and today their work is both accepted and even treasured. Others have not had the same successful judgment of history.

The immediate ramifications of the Sobrino Notification still seem a bit unclear, and my own crystal ball needs an upgrade before I can prognosticate with real assurance. According to the press, upon initial release of the Notification, the archbishop of San Salvador indicated that Sobrino could not teach within his archdiocese as a Catholic theologian until Sobrino brought his positions into conformity with the CDF critique. However, it seemed that the archbishop had erroneously believed that the CDF had attached such sanctions to Sobrino, but this was not the case. The final outcome in this and other dioceses remains to be seen, and likely there might be some differences among various bishops' approaches (e.g., I somehow doubt Bishop Fabian Bruskewitz of Lincoln, Nebraska, would allow Sobrino to speak publicly in a Catholic parish in that diocese). In canon law, in cases like this (in which the individual has not been declared excommunicated or a heretic by the Holy See) a bishop's actions have juridical force only within his own diocese.

Since the CDF imposed no sanctions of its own, it would be up to individual bishops to choose or not to choose to impose restrictions or sanctions on Sobrino's professional and/or priestly activities. This is somewhat akin to individual bishops forbidding certain individuals or groups from speaking or working in their own dioceses, or a part of their diocese. For example, in my home archdiocese of Milwaukee, Professor Daniel Maguire, a layman, is not allowed to speak in Catholic parishes, but he is still a professor in good standing at the Jesuit Marquette University where he continues to teach moral theology. Archbishop Timothy Dolan has judged Maguire to be problematic in addressing general audiences in Catholic parishes, but Dolan has *not* undertaken the canonical process required to label Maguire no longer a Catholic theologian in good standing.

Anyone with even a passing acquaintance with church history knows that there have been tensions from the time of Jesus among various theologies, among theologians, and between theologians and the magisterium. History has shown us time and time again that certain positions and individuals who have had their work questioned, criticized, silenced, and even condemned ultimately have gone on to gain considerable acceptance and approval. While this is not always the case, one need only recall just a few in the litany of great theologians whose work was at some point criticized or held suspect by official church authority: Thomas Aquinas, O.P., Karl Rahner, S.J., Cardinal Henri de Lubac, S.J., Cardinal Yves Conger, O.P., Bernard Häring, C.Ss.R., Stanislas Lyonnet, S.J., and a host of others. Following the chronology on the CDF Web site in the last dozen years, the genre of Notification has been used to raise official concerns about some of the writings of just six individuals: Roger Haight, S.J., Marciano Vidal, C.Ss.R., Jacques Dupuis, S.J., Reinhard Messner, Anthony De Mello, S.J., and Tissa Balasuriya, O.M.I. Certainly there likely have been other investigations, and while some of these might well be ongoing, many others have been concluded with no formal action on the part of the Holy See.[10] Also among these six individuals listed there is a considerable range of stated seriousness of the concerns raised by the CDF.

Perhaps it might be helpful to conclude by calling on on a very well established and respected father of the church to offer us a benediction: *In fide, unitas: in dubiis, libertas; in omnibus, caritas* ("In faith, unity; in doubt, liberty; in all things, charity"). This important principle of Christian discernment, enunciated by St. Augustine, reminds us that unity in faith is indeed important, but in cases of doubt a plurality of opinions and practices should be allowed, and, regardless, the overriding principle must always be charity toward one another.

### Notes

1. See *Lumen gentium* #25. I have elaborated at greater length on some guidelines for reading and interpreting magisterial teaching in my article "A Burden of Means: Interpreting Recent Catholic Magisterial Teaching on End-of-Life Issues," *Journal of the Society of Christian Ethics* 60, no. 2 (Fall/Winter 2006): 183-200.

2. For an example of the rare usage of *in forma specifica* see the 1997 "Instruction on

Certain Questions Regarding the Collaboration of the Non-ordained Faithful in the Sacred Ministry of Priest," which was co-promulgated by several Vatican dicasteries and adopted by Pope John Paul II *in forma specifica* so that the Instruction's practical points would carry the force of papal liturgical law.

3. For a helpful guide to Latin terms frequently used in theological and ecclesial texts, see my *Consecrated Phrases: A Latin Dictionary of Theological Terms*, 2d ed. (Collegeville, Minn.: Liturgical Press: 1998, 2003).

4. See the *NOTE of the Congregation for the Doctrine of the Faith on the Minister of the Sacrament of the Anointing of the Sick*, February 11, 2005, which states, "only priests (Bishops and presbyters) are ministers of the Sacrament of the Anointing of the Sick. This doctrine is definitive *tenenda*. Thus, neither deacons nor laypeople can exercise this ministry, and any such action would constitute simulation of the sacrament."

5. Obviously the proper interpretation of this Latin term and its concomitant application are still hotly debated. One of the most responsible and balanced voices in this discussion is the former Pontifical Gregorian ecclesiologist and current Boston College professor emeritus, Francis A. Sullivan, S.J., who has written extensively in this area. See especially his two books, *Creative Fidelity: Weighing and Interpreting Documents of the Magisterium* (New York: Paulist Press, 1996), and *Magisterium: Teaching Authority in the Catholic Church* (Dublin: Gill & Macmillan, 1983), and his two helpful articles, "Recent Theological Observations on Magisterial Documents and Public Dissent," *Theological Studies* 58 (1998): 509-15; and "The Theologian's Ecclesial Vocation and the 1990 CDF Instruction," *Theological Studies* 52 (1991): 51-68.

6. The main URL for the Holy See's Web site is www.vatican.va and the URL for the CDF Web page currently is http://www.vatican.va/roman_curia/congregations/cfaith/index.htm.

7. Technically though, these speeches would not be considered documents of the Congregation, and therefore their authority in terms of the criterion of manner would be considerably lower than a text of the Congregation itself. This can be a very important point to consider in the case of a document issued by the Congregation under its authority (usually "approved" by the pope *in forma communi*) and a commentary that might be given by the cardinal prefect of the same Congregation. The latter text carries with it generally only the weight of an individual member of the magisterium and does not include papal or dicasterial authority.

8. The URL for the document itself (available in several languages) is http://www.vatican.va/roman_curia/congregations/cfaith/documents/rc_con_cfaith_doc_20061126_notification-sobrino_en.html. Also, see pp. 255-66 below. The language of the original text was Spanish, which indicates that most likely the original push for the Sobrino investigation came from the Spanish-speaking world (likely in Central and Latin America) and that those in the CDF who did most of the original analysis and drafting of the Notification would have to have been quite fluent in Spanish, if not actual native speakers. Given these facts, and the pace at which most Vatican offices operate it would be highly unlikely that the Notification would have been much of a personal project of the current prefect, Cardinal William Levada. Interestingly, there are far fewer "live" links to the various CDF documents under Cardinal Levada's leadership than was the case with his immediate predecessor. Perhaps it's a bandwidth issue, though it could reflect a desire that only the more pertinent and authoritative documents be kept online in the CDF Web site.

9. In a few other instances the CDF supplied a commentary on its Notification, as in the 2001 case of Fr. Marciano Vidal, C.Ss.R. (2001). See http://www.vatican.va/roman_curia/congregations/cfaith/documents/rc_con_cfaith_doc_20010515_vidal-2_en.html .

10. Since virtually any individual in the entire world can contact the CDF to raise concerns about a given individual or publication, what may be surprising is not how many actual processes there are administered by the sparsely staffed office of the CDF, but how few actually result in the initialization of a formal process of inquiry; and of these, very, very few seem to result in any sort of action, such as a Notification, being taken.

# PART IV

*Moral Theology and the Christian Life*

# 14

# Radicalizing the Comprehensiveness of Mercy

*Christian Identity in Theological Ethics*

JAMES F. KEENAN, S.J.

"The principle of mercy" is treated briefly but powerfully in the first chapter of Jon Sobrino's book which bears the same name. First published by Sal Terrae in Spain in 1992,[1] *The Principle of Mercy: Taking the Crucified People from the Cross* appeared in English in 1994.[2] In taking together articles published elsewhere both before and after the martyrdom at Central American University in 1990, Sobrino digs deep to articulate and apply the principle of mercy, a principle proposed specifically for readers from the industrialized world. Yet, it is in *The Principle of Mercy*'s first chapter, "The Samaritan Church and the Principle of Mercy," that Sobrino rattles off an extraordinary number of assertions that convey, at once, how radical mercy is and how comprehensive it is.

Mercy occupies Sobrino's heart and mind, and nowhere is that more evident than in the last chapter of *The Principle of Mercy*, that is, his "Letter to Ignacio Ellacuría," which he read at Mass on November 10, 1990, nearly a year after the martyrdoms in El Salvador on November 16, 1989. He begins the letter, "Dear Ellacu, For years I've thought about what I'd be saying at the Mass of your martyrdom." He then chooses two dimensions of Ellacuría to consider, his faith and his mercy. On the latter he sums up as follows:

> This led me to the conclusion that, over and above everything else, you were a person of compassion and mercy, and that the inmost pains of you, your guts and your heart were wrenched at the immense pain of this people. Your life was not just service, then: It was the very specific service of "taking the crucified peoples down from the cross"—words very much like your own, the kind of words that take not only intelligence to invent, but intelligence moved by mercy.

He concludes the letter, "For your mercy, and for your faith, Jon." In the depths of the life of Ellacuría there was mercy, and that mercy made all of Ellacuría's life understandable.[3]

Likewise, in the book's penultimate chapter, "The Legacy of the Martyrs of the Central American University," Sobrino writes the entire legacy in the key of mercy. Mercy moved the martyrs, more than as a feeling or as a willingness, but as a "principle which guided their entire lives and work. Mercy was there in the beginning, but it stayed there throughout the entire process, shaping them as well."[4]

While mercy lives on in the martyrs at the end of the book, Sobrino begins the book with a powerfully dramatic exercise that reveals the centrality of mercy in Christianity. He captures this by demonstrating the depth (radicality) and the breadth (comprehensiveness) of mercy. In that first chapter, Sobrino unwaveringly launches his project by plowing the entire field of theology, so as to sow and to harvest mercy from Christology, soteriology, ecclesiology, biblical theology, and morality. Therein he sets deep roots for mercy.

Still, just before the first chapter, he provides an introduction to wake us up from what he calls the "sleep of inhumanity." Mercy is first based, he states, not on a commandment but on experience: In seeing another suffer, we are moved to pity. That movement precedes all others, and, as we will see later, it is that movement that is constant in the life of Jesus: he is the one, par excellence, to be moved to pity. But to be moved requires a structure for action, whence the principle of mercy; and here in the introduction, Sobrino offers four specific points on the principle.

First, there are in the world not simply suffering individuals but "crucified people." To be moved by mercy "means to do everything we possibly can to bring them down from the cross." To engage in these actions means to work for justice. Second, one who practices "a mercy that becomes justice" will automatically be persecuted. Third, this mercy must be preferred above all. Fourth, mercy depends on freedom and, in turn, furthers one's freedom.[5]

Additionally Sobrino is always concerned with idols, in particular with European and North American constructs that actually serve to immunize these populations from any sensitivity, let alone sense of responsibility, for the profound suffering in the world of those who are oppressed. In the introduction, Sobrino sees as a contrast, "the cross on which God is placed" as "the most eloquent proclamation that God loves the victimized of this world." But at the same time Sobrino demands a twofold action: a repudiation of the idols must accompany an acknowledgment of the God whom we confess. The two actions together keep either action from becoming abstract.[6]

## The Samaritan Church and the Principle of Mercy

In this first chapter, then, through four themes, Sobrino makes his case for the radical comprehensiveness of mercy: the principle of mercy, the mercy of God, the mercy of Jesus, and the mercy of the church.

First, the principle of mercy reflects the influence of the three-volume work *The Principle of Hope*, by Ernst Bloch. The comprehensiveness of Bloch's proposal as well as its apparently immediate applicability to the world makes that monumental work the model for Sobrino's.[7] Using Bloch, he argues that the concept of principle provides us with three overriding insights: that mercy stands at the *origin and basis* of all moral activity; that mercy is not one activity among others but rather that which is prior to all others; and, that mercy endures throughout the work of justice, eclipsing if you will, the entire process. The totality of his claim then comes down to this: "This principle of mercy is the basic principle of the activity of God and Jesus, and therefore ought to be that of the activity of the church."[8]

Second, Scripture reveals to us that God is the God of mercy. Sobrino finds in Exod 3:7-8 that "God stands at the origin of the salvific process." God's activity is mercy: "God hears the cries of the suffering people, and for that reason alone determines to undertake the liberative activity in question. We call this activity of love, thus structured, mercy."[9] The mercy of God not only initiates God's activity; it remains the basic constant throughout the Scriptures for describing the activity of God.

*Principle* allows Sobrino to explain these three qualities of mercy as the beginning, the essence, and the constant of all divine activity with humanity. He writes, "The mercy under consideration is not only at the origin of God's activity: It abides as a basic constant all through the Old Testament." Mercy therefore becomes the principle that best captures an *imitatio Dei*. "The fundamental exigency for the human being, and specifically for the human being, and specifically for the people of God, is that they reiterate this mercy of God's, exercising it toward others and thus rendering themselves like unto God."[10]

Reflecting on the beginning of John's Gospel he writes, "Paraphrasing Scripture, we might say that as in the absolute divine beginning "was the Word," and through the Word creation arose, so mercy is in the absolute beginning of the history of salvation, and this mercy abides as a constant in God's salvific process."[11]

Third, Sobrino finds in Jesus the expression of the "primordial mercy of God." Repeatedly, he refers to Jesus' response to one who suffers as his being moved to pity. Jesus internalizes the suffering of another as the first step to his responding: "For Jesus, to be a human being is to react with mercy."[12] Still, Sobrino acknowledges that "mercy is not the sole content of Jesus' practice, but it is mercy that stands at the origin of all that he practices; it is mercy that shapes and molds his entire life, mission, and fate."[13]

Sobrino's comprehensive claims for mercy appear as he finds mercy essential both for divinity and for humanity.

The elevation of this mercy to the status of a principle may seem minimal. But according to Jesus, without it, there is no humanity or divinity, and however minimal, it is genuinely maximal as well. The important thing to observe is that this "minimum and maximum" is the first and the last. There is nothing antecedent to mercy that might move it, nor is there anything beyond mercy that might relativize it or offer an escape from it.[14]

Clearly, the use of "principle" and the authority of Jesus play together in his theology of mercy.

Bringing these claims together and precisely as he discusses the radicality of mercy, he is finally able to offer a definition of mercy: "Mercy is a basic attitude toward the suffering of another, whereby one reacts to eradicate that suffering for the sole reason that it exists, and in the conviction that, in this reaction to the ought-not-be of another's suffering, one's own being, without any possibility of subterfuge, hangs in the balance."[15]

Fourth, "this principle of mercy ought to be operative in Jesus' church."[16] Here Sobrino proposes that the church be the Good Samaritan. He writes: "The most important thing is that the church begin to 'think itself' from without, from 'along the road,' where the wounded neighbor lies." When the church emerges from within itself, "it genuinely de-centers itself and thereby comes to resemble Jesus in something absolutely fundamental."[17]

Rather than thinking about itself, the church is to tend to the wound of the neighbor. He identifies the "wound" as the simple fact that if one is born in Haiti, Bangladesh, or Chad one has incomparably less life and incomparably less dignity than one born in the United States, Spain, or Germany. Thus "a local church that fails to tend that worldwide wound cannot claim to be ruled by the principle of mercy."[18]

As he concludes the essay, undoubtedly one written very quickly (one feels the intense energy in these pages), he states three points. One, that this principle is "nothing but a restatement" of the option for the poor. Two, that mercy is also beatitude, and therein the joy of Christ arises from the mercy of Christ. Third, a church of mercy becomes a "marked" church, marked by credibility.[19]

## Other Writings

Sobrino considered these themes in writings prior to *The Principle of Mercy*. In 1984, in "Toward a Determination of the Nature of Priesthood: Service to God's Salvific Approach to Human Beings,"[20] he reflects on an essay by Gustavo Baena. Baena studies the Letter to the Hebrews and argues that the priesthood of Jesus is founded on his mercy. He is merciful (Heb 2:17), sympathetic to our weakness (Heb 4:15), and assures us that we will receive mercy (Heb 4:16). "Jesus' mercy can be characterized as an antecedent condition for the exercise of his priesthood, but it is also more than that. An active mercy is what moves Jesus to bring salvation, and the exercise of mercy is the realization of that salvation."[21]

Hebrews calls Jesus a priest because of the pity he feels and the mercy he practices. As priest, he mediates service between God and humanity. Quoting Baena, Sobrino writes that Jesus "is expressly understood as the very mercy of God, coming in concrete form to this world."[22] He adds here that mercy is "comprehensive." "Mercy is the condensation of all the great expectancies of the messianic era. It is mercy, systematically speaking, that relates Jesus with the divine Parent and the Reign of God."[23]

In 1988, Sobrino returned to mercy and linked it to justice and liberation. In "Theology in a Suffering World," he writes that in the "massive and structural suffering that pervades the Third World, the response of mercy must be a response of justice that will bring about liberation."[24]

He develops this link, simultaneous with his essay on the Samaritan church, in "Spirituality and the Following of Jesus." Because reality is that which the person of mercy continually faces, Sobrino makes the necessary connection between justice and reality.

> To be sure, this mercy will have to be exercised in a variety of ways, depending on the nature of the wound suffered by the victim lying in the ditch. Thus it must take various forms: emergency relief, assistance and support, reconciliation, and so on. In the presence of entire crucified peoples, as in Latin America, mercy must take the form of structural justice, which is having mercy on the masses.[25]

Later in the same essay he moves from mercy to liberation, but then turns back to love. He writes:

> The merciful are those who take up the task because their hearts have been moved to compassion by the incredible suffering of the poor. This "original mercy" imbues their prophetical labors and makes their struggle a struggle waged for love. But it also requires of them that, in the practice of liberation, they continue to keep before their eyes, from first to last, the pain of the poor, which must never be reduced to the concept of the single social price to be paid for progress. . . . Structurally, pity or mercy is the manner in which they express the presence, right from the start and all through the liberation process, of a great love for the people of the poor.[26]

In two other essays, Sobrino returns to two different insights, one about Jesus being moved to pity and the other about the parable of the Good Samaritan. These essays show how, from 1988 to 1992 in particular, Sobrino deeply reflected on mercy, as expressed in his colleagues at Universidad Centroamericana and as sustained in his prayerful understanding of the saving mystery of Jesus Christ.

In "The Central Position of the Reign of God in Liberation Theology,"

Sobrino reflects on how Jesus is moved to pity in the miracles he performs. Sobrino writes:

> The basic reason for which Jesus is described as working miracles is mercy; he felt compassion for the weak and oppressed; we hear this repeatedly. "When . . . he saw the vast throng, his heart was moved with pity, and he cured their sick" (Matt. 14:14). We read that he felt compassion for a leper (Mark 1:41), for two blind persons (Matt. 20:34), for persons who had nothing to eat (Mark 8:22; Matt. 15:32), for those who were sheep without a shepherd (Mark 6:34; Matt. 9:36), for a widow who had just lost her son (Luke 7:13). It is also this mercy that also appears in the miracle accounts. On at least four occasions, Jesus performs a cure upon hearing, "Have pity on me/us!" (Matt. 20:29-34; and par.; 15:21-28 and par.; 17:14-29; Luke 11:19).[27]

In 1991 Sobrino writes about the Good Samaritan in "Rich and Poor Churches and the Compassion Principle":[28]

> When Jesus wishes to give an example of the perfect human being, he tells the parable of the Good Samaritan. This is a solemn moment in the Gospel which goes farther than the curiosity of finding out which commandment carries the most weight. The parable seeks to tell us, in a word, what human beings are. Thus, the perfect human being is the one who saw a beaten man on the roadside, reacted and aided him in every way he could.[29]

Finally, it is in the "Spirituality and the Following of Jesus," that we get perhaps the best of a summary statement on mercy. Herein, we find the comprehensiveness of mercy radicalized.

> Mercy is the primary and ultimate, the first and last of human reactions. It is that in terms of which all dimensions of the human being acquire meaning and without which nothing else attains to human status. In this mercy, the human being is perfected, becomes whole, as Luke teaches in the parable of the Good Samaritan. The gospels use it to typify Jesus himself, who so often acts after being "moved with compassion." The Bible actually uses it to typify God whose bowels grow so tender that the divine Father welcomes and embraces the prodigal. Mercy, then, is the correct manner of responding to concrete reality—as well as the ultimate and decisive manner thereof, as we learn from the parable of the Last Judgment. Everything—absolutely everything—turns on the exercise of mercy. On it depends not only transcendent salvation, but our living here and now, in concrete history, as saved human beings.[30]

## The Distinctiveness of Roman Catholic Ethics

If we realize that liberation theology includes a theological ethic, then Sobrino is locating the distinctiveness of Roman Catholic theological ethics in mercy. To make this case, I want to track three issues in Christian ethics: the debate on the specificity of Christian ethics; the centrality of mercy in the New Testament; and the centrality of mercy in the tradition.

The specificity of Christian ethics arose from the proposal of certain German theological ethicists—above all, Alfons Auer—of an autonomous ethics in the context of faith. In recent years, this ethics has undergone a significant shift.[31] In its earlier expression, Auer proposed an autonomous ethic as an *ethical* thesis: the autonomy of moral reasoning refers to the unique yet rational character of moral statements. This means that in conscience an individual Catholic moved by the light of faith makes inquiry into what is being asked of her/him. As a *theological* thesis, the autonomy of moral reasoning protects the specificity of Christian ethics from being reduced to specific material content. In effect, the specificity of Christian ethics, according to Auer, was in the call of conscience to determine the morally right.

Still, for Auer, faith provides a new horizon of meaning (*einen neuen Sinnhorizont*). Norms are not derived from faith; faith does not replace the responsibility of human reason, but it exerts an integrating, criticizing, and stimulating effect on the reasoning process. As a thesis about *church teaching,* the autonomy of moral reasoning helps protect the moral norm from being imposed by any outside authority, in general, or the magisterium, in particular. The norms actually derive from the acting conscience of the Christian.[32]

On the other side of this debate came a robust salvo from Joseph Ratzinger and Hans Urs von Balthasar in 1975.[33] Their argument highlighted the need to continue the work of the apostolic church by consistently proclaiming the normative teaching of Christ expressed by the more recently articulated claims of the magisterium. They offer an ethics of faith that purifies reason.[34] But they are quite clear about specific moral norms coming from the magisterium as deriving from the faith. In a manner of speaking, the Christian distinctiveness that they propose is something that looks more like *Humanae vitae* or *Casti connubii,* than, say, the Gospels.

For many in theological ethics, the debate represented a significant stalemate. One side said effectively that moral motivation was what distinguished Christian ethics, while the other side argued that the continuous normative teachings of the church captured Christian identity. Most theological ethicists were looking for something in between these extremes, that is, a Christian ethics that was more than motivation but less than concrete yet very historically based specific norms, mostly related to sexual conduct.

Progressively, people found the common ground in a wide range of topics from a virtue ethics, broadly construed to include a character-based ethics, to a more generous responsibility ethics that was based on a person-based as opposed to an action-based ethics. These alliances, which really arose from the major works of revision of the twentieth century, namely Odon Lottin,[35] Fritz Tillmann,[36] Gerard Gilleman,[37] and Bernard Häring,[38] underlined that the contents of a distinctively Christian ethics were found more in Gospel virtues than in magisterial norms.

The middle position turns as Tillmann did to the Gospels to find the predominant expressions of distinctive moral teaching. While von Balthasar and Ratzinger turn to the particulars of (very) local and historical teachings, for instance, the teachings of Pope Paul VI in *Humanae vitae,* as having some real contact with the heart of what it means to be Catholic, and while Auer and his disciples sought to eradicate the contents of Christian morality by insisting on the uniqueness of Christian motivation (and perhaps they were doing no more than casting adrift the claims of von Balthasar and Ratzinger), more moderates were looking to find in the Gospels something distinctively virtuous about Christian ethics. The more moderate quest was to find the distinctiveness of Christian ethics in church teaching from Scripture that was not narrow nor vacuous.

Sobrino belongs to this middle camp, for clearly, as can be deducted from the material above, Sobrino could not accept the position of Auer that Christian conduct was nothing more than a Christian willingness, nor could he accept, at the other extreme, a very German outlook on Christian ethics that found Christian identity singularly in long held (predominantly sexual) teachings by an elite hierarchy.

Theologians such as Odon Lottin, who wrote on the relevance of Christian virtue, Fritz Tillmann who treated the distinctiveness of the triple love command from the Gospels, and Gerard Gilleman who wrote on the primacy of charity found the distinctiveness of Christian ethics in the theological virtues.

Typical of the liberation theologians, they too turn to the Scriptures to find both Christian identity and ethical directives, and no less than Jon Sobrino finds it in the Gospel virtue of mercy.

## Mercy in the Bible

To continue making my case for the validity of Sobrino's claim for the central distinctiveness of mercy, I want to turn to three insights from the New Testament. First, the parable of the Good Samaritan (Luke 10:29-37) portrays mercy as the definitive expression of the love of neighbor command. It is important for us to remember why Jesus tells this parable. He has just given the commandment to love one another. In response, one of the scribes asked Jesus, "Who is my neighbor?" Jesus responds by telling the parable of the Good Samaritan; a close reading of the story reveals that Jesus is offering a very surprising answer to the question.

At the beginning of the story we are thinking that the answer to the question "who is my neighbor?" is the man lying wounded on the road. But by the end of the story we are no longer looking at the neighbor who is wounded but rather at the neighbor who is acting. The scribe, therefore, answers that the neighbor is the one who shows mercy. In the beginning we think the parable is about whom we should assist. But the end is really about who we are called to be. We are called to be like the Good Samaritan, that is, to be a neighbor.

Like the surprise ending, many of us forget that this parable was never primarily a moral one. Throughout the tradition many preachers and theologians saw in the story of the Good Samaritan the narrative (in miniature) of our redemption by Christ. Starting with Clement of Alexandria (ca. 150-ca. 215), then Origen (ca. 184- ca. 254), Ambrose (339-390), and, finally, Augustine (354-430), the Good Samaritan parable is the merciful narrative of our redemption. Later, from Venerable Bede (673-735) to Martin Luther (1483-1546), preachers and theologians appropriate and modify the narrative, but in each instance, the narrative is first and foremost christological.[39]

The basic allegorical expression of the parable was this: the man who lies on the road is Adam, wounded (by sin), suffering outside the gates of Eden. The priest and the Levite (the Law and the prophets), are unable to do anything for Adam. Along comes the Good Samaritan (Christ), a foreigner, one not from here, who tends to Adam's wounds, takes him to the inn (the church), gives a down payment of two denarii (the two commandments of love), leaves him with the innkeeper (St. Paul), and promises to return for him (the second coming) when he will pay in full for the redemption and take him with him into his kingdom.

The parable, then, is first and foremost not a story about how we should treat others but rather the story of what Christ has done for us. We are called to follow the actions of the Good Samaritan not because the parable is an attractive one, but because it is a retelling of the entire Gospel. Thus, though Sobrino, like William Spohn,[40] recognizes in the parable itself the paradigm of mercy for Christian discipleship, we can add to his insight the fact that the tradition of interpretation gave it pride of place for not only modeling Christian discipleship but, more importantly, for being in itself the kerygma in narrative form. The parable is not, then, one among many: besides serving as the foundational explanation of the love command, it is also the allegorical account of salvation history.

This leads to the second point, namely, that the Scriptures name mercy as the condition for salvation. This is made clear in the last judgment in Matthew 25 where the saved are those who performed what we later called the corporal works of mercy. The parable of Matthew 25 is striking in that everyone is surprised by the judgment. The sheep never realized that in feeding the hungry, they were feeding the king; unfortunately, the goats never realized that by not visiting the sick, they were not visiting the Lord. For the Gospel writers, we will be judged by whether we practiced mercy, and we will not be excused if we did not know we should practice it. Thus, like Matthew's goats, the rich man in Luke 6 learns this "moral" in Hades; he never showed mercy to poor Lazarus begging at his gate. The practice of mercy is the measure of our judgment.

Third, our entire theological tradition is expressed in terms of mercy, which I define as the willingness to enter into the chaos of another. Like the Good Samaritan stopping for wounded Adam, attending to someone in need is no simple affair. Helping anyone in need is entering into the entire "problem" or "chaos" of their situation.[41]

Thus, the creation is bringing order out of the chaos of the universe; the incarnation is God's entry into the chaos of human existence; and the redemption is bringing us out of the chaos of our slavery to sin. Christ's own entrance into the chaos of death occasions our hope in the risen life, and his pledge to return again is a pledge to deliver us from the chaos of our own lives. Every action of God is aimed at rescuing us from chaos, not unlike Sobrino's own claims for mercy.

## Mercy in the Tradition

In looking for the singularity of mercy as distinctive for Christian ethics, I want to turn to two places: the early church and the *Summa Theologiae* of Thomas Aquinas.

Listening and responding to the sufferer as an embodied subject has always been the vocation of the Christian disciple, as Rodney Stark argues in his brilliant work *The Rise of Christianity: A Sociologist Reconsiders History*. There Stark argues that at its inception Christianity was an urban movement in dreadfully overpopulated cities.[42] Moreover, these cities were not settled places whose inhabitants descended from previous generations. With high infant mortality rates and short life expectancies, the cities required a substantial stream of newcomers in order to maintain their population levels. These cities then were comprised of strangers, and these strangers were hospitably treated by some Christians, who were anything but poor.[43]

As distinct from Christians, the ethical demands imposed by the gods of the pagans were substantively ritual, and, while pagan Romans practiced generosity, their generosity did not stem from any divine command. On the contrary, Roman philosophers opposed the practice of mercy. "Pity was a defect of character unworthy of the wise and excusable only in those who have not yet grown up. It was an impulsive response based on ignorance."[44] Against this background, Stark highlights the distinctive significance of Christian mercy.

This was the moral climate in which Christianity taught that mercy is one of the primary virtues—that a merciful God requires humans to be merciful. Moreover, the corollary that *because* God loves humanity, Christians may not please God unless they *love one another* was entirely new. Perhaps even more revolutionary was the principle that Christian love and charity must extend beyond the boundaries of family and tribe, that it must extend to "all those who in every place call on the name of our Lord Jesus Christ" (1 Cor. 1:2). . . . This was revolutionary stuff. Indeed, it was the cultural basis for the revitalization of a Roman world groaning under a host of miseries.[45]

Along with Stark, biblical scholars Wayne Meeks[46] and Abraham Malherbe[47] direct us to the social research that highlights hospitality and mercy as central identifiable traits of early urban Christian ethics. The social historian Peter Brown likewise reflects on the first Christians and again addresses the urban context, the virtue of mercy, and the imaginative responses.[48]

Moreover, this mercy was effective. Stark provides us with a summary:

Christianity revitalized life in Greco-Roman cities by providing new norms and new kinds of social relationships able to cope with many urgent urban problems. To cities filled with the homeless and impoverished, Christianity offered charity as well as hope. To cities filled with newcomers and strangers, Christianity offered an immediate basis for attachments. To cities filled with orphans and widows, Christianity provided a new and expanded sense of family.[49]

Mercy, then, was constitutive of early Christian identity, and therefore the ethics of Christianity was distinctively marked by the call of mercy.

Though Sobrino, on several occasions, tries to distance the normativity of the principle of mercy from the corporal works of mercy, still, in the tradition, by engaging the corporal works, one experienced a sustained encounter of solidarity with persons who were suffering, be they prisoners, sick, homeless, starving, and so on. The experience of that encounter should lead and often does to the quest to understand more systematically the causes of the suffering. This, in turn, leads naturally to trying to articulate the right systematic responses to these causes.

In the Christian tradition, visiting the prisoner led to working for prison reform; sheltering the homeless prompted such agents to discover and rectify the social causes of homelessness; feeding the hungry helped Christians understand the underlying discriminatory practices that cause hunger.

Like Sobrino's insight, this practice of mercy leads to the enduring work of justice; but that mercy, that felt human solidarity that prompted the action in the first place, is the underlying principle of the works of justice. In fact, throughout all our work for justice, it is that principled, driving mercy that sustains our work and also our relatedness to the one suffering from injustice.

Thus, the priority that Sobrino gives to mercy is, as he says, nothing new. I close by looking at Thomas Aquinas, who essentially makes the same affirmation. In entertaining the question "whether mercy is the greatest of the virtues," Thomas remarks, "In itself, mercy takes precedence over other virtues, for it belongs to mercy to be bountiful to others, and what is more, to succor others in their wants, which pertains chiefly to one who stands above. Hence mercy is accounted as being proper to God: therein His omnipotence is declared to be chiefly manifested."[50] Thomas adds, "mercy likens us to God as regards similarity of works."[51]

While Sobrino tells us that the root and breath of all Christian moral activity are inevitably caught by mercy, Aquinas similarly remarks that as regards any moral action, the "sum total of the Christian religion consists in mercy."[52] On mercy, Sobrino takes us to the traditional heart of Catholicism.

## Notes

1. Jon Sobrino, *El Principio-Misericordia: Bajar de la cruz a los pueblos crucificados* (Santander: Sal Terrae, 1992).

2. Jon Sobrino, *The Principle of Mercy: Taking the Crucified People from the Cross* (Maryknoll, N.Y.: Orbis Books,1994) (hereafter, *Principle*).

3. Sobrino, "Letter," in *Principle*, 188. See also the comments in Kevin Burke, *The Ground beneath the Cross: The Theology of Ignacio Ellacuría* (Washington, D.C.: Georgetown University Press, 2000), 214-15.

4. Sobrino, "The Legacy of the Martyrs of the Central American University," in *Principle*, 176.

5. Sobrino, "Awakening from the Sleep of Inhumanity," in *Principle*, 10.

6. Ibid., 9.

7. Sobrino, "Preface," in *Principle*, viii.

8. Sobrino, "The Samaritan Church and the Principle of Mercy," in *Principle*, 16. The essay originally appeared in the journal *Sal Terrae* 927, no. 10 (1990): 665-78.

9. Ibid., 16.

10. Ibid., 17.

11. Ibid. See also Burke, *Ground beneath the Cross,* 159-60.

12. "Samaritan Church and the Principle of Mercy," 17.

13. Ibid., 19-20.

14. Ibid., 18.

15. Ibid.

16. Ibid., 20.

17. Ibid., 21-22.

18. Ibid., 22.

19. Ibid., 23-24.

20. Sobrino, "Toward a Determination of the Nature of Priesthood: Service to God's

Salvific Approach to Human Beings," in *Principle*, 105-43; originally appeared in *Revista Latinoamericana de Teología* (1984).

21. Ibid., 132. Gustavo Baena, "El sacerdocio de Cristo," *Diakonia* 26 (1983): 122-34. I found several of these texts coming from works beyond *Principle* in the insightful dissertation by Kathleen Bozzuti-Jones, "Groundwork for an Ethic of Mercy: For Privileged Christians Desiring Restoration and Repair" (Ph.D. diss., Boston College, May 2005).

22. Baena, "El sacerdocio de Cristo," 130, at Sobrino, *Principle*, 132.

23. Sobrino, *Principle*, 133.

24. Sobrino, "Theology in a Suffering World," *Principle*, 27-46, at 45, originally published in *Pluralism and Oppression*, ed. Paul Knitter (Annual of the College Theology Society, 1988).

25. Sobrino, "Spirituality and the Following of Jesus," in *Mysterium Liberationis: Fundamental Concepts in Liberation Theology*, ed. Ignacio Ellacuría and Jon Sobrino (Maryknoll, N.Y.: Orbis Books, 1993), 677-701, at 682.

26. Sobrino, "Spirituality and the Following of Jesus," 692.

27. Sobrino, "The Central Position of the Reign of God in Liberation Theology," in *Mysterium Liberationis*, ed. Ellacuría and Sobrino, 350-88, at 363.

28. Curiously, Sobrino acknowledges that in Spanish the word *misericordia* can mean both "mercy" and "compassion." He uses the latter word because he thinks it more appropriate, but, fortunately, subsequent editors and translators kept the principle as "mercy," with this being the only exception. Moreover, he acknowledges that much of what he has to say has already been developed in the 1990 *Sal Terrae* article on the Samaritan Church (see n. 8 above); also, Jon Sobrino, "Rich and Poor Churches and the Compassion Principle," in *A Spirituality for Contemporary Life*, ed. David Fleming (St. Louis: Review for Religious, 1991), 44-63, at 44 and 63 respectively.

29. Ibid., 50.

30. Sobrino, "Spirituality and the Following of Jesus," 682.

31. See Franz Furger, "Christlich-theologische Ethik—angefragt und in Frage gestellt," *Theologie der Gegenwart* 39 (1996): 209-34; James Keenan and Thomas Kopfensteiner, "Moral Theology out of Western Europe," *Theological Studies* 59 (1998): 107-35.

32. See the recent collection of Auer's work; in particular, "Die Bedeutung des Christlichen bei der Normfindung," in *Zur Theologie der Ethik* (Freiburg: Herder, 1995), 208. His interest in the thesis from an ecclesiological perspective stems from an early article, "Nach dem Erscheinen der Enzyklika 'Humanae vitae'—Zehn Thesen über die findung sittlicher Weisungen," *Theologische Quartalschrift* 149 (1969): 78-85; the classical work remains his *Autonome Moral und christlicher Glaube* (Düsseldorf: Patmos, 1984).

33. Heinz Schurmann, Joseph Ratzinger, Hans Urs Von Balthasar, *Principles of Christian Morality* (San Francisco: Ignatius Press, 1986) (German original, *Prinzipien Christlicher moral*, 1975).

34. The major essays in the debate appeared in Charles E. Curran and Richard McCormick, eds., *Readings in Moral Theology, No. 2: The Distinctiveness of Christian Ethics* (New York: Paulist Press, 1980). See a fine treatment of the debate in Eric Gaziaux, *Morale de la foi et morale autonome* (Leuven: Peeters, 1995); and idem, *L'autonomie en morale: Au croisement de la philosophie et de la théologie* (Leuven: Leuven University Press, 1998).

35. Odon Lottin, *L'Âme du culte: La vertu de religion* (Louvain: Abbaye du Mont César, 1920); idem, *Psychologie et morale aux XIIe et XIIIe siècles* (Gembloux: J. Duculot, 1942-1960); idem, *Principes de morale* (Louvain: Abbaye du Mont César, 1946); idem, *Aux Sources*

*de notre grandeur morale* (Louvain: Abbaye du Mont César, 1946); idem, *Morale fondamentale* (Tournai: Desclée, 1954); idem, *Au Coeur de la morale chrétienne* (Tournai: Desclée, 1957). See also Mary Jo Iozzio, *Self-Determination and the Moral Act: A Study of the Contributions of Odon Lottin, O.S.B.* (Leuven: Peeters, 1995).

36. Theodor Steinbüchel, *Die philosophische Grundlegung der katholischen Sittenlehre;* Theodor Müncker, *Die psychologische Grundlegung der katholischen Sittenlehre;* Fritz Tillmann, *Die katholische Sittenlehre: Die Idee der Nachfolge Christi,"* vols. 1, 2, and 3 of *Die katholische Sittenlehre,* ed. Fritz Tillmann (Dusseldorf: Patmos, 1934); Tillmann, *Der Meister Ruft* (Düsseldorf: Patmos, 1937), Eng. trans., *The Master Calls: A Handbook of Christian Living* (Baltimore: Helicon Press, 1960).

37. Gerard Gilleman, *The Primacy of Charity in Moral Theology,* trans. William Ryan and André Vachon (Westminister, Md.: Newman Press, 1959). Vincent Leclercq, "Le primat de la charité de Gilleman et la conscience de Carpentier: Le renouveau théologal de la vie morale," *Studia Morale* 44 (2006): 353-75.

38. Bernard Häring, *The Law of Christ,* trans. Edwin Kaiser (Westminster, Md.: Newman Press, 1961).

39. See, for instance, Augustine, *Quaestiones Evangeliorum* 2.19; Bede, *Lucae Evangelium Expositio,* III (Patrologia latina 92: 467-70). See also Robert Stein, *An Introduction to the Parables of Jesus* (Philadelphia: Westminster, 1981) 42-52.

40. William C. Spohn, *Go and Do Likewise: Jesus and Ethics* (New York: Continuum, 1999), 89-90.

41. See my *The Works of Mercy: The Heart of Catholicism,* 2d ed. (Lanham, Md.: Sheed & Ward, 2007).

42. Rodney Stark, *The Rise of Christianity: A Sociologist Reconsiders History* (Princeton: Princeton University Press, 1996), 149-50. At the end of the first century, Antioch's population was 150,000 within the city walls or 117 persons per acre. Today, New York City has a density of 37 overall, and Manhattan with its high-rise apartments has 100 persons per acre.

43. Ibid., 28-47. See also Robin Scroggs, "The Social Interpretation of the New Testament," *New Testament Studies* 26 (1980): 164-79; Marta Sordi, *The Christians and the Roman Empire* (Norman: University of Oklahoma Press, 1986).

44. E. A. Judge, "The Quest for Mercy in Late Antiquity," in *God Who Is Rich in Mercy,* ed. P. T. O'Brien (Sydney: Macquarie University Press, 1986): 107-21, at 107. As quoted in Stark, *The Rise of Christianity,* 212.

45. Stark, *The Rise of Christianity,* 212. See also John Elliott, *A Home for the Homeless: A Sociological Exegesis of I Peter, Its Situation and Strategy* (Philadelphia: Fortress, 1981).

46. Wayne Meeks, *The Origins of Christian Morality* (New Haven: Yale University Press, 1993); and idem, *The First Urban Christians* (New Haven: Yale University Press, 1983).

47. Abraham Malherbe, *Social Aspects of Early Christianity* (Baton Rouge: Louisiana State University, 1977).

48. Peter Brown, *Late Antiquity* (Cambridge, Mass.: Belknap Press of Harvard University Press, 1998).

49. Stark, *The Rise of Christianity,* 161.

50. Thomas Aquinas, *Summa Theologiae,* 2d ed.; trans. Fathers of the English Dominican Province (London: Burns, Oates & Washbourne, 1921), II.II.30. 4c.; vol. 9, 396.

51. Ibid., 30. 4. ad 3., 397.

52. Ibid., 30.4. ad 2., 397.

# 15

# Mercy and Justice in the Face of Suffering
*The Preferential Option for the Poor*

JOSEPH CURRAN

The recent Notification on the Works of Father Jon Sobrino, S.J., issued by the Congregation for the Doctrine of the Faith, is introduced with an Explanatory Note that acknowledges Sobrino's concern for the poor and oppressed, a "preoccupation" shared by the universal church.[1] This cover letter affirms the church's commitment to the preferential option for the poor and repeats the warnings of *Libertatis nuntius*[2] and *Libertatis conscientia*[3] that official critiques of liberation theology and liberation theologians are not to be interpreted as a retreat from that commitment. By placing the Notification in this context, the Congregation seems to suggest that the criticisms of some aspects of Sobrino's theology evaluated elsewhere in this volume should not be construed as a rejection of the preferential option for the poor, which he advocates.

The phrase "preferential option for the poor" has been widely used but not always precisely defined. The Catholic bishops of Latin America defined the preferential option as a "pastoral guideline" calling the church to special solidarity with the poor;[4] John Paul II described it as a moral principle governing the use of goods by all Christians, and directing all Christians to solidarity with the materially poor.[5] The Catholic bishops of the United States have argued that the preferential option requires public policy decisions to be assessed first in light of their impact on the poor.[6] The preferential option has also been described as an orientation that characterizes all of Catholic social teaching.[7]

To this complex and diverse discussion, Sobrino brings a challenging clarity. For Sobrino, the preferential option for the poor is a reaction to the suffering of the poor and oppressed which directs the church and its members to locate themselves with the poor and work to eliminate that suffering. It finds its authority in the life and example of Jesus and directs every aspect of the life of the one who makes the preferential option. This commitment will take those who make it literally out of their way, and in fact this "de-centering" is the sure sign that the preferential option is being practiced. This chapter will explore, first, the roots of Sobrino's account of the preferential option in his analysis of the life of Jesus, and then his systematic treatment of the preferential option as the "principle of mercy" in "The Samaritan Church and the Principle of Mercy," both with reference to Archbishop Oscar Romero, who is Sobrino's paradigm for the preferential option at the personal and institutional level.

## The Preferential Option and Discipleship

Sobrino regards Jesus Christ as the foundation of all Christian thought and life. Christian ethics "finds in Christ, meaning here the Jesus of history, its criterion for formulating the principles and tasks of morality."[8] Rather than attempt to reconstruct or recover the historical reality of Jesus that lies behind the Gospel accounts of his life, Sobrino argues that Christology can recognize a consensus about the historical accuracy of some of the "fundamental data" of Jesus' life.[9] The spirit and practice of Jesus are handed down by the Christian community, primarily through the Gospels, and this tradition renders "a historical version" of Jesus without giving full access to the "real Jesus."[10] Specific facts about Jesus' life should not be abstracted from these accounts in any attempt to reconstruct the "real" Jesus. In this manner, Sobrino distances himself from the project of reconstructing a historical Jesus.[11]

Sobrino concludes that the announcement of the kingdom of God is the center of Jesus' mission, although "Jesus often speaks of the Kingdom of God, but never says what it actually is."[12] Sobrino argues that Jesus' concept of the kingdom of God is rooted in the Hebrew Scriptures' picture of an oppressed people who hope for justice in history.[13] Jesus' announcement of the coming of the kingdom appealed to this hope, which emerges within the context of negative situations, for example, slavery in Egypt, or exile in Babylon.[14] The kingdom of God was expected to transform an unjust situation into a just one. One thing that can be said definitively about the kingdom of God is that it constitutes good news to the poor, and something of the nature of the kingdom of God can be inferred from this.[15] Jesus identified the poor as special recipients of the good news of the kingdom of God in Luke's beatitudes (Luke 6:20), and Jesus repeatedly identified himself as the one who brings good news to the poor (e.g., Luke 4:18 and 7:22; Matt 11:5). Sobrino argues that "the poor" to whom Jesus refers throughout the Gospel narratives includes sinners, toll collectors, and others who were socially excluded even if they were not materially poor.[16]

John Meier has criticized some aspects of Sobrino's interpretation of the meaning of "the poor" in the Gospels, as well as Sobrino's assertion that Jesus showed partiality toward the poor.[17] Meier argued that in referring to Jesus' partiality to "the poor, the oppressed, and sinners," Sobrino conflated several distinct and materially different groups. Meier also objected to Sobrino's suggestion that this partiality contributed to Jesus' death: "there is not proof that Jesus' concern for economically poor or uneducated people caused a major scandal or persecution, or was the major reason for his execution."[18] Meier argued that Jesus alienated Jews from across the sociopolitical spectrum through his offer of forgiveness to tax collectors who were "economic oppressors," and not in any sense "poor."[19]

However, even Sobrino's early work recognized that Jesus' death cannot be attributed to any one aspect of his ministry. In *Christology at the Crossroads*, Sobrino argued that Jesus' revelation of the reality of God, including but not limited to his partiality to the poor, was the cause of his death.[20] Also, in *Jesus the Liberator*, Sobrino describes the poor as falling into two broad categories— the "economic poor," that is, those who have trouble getting enough material goods for survival, and the "sociologically poor," that is, those who are outcasts, such as the sinners and tax collectors of the Gospels.[21] In the Gospels, these groups often comprised different members, but Sobrino points out that today in Latin America, the economically poor are, in fact, also the despised and excluded. Sobrino recognizes that fine points of his interpretation may be called into question, but he believes that "a basic vision of what the poor meant to Jesus" is clear, and that they are "those who are at the bottom of the heap of history and those who are oppressed by society and cast out from it."[22] By referring collectively to "the poor," Sobrino makes a generalization, but he does so with some attention to historical-critical issues. He does not suggest that poverty as a socioeconomic reality today corresponds exactly with the poor of the Gospels; he simply suggests that the best modern analogue to the people to whom Jesus is partial in the Gospels are the materially poor people of Latin America. Meier's criticisms reveal that Sobrino often treats scriptural texts without an exegete's precision. Meier, however, does not challenge the basic argument that structures Sobrino's preferential option for the poor—that Jesus showed special concern for those "at the bottom of the heap of history," that Christians should follow his example, and that the concern should be directed to the materially poor, particularly of Latin America.

Sobrino argues that the universality of the kingdom of God is expressed through a special concern for this group, as in the story of the Exodus, when God revealed his universal care for humanity through a partiality for the Israelites. Jesus reveals God's universal care for the world through his care for those who have the least reasonable expectation of receiving such care.[23] Sobrino argues that since the poor are the ones whose lives are threatened, good news to them would offer security. Therefore, the kingdom of God, as good news to the poor, is that which brings "authentic liberation at every level of human existence."[24] The kingdom of God liberates from oppression as Jesus liberated from blindness, sin, paralysis, and other forces; we may infer the content of the kingdom from the actions of Jesus—that is, praying, healing, exorcizing, raising the dead, and forgiving as well as teaching.[25] However, "God's action does not simply affirm the positive aspect of human existence. Rather it affirms through a negation—which is to say, through a liberation."[26] Sobrino concludes that preaching the kingdom of God includes confronting and denouncing the "anti-reign."[27]

Jesus denounces with actions and words. In several incidents in the Synoptic Gospel, Jesus' actions constitute a prophetic denunciation of religious ritual structures that oppressed and enslaved. These controversies include the healing and forgiving of the paralytic (Mark 2:1-12; Matt 9:1-18; Luke 5:17-26), Jesus' habit of eating with known sinners (Mark 2:15-17; Matt 9:9-13; Luke 5:27-32), Jesus' answer to the question about fasting (Mark 2:18-22; Matt 9:14-17; Luke 5:33-39), Jesus' disciples' plucking and eating grain on the Sabbath (Mark 2:23-28; Matt 12:1-8; Luke 6:1-5), and Jesus' curing on the Sabbath (Mark 3:1-6; Matt 12:9-14; Luke 6:6-11). According to Sobrino, in each of these cases, Jesus by his words and actions asserted that "his God is a God of life and that this is the basis on which the goodness or badness of religious and social rules and practices must be judged."[28] Jesus showed that "God does not wish religious observance to get in the way of human observance."[29] Sobrino suggests that Jesus was intentionally provocative, for example, by healing on the Sabbath when such healing might have been done later, precisely to condemn religious observances that contradict God's compassion.[30]

In addition to these prophetic actions, Jesus directly denounced the rich, the scribes and Pharisees, and the priests in particular because of their opposition to the reign of God. Jesus juxtaposed the rich and the poor in the story of Lazarus and the rich man (Luke 16:19-31) and in the beatitudes and woes (Luke 6:20-26). Sobrino argues that these stories show that Jesus found the coexistence of wealth and poverty "insulting and intolerable," a social evil that is an affront to God.[31] Jesus also suggested on several occasions (e.g., Matt 6:24; Luke 16:13; 18:23) that the possession of riches is incompatible with serving God.

Jesus most often denounces the scribes and Pharisees (Luke 11:37-53; Matt 23:1-36) for their vanity and hypocrisy, but Sobrino points out that Jesus also denounced them for oppressing the people. Jesus denounces the scribes for "oppression and objective wickedness,"[32] because they "load the people with burdens too hard to bear" (Luke 12:46). In Mark, the scribes "devour widows' houses and for the sake of appearances say long prayers" (Mark 12:38-40). Sobrino finds in these denunciations and the attendant warnings an echo of the prophet Hosea, "they feed on the sins of my people; they are greedy for their iniquity" (4:8).[33] Jesus denounced the priests as he purified the temple (Mark 11:15-19; Matt 21:12-17; Luke 19:45-48), echoing the prophets' denunciation of the exploitation of the people (e.g., Jer 7:11 and Isa 65:7). Sobrino concludes that Jesus' preaching of the kingdom of God included denouncing structures that were in opposition to the kingdom. In doing this, Jesus struck at "the roots of a society oppressed by all sorts of power: economic, political, ideological, and religious."[34] These denunciations were part of the tension and conflict that contributed to Jesus' death. Sobrino argues repeatedly that such tension and conflict is a sign that God's reign is being preached, both in Jesus' time and today.[35]

Sobrino defines Christian discipleship as continuing the practice of Jesus in one's own context.[36] Jesus' practice must be considered in light of the "spirit with which he engaged in it and with which he imbued it,"[37] a spirit characterized by special attention to the plight of the poor. Extending this spirit and practice into one's own context requires an analysis to determine who the "poor" are in that context. Sobrino argues that such an analysis today shows a world characterized more profoundly by the suffering of material poverty than by any other reality. Other characteristics of the world—for example, religious pluralism and cultural diversity—may be important, but poverty is the world's "primary reality."[38] Liberation theology recognizes the suffering of the materially poor—the "crucified peoples" as the "major form" of suffering in the world.[39] This is the most extreme form of what Sobrino calls "historical suffering," that is, suffering that some people deliberately inflict on others, because it is both widespread and terminal.[40] Therefore, Sobrino argues that poverty is the most massive form of historical suffering both in severity and extent.[41]

By emphasizing the priority of material suffering, Sobrino may seem to overlook the significance of spiritual suffering, as has been suggested by the Congregation for the Doctrine of the Faith.[42] Thomas Aquinas argued that good works which succor the spirit are more excellent than those that succor the body, because the soul is higher than the body.[43] Sobrino regards such "spiritual suffering" as "doubts, guilt, failure, meaninglessness" as simply one of several categories of suffering.[44] These positions, however, are not as far apart as they appear. Thomas's general precept that spiritual almsgiving is more excellent than corporal almsgiving has a number of exceptions for particular cases, most often in the case of extreme physical or material need.[45] Sobrino describes the poverty of Latin America and the rest of the Third World as a terminal condition that "brings death slowly and violently" to untold millions each year, that is, an extreme case of physical and material need.[46] Sobrino is not arguing for the absolute priority of the needs of the material suffering but for the priority of those needs in the case of the world as it is. Sobrino's insistence on the priority of material suffering grows out of his examination of the state of the world today and his analysis of the practice of Jesus—not out of an a priori determination that material suffering is more serious than spiritual suffering. It seems consistent with Thomas's classic understanding of the relationship of spiritual and physical needs.

In order to make a preferential option for the poor, the church must denounce the oppression of the poor and announce the reign of God as Jesus did. The church, however, as an institution tends toward stability and self-preservation, which are often in tension with prophetic denunciation. In *The True Church and the Poor,* Sobrino describes the interplay between the prophetic and institutional roles of the church. The institutional aspect of the church is comprised of the doctrinal, administrative, and liturgical structures by which it carries out the mission of Christ. This institutional presence makes the embodiment of Jesus by the Christian community more universally effective, and without the institutional aspect there would be no church.[47] The institutional aspect of the church also keeps the community from becoming "a minority group of ethically superior individuals." However, it also tends to "avoid conflict and distrust the new until its truth has been theologically justified."[48]

In contrast, the prophetic aspect of the church is committed to the utopian horizon of the reign of God. According to Sobrino, the prophetic church will constantly remind the institutional church that the church itself is not the reign of God. This is why prophecy usually entails conflict with the institutional church.[49] Such conflict, however, pushes the entire church to take a prophetic stance in society, a stand that it might not otherwise take. Sobrino argues that without such pressure, the institutional church might retreat from the need to engage in truly prophetic work, for example, by endorsing human rights in a general way without denouncing the societal structures that give rise to a concrete situation of violence.[50]

In his account of the prophetic nature of the preferential option for the poor, Sobrino acknowledges that most individual Christians belong to "the vast majority of human beings who by reason of the social structure of the race cannot be prophets."[51] Some people, however, find themselves in positions of social prominence that allow them to take an effective prophetic stance on behalf of the poor. Archbishop Oscar Romero was such a person. Sobrino describes Romero's denunciation of oppression as rooted in a faith like that of Jesus, a faith in a God who will bring about a more just society.[52] Romero repeatedly condemned the oppression of the people in spite of the threats to the security and well-being of the institutional church of which he was the leader. In so doing, he "made the defense of the poor and oppressed a specific and basic function of his episcopal ministry."[53] Romero also placed the resources of his archdiocese at the disposal of the poor, and thereby "effectively institutionalized the preferential option for the poor."[54] Romero's defense of the poor in the form of an attack on their oppressors led the Salvadoran church into conflict with the powerful; Sobrino argues that such conflict is a mark of the presence of the true church[55] and an inevitable result of the church's attempt to carry out its mission of realizing God's reign in history.[56]

Romero illustrates how a preferential option for the poor functions as a prophetic stance, one that requires the church to denounce the structures and powers that cause and perpetuate poverty, one that takes the church out of its way. The story of Jesus provides the authority for this denunciation and an example of how it is to be done. An even more systematic treatment of the preferential option as a prophetic stance at both the personal and institutional level is found in the *Principle of Mercy*, Sobrino's formulation of the preferential option for the poor based on the story of the Good Samaritan.

## The Principle of Mercy

The Good Samaritan functions as both a systematic treatment of the preferential option and as another concrete example of a person making the preferential option. In an essay entitled "The Samaritan Church and the Principle of Mercy," Sobrino indicates that the principle of mercy is "nothing but a restatement, in other language, of the option for the poor that the church is obliged to make according to the definitions of the institutional church itself."[57] For this particular restatement of the preferential option, Sobrino draws on the parable of the Good Samaritan, in addition to amplifying some of the reflections on the life of Jesus described above.

Sobrino argues that mercy is a guiding principle in the life of Jesus and is therefore a defining mark of the church.[58] Mercy is the "most structuring" element of the life of Jesus and therefore must be the most structuring element in the life of the church, which properly resembles Jesus.[59] The mercy of Jesus is not merely an occasional sentimental movement to alleviate isolated cases of suffering, but a lifetime commitment to eradicate the root causes of suffering; this is why Sobrino calls it a principle. The principle of mercy is a love that initiates and animates a process of activity aimed not only at alleviating specific needs but also at transforming the structures of injustice that are at the root of these needs.

*The Principle of Mercy* draws on Sobrino's previous descriptions of a preferential option for the poor. Sobrino argues that Jesus' practice of mercy "shapes his life and seals his fate."[60] Mercy led Jesus to heal on the Sabbath even though this practice exposed him to controversy and even danger.[61] Jesus healed those who were sick or suffering out of mercy and nothing else, as God saved his people from the Egyptians out of mercy for their suffering and nothing else.[62] Jesus preached, "Blest are they who show mercy," suggesting that by showing mercy one is living as an authentic human being.[63] Sobrino, therefore, sees mercy as the most structuring element of Jesus' life. There are other important elements of Jesus' life but mercy is "absolutely necessary" to define Jesus.[64] For Jesus, to be a human being was to react with mercy, to allow oneself to be transformed by the suffering of the other. Failure to do so attacks the essence of humanity "at its very root."[65]

According to Sobrino, the parable of the Good Samaritan (Luke 10:25-37) illustrates the nature of the principle of mercy because it presents the ideal human being as "one who has seen someone else lying wounded in the ditch along the road, has re-acted, and has helped the victim in every way possible."[66] Jesus offers the parable as a response to a question about the command to love one's neighbor, but the story does not suggest that the Samaritan acted to fulfill any commandment. Instead, Sobrino argues that the Samaritan's action is a radical response to the plight of the wounded man, prompted by a movement of pity. The parable depicts a love that is prompted by suffering, a love that moves the Samaritan to alleviate that suffering as completely as he can "for the sole reason that it exists."[67]

Suffering in Sobrino's usage refers to what is inflicted on some people by others. As he has done elsewhere, Sobrino argues that this is the form of suffering that is most significant to theology, most urgent, and has the first claim on the mercy of the Christian community.[68] For the church to be animated by the principle of mercy, it must "de-center" itself, allowing itself to be taken out of its way as the Samaritan was, to react to this suffering with mercy. The suffering of the poor, which wounds the entire planet and involves millions of people, is the suffering that most cries out for the church's attention. This does not preclude a merciful response to other forms of suffering at the same time, but the universal church and every local church are required, according to Sobrino, to deal with the suffering of poverty if they are to be governed by the principle of mercy.[69]

Sobrino suggests that a church truly motivated by the principle of mercy will be more concerned with alleviating the suffering of "the other," the poor, than it will be with correcting injustices within the institutional church itself. The academic freedom of theologians, for example, is an important issue within the church, but it is not as pressing as the need to attend to the poor who are wounded by the side of the road.[70] This is not to say that one must compete against the other. Sobrino argues for the priority of material suffering in order to overcome ideological resistance to the preferential option, but the church does not have to choose between either pursuing justice within the church or practicing mercy outside of it.

Like the Samaritan, the church's response should also seek to alleviate the suffering of the wounded ones as thoroughly as possible. Therefore, the response cannot be limited to isolated acts of mercy alone. The church must challenge the unjust structures and systems that are at the roots of suffering. For Sobrino, the parable illustrates a reality "shot through with mercilessness," not merely because of the actions of the robbers but also the failure of the priest and the Levite to show any mercy.[71] The church must challenge this reality and deal directly with the forces of anti-mercy. Such forces will tolerate limited tending of wounds, but not the kind of comprehensive practice of mercy that will truly correct unjust situations and save the innocent from falling into the hands of the robbers once again.[72]

Clearly "The Samaritan Church and the Principle of Mercy" is not intended as a thorough historical-critical exegesis of the parable of the Good Samaritan.

Sobrino cites no exegetical literature, and the form and language of the article suggests a theological and pastoral reflection on the parable rather than a rigorous exegetical analysis. It should also be noted that Sobrino's definition of the principle of mercy does not come exclusively from the parable. To support his complex and rich notion of the principle of mercy Sobrino also refers to the general shape of the life of Jesus, as well as to some other specific stories of Jesus' activities in the Gospel.

This is necessary because it is quite clear that the story of the Good Samaritan alone does not suffice to illustrate every aspect of the preferential option. First of all, the story itself is about an individual's act of mercy, but Sobrino attempts to apply the lesson of the parable to the life of the Christian community as a whole and the church as an institution. Sobrino argues that the mercy illustrated in the story must go beyond isolated acts of mercy, yet the story is about only one act of mercy. Further, the story does not necessarily illustrate a motivation for one to attack the root of evil, that is, the structures of injustice, the forces of anti-mercy.[73] The Samaritan does not address the cause of the wounded man's distress, or confront or condemn the robbers, nor does Jesus condemn the robbers, the root cause of the man's suffering. Sobrino claims that "the parable exemplifies the condition of the concrete historical phenomenon as a reality shot through with mercilessness. The priest and the Levite show no mercy, and Jesus is horrified."[74] Such horror, however, must be inferred; Jesus passes over their failure to help without comment. He leaves it to the lawyer to pass judgment on the story's cast. Sobrino argues that the practice of mercy necessarily brings resistance, even persecution, on those who make mercy the principle of their lives. Yet no one resists the Samaritan's actions; in fact, he encounters cooperation from the innkeeper.

This does not suggest that a confrontation with the perpetrators of injustice is not required of those who practice mercy. In fact, Sobrino's experience and that of the church in Latin America seems to indicate that such a confrontation is necessary. But such a confrontation is not found in the parable of the Good Samaritan. A simple and vivid story such as the Good Samaritan can be a fine illustration of moral values and principles, but it is not sufficient fully to illustrate the preferential option for the poor as Sobrino describes it, that is, as a principle that orders and motivates one's entire life and the entire ministry of the church. In order to make these points, Sobrino is forced to import to the story elements not found there. He interprets the role of the robbers and the relationship between the robbers and the one who practices mercy in light of the experience of the church in Latin America, rather than the other way around. By comparing the robbers to the contemporary forces of anti-mercy, Sobrino only draws attention to the absence of any such action by the robbers in the story itself. The reality of anti-mercy in the world is better illustrated by other narratives, which Sobrino uses in this article and elsewhere.

## Assessment

Although the Good Samaritan as an illustration of the principle of mercy has apparent shortcomings, taken together with Sobrino's other work, it completes a clear, detailed, and challenging definition and illustration of the preferential option for the poor.

The preferential option is presented by Sobrino as a prophetic stance. Sobrino considers prophecy to be more than social criticism, more than the condemnation of unjust social structures and the annunciation of a better way, more than even delivering messages for God. The prophetic stance of the preferential option includes all of these things but is most fundamentally an individual or institutional choice about one's own social location.

Sobrino recognizes that the church as institution will tend to resist involvement in the often-dangerous activities of prophecy, as was usually the case with the Salvadoran church.[75] Sobrino argues that this tension, even conflict, was a sign that the church was doing what it should. *The Principle of Mercy* argues that the church's willingness to practice mercy toward the poor is represented by its willingness to condemn the structures and forces that cause poverty, and that the absence of "threats, assaults and persecutions" would indicate only the church's failure to carry out its mission "to the last."[76] Sobrino quotes Romero with approval: "So they have destroyed our radio and murdered our priests? Then let them know they have done us no harm."[77] Sobrino also describes the utopian announcement of the reign of God, but this seems to be less prominent than his denunciation of the structures of injustice and the persecution that this denunciation brings.

Sobrino's willingness to expose the church to conflict and repression can be counterproductive. Romero's prophetic utterances were effective in part because they came from the head of the institutional church of El Salvador, so that the church as an institution enabled him to be an effective prophet. Other missions of the church—the forgiveness of sins, the practice of mercy through direct aid, evangelization, the administration of the sacraments—are also carried out through institutional forms and structures. Sobrino's description of mercy, "consistent to the last," suggests that there is no point at which the church's institutional well-being, or even the church's institutional existence, takes precedence over the denunciation of structures of injustice. Paradoxically, Sobrino seems to suggest that the church should advocate for the poor even if doing so leads to the church's being silenced, which would leave the poor with no advocate.

This is not to argue that the church should never be placed in a dangerous position or that the protection of the church's institutional status and prerogatives is an absolute value. Sobrino rightly points out that the church is not the kingdom of God, and is therefore not indispensable. However, the prophetic denunciation of structures of injustice is not the entirety of the kingdom of God either. Like all functions and ministries of the church, the denunciation of injustice must be reviewed and evaluated in light of the mission of the church to proclaim the kingdom of God.

Sobrino's formulation of the preferential option lacks the kind of moral discourse that directs personal moral choices. Those who act as prophets must have the prominence and public voice effectively to announce and denounce, and to claim some kind of authority for these annunciations and denunciations. Sobrino acknowledges the "vast majority of human beings who by reason of the social structure of the race cannot be prophets," although they might follow the path outlined by the prophets.[78] However, Sobrino does not describe *how* such people might follow the path of the prophets, how the preferential option for the poor may direct their personal moral choices. This dimension of the preferential option, a personal preferential option for the poor, remains unexplored.

However, Sobrino's preferential option for the poor includes the personal dimension in one important area, and that is his understanding of the preferential option as a response to the experience of contact with those who are suffering from poverty. In the case of the Good Samaritan, Jesus, Romero, and even Sobrino himself, the fundamental choice to act to alleviate suffering begins with the encounter with that suffering. Sobrino clearly states that the beginning of the preferential option is this encounter; the option itself is a response to suffering. To make the preferential option, one must know something of the suffering of poverty; in this way the preferential option is connected to solidarity. This also suggests that, although the full extent and nature of the preferential option on the personal level may not be specified, such a personal preferential option begins, at the very least, with having contact with those who are poor and oppressed. This also provides a basis for correlating the preferential option for the poor with similar commitments that do not depend on explicitly Christian affirmations.

Taking all of Sobrino's work on the preferential option for the poor together, we see a fundamental orientation that functions as a personal moral principle, a guide for prophetic discourse, and criteria for assessing policy, but is not limited to any one of these. Sobrino emphasizes the notion that the preferential option for the poor calls the church and Christians out of their way, asks them to locate themselves with the poor. Here, the concrete example of the Good Samaritan illustrates what is most challenging about Sobrino's preferential option for the poor. Contact with suffering changes a person or an institution, and that transformation is most complete when the church and its members choose to located themselves with the poor, share in some measure their suffering, and work from that perspective to alleviate that suffering. Sobrino describes the preferential option as a principle in the classic sense, a fundamental choice and orientation that animates a whole range of activity.

Sobrino puts forward a comprehensive and uncompromising vision; and while it may not provide a set of guidelines for making a personal preferential option for the poor, it does provide a challenging framework within which to establish these guidelines, and an important starting point for making the preferential option.

## Notes

1. Congregation for the Doctrine of the Faith, "Explanatory Note on the Notification on the Works of Father Jon Sobrino, S.J." section 1. Accessed August 29, 2007, at http://www.vatican.va/roman_curia/congregations/cfaith/documents/rc_con_cfaith_doc_20061126_nota-sobrino_en.html.

2. Congregation for the Doctrine of the Faith, "Instruction on Certain Aspects of the Theology of Liberation," in *Liberation Theology: A Documentary History*, ed. Alfred T. Hennelly (Maryknoll, N.Y.: Orbis Books, 1990), 393-414. See, for example, XI.1.

3. Congregation for the Doctrine of the Faith, "Instruction on Christian Freedom and Liberation," XI. 1-2, in *Liberation Theology*, ed. Hennelly, 461-97. See, for example, nos. 68-70.

4. See Archbishop Marcos McGrath, "The Puebla Final Document, Introduction and Commentary," in *Evangelization in Latin America's Present and Future: Final Document of the Third General Conference of the Latin American Episcopate*, ed. John Eagleson and Philip Sharper (Maryknoll, N.Y.: Orbis Books, 1979), 87-110, at 104.

5. See, for example, *Sollicitudo rei socialis* nos. 42 and 46, *Centesimus annus* no. 36, in David J. O'Brien and Thomas Shannon, *Catholic Social Thought: The Documentary Heritage* (Maryknoll, N.Y.: Orbis Books, 1992).

6. United States Conference of Catholic Bishops, *Economic Justice for All*, in O'Brien and Shannon, no. 86.

7. Donal Dorr, *Opting for the Poor* (Maryknoll, N.Y.: Orbis Books, 1992), 1.

8. Jon Sobrino, *Christology at the Crossroads*, trans. John Drury (Maryknoll, N.Y.: Orbis Books, 1978), 109.

9. Jon Sobrino, *Jesus the Liberator*, trans. Paul Burns and Francis McDonagh (Maryknoll, N.Y.: Orbis Books, 1994), 61. Sobrino makes a distinction here between the common understanding of the term "historical Jesus" in European circles and what is meant in Latin American liberation theology; see Sobrino, *Jesus the Liberator*, 47-48.

10. Ibid., 61.

11. Ibid., 51. Sobrino's detailed definition of the historical Jesus seems to be a reaction to criticism such as that of John Meier, who found Sobrino's treatment of the historical Jesus in *Jesus in Latin America*, "fuzzy" (John Meier, "The Bible as a Source for Theology," CTSA *Proceedings* 43 [1988], 1-14, at 3). These criticisms indicate a need for clarification of some of Sobrino's early work, but it should be noted that Sobrino never attempts to establish "criteria for authenticity" in order to reconstruct "the real Jesus."

12. Sobrino, *Jesus the Liberator*, 69.

13. Ibid., 74-75.

14. Ibid., 71-72.

15. Ibid., 69-70.

16. Ibid., 82.

17. Meier, "The Bible as a Source for Theology," 3.

18. Ibid., 4.

19. Ibid., 4.

20. Sobrino, *Christology at the Crossroads*, 203-4.

21. Sobrino, *Jesus the Liberator*, 80.

22. Ibid., 80.

23. Ibid., 82.

24. Sobrino, *Christology at the Crossroads*, 44.

25. Ibid., 41-43; Sobrino, *Jesus the Liberator*, 87-104. Sobrino takes more liberties than Meier, going beyond the sayings that mention the reign of God or imply its presence in Jesus' ministry. Jesus, however, does make an explicit connection between his own actions and the reign of God (e.g., Luke 11:20, "If by the finger of God I cast out demons, then the Kingdom of God has come upon you"). In light of such sayings, and in light of the evident importance of the reign of God to Jesus' teaching and ministry, casting a wide net to determine the nature of the reign of God, as Sobrino does, is certainly defensible.

26. Sobrino, *Christology at the Crossroads*, 47.

27. Sobrino, *Jesus the Liberator*, 170; see also Sobrino, *Christology at the Crossroads*, 53.

28. Sobrino, *Jesus the Liberator*, 163.

29. Ibid., 164.

30. Ibid., 195. For a slightly different description of these incidents, see Jon Sobrino, *The Principle of Mercy* (Maryknoll, N.Y.: Orbis Books, 1994), 19.

31. Sobrino, *Jesus the Liberator*, 172.

32. Ibid., 175.

33. Ibid., 175-76.

34. Ibid., 179.

35. Sobrino, *Jesus the Liberator*, 83; Sobrino, *Christology at the Crossroads*, 355.

36. Sobrino, *Jesus the Liberator*, 49.

37. Ibid., 52.

38. Sobrino, *Principle of Mercy*, 27.

39. Ibid., 25, 29.

40. Ibid., 29.

41. Ibid., 33.

42. In the cover letter to the Notification, the Congregation agrees with Pope Benedict XVI that "the first poverty among people is not to know Christ" (Congregation for the Doctrine of the Faith, "Explanatory Note on the Notification on the Works of Father Jon Sobrino, S.J.," section 1, n. 2).

43. Thomas Aquinas, *Summa Theologiae*, trans. Fathers of the English Dominican Province (New York: Benziger Brothers, 1947-48), II-II 32.4.

44. See Sobrino, *Principle of Mercy*, 29.

45. Aquinas writes, "A man in hunger is to be fed rather than instructed, and as the philosopher observes, for a needy man money is better than philosophy, although the latter is better simply" (*Summa Theologica*, II-II 32.4).

46. Sobrino, *Principle of Mercy*, 29.

47. Jon Sobrino, *The True Church and the Poor*, trans Matthew J. O'Connell, (Maryknoll, N.Y.: Orbis Books, 1984), 217.

48. Ibid., 212; see also 214-15.

49. Ibid., 212.

50. Ibid., 218.

51. Ibid., 217.

52. Jon Sobrino, "A Theologian's View of Oscar Romero," in Oscar Romero, *Voice of the Voiceless: The Four Pastoral Letters and Other Statements*, trans. Michael J. Walsh (Maryknoll, N.Y.: Orbis Books, 1985), 22-51, at 23 and 24-25.

53. Ibid., 30.

54. Ibid., 31.

55. See Sobrino, *Principle of Mercy*, 24.

56. See Sobrino, *True Church and the Poor*, 208-10.

57. Sobrino, *Principle of Mercy*, 25.

58. The article was originally written for an issue of *Sal Terrae* titled "The Other Marks of the Church"; see Sobrino, *Principle of Mercy*, 15.

59. Ibid., 15-16.

60. Ibid., 17.

61. Ibid., 19.

62. Ibid., 16. Sobrino argues that the loving action of God stands at the beginning of the process of salvation and notes that the reason God gives to Moses for coming to rescue his people is simply that he has "observed the misery of my people who are in Egypt, I have heard their cry on account of their taskmasters. Indeed I know their sufferings . . . " (Exod 3:7-8).

63. Sobrino, *Principle of Mercy*, 19.

64. Ibid., 17.

65. Ibid., 17-18.

66. Ibid., 17.

67. Ibid., 18.

68. Ibid., 29.

69. Ibid., 22.

70. Ibid., 21-22.

71. Ibid., 19.

72. Ibid., 23.

73. Ibid.

74. Ibid., 19.

75. Ibid., 24.

76. Ibid., 23.

77. Ibid., 24.

78. Sobrino, *True Church and the Poor*, 217.

# 16

# Power and the Preferential Option for the Poor

At our weekly women's house meeting one Friday night at the St. Peter Claver Catholic Worker community in South Bend, one of our new guests began describing her week by joyfully giving thanks to God for being able to rest in safety. Along with her sixteen-year-old daughter, she had just moved in two days earlier to escape an abusive living situation. She recounted that as she was gathering their few possessions to leave, someone asked whether she was certain that it was the right course of action. She responded, "There are only two things in this life about which I'm sure: that Jesus Christ will come again and that God is God."

As I listened, it occurred to me that apart from Scripture, I had never encountered such a firm, clear, and courageous articulation of these tenets of the Christian faith. Her setting or social location—as an African American mother with no material resources, no family in the area, and suddenly with nowhere to rest her head or shelter her daughter—distilled her expression of deep, lifelong faith down to the essentials. In the process, she evangelized our community through her steadfast, humble witness of Christian faith in the midst of severe trials, true to the church's mission rooted in the apostolic tradition.

With this experience in mind, I have pondered Jon Sobrino's argument in *Jesus the Liberator: A Historical-Theological View,* as quoted in and critiqued by the Congregation for the Doctrine of the Faith's (CDF) "Notification on the Works of Father Jon Sobrino, S.J.":

> "Latin America Christology . . . identifies its setting, in the sense of a real situation, as the poor of this world, and this situation is what must be present in and permeate any particular setting in which Christology is done" (*Jesus the Liberator*, 28). Further, "the poor in the community question Christological faith and give it its fundamental direction" (Ibidem, 30) and

"the Church of the poor . . . is the ecclesial setting of Christology because it is a world shaped by the poor" (Ibidem, 31). "The social setting is thus the most crucial for the faith, the most crucial in shaping the thought pattern of Christology, and what requires and encourages the epistemological break" (Ibidem).

While such a preoccupation for the poor and oppressed is admirable, in these quotations the "Church of the poor" assumes the fundamental position which properly belongs to the faith of the Church. It is only in this ecclesial faith that all other theological foundations find their correct epistemological setting.[1]

Epistemologically, the narrative of our new Catholic Worker guest has influenced my understanding of both Sobrino's claims and the CDF's concerns, inducing the sort of "break" that Sobrino describes. Considered correlatively, her witness provides three relevant conceptual hooks. First, epistemologically, her social setting established the ground of understanding from which her articulation of Christian faith arose. Second, methodologically, in no way did her situation of dire poverty and structural violence usurp the "fundamental position" of the faith of the church in her life. On the contrary, her social setting impelled her to grasp the tried and true handholds of the Christian faith with even greater resolve and tenacity, to a degree that nonpoor members of the church, myself included, may never be able to comprehend fully precisely because of our own setting of relative material comfort and social security. And lastly, through her witness, she invited the members of our community into "a privileged setting for knowing God and discovering his will."[2] In this respect, her joy was at once evangelizing and subversive, qualities emblematic of what Gustavo Gutiérrez has called the transformative power of the poor in history.[3]

Our guest's narrative, I suggest, illuminates the interrelated issues of epistemology, method, and power that underpin the CDF's critique of Sobrino's work. His understanding of the church of the poor as the ecclesial setting for Christology represents a theological application of the traditional Catholic social teaching principle of the preferential option for the poor. Methodologically, this involves a commitment to view reality from the interpretive standpoint of the marginalized. From that perspective, the destructive effects of dominative exercises of power come into sharp focus, and a contrasting form of power, one emanating from the Holy Spirit, presents itself, by grace, to those disposed to partake in it.

The church of the poor, in Sobrino's theological epistemology, finds its wellspring in pneumatological power. Precisely through their evangelizing witness of the faith of the church, the poor illuminate for the people of God the way of the cross as the path of salvation from the idolatrous grip of sinful structures of domination, even those afflicting the institutional church itself.

### Epistemology: The Preferential Option for the Poor

In an Explanatory Note accompanying the Notification, the CDF reiterated its critique of Sobrino's theological method by calling particular attention to "the affirmation that the 'Church of the poor' is *the* ecclesial 'setting' of Christology and offers it its fundamental orientation. This disregards the fact that it is only the *apostolic faith* which the Church has transmitted through all generations that constitutes the ecclesial setting of Christology and of theology in general."[4] Stated twice and with such vigor, this particular concern invites a closer reading of *Jesus the Liberator*, beginning with a fuller contextual view of the passage quoted earlier. Sobrino writes,

> Just because they are poor, the poor make a difference to the faith of those who are not poor, so that in the church there cannot be mere addition of individual faiths, but complementarity—put more precisely, *solidarity*—a mutual carrying of one another in faith, allowing oneself to be given faith by the poor and offering them one's own faith. Then, and at the level of content, since the poor are those to whom Jesus' mission was primarily directed, *they ask the fundamental questions of faith and do so with power to move and activate the whole community in the process of "learning to learn" what Christ is.* Because they are God's preferred, and because of the difference between their faith and the faith of the non-poor, the poor, within the faith community, question christological faith and give it its fundamental direction.[5]

In this longer excerpt, Sobrino does affirm the centrality of faith in Christian ecclesial life, but he trains his attention on the methodological fact that one's personal appropriation of faith necessarily takes shape within a particular context or setting, and that in turn determines one's epistemological departure point for understanding and giving expression to faith. By positing the church of the poor as the ecclesial setting of Christology, Sobrino adopts the theological epistemology of the preferential option for the poor.

In *Sollicitudo rei socialis*, Pope John Paul II describes this traditional Catholic social teaching principle as "a *special form* of primacy in the exercise of Christian charity, to which the whole tradition of the Church bears witness. It affects the life of each Christian inasmuch as he or she seeks to imitate the life of Christ, but it applies equally to our *social responsibilities* and hence to our manner of living, and to the logical decisions to be made concerning the ownership and use of goods."[6] Like Sobrino, John Paul II links the expression of faith, *imitatio Christi*, to the praxis of preferentially opting for the poor in the concrete circumstances of one's life. Later in this same document, he calls on the sons and daughters of the church to serve as moral exemplars for the rest of the world by committing themselves to solidarity and the option for the poor "in conformity with the program announced by Jesus himself in the synagogue at Nazareth, to 'preach good news to the poor . . . to proclaim release to the captives and recovering of sight to the blind, to set at liberty those who are oppressed, to proclaim the acceptable year of the Lord' (Luke 4:18-19)."[7]

The resonance between Sobrino's account of the church of the poor and John Paul II's understanding of the option for the poor emerges clearly in light of the pope's treatment of structural sin, a term developed through the scholarship of many liberation theologians, including that of Sobrino. John Paul II first invoked the language of social sin in an address given in 1979 at the Basilica of Our Lady of Zapopán in Guadalajara, Mexico, in preparation for the Third Conference of the Latin American Bishops in Puebla. Affirming the significance of Mary for Mexico and for the entire continent, he observed that as the refuge of sinners, she "enables us to overcome the multiple 'structures of sin' in which our personal, family, and social life is wrapped."[8] The final Puebla document followed the pope's lead in calling attention to the structures of sin threatening their continent, bearing lethal consequences for the poor in particular.[9]

In *Sollicitudo rei socialis*, John Paul II deliberately chose and emphasized the global reality of structural sin as the epistemological framework for his theological argument. "'Sin' and 'structures of sin' are categories which are seldom applied to the situation of the contemporary world. However, one cannot easily gain a profound understanding of the reality that confronts us unless we give a name to the root of the evils which afflict us."[10] In the face of such moral evil, he wrote, the virtue of solidarity and the preferential option for the poor represent necessary, even urgent, theological responses. "These . . . 'structures of sin' are only conquered—presupposing the help of divine grace—by a *diametrically opposed attitude*: a commitment to the good of one's neighbor with the readiness, in the gospel sense, to 'lose oneself' for the sake of the other instead of exploiting him, and to 'serve him' instead of oppressing him for one's own advantage (cf. Matt. 10:40-42; Mark 10:42-45; Luke 22:25-27)."[11] Using the epistemology of the option for the poor, John Paul II, like Sobrino, placed the poor at the center of an ecclesial life and mission of solidarity in faith expressed through praxis.

## The Pneumatological Power of the Poor

Epistemologically, the setting of the church of the poor allows the ecclesial community to experience the transformative power of evangelization from the societal margins. Drawing on the Puebla document, Sobrino emphasizes that the poor serve the church, first, by prompting it to conversion. "They move it to conversion because in their own flesh—human table scraps in many cases—they are asking the church the great question of God: 'What have you done to your brother?' And if those poor, inconcealable because they are at the very center of the church, do not move it to conversion, nothing will."[12] Second, the poor evangelize the church through gospel values, "by their openness to God, by their solidarity, by their sense of community."[13] By virtue of their evangelical witness in faith, the poor become the center of ecclesial life, just as they were in Jesus' life and ministry.

For the nonpoor, the process of being "moved and activated" by the witness of courageous fidelity to gospel values in the midst of life-threatening structural violence implies a radical conversion, a shift from the center of social and ecclesial power structures to the margins that opens new ground for the encounter with Jesus Christ in faith. This movement unfolds inductively, as Sobrino's own narrative attests. He remembers the epistemological epiphany of coming to see reality from the perspective of the poor majority, beginning simply with a disposition to learn from the poor: "When I arrived in El Salvador in 1957 I witnessed appalling poverty, but even though I saw it with my eyes, I did not really see it; thus that poverty had nothing to say to me for my own life as a young Jesuit and as a human being. It did not even cross my mind that I might learn something from the poor."[14] Through this experience, Sobrino realized that the option for the poor inexorably demands conversion of highly educated Westerners, providing an impetus "to admit that we don't know everything, and maybe we don't know the most basic things, and we don't know them because we do not have the eyes of the poor."[15] In attempting to forge relationships of solidarity, the nonpoor begin from a place of epistemological disadvantage, hampered by manifold privilege secured through structures of dominative power. Coming to see one's own blindness, though, represents the beginning of a certain epistemological humility.

The word "humility" stems from the Latin root *humus,* meaning "ground" or "soil." Because poverty means physical death for countless human beings, the option for the poor entails an experiential grounding in the fragile liminality between life and death. Thus, as Sobrino and others have indicated, the reality of the poor actually affords an epistemological advantage: "In the world of the poor there is a light that enables the intellect to see objects that are hard to see without this light."[16] Humbly allowing God to claim oneself through and with the poor, one strives to take in the whole horizon of reality, but one also becomes attuned to previously unknown layers within each present moment, dimensions of the concrete particularity of reality revealed to those who follow Jesus to the margins. Entering deeper into personal relationships of love with flesh-and-blood human beings who lack the basic necessities of a dignified life raises ultimate questions of life and death, breaking open interior space for contemplative awareness at the foot of the cross. Grounded in the *humus,* one begins to perceive and to touch the wounds of crucified humanity rendered visible by the light of God's love. Remembering his own journey, Sobrino recounts,

> Little by little I came face to face with the truly poor, and I am convinced that they were the ones who brought about the final awakening. Once awakened, my questions and especially my answers became radically different. The basic question came to be: Are we really human and, if we are believers, is our faith human? The reply was not the anguish which follows an awakening from dogmatic sleep, but the joy which comes when we are willing not only to change the mind from enslavement to liberation, but also to change our vision in order to see what had been there, unnoticed, all along, and to change hearts of stone into hearts of flesh—in other words, to let ourselves be moved to compassion and mercy.[17]

Moved and activated by the faith of the poor, Sobrino entered into their experience of the subversive joy of God's love. The poor, once on the margins of his theological epistemology, became the center by witnessing to the power of that love.

The same illuminative quality by which the world of the poor reveals God's presence in the infinite layers of reality also adumbrates all that opposes the power of divine love. From the perspective of those treated as the "human table scraps" of society, the lethal effects of dominative power come into sharp relief. The option for the poor, as a decisive choice for the God of life, involves the simultaneous rejection of the coercive methods of dominative power and a contemplative awareness and embrace of the power of the Holy Spirit available on the margins. This pneumatological form of power springs from and continually nourishes the sort of ecclesial communion that Sobrino describes as the temple of the Spirit,

> that is, of believers with spirit, of believers who in the reality of their life show the spirit of mercy, which means justice for the popular majorities; the spirit of a clean heart, of truth, of seeing, analyzing, denouncing, and unmasking reality as it is; the spirit of peace, active peace for which one must struggle and not only pray or hope with arms crossed; the spirit of strength to withstand the many risks, threats, and attacks that come from the struggle for justice; the spirit of joy, because under persecution they are a little more like Jesus; the spirit of the highest love to give up their lives for their brothers and sisters; the spirit of generosity, of having received from God—often from the hidden God in the poor—new ears to hear God's word, new eyes to travel new ways, and new hands to transform it;

the spirit of prayer, of calling God "Father"; and the spirit of celebration in calling God "our" Father, as Jesus did.[18]

Through their evangelizing witness, the poor mediate these fruits of the Spirit, illuminating the dynamic features of pneumatological power. First, it appeals to human freedom and rejects methods of violent coercion.[19] Second, it assigns value to self-sacrificial love rather than material possession. Third, it is radically inclusive and seeks to restore God's creation to wholeness by beginning with the poor, whose lives are most endangered by the lethal effects of structural sin. Finally, it involves an epistemological de-centering of knowledge as power, relying not on the dominant influence of certain individuals or institutions, but rather working through each member of a community and all together to nurture the common good.[20]

The pneumatological power available on the periphery of society has the potential to disarm structures of dominative power. Both the materially poor and those who live in solidarity with them are well positioned to experience the radically liberating love of God through Jesus Christ in the Spirit, freeing them to enter into the reality of the present moment more deeply, there to discover and create new ways, as Sobrino puts it, "to Christianize every kind of power—as Jesus did—by putting it at the service of the oppressed."[21]

This task can only be accomplished through the apostolic faith of the church because pneumatological power works through believers but cannot be claimed by them as a personal possession. Ultimately, it is divine power that liberates the world from the powers of domination.[22] The church, the Body of Christ in history, takes up the apostolic mission of transforming these powers to serve the God of life, beginning precisely from the point at which life is most threatened and drawing on the power of God's Spirit available there. For this reason, Gutiérrez identifies the poor as "history's transforming power, the agents of a liberating praxis." They evangelize and subvert simultaneously, "for these two praxes are bound up together at the very heart of history."[23]

By their very existence, but particularly by partaking in pneumatological power, the poor and those who live in solidarity with them necessarily enter into conflict with those wielding dominative power. Thus the poor, Sobrino writes, "may also be defined as those who have ranged themselves against all the powers of this world."[24] The conflict emerges not merely from the gross material disparities dividing those human beings deemed expendable from those gripped by their own insatiable need to possess the goods of creation in superabundance, even at the expense of human life. It also stems from the fact that pneumatological power exposes the dominative variety as a form of idolatry designed to lure humans to worship it as divine.[25]

Faith finds its contrary, notes Sobrino, not in unbelief but rather in idolatry.[26] John Paul II explored the ethical contours of this opposition in *Sollici-*

*tudo rei socialis* when he called attention to two idolatrous dispositions and their attendant structural settings, "on the one hand the *all-consuming desire for profit*, and on the other, *the thirst for power*, with the intention of imposing one's will upon others. In order to characterize better each of these attitudes, one can add the expression: 'at any price.' In other words, we are faced with the *absolutizing* of human attitudes with all its possible consequences."[27]

The pope's assessment finds vivid confirmation in El Salvador. There, Sobrino has repeatedly called attention to the doctrine of national security and the absolutization of capitalism as particularly virulent forms of idolatry that have exacted a bloody price, beginning first with the lives of the poor.

> Idols dehumanize their worshipers, but their ultimate evil lies in the fact that they demand victims in order to exist. If there is one single deep conviction which I have acquired in El Salvador, it is that such idols are real; they are not the inventions of so-called primitive peoples but are indeed active in modern societies. We dare not doubt this, in view of such idols' innumerable victims: the poor, the unemployed, the refugees, the detainees, the tortured, the disappeared, the massacred.[28]

Precisely from the vantage point of idolatry's victims, its falsehood comes to light. By opting for the poor, the church is better situated to discern the moral evil of idolatrous structures and to disarm them through the methods of pneumatological power as a constitutive dimension of its evangelizing mission.

The practice of ecclesial solidarity with idolatry's victims enfleshes the church of the poor as the Body of Christ in history, firmly rooting the people of God in the same *humus* as the cross of Jesus. And like Jesus, the church can expect persecution, even to the point of martyrdom, a time-honored mark of the apostolic faith. "In order [for the church] to gain credibility in El Salvador, persecution has been important," Sobrino attests. "Why? Because for the first time in many years—maybe centuries—the poor people have understood that if what happens to them—oppression, repression—happens to the church then it is true that the church is with the poor . . . that the Christ preached by the church is a Christ of the poor . . . that the God preached by the church is a God of the poor."[29]

## At the Intersection of Theological Method and Ecclesial Power

Ecclesiologically, the church of the poor embraces the way of the cross as the setting of pneumatological power, capable of leading the people of God to ground their ecclesial identity in the orthopraxis of faith. "To say it from the beginning," Sobrino insists, "a church of Jesus, centered in the poor, inspired by them and placed at the service of the Kingdom of God, will generate one type of evangelical and Christian communion, beneficial to the church itself and, above all to the kingdom of God and the poor of this world. . . . Not every communion is Christian and desirable, but only that which arises around the crucified of this world."[30] Viewing the life of the ecclesial community from the perspective of the world's crucified offers the church an ethical framework for discerning whether its institutional practices align with its mission.

At Vatican II, the world's bishops took up this issue quite explicitly. Their negotiation of the intersection between theological method and ecclesial power, I suggest, proves evocative in relation to the questions of procedural justice that arise in the CDF's handling of Sobrino's case. Born of a desire to free the church from intra-ecclesial structures of domination, their insights resonate with the ethos of the church of the poor.

As the council considered a draft of what would become the *Decree on the Bishops' Pastoral Office in the Church*, Cardinal Frings of Cologne made an intervention on November 8, 1963, critiquing the methods of the Supreme Congregation of the Holy Office. In the estimation of Henri Cardinal de Lubac, his statement paved the way for the dissolution of that office and the formation of the Congregation for the Doctrine of the Faith.[31] Frings argued that the methods of the Holy Office did not cohere with the times and were in fact detrimental to the church, even to the point of scandal. His remarks met with sustained applause among those gathered for the 63rd General Congregation—notwithstanding a stern, defensive response from Cardinal Ottaviani. Notably, almost all of the twenty-one bishops who signed in support of Frings's view represented dioceses in Latin America, and the principal author of Frings's intervention was his *peritus,* Joseph Ratzinger.[32]

The final document, *Christus Dominus*, echoes Frings's words: "The Fathers of this most sacred Council, however, strongly desire that these departments [of the Roman Curia] . . . be reorganized and better adapted to the needs of the times, and of various regions and rites. This task should give special thought to their number, name, competence, and particular method of procedure, as well as to the coordination of their activities."[33] In a *motu proprio* issued shortly after the promulgation of *Christus Dominus*, Paul VI abolished the Holy Office and instituted the Congregation for the Doctrine of the Faith, outlining procedural methods such as dialogical consultation with concerned parties in particular cases, including regional bishops and theological experts.[34]

This methodological outline of the CDF's role, born of a Vatican II ecclesiological disposition toward *aggiornamento*, provides a normative setting in which to interpret the procedure followed in Sobrino's case. In the Explanatory Note, the CDF stated that it adopted an abbreviated process because of perceived "grave deficiencies" in Sobrino's method coupled with the wide diffusion of his works, especially in Latin America. Remarkably, it made no mention of consultation with regional bishops nor did it acknowledge any efforts to seek a range of theological opinion regarding Sobrino's work. In terms of procedural justice, these steps would seem to have been warranted according to the original charge given to the CDF by Pope Paul VI.

Instead, a decidedly nondialogical process unfolded. In a December 2006 letter to Jesuit Superior General Hans-Peter Kolvenbach, Sobrino remarked, "It is not easy to dialogue with the Congregation [for the Doctrine of the Faith]. At times, it seems impossible. It appears obsessed to find whatever limitation or error. . . ."[35] Along with other theologians, Sobrino has observed a strong hermeneutic of suspicion among Vatican officials toward his work and toward liberation theology in general. Left unchecked, this methodological predisposition toward finding fault has functioned as a coercive exercise of power, and, as such, it appears to have vitiated the value of the Notification as an instrument of service to the church in a number of ways. First, the Notification reflects such a narrow interpretive lens as to call into question the fairness of its method and therefore the accuracy of its assessment, leading Bernard Sesboüé to assert that "with such a deliberately suspicious method, I could read many heresies in the encyclicals of John Paul II."[36]

Second, Sesboüé, along with a number of other respected theologians, such as José Ignacio González Faus, Carlo Palacio, and Martin Maier, carefully examined Sobrino's work and found no doctrinal errors; yet their views were not formally recognized in the Notification nor is it clear whether they were even considered in the CDF's abbreviated process. This ambiguity, if not intentional omission, recalls the structural concerns expressed by Frings at Vatican II regarding the Holy Office. In the CDF's process, whether in general or abbreviated form, which theological methods are given credence, by whom, and with what justification?

Finally, though the Notification is dated November 26, 2006, the Feast of Christ the King, it was published on March 14, 2007. Those familiar with El Salvador's tragically extensive martyrology will recall that March 12 marked the thirtieth anniversary of Fr. Rutilio Grande's assassination and March 24 the twenty-seventh year since Archbishop Romero was gunned down while consecrating the Eucharist. Measured by the faith of a church firmly rooted in and nourished by the witness of its martyrs, mindfully marking time over millennia through the rhythmic remembrance of their feast days, the timing of the Notification represents a breathtaking epistemological blindness to the significance of local context for the practice of fidelity to the ecclesial tradition of the church. The CDF's choice of March 14 as the date to publicize its critique of Sobrino's work evokes lament, akin to that of Frings when faced with the scandal of the Holy Office's methods.

Remembering John Paul II's prescription of solidarity as the antidote for the idolatrous dispositions toward greed and lust for power plaguing the world, I suggest that it is precisely by becoming the church of the poor that the people of God can resist the allure of dominative power and instead embrace the power of the Spirit available on the societal margins. An ecclesiology that places the integral well-being of the poor at the center of Christian awareness springs from the heart of the gospel (Matt 25:31-46). Jesus' parable of the last judgment happens to be one of the readings in the lectionary cycle for the Feast of Christ the King, the actual date of the Notification. "Then the just will ask him: 'Lord, when did we see you hungry and feed you or see you thirsty and give you drink? When did we welcome you away from home or clothe you in your nakedness? When did we visit you when you were ill or in prison?' The king will answer them: 'I assure you, as often as you did it for one of my least brothers, you did it for me.'"[37]

Among Sobrino's many theological contributions, perhaps the most important is his courageous witness to this truth of the Christian faith. The poor majority of human beings continually sets before the church the gift and the task of fulfilling its evangelical mission of solidarity with the "human table scraps" of society. Illuminating the way of Jesus' cross as the path of salvation, the poor, the crucified of this world, incarnate Jesus' invitation to his church to reject the methods of dominative power and to surrender humbly to the power made available through the Holy Spirit when the poor become the epistemological center of ecclesial life in faith.

## Notes

1. Congregation for the Doctrine of the Faith (CDF), "Notification on the Works of Father Jon Sobrino, SJ," no. 2. See pages 255-66 below; also available at http://www.vatican.va/roman_curia/congregations/cfaith/documents/rc_con_cfaith_doc_20061126_nota-sobrino_en.html.

2. Jon Sobrino, "The 'Doctrinal Authority' of the People of God," in *The Teaching Authority of Believers*, ed. Johannes-Baptist Metz and Edward Schillebeeckx, English trans. ed. Marcus Lefébure (Edinburgh: T&T Clark, 1985), 58.

3. Gustavo Gutiérrez, *The Power of the Poor in History,* trans. Robert R. Barr (Maryknoll, N.Y.: Orbis Books, 1983),105.

4. CDF, "Explanatory Note on the Notification on the Works of Father Jon Sobrino." See also "Notification," no. 2.

5. Jon Sobrino, *Jesus the Liberator. A Historical-Theological View,* trans. Paul Burns and Francis McDonagh (Maryknoll, N.Y.: Orbis Books, 1993), 30 (emphasis added).

6. John Paul II, *Sollicitudo rei socialis* (On Social Concern, 1987), in *Catholic Social Thought. The Documentary Heritage,* ed. David J. O'Brien and Thomas A. Shannon (Maryknoll, N.Y.: Orbis Books, 1992), no. 42.

7. *Sollicitudo rei socialis,* no. 47.

8. John Paul II, "Responsible for One Another" (Address at the Basilica of Our Lady of Zapopán, Guadalajara, January 30, 1979). *L'Osservatore Romano* (February 19, 1979), 3.

9. See CELAM, *Evangelization in Latin America's Present and Future: Final Document of the Third General Conference of the Latin American Episcopate* (Puebla de los Angeles,

Mexico, January 27 - February 13, 1979), in *Puebla and Beyond*, ed. John Eagleson and Philip Scharper, trans. John Drury (Maryknoll, N.Y.: Orbis Books, 1979), no. 28. See also nos. 73, 281, 482, 487, 1032.

10. *Sollicitudo rei socialis*, 36.

11. *Sollicitudo rei socialis*, 38. His argument was later affirmed by the Pontifical Council for Justice and Peace in the *Compendium of the Social Doctrine of the Church* (Vatican City: Libreria Editrice Vaticana, 2004), nos. 182, 193, 332, and 449.

12. Jon Sobrino, "Communion, Conflict, and Ecclesial Solidarity," in *Mysterium Liberationis: Fundamental Concepts of Liberation Theology*, ed. Ignacio Ellacuría and Jon Sobrino (Maryknoll, N.Y.: Orbis Books, 1993), 624.

13. Ibid., 624.

14. Jon Sobrino, "Awakening from the Sleep of Inhumanity," *Christian Century* 108, no. 11 (April 3, 1991): 364.

15. Jon Sobrino, "Poverty Means Death to the Poor," *Cross Currents* 36, no. 3 (Fall 1986): 269; see also "Communion, Conflict, and Ecclesial Solidarity," 635.

16. *Jesus the Liberator*, 33. Sandra Harding makes a similar point in "Rethinking Standpoint Epistemology: What Is 'Strong Objectivity'?" in *Feminist Epistemologies*, ed. Linda Alcoff and Elizabeth Potter (New York: Routledge, 1993), 54.

17. "Awakening," 365-66.

18. "Communion, Conflict, and Ecclesial Solidarity," 621.

19. On the power of coercive influence, see John R. P. French, Jr., and Bertram Raven, "The Bases of Social Power," in *Studies in Social Power*, ed. Dorwin Cartwright (Ann Arbor: University of Michigan Press, 1959), 157.

20. I have developed an account of these characteristics of pneumatological power in a slightly different form in "Wise as Serpents, Innocent as Doves: Strategic Appropriation of Catholic Social Teaching," in *Prophetic Witness: Catholic Women's Strategies for the Church*, ed. Colleen Griffith, Century 21 Series, ed. James Keenan and Patricia De Leeuw (New York: Crossroad, forthcoming).

21. "Communion, Conflict, and Ecclesial Solidarity," 633.

22. For a compelling account of this liberating process, see Hendrik Berkhof, *Christ and the Powers*, trans. John Howard Yoder (Scottsdale, Pa.: Herald Press, 1977, first published in Dutch in 1953).

23. *Power of the Poor in History*, 105.

24. "Awakening," 366; see also "Poverty Means Death," 269. For a similar argument from the perspective of social psychology, see Ignacio Martín-Baró, *Sistema, Grupo, y Poder. Psicología Social desde Centroamerica*, vol. 2 (San Salvador: UCA Editores, 1989), 97.

25. See Walter Wink, *Engaging the Powers: Discernment and Resistance in a World of Domination* (Minneapolis: Fortress Press, 1992), 300.

26. "Poverty Means Death," 269.

27. *Sollicitudo rei socialis*, 37.

28. "Awakenings," 368; see also "Poverty Means Death," 269.

29. "Poverty Means Death," 275-76.

30. "Communion, Conflict, and Ecclesial Solidarity," 616.

31. Henri de Lubac, *Entretien autour de Vatican II: Souvenirs et réflexions* (Paris: Cerf, 1985), 123.

32. Cardinal Josef Frings (Archbishop of Cologne), Intervention, November 8, 1963,

General Congregation LXIII, *Acta Synodalia Sacrosancti Concilii Oecumenici Vaticani II*, vol. 2, part 4 (Vatican City: Typis Polyglottis Vaticanis, 1972), 616-18.

33. *Christus Dominus* (Decree on the Bishops' Pastoral Office in the Church), in *The Documents of Vatican II*, ed. Walter M. Abbott (New York: Herder & Herder, 1966), no. 9.

34. Paul VI, *Integrae servandae* (*motu proprio*), December 7, 1965, *Acta Apostolicae Sedis* 57 (1965): 954.

35. Jon Sobrino, letter to Hans-Peter Kolvenbach, December 13, 2006, p. 4; available at http://chiesa.espresso.repubblica.it/articolo/127601.

36. Quoted in "Letter to Kolvenbach," and in John L. Allen, Jr., "Vatican Censures Sobrino, Who Calls Procedures 'Not Honest,'" *NCR Conversation Cafe*, March 14, 2007, available at http://ncrcafe.org.

37. *Lectionary for Mass* (New York: Catholic Book Publishing, 1970), Last Sunday of the Year, Christ the King, Cycle A, p. 256; New American Version Scripture translation.

# 17

# Liberation Theology and Catholic Social Teaching

KENNETH R. HIMES, O.F.M.

In its first extended treatment of the movement called liberation theology the Congregation for the Doctrine of the Faith (CDF) issued an "Instruction on Certain Aspects of the 'Theology of Liberation.'" At that time the CDF commentary included the following:

> One of the conditions for necessary theological correction is giving proper value to the *social teaching of the Church*. This teaching is by no means closed. It is, on the contrary, open to the new questions which are so numerous today. In this perspective, the contribution of theologians and other thinkers in all parts of the world to the reflection of the Church is indispensable today.[1]

For most of its history the dominant voices and concerns of the church's social teaching were those of Western European societies. In the latter part of the twentieth century, however, Catholic social teaching became informed by other regions of the globe and, in a particular way, by Latin America.

Paul VI's statement, *Octogesima adveniens*, provides the clearest papal support for the church in Latin America to develop its own distinctive voice. After noting the extent of diversity in the world in which Christians find themselves, the pope embraced a local and pluralist solution.

> In the face of such widely varying situations it is difficult for us to utter a unified message and to put forward a solution which has universal validity. Such is not our ambition, nor is it our mission. It is up to the Christian communities to analyze with objectivity the situation which is proper to their own country, to shed on it the light of the Gospel's unalterable words and to draw principles of reflection, norms of judgment and directives for action from the social teaching of the Church.[2]

At the same time, Paul VI did not desire or expect that local and regional responses would be developed on their own apart from the wider family of faith. The pope encouraged a dialogue that would be mutually enriching between Catholic social teaching and a local church. It is that hope for a true dialogue that is then reaffirmed by the CDF's statement, "the contribution of theologians and other thinkers in all parts of the world" is "indispensable" to the ongoing development of the church's social mission, both its practice and teaching.

In this essay I will explore some of the fruits of the dialogue between liberation theology and Catholic social teaching. The focus will be on how liberation theology has contributed to Catholic social teaching. The other side of the dialogue, how Catholic social teaching can enrich liberation theology, is a useful point to explore, but I will not take it up in this essay. The contribution that liberation theology has made will be treated under four headings. The first concerns the way in which liberation theology constitutes a response by Latin American thinkers, such as Jon Sobrino, to the needs of the local church in the aftermath of Vatican II.

## The Import of Local Church Initiatives for Catholic Social Teaching

Throughout history one can easily see a variety of models for the relationship between church and world. The minority sect of the apostolic church is very different from the model after Constantine's reign. The church of European Christendom is dramatically different from the church of contemporary Asia. The Catholic subculture that developed among nineteenth-century immigrants in the United States is quite distinct from the alliance of cross and crown that occurred in colonial Latin America.

One part of the agenda at Vatican II was the need to address the changed nature of the relationship of church and world as experienced in postwar Europe. At the same time, the council fathers were increasingly aware that the European approach would not be possible in other parts of the world that had a different history and demographic reality.

At Vatican II the voice of the Latin American bishops was not very strong. It was the council itself that initiated the process for many of the Latin American prelates to develop a sense of themselves as leaders of a regional church and to foster ties with one another. The outcome of this process is best seen not in the role of the Latin Americans at Vatican II but later when they met in Medellín, Colombia.

When the bishops returned to their home dioceses after the council, they began to plan just the second meeting ever held of the Conference of Bishops of Latin America (CELAM). At that meeting in 1968 the bishops were reluctant simply to *apply* the teaching of Vatican II to the Latin American church. Instead, there was a desire to *interpret* Vatican II for the region.

When the bishops at Medellín investigated the "signs of the times" in their part of the globe they saw a contradiction between the gospel's vision of life and the crushing poverty of everyday experience. They discerned that political colonialism may have ceased but that economic colonialism had replaced it. The failure to alleviate the suffering among the mass of people in the region required theological reflection.

Medellín made the option for the poor the specification of what it means to be a committed Christian in Latin America. Certainly there were theologians and church leaders in Europe and North America who were also wrestling with the relationship of the church and the world. From the perspective of a more affluent context, however, the problems appeared to be the "privatization" of religious belief and the growing secularism of a culture shaped by scientific rationalism. Participants at Medellín, however, saw oppression as the chief feature of their context. The audience for their message was not the nonbelievers of modernity, but those "nonpersons" living in the shadows of desperate poverty.

The Latin American bishops made a decisive move in that the option for the poor signaled a break with the historic alliance of the colonial church and the state. The close ties between cross and sword had led to pastoral strategies focused on the elites of a society rather than on the mass of people. Through a preferential option for the poor a new set of priorities emerged. Of course, this shift was not uniformly adopted or even recognized by all, but the clear impact of Medellín should not be missed. Working in concert, a majority of bishops gave formal support to a new movement of theologians that would name and then work to transform the Latin American reality.

The centrality of a person's concrete situation in the process of theological reflection has led to a misunderstanding between the CDF and Sobrino. In the second paragraph of the Notification that examines his work, the CDF quotes from his writing and then offers a correction to it.

> Father Sobrino affirms: "*Latin American Christology . . . identifies its setting, in the sense of a real situation, as the poor of this world, and this situation is what must be present in and permeate any particular setting in which Christology is done*" (*Jesus the Liberator*, 28). Further, "*the poor in the community question Christological faith and give it its fundamental direction*" (*Ibidem*, 30), and "*the Church of the poor . . . is the ecclesial setting of Christology because it is a world shaped by the poor*" (*Ibidem*, 31). "*The social setting is thus the most crucial for the faith, the most crucial in shaping the thought pattern of Christology, and what requires and encourages the epistemological break*" (*Ibidem*).

While such a preoccupation for the poor and oppressed is admirable, in these quotations the "Church of the poor" assumes the fundamental position which properly belongs to the faith of the Church. . . .

The ecclesial foundation of Christology may not be identified with "the Church of the poor", but is found rather in the apostolic faith transmitted through the Church for all generations.

In writing subsequent to the CDF Notification, Sobrino has made clear the distinction that has led to the confusion. He distinguishes between "setting" and "source":

"Setting" means the reality from which the believer believes and the theologian reflects. "Setting" thus understood is not at all opposed to "sources" of theological knowledge—scripture, tradition, and the authoritative magisterium. "Setting" and "source" are formally distinct realities, although they do not need to exclude each other.[3]

It is apparent that Sobrino does not deny the point of the CDF assertion that the apostolic tradition is the foundation for Catholic theology. What he brings into bold relief, however, is that the context (setting) in which one does theology plays a decisive role in shaping the questions one asks of the sources and how one reads them. Like other liberation theologians, Sobrino insists we not presume that theology is done from a neutral, objective situation; it is always contextual.

This emphasis on context is important because it serves as a corrective to some ways of interpreting Catholic social teaching. There is always a risk that this teaching, when it abstracts from its particular context, can propose an insight for one context that is not helpful in a different setting. Teachings on slavery, usury, and religious liberty are commonly cited examples from the past where context played a key role.[4] More recently, there are teachings on gender roles in the workplace, property rights, and capital punishment that have been decisively influenced by the context in which they were formulated.

Although Latin American liberation theology is not the only source of the insight, it is true that theologians such as Sobrino have made an important contribution by insisting that "setting" is crucial to the process of theological reflection. This is especially the case with Catholic social teaching, a tradition of reflection that requires many judgments about highly contingent factors. It is imperative, therefore, that we be self-conscious of the perspective from which we interpret the world around us. For Sobrino and other liberation theologians, it is a commitment to the poor that provides the most appropriate setting for the doing of theology in our time.

## The Option for the Poor

While the option for the poor has been identified with liberation theology, the idea of the church having a special concern for the poor has its origins in ancient times. Throughout Scripture, and particularly in the prophets, one reads that Yahweh has a special concern for the widow, the orphan, and the alien. The classical prophets attacked those who defrauded the poor and lacked compassion for the suffering. Jesus' storytelling as well as his actions all attest to his love of the poor.

Certainly, the early church saw itself as a community dedicated to caring for the poor.[5] Monastic and mendicant movements in later centuries exhibited a commitment to the temporal as well as spiritual welfare of the poor. Throughout the history of the church in the modern era there have been individuals, communities, and movements that reflected the commitment of the church to ease the burden of the poor.

Hence, the CDF was correct to say in its second statement on liberation theology that "those who are oppressed by poverty are the object of a love of preference on the part of the Church. . . . She has done this through numberless works of charity which remain always and everywhere indispensable."[6] In that same 1986 statement, however, the CDF may have been too quick to state without qualification that "through her social doctrine" the church "has sought to promote structural changes in society so as to secure conditions of life worthy of the human person."[7] The needed qualification is that despite the teaching's concern for the poor, the actual practice of church leaders sometimes put the church on the side of societal elites in resisting political and economic reforms that could have transformed the situation of the poor. Social charity has been a hallmark of the church throughout history; action on behalf of social justice presents a less consistent pattern.

For Leo XIII, and within the formal magisterial tradition of social teaching, the poor loom large. At the beginning of the landmark encyclical *Rerum novarum*, Leo wrote, "some remedy must be found, and quickly found, for the misery and wretchedness which press so heavily at this moment on the large majority of the very poor."[8] The poor in the forefront of Leo's consciousness were those who had suffered during the painful transition from a European economy that was largely rural and agrarian to a new order that was urban and industrial. His focus was on the plight of workers who were defenseless at a time when laws addressing minimum wage, child labor, workplace safety, length of workday and workweek, as well as the right to organize, were largely nonexistent.

At the same time, Leo was greatly concerned to combat the rising popularity of socialism among the European working class. He defended the church as the true friend of the poor while portraying socialism as a false hope in the effort to improve the lives of the working poor.[9] In part, this reflected the social conservatism of the church after it had been buffeted not only by the French Revolution but also the liberal revolutions of 1848, as well as the anticlericalism of a variety of movements on the left. Consequently, what Donal Dorr has called the "Catholic ethos" of the period promoted interpretations of Catholic social teaching that were of a conservative nature whenever concrete judgments of political and economic policy were made.[10] This pattern continued in later papacies where fear of the left almost always trumped anxieties about the right in European societies.

With the papacy of John XXIII and his encyclical *Mater et magistra*, we see a movement away from identifying the church with alliances of power and wealth in European life. Paul VI continued this shift, and his major social encyclical, *Populorum progressio,* raised the issue of global poverty to new heights in the consciousness of church members. Nonetheless, as a number of commentators have pointed out, even in this encyclical Paul envisions change from the top down, as the powerful voluntarily make social changes on behalf of the poor.

Liberation theology, on the other hand, sees the option for the poor as entailing a committed choice to foster the kinds of change that allow the poor to have a more equitable share of power as well as material goods. The option for the poor is not limited to social charity that makes the poor *objects* of concern; it also includes social justice that sees the poor as *agents* of change. This idea is not novel to Catholic social teaching, yet the magisterial teaching has frequently been ahead of the institutional practice. Sobrino and others have been intent on overcoming this gap. That is one reason why liberation theologians so often emphasize what is needed is a commitment to a liberating praxis in order to do theology.[11]

"Praxis," as the word is employed by Sobrino, is not simply action as practice, but refers instead to a particular form of behavior. Praxis is behavior that participates in the larger movement of history; Sobrino views it as a movement guided by the Spirit of God. And God's Spirit is leading humankind away from what enslaves and oppresses and toward what liberates and gives life. Thus, to make an option for the poor is to put oneself on the side of God's action in history, leading those who are oppressed into freedom. To commit oneself to a liberating praxis with and for the poor places the theologian in a setting that is particularly apt in the present moment of Latin America and other parts of the world.

In this way, Sobrino and other liberation theologians, who make an option for the poor, prod those who embrace Catholic social teaching to concretize and further specify the meaning of adopting a political and economic ethic that is aimed at social change as well as social service. The increased willingness of the church to take a prophetic stance within a society, even when the church's institutional interests are not under attack in that society, is an example of how the option for the poor has influenced Catholic social thought. Documents such as Paul VI's *Octogesima adveniens,* John Paul II's *Sollicitudo rei socialis,* and episcopal statements such as Medellín and Puebla from CELAM, or those of the Philippine bishops during the Marcos regime are examples of the new direction and tone of Catholic social teaching.

## Spirituality and Justice

Among the significant weaknesses within the tradition of Catholic social thought is the lack of a developed spirituality to motivate and sustain a commitment to justice. While the tradition presents many compelling arguments and rationales for why justice is a central component of Christian faith, there is a shortage of writing on the spirituality of justice.

Some of the earlier texts, such as *Rerum novarum, Quadragesimo anno,* and *Mater et magistra,* were couched largely in the language of natural law, and that partly accounts for the lack of spirituality. Recent texts have employed more scriptural language, but the attention to spirituality continues to falter. The movement of liberation theology, on the other hand, has produced a significant amount of writing on spirituality. This is not surprising given the concern for a liberating praxis. With such a goal in mind, spirituality becomes a key component in keeping alive a commitment to transform an oppressive reality into a life-giving one.

A number of Latin American theologians, including Sobrino, are committed to linking mysticism and politics, or practicing contemplation amidst working for justice.[12] Sobrino suggests that any valid spirituality requires several things. The first feature is an encounter with reality; to respect the truth one finds when being attentive to what actually is going on. The second, to respond honestly to *la realidad,* the reality, which, in the case of Latin America, is to respond to the fact of great and widespread suffering among people. This leads to the quality of mercy, the ability to see oneself as united with the suffering other. Compassion is another term for this dimension of spirituality, the ability to react to the pain of others by entering into it oneself.

The third characteristic of a true spirituality is fidelity to "the real." Throughout history there is a temptation to disguise "the real," to make it seem less painful because it is difficult to sustain the initial response of mercy. Therefore, it is necessary to have hope in the possibility of *la realidad* being transformed, not as an act of fantasy but in response to actual signs of hope within the reality encountered.

The fourth feature of spirituality is the human ability to tap into the deeper currents of reality, those elements that give rise to hope. This implies that within each person there is a creative force. This force not only places ethical obligations on us to act justly but also offers a sense of the opportunities that are presently embedded in reality. The four dimensions noted above are found in any spirituality that is truly human, according to Sobrino.[13]

While spirituality is a category that transcends Christianity, it is the particularity of Christian spirituality that is the concern of liberation theologians. One can readily see how Christians will name and interpret the features above: grace, sacrament, virtue, sin, and conversion are all words that could be used in describing the four dimensions of what Sobrino calls a "fundamental human spirituality," as outlined above. The particularity of Christian spirituality is "no more and no less than a living of the fundamental spirituality that we have described, precisely in the concrete manner of Jesus and according to the spirit of Jesus."[14]

Liberation theology places great weight on the New Testament's portrayal of Jesus' actual life and ministry, his historical praxis, especially as portrayed in the Synoptic Gospels. This leads liberation theology to develop a spirituality of discipleship, the following of Jesus. Such an approach suggests two necessary dimensions, christological and pneumatological. The christological is the establishment of the historical Jesus as the *norma normans* for our understanding of discipleship. The pneumatological dimension is the power of the Spirit that allows Jesus to be actively present today, and not merely as a figure of historical memory.

This means that following Jesus is "a constant in the history of Christians who have lived with spirit. However, it adopts a particular guise in this or that particular era. . . . Jesus should be followed, continued, updated in history—not imitated." It is the Spirit that gives the disciple the ability to adapt Jesus to a given historical reality, to "actualize Jesus" for a particular time and place. At the same time the Spirit calls upon disciples to follow Jesus, not any other master.[15]

To truly be a disciple, then, demands that a disciple follow Jesus, under the inspiration of the Spirit, by living as Jesus would within the given historical reality that the disciple encounters. For liberation theologians, the overwhelming reality is the "irruption of the poor in history" and how the encounter with that reality makes demands upon, and offers opportunities to, those men and women who would seek to live as Jesus lived.

Liberation theologians offer a wide array of reflections on how such a spirituality leads disciples to undertake a liberating praxis. A common strand in these writings is that the praxis is inspired by the historical Jesus, whose preaching of the reign of God is the telltale characteristic of his life and ministry.

In an important essay, Sobrino takes up the centrality of the reign of God for liberation theology.[16] He acknowledges that the historical Jesus never defines the meaning of the reign of God, nor describes it analytically, only parabolically. Nonetheless, some understanding of the reign of God can be gleaned by employing three methods. Using historical-critical methods, we can learn what the term meant for a Jew in the first century A.D. This approach, which

Sobrino calls the "notional" method,[17] offers competing versions, so the reign of God may remain vague. Nonetheless, the idea, however understood, functioned as a principle of hope for a Jewish person.

A second approach examines the praxis of Jesus, because what Jesus did reveals the reign of God. Here Sobrino focuses on three aspects of the praxis of Jesus—his miracles, his denunciations, and, what Sobrino calls, his "lot." The miracles of Jesus were concrete events in which, motivated by mercy, he met immediate needs of people. The miracles do not remove all illness, all suffering in the world. They are particular instances of God's salvific reign coming into the life of a given person. According to Sobrino, this suggests that salvation is both concrete and plural.

The denunciations of Jesus show us what is opposite to the reign of God. God's reign entails the fullness of life, as God desires it for creation. The opposite of God's reign is the use of power to create victims; to oppress others. To have power in order to engage in death-dealing behavior is to stand against the reign of God. God's reign may be construed as the use of power to give life, to prevent turning another person into a victim. Thus, we can know something of the reign of God by knowing its opposite: oppression, victimization, and death.

Jesus' lot, the opposition to him, and the consequent passion and death that he suffered teach us that he did not die because he preached some abstraction called the reign of God. Because of the specific mediations of God's reign that he proclaimed and brought about, he was put to death. The way that the reign of God appeared in the life of Jesus threatened the powers of the anti-reign, whether those powers be represented in political or religious realms. We can infer a good deal about the reign of God that Jesus embodied from the miracles he performed, the evils he denounced, and the course of his fate.

Another way to understand the reign of God is to consider to whom it was addressed in the New Testament. Sobrino argues that the primary audience was the poor, those who found life a burden and who knew suffering as a regular experience. The reign of God is a new reality in which life and dignity are made possible for those who are denied these now. This is so because of who God is; not simply, love, but the one who loves the poor and weak and neglected of this world.[18]

The emphasis that liberation theology has given to developing a scripturally based spirituality that links faith with justice is a signal achievement that has enriched Catholic social teaching. While the more analytical tone and method of Catholic social teaching have their strengths, they are not sufficient to foster an ongoing commitment to social justice by faithful Catholics. We also need a clear and tight connection between the experience of faith and the work of social transformation. Liberation theology, by its promotion of a spirituality of justice grounded on the experience of following Jesus, has made an important contribution to Catholic social teaching.

## The Idea of Structural, or Social, Sin

In 1971 Catholic bishops from around the world gathered in a Roman synod, noted the reality of "sin in its individual and social manifestations,"[19] and lamented "the objective obstacles which social structures place in the way of conversion of hearts."[20] A popular textbook in Catholic moral theology, published in 1989, observed that the idea of social sin was "a relatively new theological concept" at the time.[21] And an article published ten years later made the case that the emergence of the idea of social or structural sin was a legitimate development in the teaching of the church.[22]

These references suggest that the idea of structural, or social, sin, first advanced by liberation theologians, has in a brief period of time worked its way into the tradition of Catholic social teaching. The idea is not difficult to understand. Catholicism has long maintained that there are privileged structures of grace; that certain institutional structures—the church's sacramental order, for example, or the vowed life of religious—are privileged mediations of grace in our world. The idea of social sin merely points out the fact that evil also can be embodied in particularly effective historical mediations, that social organizations can violate the moral norms reflective of God's purposes.

Sobrino has written about demonic forces that are anti-Christian, that oppose the life and dignity of all persons. These forces are the "historical project of human wills, crystallized in structures that produce injustice."[23] Like other liberation theologians, he utilized the language of structural sin to portray the theological significance of efforts to overcome injustices embedded in the social systems governing Latin American life. These systems may be cultural and political patterns inherited from the colonial past, or economic and social practices resulting from Latin America's role in global capitalism. Liberation theologians insist that past human decisions are behind the present misery of the mass of people and that human choices continue to sustain the present structural arrangements that violate the dignity of the majority of people.

Commenting on the papal reaction to social sin, Adam DeVille shows that John Paul II offered a diagnosis of the idea of social sin in 1984 that reflected a wary openness to the idea. The pope noted that sin could be understood as social in the sense that each individual sin affects others, however indirectly. He also observed that some sins involve a direct attack on one's neighbor, graphically violating the norm of love of neighbor, and that this was a particular instance of sin that could be viewed as social. Such illustrations, however, failed to capture the insight of the liberationist approach. With his third example, sin as descriptive of certain "relationships between various human communities,"[24] the pope was getting closer to the Latin American approach. Still, John Paul insisted that this usage of sin is analogical, mainly because he feared the loss of a sense of individual accountability for sin if the language of social sin became too common.

Just three years later, John Paul returned to the theme in his encyclical *Sollicitudo rei socialis*. He did so with fewer caveats and with an approach much closer to the way that Sobrino and other Latin Americans use the term. Without forgoing his concern about connecting sin to individual responsibility, the pope discussed "rigid ideologies" that sustain competing "blocs" guilty of "different forms of imperialism." He warned that the end result "can only be a world subject to structures of sin." John Paul continued, "'Sin' and 'structures of sin' are categories which are seldom applied to the situation of the contemporary world. However, one cannot easily gain a profound understanding of the reality that confronts us unless we give a name to the root of the evils which afflict us."[25]

John Paul's teaching on the topic continued to evolve, as is evidenced by the 1995 encyclical *Evangelium vitae*. In this document, the pope was concerned with what he saw as the growing tendency in modern societies to denigrate the dignity and value of human life. In the first chapter of the text, he returned to the theme of structural sin.

> While the climate of widespread moral uncertainty can in some way be explained by the multiplicity and gravity of today's social problems, and these can sometimes mitigate the subjective responsibility of individuals, it is no less true that we are confronted by an even larger reality, which can be described as a veritable *structure of sin*. This reality is characterized by the emergence of a culture which denies solidarity and in many cases takes the form of a veritable "culture of death."[26]

In continuity with his earlier statements, John Paul does not deny individual responsibility for social sin, but he admits that it is not always easy to demarcate.[27]

What is easy to distinguish, according to Sobrino, is the divide between the saving work of God and reality experienced by the oppressed poor of Latin America. The emphasis on social sin stems from a dialectical rather than analogical perspective. The contrast between God's desire to give abundant life to humans and the abysmal reality of the poor is so stark that knowing what is evil becomes all too evident. Thus, the emphasis on structural sin is an understandable strategy.[28]

At the same time, Sobrino's reliance on structural sin to describe the experience of the poor does not lead him to endorse a purely social reading of redemption. Salvation does not come simply by transforming social structures: "evangelizers must not equate the complete renewal of the person (the 'new man') with a transformation of structures," even if they ought to be deeply committed to new structures.[29] In sum, the stress that liberation theologians have given to the dimension of sin that is captured by the term "structural sin" has not led to an avoidance of the personal dimension of sin. It is a classic Catholic "both/and" rather than "either/or" approach to the topic. The insight of Sobrino and other liberation theologians regarding the structural nature of human sinfulness has brought new depths to Catholic social teaching.

DeVille shows that the papal diagnosis of social sin developed to the point that by the mid-nineties John Paul saw four "types," or illustrations, of social sin: (1) dehumanizing structures; (2) cultural symbology that denigrates the human; (3) false consciousness that infects the minds of people; and (4) the collective complicity of a group in a social wrong.[30] He concludes his essay with the judgment that John Paul "has given legitimacy to the discussion about structural sin and noted its authenticity as a category of social and moral analysis. The capacity of the Church for moral teaching has been developed and enriched by the addition of this new analytic tool and category of insight."[31]

## Conclusion

The conversation between liberation theology and the magisterium has known its difficult moments. Gifted and faithful theologians have sometimes been put under suspicion, and the entire movement has been subjected to criticism. Despite these controversies, it is also clear that liberation theology has enriched the church in a variety of ways, not least in the area of Catholic social teaching.

Paul Lakeland has suggested that the debt that the universal church in its social teaching owes to liberation theology has gone unacknowledged.[32] In an article that examined the teaching of John Paul in *Sollicitudo rei socialis*, Lakeland argued that the pope clearly learned from, and borrowed, two key ideas: the option for the poor and structural sin. He then notes that almost all the abundant footnotes of the letter refer to previous papal teaching and Scripture. He concludes, "when ideas become central which were only too long forgotten by the tradition, some recognition of where and how the Spirit of God reminded the church of its lapse of memory would not seem to be out of place."[33]

When future students of Catholic social teaching review the history of its development, the period following Vatican II will be seen as a time of significant progress, both in articulating the teaching and in expanding its impact. There is little doubt that the influence of liberation theologians will be seen to be among the most important factors in the development of the teaching. And, furthermore, there is no question that Sobrino will be viewed as among the foremost contributors to that movement of the Spirit in our time that is called liberation theology.

## Notes

1. Congregation for the Doctrine of the Faith, "Instruction on Certain Aspects of the 'Theology of Liberation'" (*Libertatis nuntius*), (Vatican City: Vatican Polyglot Press, 1984), no. 12.

2. Paul VI, "A Call to Action" (*Octogesima adveniens*), 1971, no. 4 in *Catholic Social Thought: The Documentary Heritage,* ed. David O'Brien and Thomas Shannon (Maryknoll, N.Y.: Orbis Books, 1995).

3. "Epilogue," in Ecumenical Association of Third World Theologians, *Getting the Poor Down from the Cross: Christology of Liberation* (first digital edition, version 1.02), 291-300, at 299 (accessed July 1, 2007).

4. John Noonan, *A Church That Can and Cannot Change* (Notre Dame, Ind.: University of Notre Dame Press, 2005).

5. William Walsh and John Langan "Patristic Social Consciousness" in *The Faith That Does Justice,* ed. John Haughey, S.J. (New York: Paulist Press, 1977), 113-51.

6. Congregation for the Doctrine of the Faith, "Instruction on Christian Freedom and Liberation" (*Libertatis conscientia*) (Washington, D.C.: United States Catholic Conference, 1986), no. 68.

7. Ibid.

8. Leo XIII, "On the Condition of Labor" (*Rerum novarum*), 1891, no. 2, in *Catholic Social Thought,* ed. O'Brien and Shannon. For commentaries on this encyclical and other major documents of official Catholic social teaching, see Kenneth R. Himes, ed., *Modern Catholic Social Teaching: Commentaries and Interpretations* (Washington, D.C.: Georgetown University Press, 2005).

9. Ibid., nos. 22-24 especially.

10. Donal Dorr, *Option for the Poor,* rev. ed. (Maryknoll, N.Y.: Orbis Books, 1992), 353.

11. "Latin American theology is more interested in the crisis within reality and less in the repercussions of this crisis on the subject who may be ideologically affected by it. . . . It is not so much concerned that the hunger of the masses seems senseless to the contemporary world; its concern is the hunger. . . . The aim is . . . to confront the reality of hunger and not the threat that widespread hunger may represent to the meaningfulness of the subject's faith" (Jon Sobrino, *The True Church and the Poor* [Maryknoll, N.Y.: Orbis Books, 1984], 17).

12. "In Latin America the theology of liberation has been very attentive to spirituality, and the performance of its task has been steeped in a particular spirit from the very start. . . . It is because this theology wishes to take account of, and constitute a response to, concrete, historical church reality, with its real cries and real hopes" (Jon Sobrino, "Spirituality and the Following of Jesus," in *Mysterium Liberationis: Fundamental Concepts of Liberation Theology,* ed. Ignacio Ellacuría and Jon Sobrino [Maryknoll, N.Y.: Orbis Books, 1993], 677-701, at 703).

13. Ibid., 681-85.

14. Ibid., 686.

15. Ibid., 687.

16. Jon Sobrino, "Central Position of the Reign of God in Liberation Theology," in *Mysterium Liberationis,* 350-88.

17. Ibid., 358.

18. Ibid., esp. 358-70.

19. Synod of Bishops, "Justice in the World" (*Justitia in Mundo*), 1971, chap. 3 in *Catholic Social Thought,* ed. O'Brien and Shannon.

20. Ibid., chap. 1.

21. Richard Gula, *Reason Informed by Faith* (New York: Paulist Press, 1989), 216.

22. Adam DeVille, "The Development of the Doctrine of 'Structural Sin' and a 'Culture of Death' in the Thought of Pope John Paul II," *Église et Théologie* 30 (1999): 307-25. Some authors use the modifier "social" while others prefer "structural" to describe the reality under discussion. I shall use the terms interchangeably in this essay.

23. Sobrino, *The True Church and the Poor,* 166.

24. John Paul II, "Reconciliation and Penance" (*Reconciliatio et paenitentia*), 1984, no. 16. Available at http://www.vatican.va/holy_father/john_paul_ii/apost_exhortations/documents/hf_jp-ii_exh_02121984_reconciliatio-et-paenitentia_en.html (accessed December 5, 2007).

25. John Paul II, "On Social Concern" (*Sollicitudo rei socialis*), 1987, no. 36 in *Catholic Social Thought,* ed. O'Brien and Shannon. The change in papal tone and understanding from 1984 to 1986 is mirrored in the two documents on liberation theology issued by the CDF. The initial statement was suspicious that social sin might undercut individual responsibility and accountability for sin. But in the 1986 statement there is a clear acknowledgment that "one can therefore speak of structures marked by sin" and that these are "sets of institutions and practices which people find already existing or which they create" and that such structures can become "fixed and fossilized." "Relatively independent of the human will," these structures end up "paralyzing or distorting social development and causing injustice" (*Libertatis conscientia,* no. 74).

26. John Paul II, "The Gospel of Life" (*Evangelium vitae*), 1995, no. 12. Available at http://www.vatican.va/edocs/ENG0141/_INDEX.HTM (accessed December 5, 2007).

27. For an earlier attempt at sorting through the question of individual responsibility and social sin, see my essay "Social Sin and the Role of the Individual," *The Annual of the Society of Christian Ethics* (1986): 183-218.

28. Sobrino, *The True Church and the Poor,* 27.

29. Ibid., 280.

30. DeVille, "Development of the Doctrine of 'Structural Sin,'" 319-21.

31. Ibid., 325.

32. Paul Lakeland, "Development and Catholic Social Teaching: Pope John Paul's New Encyclical," *The Month* 21 (June 1988): 706-10 at 710.

33. Ibid., 710.

# 18

# Christ and Kingdom
*The Identity of Jesus and Christian Politics*

Politics is inscribed in the identity of Jesus Christ, required by the gospel, and inherent in the practice of the kingdom of God. Politics is not related to Christian identity as a derivative application, much less as a mere afterthought, and even less as a superfluous add-on. Far from undermining the divinity of Jesus Christ, Christian political commitment is empowered by the incarnation and derives its hope from it. Expressed another way, the resurrection of Jesus Christ empowers the Body of Christ to exist with radical newness of life and to inaugurate the transformation of all creation.

## Sobrino's Political Christology

Jon Sobrino orients both his Christology and his politics around God's transformative solidarity with the victims of history. This solidarity is embodied in Jesus' preaching of the kingdom or reign of God, as well as in his whole life and his death on the cross. But the cross cannot be preached without the resurrection. The resurrection bestows transformative power on the experience of the cross for us. And neither the cross nor the resurrection can be understood rightly unless one shares in the praxis of the kingdom of God.

These are the themes of Sobrino's major christological work, *Christ the Liberator*.[1] Acting with love and mercy, Jesus manifests the action of God's Spirit in history. To be a disciple of and a believer in Jesus is to adopt the way of life he embraced, the politics of the kingdom of God. Any Christology that is faithful to the New Testament must take as fundamental both the experience of Jesus' resurrection and the memory of his earthly life, especially his ministry of the kingdom.[2] This experience and this memory give rise to the proclamation of Jesus Christ as human and divine, and as forming Christian identity and action. The politics of the kingdom is an essential part of the gospel, and it is only by living the gospel that it is possible to reach greater insight into the reality and role of Christ. "The way that leads to knowledge of Jesus Christ is 'following with spirit' but not the action of the spirit cut off from following."[3]

To follow Jesus Christ requires faith in his humanity as well as in his divinity. His divinity brings us God's power to transform human sinfulness and evil, while his humanity makes that power our own and shows us what transformed existence looks like. Transformed existence means forgiveness, reconciliation, compassion, service, and inclusion of the rejected and the oppressed. Toward the end of *Christ the Liberator*, Sobrino observes that the scandal of God's true, particular, and historical humanity in Christ—God's "will to become real in the flesh of not just anyone but of the poor and the victims"—has been hard to accept from the beginning.[4] To deny or diminish the humanity of Christ and the politics for which it calls is to repudiate the Jesus of the Gospels and the formulations of Chalcedon. It is also to deprive the church of its transformative power for humanity and to destroy the hope of those whom Sobrino calls "the crucified peoples." Nevertheless, "right down to the present, the major problem is still *Docetism* in Christology and *unreality* in the church."[5] Those who deny or downplay the true and full humanity of Jesus Christ also disconnect the church from its social and political mission in history, the mission of the kingdom of God.

## Sobrino's Critics

Sobrino's writings have been attacked for failing to do justice to the divinity of Christ, and for supposedly reducing the gospel message to social action. In 2007, the Vatican Congregation for the Doctrine of the Faith warned Sobrino on these and other points.[6] Specifically, the Congregation named Sobrino's method of beginning theological reflection by attending to the situation of the poor, and his positions on the divinity of Jesus Christ, the incarnation of the Son of God, the relationship between Jesus and the kingdom, the self-consciousness of Jesus, and the salvific value of Jesus' death.[7] A key accusation is, "A number of Father Sobrino's affirmations tend to diminish the breadth of the New Testament passages which affirm that Jesus is God"; "he fails to affirm the divinity of Jesus with sufficient clarity."[8]

Such complaints are rooted in the facts that Sobrino views the confession of Christ as divine to have developed on the basis of the resurrection experiences of his disciples,[9] and to have been specified and clarified only over centuries, through a historical process involving church councils at Nicaea, Chalcedon, and Constantinople.[10] During and after this process, he believes that the humanity of Christ was unjustifiably depreciated. Moreover, Sobrino's predications of divinity in relation to Jesus Christ can sound equivocal, as when he states that the title "Son of God" in the New Testament does not express a "metaphysical" nature but a "salvational" role; or when he says that "since the incarnation the human Jesus is the real symbol of God."[11] However, the fact is that the New Testament does include a variety of unsynchronized ways of expressing the status of Christ, including a two-stage Christology in which Christ is "exalted" at the resurrection, as well as what Larry Hurtado has termed "binitarian" subordinationism, in which only the Father and the Word or Son are divine, and the Father is the source of the "less divine" Son.[12] Although Christians worshipped Christ as God from earliest times, it requires the totality of the New Testament canon, and several hundred years' worth of church councils, to reconcile this confession of Christ with Jewish monotheism (at least to the satisfaction of the Christians, if not the Jews), and to construe acceptable and unacceptable ways of explaining its meaning theologically.

Moreover, and most importantly, the christological formulations of Chalcedon affirm the fullness of Christ's human and divine natures (never to be mixed or confused but also never to be divided or separated) without stipulating in any specific way which theological constructions of the human–divine relation in Jesus Christ are or are not adequate. The manner of relation of divine and human is, as Sobrino well sees, an "ultimate mystery," calling for "chastity of understanding" on the part of systematizing theologians.[13] Theological strategies such as the *communicatio idiomatum* (a point of contention between Sobrino and the Vatican[14]), or the well-established idea that the one subject of the person Jesus Christ is the Word (and not a human subject[15]) are just that: theological strategies and not definitive doctrine. Hence, Sobrino is not wrong to appeal to the facts of theological development and pluralism to create a space for his theological explorations of the identity of Jesus Christ.

As far as Christian ethics and politics are concerned, suffice it to say that humanity and divinity are both essential. Christ's divinity brings humanity into proper alignment with God, and brings God into the human equation in a saving and restorative way. Christ's humanity both illustrates the fullness of human life in relation to God and includes other humans eschatologically in Christ's ability to embody this fullness. The primary focus of the present essay will be the importance of the kingdom of God to the saving mission of Jesus Christ as human and divine, since the kingdom of God is both central to Sobrino's thought and essential to Christian ethics and politics.

The Notification takes issue with Sobrino's reading of the kingdom of God, though it accepts ministry to the poor as valid. According to the Notification, Sobrino's political Christology undercuts the divinity of Christ, partly because "kingdom" is misinterpreted. Rather enigmatically, the Notification quotes Origen, against Sobrino, to the effect that "Jesus is the Kingdom of God in person." The apparent relevance of this is that the kingdom of God cannot, in the view of the author(s) of the Notification, be separated from Christ the Mediator as a distinct reality that is mediated.[16] This assertion in effect makes it impossible to talk about the kingdom of God as a transformed community, whose relations have been reordered according to God's love, mercy, forgiveness, and power. Interestingly, in *Christ the Liberator*, Sobrino quotes the same metaphor ("the kingdom of God in person"), adding, however, that an unfortunate consequence of Origen's use of this metaphor was a christological shift in which the kingdom of God "ceased to be the type of historical-social-collective reality that Jesus preached and became a different sort of reality, a personal one. . . ."[17]

Near the time of the publication of this warning about the dangerous character of Sobrino's Christology, a competing theological interpretation, *Jesus of Nazareth*, was published by Joseph Ratzinger, Pope Benedict XVI.[18] Perhaps unsurprisingly, this work has striking points in common with the theology of the Notification. Salient among them is a clear and overriding emphasis on the divinity of Christ, to the extent that the kingdom of God in the preaching of Jesus is nowhere associated with a Christian mandate to undertake political action on behalf of the poor. Instead, like the Notification, Ratzinger calls Jesus "the Kingdom of God in person," citing Origen.[19] Ratzinger's Christology falls into the consequent apolitical trend identified by Sobrino, in which the kingdom comes to represent personal communion with God in Christ, without integral connection to action in the world on behalf of excluded or oppressed peoples. Ratzinger seems to interpret any claim that the kingdom has political ramifications as necessarily reductionistic with regard to the divine identity and mission of Jesus Christ.

Ratzinger agrees with Sobrino that the core content of the gospel is that the kingdom of God is at hand, and that the announcement of the kingdom by Jesus comes with "efficacious power that enters into the world to save and transform."[20] But this transformation concerns primarily, and is largely limited to, personal faith and spirituality. First of all, the symbol "kingdom of God" means that Christ himself is God's presence, that is, its main function is to affirm the divinity of Christ. Second, also following Origen, Ratzinger proposes a complementary "mystical interpretation" that "sees man's interiority as the essential location of the Kingdom of God."[21] The kingdom of God is present when the soul is in communion with God.

Another interpretation is considered by Ratzinger to be objectionable: an "ecclesiastical" interpretation, in which the kingdom of God and the church in history are closely related.[22] A reader might expect here a discussion of the problems that arise when the imperfect, historical church is identified too closely with the eschatological reality of God's transforming grace. This is not the line of thought pursued by Ratzinger. Instead, he identifies three different versions of this unacceptable "ecclesiastical" interpretation. One is a liberal view of the kingdom in which it is associated with individual moral action and loving good works. A second is an eschatological expectation of an imminent end of the world, as attributed to Jesus himself by some (not all) historical critics of the Bible. Finally, there is a "secularist" view of the kingdom (especially pernicious, Ratzinger believes, in post–Vatican II Catholic theology). Here Jesus' message "is simply the name for a world governed by peace, justice, and the conservation of creation. It means no more than this." "The main thing that leaps out is that God has disappeared."[23] Ratzinger's delineation of this final interpretation suggests reasons, however ill-founded, for *magisterial* resistance to Sobrino's Christology and to liberation theology in general.

Ratzinger's own constructive reading of the kingdom of God is that with this symbol Jesus proclaims the divine lordship, "God's dominion over the world and over history."[24] What are the results of this lordship? On the one hand, "Jesus' message of the Kingdom" has "meager dimensions within history."[25] It has few if any visible social or political effects. On the other, "it is present as a life-shaping power through the believer's prayer and being: by bearing God's yoke, the believer already receives a share in the world to come." The kingdom of God, then, offers the opportunity for the individual person of faith to enter into communion with God, transcending history in a sense, through the grace of God's action in Christ as divine. Ratzinger takes a strong stand in defense of the real possibility of spiritual contact with the divine through the person of Jesus Christ, a stand that will appeal to many.[26] Yet it is all too clear that Ratzinger has validated Sobrino's worries about Origen's metaphor leading to a politically detached, individualist piety, as well as to a church that Sobrino would no doubt regard as "unreal" in its lack of concern for the victims of history, whom he considers to take Christ's place on the cross.

Is Ratzinger right that modern historical-critical methods invariably serve up a nondivine Christ, or that political interpretations necessarily eliminate God from the picture? Or does recent study of the New Testament, particularly hypotheses about the teaching and effect of Jesus during his lifetime, validate Sobrino's conviction that the kingdom of God has social-ethical and political content? Theologically speaking, is this content compatible with and even demanded by faith in the person of Jesus Christ as human and divine? Historically informed biblical scholarship may assist discernment of what is the most adequate interpretation of the preaching of the kingdom by Jesus.

## The Historical Jesus and the Kingdom of God

Historical study of Jesus of Nazareth has been of high interest to theologians and biblical scholars since at least the eighteenth century. It informs the work of Sobrino, for whom the historical meaning and social significance of Christ's kingdom preaching and practices establish the content of a Christian politics, a politics which on theological grounds is connected with salvation.

As with any other historical figure it is impossible to return to Jesus' lifetime and know him just as did his personal acquaintances, friends, family, followers, and adversaries. Moreover, the Gospels—which provide Christians with their major impressions of his life—were not written for the purpose of providing historical records in the modern sense. They were written to communicate an experience of the risen Jesus Christ, an experience that from the beginning subsumed and reinterpreted historical memories of the life and death of the man known as Jesus of Nazareth. Hence, historical research aims neither to recapture Jesus "as he really was" in his own day, nor to validate (or *in*validate) the present reality of Jesus Christ as risen and present to the church. Instead, it employs critical historical tools to learn what can be known with certainty or probability about Jesus of Nazareth as a historical figure, accessible to the methods of the historian; or about the first-century Palestinian environment in which he lived, taught, and finally was killed ("social history").[27]

The various phases, branches, and authors of historical criticism have produced different pictures of Jesus, depending, for instance, on the weight they give to his similarity to his Jewish context, the context of Greco-Roman culture and religion, the reliability of the Gospels as offering historical information within their overriding theological concerns, the historical ordering of and influences on the Gospels and their portraits, the correspondence of details in the Gospels to information available from non-Christian authors from the same or slightly later time periods, and the relevance of noncanonical Gospels to understanding Jesus (e.g., *Gospel of Thomas*). Despite this variety, there is a scholarly consensus that the kingdom of God was central to the teaching of Jesus; that he saw himself in relation to God's momentous action to establish a new order; and that his ministry was marked by an iconoclastic willingness to share table with "rejects" and undesirable riffraff whom others take to be anything but members of God's renewed community.[28]

A first methodological task for Christology is to show why historical research on Jesus is pertinent in the first place. Ratzinger thinks it is not. There are other theologians who are at least highly skeptical about the usefulness and aims of the work of historical scholars. For example, Luke Timothy Johnson generalizes that some "recent historical Jesus books" share "certain standard features." These include rejecting the Gospels as reliable sources of information, portraying Jesus and his mission as about social and cultural reform "rather than" about religious and spiritual realities; and assuming that nothing that cannot be verified historically can be held by Christian faith.[29] Ratzinger is on the same wavelength. Yet, despite the selective and derogatory characterizations of Sobrino in the Notification, Sobrino clearly holds Jesus Christ to be "divine." Indeed, he regards the denial of Christ's divinity to be "intolerable for Christian faith."[30] Remaining questions are whether the New Testament affirms Christ's divinity in the same way and as clearly as later councils, what precisely "divinity" means when ascribed to Christ, whether it must be defined in "ontological" terms, and how it is related to his humanity. However, it is clear that the use of historical research as such means neither that an author rejects Christ's divinity nor that he or she denies that the Gospels were written from the perspective of resurrection faith, a perspective that theological interpretation must ultimately share. (Historical critics as diverse as John Meier, N. T. Wright, E. P. Sanders, Marcus Borg, and Daniel Harrington evidently share it also.)

Historical research can aid theology. It can enhance understanding of the New Testament by illuminating the circumstances in which it was written, as well as the (earlier) religious, social, and political contexts of Jesus himself. Historical understanding brings new dimensions to our reading of New Testament accounts and may help eliminate faulty readings that are unlikely to reflect how Jesus was heard and received in his own era, or what his first followers meant by their proclamations of Jesus as Christ, Lord, and Messiah. Historical understanding can also suggest or support new directions for constructive theologies, including Christology, for example, by opening windows into first-century sources and meanings of titles ascribed to Jesus. (Sobrino uses it for this purpose in *Christ the Liberator*, part 2, on christological titles.)

Social ethicists and liberation theologians take it for granted that Jesus acted and spoke in certain ways himself, and that his example sets the standard for Christian politics. Jesus exemplified and preached the message that to live according to God's will is to live in transformed relationships and communities of compassion and reconciliation. This means that enemies are forgiven, the poor and oppressed are served, and all kinds of human-status boundaries are overcome to constitute a new way of life under God's reign (see, e.g., the "hard sayings" of Matt 5:38-48, the "parable of judgment" in Matthew 25, and the baptismal formula of Gal 3:28). The parable of the Good Samaritan (among others) illustrates such a way of life, portraying an "outcast" who overcomes boundaries of religion and ethnicity to help a vulnerable stranger at significant personal inconvenience and expense (Luke 10:25-37). The story is told by Jesus to illustrate the meaning of love of neighbor, a precondition of inheriting eternal life. This same love as service characterizes kingdom life now, just as it did in the time of Jesus.

Kingdom life is possible historically, though partially and in anticipation of God's future fulfillment (Luke 17:21; 11:20; Matt 12:28; and perhaps Mark 1:15). Jesus actually changed and changes people and their relationships. And the virtues and relationships of the kingdom are more than personal spiritual experiences; they are social experiences, and their effects are not limited to relationships among the disciples. They have political ramifications that affect the roles of Christians and their communities in the world. It is true that Jesus did not have an explicit sociopolitical "agenda," nor was he a revolutionary who tried to change the world around him using expressly political, much less violent, measures. Yet the changes that he called for—especially through his ministry to "tax collectors and sinners," to women, and to those ostracized because of illness or disability—present a radical challenge to every society and make it clear whose side he was on. To live in the kingdom is to make an option for the poor and to be committed to social justice—just as Jesus was.

Sobrino particularly makes the point, as we have seen, that this commitment is required by the humanity of Jesus. Jesus Christ is not only the Word Incarnate, he is a human person in history, Jesus of Nazareth. In fact, although his humanity was evident to all who knew him and certainly to the earliest Christians, it was illegitimately submerged in the later tradition (despite the affirmations of Nicaea and Chalcedon). Yet it is by Jesus' humanity that we know what is demanded of us concretely—and what is possible for us—in the Christian life.

> According to the New Testament, true humanity consists of faithfulness to God, letting God be God, mercy toward other people; and surrender of self. It also involves fellowship and solidarity, which is why Christ is presented in the New Testament as not only human but as a brother (Heb 2:11). Finally it also means upholding these specifications, journeying to the end and in preparedness to surrender one's very life.[31]

A critic could raise several questions about these assumptions or interpretations. Why is it so clear that Jesus expected to change society, or at least expected his later followers to do so? And, in any event, should not Christian faith, theology, and ethics be based on the resurrection as validating the divine origin of Christ, the salvation of the soul, and the person's ultimate destiny of union with God—not as communicating a message about social action? If his entire life must be seen from the perspective of the resurrection faith of the church, does that not require Christians to prioritize the proclamation of Christ's divinity?

One avenue to address such questions is historical research on the life and death of Jesus, which enlightens both the meaning his reported words and deeds might have had in their original context, and the historical development of the Gospel accounts themselves. One among many relevant areas in which considerable recent research has been done is the Jewishness of Jesus, his resemblance to his Jewish environment, and the Jewish origins of titles such as "Messiah," "Son of Man," and "Son of God." Needless to say, Jesus is not similar in every respect to his context; and that context itself is pluralistic. Nevertheless, the theological process of interpretation that is essential to Christology is helpfully informed by such studies. In the words of the respected (and moderate) Catholic biblical scholar Daniel J. Harrington,

> Most of Jesus' teachings about God, creation, covenant, obedience to God's will, righteousness, and eschatology are consistent with his Jewish theological heritage. Furthermore, the early Christian beliefs about Jesus—his

relationship to God as Father, his identity, the significance of his life, the movement he began, his teachings about the coming kingdom of God, and his instructions about human attitudes and actions—use the language and concepts of Judaism. To say the same thing in other terms Christian theology, Christology, soteriology, ecclesiology, eschatology, and ethics are rooted in Judaism.[32]

To say that early Christians (or Jesus himself) used Jewish symbols and concepts is not to deny that they used them creatively and modified their significance.[33] But it is to suggest (*pace* Ratzinger[34]) that to have greater knowledge of their origins is to understand better their ultimate Christian meanings.

As Harrington indicates, it is instructive for a Christian politics to examine Jesus' "teachings about the coming kingdom of God" and about political ethics in their historical setting, especially their Jewish setting. That the kingdom is a central part of Jesus' teaching, and that it has a long history in Judaism as symbolizing God's kingly rule, can hardly be denied.[35] In Jewish usage in Jesus' day, the symbol has an especially strong connection with eschatological or apocalyptic beliefs, expressing hope in God's definitive salvation, vindication, and restoration of Israel in the future, a hope that Jesus does not reject.[36] Yet Jesus' use of the symbol has distinctive notes. One is the idea of reversal, of insiders becoming outsiders, and outsiders becoming insiders at the final banquet (Matt 8:11-12; Luke 13:28-29). Gentiles will be included, while Jesus' opponents even within Israel will be excluded.[37] Jesus proclaimed the "loving forgiveness of God the Father, a prodigal father who freely bestows his forgiveness on sinners who have no strict claim on God's mercy. . . ." God's action brings a "revolution" to the present world.[38]

Furthermore, this revolution is in some sense already accomplished in the words and deeds of Jesus[39]—raising the critical and ultimately divisive Jewish-Christian question of the source of Jesus' power and authority. Jesus' offer of table fellowship to all, including "lowlifes" like tax collectors, prostitutes, and other sinners, "was meant to foreshadow the final eschatological banquet and to give a foretaste of that banquet even during his public ministry."[40] His healings and exorcisms, likewise, signified the inbreaking power of God, who would restore to community all those who are alienated, afflicted, or rejected. Although an incident in the Jerusalem temple, as reported variously in the Gospels, was the immediate precipitating event that led to Jesus' execution by the Roman authorities, with the apparent collusion of Jewish religious leadership, it is not unlikely that the socially challenging and disruptive effects of his practices and teachings were contributory to his imprisonment, trial, and death.

It is true to say, with John Meier, that Jesus "did not issue pronouncements about concrete social and political reforms." Yet Meier goes further than warranted when he asserts that Jesus "was not interested in" and "was not proclaiming" the reform of the world, or of particular social and political relationships and institutions.[41] Rather, one may, with Sobrino, see Jesus' compassion for and practical inclusion of the "lowlifes," which brought social disapprobation and danger, as a profound revision of the status quo, in the name of the power and authority of God, and in expectation of the incipient reordering of history. Jesus "both challenged the existing social order and advocated an alternative,"[42] guided by compassion, and giving voice to the sufferings of the peasant classes, as well as to those oppressed by inauthentic, class- and gender-biased interpretations of purity and holiness. In this way, Jesus fits into the tradition of the Jewish prophets, for whom there was certainly no breach between covenant faithfulness to God and responsibility for the way social arrangements affect the oppressed and the vulnerable.

## Emissaries of the Kingdom: Christians and Political Change

As Mark Allan Powell remarks, a dichotomous understanding of Jesus as either a purely religious figure or the leader of a political movement is no longer necessary.[43] The consensus is in favor of his political significance, despite scholarly differences over the relation he claimed to God the Father, the nature of his eschatological or apocalyptic expectations, and the degree of his reliance on Jewish or Hellenistic worldviews. By preaching and inaugurating the kingdom of God, "Jesus posed a real threat to the political system of his day, indeed a greater threat ultimately than those who thought they would change society by overthrowing this or that particular tyrant."[44]

With Sobrino, then, the theologian may use historical research to bolster and augment theological claims about Jesus, not to reject them. In fact, some historical critics now even raise the question whether the older "scientific" paradigm of historical research and knowledge should be adjusted or replaced to reflect experiential and historical "data" that cannot otherwise be explained.[45] In any event, Sobrino would claim, the humanity of Jesus demands that the theologian take his historical reality into account in building a Christology; Christology must not lose sight of the fact that Jesus' reality involved a prophetic challenge to society and politics. Humanity and divinity are equally important to Christ's salvific role. The divinity of Christ and Christ's resurrection demand that Christians see society and politics as eschatologically transformed by Christ. And Christ's own preaching and practice of the kingdom of God attest that social and political transformation is a reality that can begin even now, a reality that his followers are called to embody. Sobrino thus rightly defines the Christian vocation as one that includes a praxis of hope in favor of the victims of history. This is the praxis of the kingdom of God, a politics that embodies resurrection life and attests to the truth of the incarnation.

## Notes

1. Jon Sobrino, *Christ the Liberator: A View from the Victims*, trans. Paul Burns (Maryknoll, N.Y.: Orbis Books, 2001).

2. Ibid., 334.

3. Ibid., 328.

4. Ibid., 289.

5. Ibid., 290.

6. Congregation for the Doctrine of the Faith, "Notification on the Works of Father Jon Sobrino, S.J." See pages 255-66 below. Also available at http://www.vatican.va/roman _curia/congregations/cfaith/documents/rc_con_cfaith_doc_20061126_notification-sobrino_en.html (accessed July 31, 2007).

7. Ibid., no. 1.

8. Ibid., no. 4.

9. *Christ the Liberator*, 98-103, 113-14.

10. Ibid., 107-10, 275-84.

11. Ibid., 174, 319.

12. See Larry W. Hurtado, *Lord Jesus Christ: Devotion to Jesus in Earliest Christianity* (Grand Rapids/Cambridge, U.K.: Eerdmans, 2003); Richard N. Longenecker, *New Wine into Fresh Wineskins: Contextualizing the Early Christian Confessions* (Peabody, Mass.: Hendrickson, 1999); and James D. G. Dunn, *Christology in the Making: A New Testament Inquiry into the Origins of the Doctrine of the Incarnation*, 2d ed. (Grand Rapids: Eerdmans, 1996).

13. *Christ the Liberator*, 285.

14. See the Notification, no. 6. The *communicatio idiomatum* (the precise term apparently arose only in the Middle Ages) refers to the idea that attributes of one nature, human or divine, can be predicated of the other in an analogous way, in view of the fact that the two natures are united in Christ. This was the view of Cyril of Alexandria against Nestorius, who maintained that Mary could not be called the "mother of God" (*Theotokos*). Some later authors, however, including Thomas Aquinas and Karl Rahner, turned the strategy on its head by denying that attributes of the divine could be attributed to the human, and vice versa. Rather, each could be predicated of the one person Jesus Christ—thus avoiding the idea that God can, for instance, suffer. Other authors, including Martin Luther, Dietrich Bonhoeffer, Jürgen Moltmann, Hans Urs von Balthasar, Jon Sobrino, and most other liberation and feminist theologians see a "suffering God" as an appropriate explanation of the meaning of the cross. A crucial point is that any human characteristic predicated of God (whether suffering, compassion, justice, mercy, wrath, or love) must in the nature of the case be analogous attributions. Suffering is no more vulnerable on this score than the others.

15. See Anthony Baxer, "Chalcedon, and the Subject in Christ," *Downside Review* 107, no. 366 (1989): 1-21.

16. Notification, no. 7.

17. *Christ the Liberator*, 334.

18. Joseph Ratzinger (Pope Benedict XVI), *Jesus of Nazareth: From the Baptism in the Jordan to the Transfiguration*, trans. Adrian J. Walker (New York/London/Toronto: Doubleday, 2007).

19. *Jesus of Nazareth*, 49.

20. Ibid., 47.

21. Ibid., 49.

22. Ibid., 50.

23. Ibid., 51-54.

24. Ibid., 57.

25. Ibid., 57-58.

26. Peter Steinfels, "The Face of God: What Benedict's Jesus Offers," *Commonweal* (August 17, 2007): 8-9.

27. For an excellent overview of these and related issues, as well as of major contributors in the field, see Mark Allan Powell, *Jesus as a Figure in History: How Modern Historians View the Man from Galilee* (Louisville/London: Westminster John Knox, 1998).

28. See *Jesus as a Figure in History*, 174-76.

29. Luke Timothy Johnson, "The Real Jesus: The Challenge of Current Scholarship and the Truth of the Gospels," in *The Historical Jesus through Catholic and Jewish Eyes*, ed. Bryan F. LeBeau, Leonard Greenspoon, and Dennis Hamm, S.J. (Harrisburg, Pa.: Trinity Press International, 2000), 53-54.

30. *Christ the Liberator*, 240.

31. Ibid., 287.

32. Daniel J. Harrington, S.J., "Retrieving the Jewishness of Jesus: Recent Developments," in *Historical Jesus through Catholic and Jewish Eyes*, 68.

33. The criterion of "dissimilarity" to authenticate the sayings and deeds of Jesus by contrasting them with prevailing Jewish or Christian norms originated in the 1960s with Norman Perrin, and has stood the test of time. But, as N.T. Wright has argued more recently, recognizing Jesus' similarity to his Jewish background also helps us understand his historical reality and the meaning of his teaching and deeds against that backdrop. For a discussion, see *Jesus as a Figure in History*, 46-50, 150-52, 168-69.

34. In *Jesus of Nazareth*, Ratzinger in fact emphasizes the radical difference between Christianity, which claims that Jesus is divine, and Jewish monotheism. While this difference is real, it is arguable historically (and is suggested by Sobrino) that it developed progressively, coming to clarity only after Jesus' lifetime, and required refinement even after the New Testament accounts were composed, at Chalcedon and later. Ratzinger claims that Jesus was recognized as divine already during his lifetime, a claim that can be regarded as highly debatable without in any way rejecting the confession of Christ as divine and human (see *Christ the Liberator*, 114-16). To make his argument, Ratzinger takes Gospel accounts, based on the experience of the resurrection, as historical records of events in the life of Jesus (e.g., the Transfiguration). He does this in the name of taking history seriously and avoiding "Gnosticism." As one reviewer puts it, Ratzinger "parts company with the critical majority in treating even this floridly mythological episode [the Transfiguration] as a historical event no more problematical for open-minded historians than Jesus' birth in Palestine" (Jack Miles, "Between Theology and Exegesis," *Commonweal* [July 13, 2007]: 21). Ratzinger fails to differentiate between aspects of the Gospels that are more and less likely to reflect historical events, having dismissed the relevance of historical research. Historical facts are posited on the basis of special revelation—after all, a gnostic move?

35. John P. Meier, *A Marginal Jew: Rethinking the Historical Jesus, Volume Two: Mentor, Message, and Miracles* (New York/London/Toronto: Doubleday, 1994), 237-38.

36. Ibid., 269-70.

37. Ibid., 330.

38. Ibid., 331.

39. Ibid., 351, 453.

40. Ibid., 966.

41. Ibid., 331.

42. Marcus J. Borg, *Jesus in Contemporary Scholarship* (Valley Forge, Pa.: Trinity Press International, 1994), 98.

43. *Jesus as a Figure in History*, 174.

44. Ibid., 176.

45. For a discussion, see *Jesus as a Figure in History*, 178-81.

# Appendix 1

### *NOTIFICATION*
### *on the Works of Father Jon SOBRINO, SJ:*

*Jesucristo liberador. Lectura histórico-teológica*
*de Jesús de Nazaret* (Madrid, 1991)[1]
and
*La fe en Jesucristo. Ensayo desde las víctimas* (San Salvador, 1999)[2]

## Introduction

1. After a preliminary examination of the books *Jesucristo liberador. Lectura histórico-teológica de Jesús de Nazaret* (*Jesus the Liberator*) and *La fe en Jesucristo. Ensayo desde las víctimas* (*Christ the Liberator*) by Father Jon Sobrino, SJ, the Congregation for the Doctrine of the Faith, because of certain imprecisions and errors found in them, decided to proceed to a more thorough study of these works in October 2001. Given the wide distribution of these writings and their use in seminaries and other centers of study, particularly in Latin America, it was decided to employ the "urgent examination" as regulated by articles 23-27 of *Agendi Ratio in Doctrinarum Examine.*

As a result of this examination, in July 2004 a list of erroneous or dangerous propositions found in the abovementioned books was sent to the Author through the Reverend Father Peter Hans Kolvenbach, SJ, Superior General of the Society of Jesus.

In March of 2005, Father Jon Sobrino sent a *Response to the text of the Congregation for the Doctrine of the Faith* to the Congregation. This *Response* was studied in the Ordinary Session of the Congregation on 23 November 2005. It was determined that, although the author had modified his thought somewhat on several points, the *Response* did not prove satisfactory since, in substance, the errors already cited in the list of erroneous propositions still remained in this text. Although the preoccupation of the Author for the plight of the poor is admirable, the Congregation for the Doctrine of the Faith has the obligation to indicate that the aforementioned works of Father Sobrino contain notable discrepancies with the faith of the Church.

For this reason, it was decided to publish this *Notification,* in order to offer the faithful a secure criterion, founded upon the doctrine of the Church, by which to judge the affirmations contained in these books or in other publications of the Author. One must note that on some occasions the erroneous propositions are situated within the context of other expressions which would seem to contradict them[3], but this is not sufficient to justify these propositions. The Congregation does not intend to judge the subjective intentions of the Author, but rather has the duty to call to attention to certain propositions which are not in conformity with the doctrine of the Church. These propositions regard: 1) the methodological presuppositions on which the Author bases his theological reflection, 2) the Divinity of Jesus Christ, 3) the Incarnation of the Son of God, 4) the relationship between Jesus Christ and the Kingdom of God, 5) the Self-consciousness of Jesus, and 6) the salvific value of his Death.

## I. Methodological Presuppositions

2. In his book *Jesus the Liberator: A Historical-Theological View,* Father Sobrino affirms: *"Latin American Christology . . . identifies its setting, in the sense of a real situation, as the poor of this world, and this situation is what must be present in and permeate any particular setting in which Christology is done"* (*Jesus the Liberator,* 28). Further, *"the poor in the community question Christological faith and give it its fundamental direction"* (*Ibidem,* 30), and *"the Church of the poor . . . is the ecclesial setting of Christology because it is a world shaped by the poor"* (*Ibidem,* 31). *"The social setting is thus the most crucial for the faith, the most crucial in shaping the thought pattern of Christology, and what requires and encourages the epistemological break"* (*Ibidem*).

While such a preoccupation for the poor and oppressed is admirable, in these quotations the "Church of the poor" assumes the fundamental position which properly belongs to the faith of the Church. It is only in this ecclesial faith that all other theological foundations find their correct epistemological setting.

The ecclesial foundation of Christology may not be identified with "the Church of the poor," but is found rather in the apostolic faith transmitted through the Church for all generations. The theologian, in his particular vocation in the Church, must continually bear in mind that theology is the science of the faith. Other points of departure for theological work run the risk of arbitrariness and end in a misrepresentation of the same faith.[4]

3. Although the Author affirms that he considers the theological fonts "normative," the lack of due attention that he pays to them gives rise to concrete problems in his theology which we will discuss below. In particular, the New Testament affirmations concerning the divinity of Christ, his filial consciousness and the salvific value of his death, do not in fact always receive the attention due them. The sections below will treat these specific questions.

The manner in which the author treats the major Councils of the early Church is equally notable, for according to him, these Councils have moved progressively away from the contents of the New Testament. For example, he affirms: "*While these texts are useful theologically, besides being normative, they are also limited and even dangerous, as is widely recognized today*" (*Christ the Liberator*, 221). Certainly, it is necessary to recognize the limited character of dogmatic formulations, which do not express nor are able to express everything contained in the mystery of faith, and must be interpreted in the light of Sacred Scripture and Tradition. But there is no foundation for calling these formulas dangerous, since they are authentic interpretations of Revelation.

Father Sobrino considers the dogmatic development of the first centuries of the Church including the great Councils to be ambiguous and even negative. Although he does not deny the normative character of the dogmatic formulations, neither does he recognize in them any value except in the cultural milieu in which these formulations were developed. He does not take into account the fact that the *transtemporal* subject of the faith is the believing Church, and that the pronouncements of the first Councils have been accepted and lived by the entire ecclesial community. The Church continues to profess the Creed which arose from the Councils of Nicea (AD 325) and Constantinople I (AD 381). The first four Ecumenical Councils are accepted by the great majority of Churches and Ecclesial Communities in both the East and West. If these Councils used the terminology and concepts expressive of the culture of the time, it was not in order to be conformed to it. The Councils do not signify a hellenization of Christianity but rather the contrary. Through the inculturation of the Christian message, Greek culture itself underwent a transformation from within and was able to be used as an instrument for the expression and defense of biblical truth.

## II. The Divinity of Jesus Christ

4. A number of Father Sobrino's affirmations tend to diminish the breadth of the New Testament passages which affirm that Jesus is God: "*[The New Testament] makes clear that he was intimately bound up with God, which meant that his reality had to be expressed in some way as a reality that is of God (cf. Jn 20:28)*" (*Christ the Liberator*, 115). In reference to John 1:1, he affirms: "*Strictly speaking, this logos is not yet said to be God (consubstantial with the Father), but something is claimed for him that will have great importance for reaching this conclusion: his preexistence. This does not signify something purely temporal but relates him to the creation and links the logos with action specific to the divinity*" (*Christ the Liberator*, 257). According to the Author, the New Testament does not clearly affirm the divinity of Jesus, but merely establishes the presuppositions for it: "*The New Testament . . . contains expressions that contain the seed of what will produce confession of the divinity of Christ in the strict sense*" (*Ibidem*). "*All this means that at the outset Jesus was not spoken of as God, nor was divinity a term applied to him; this happened only after a considerable interval of believing explication, almost certainly after the fall of Jerusalem*" (*Ibidem*, 114).

To maintain that John 20:28 affirms that Jesus is "of God" is clearly erroneous, in as much as the passage itself refers to Jesus as "Lord" and "God." Similarly, John 1:1 says that the Word is God. Many other texts speak of Jesus as Son and as Lord.[5] The divinity of Jesus has been the object of the Church's faith from the beginning, long before his consubstantiality with the Father was proclaimed by the Council of Nicea. The fact that this term was not used does not mean that the divinity of Jesus was not affirmed in the strict sense, contrary to what the Author seems to imply.

Father Sobrino does not deny the divinity of Jesus when he proposes that it is found in the New Testament only "in seed" and was formulated dogmatically only after many years of believing reflection. Nevertheless he fails to affirm Jesus' divinity with sufficient clarity. This reticence gives credence to the suspicion that the historical development of dogma, which Sobrino describes as ambiguous, has arrived at the formulation of Jesus' divinity without a clear continuity with the New Testament.

But the divinity of Jesus is clearly attested to in the passages of the New Testament to which we have referred. The numerous Conciliar declarations in this regard[6] are in continuity with that which the New Testament affirms explicitly and not only "in seed." The confession of the divinity of Jesus Christ has been an absolutely essential part of the faith of the Church since her origins. It is explicitly witnessed to since the New Testament.

## III. The Incarnation of the Son of God

5. Father Sobrino writes: *"From a dogmatic point of view, we have to say, without any reservation, that the Son (the second person of the Trinity) took on the whole reality of Jesus and, although the dogmatic formula never explains the manner of this being affected by the human dimension, the thesis is radical. The Son experienced Jesus' humanity, existence in history, life, destiny, and death"* (*Jesus the Liberator*, 242).

In this passage, the Author introduces a distinction between the Son and Jesus which suggests to the reader the presence of two subjects in Christ: the Son assumes the reality of Jesus; the Son experiences the humanity, the life, the destiny, and the death of Jesus. It is not clear that the Son is Jesus and that Jesus is the Son. In a literal reading of these passages, Father Sobrino reflects the so-called theology of the *homo assumptus*, which is incompatible with the Catholic faith which affirms the unity of the person of Jesus Christ in two natures, divine and human, according to the formulations of the Council of Ephesus,[7] and above all of the Council of Chalcedon which said: "... *we unanimously teach and confess one and the same Son, our Lord Jesus Christ, the same perfect in divinity and perfect in humanity, the same truly God and truly man composed of rational soul and body, the same one in being with the Father as to the divinity and one in being with us as to the humanity, like us in all things but sin (cf. Heb 4:15). The same was begotten from the Father before the ages as to the divinity and in the latter days for us and our salvation was born as to His humanity from Mary the Virgin Mother of God; one and the same Christ, Son, Lord, only-begotten, acknowledged in two natures which undergo no confusion, no change, no division, no separation."* [8] Similarly, Pope Pius XII declared in his encyclical *Sempiternus Rex*: *". . . the council of Chalcedon in full accord with that of Ephesus, clearly asserts that both natures are united in 'One Person and subsistence', and rules out the placing of two individuals in Christ, as if some one man, completely autonomous in himself, had been taken up and placed by the side of the Word."* [9]

6. Another difficulty with the Christological view of Father Sobrino arises from an insufficient comprehension of the *communicatio idiomatum*, which he describes in the following way: *"the limited human is predicated of God, but the unlimited divine is not predicated of Jesus"* (*Christ the Liberator*, 223, cf. 332-333).

In reality, the phrase *communicatio idiomatum*, that is, the possibility of referring the properties of divinity to humanity and vice versa, is the immediate consequence of the unity of the person of Christ "in two natures" affirmed by the Council of Chalcedon. By virtue of this possibility, the Council of Ephesus has already defined that Mary was *Theotokos*: *"If anyone does not confess that Emmanuel is truly God and, therefore, that the holy Virgin is the Mother of God (theotokos) since she begot according to the flesh the Word of God made flesh, let him be anathema."* [10] *"If anyone ascribes separately to two persons or hypostases the words which in the evangelical and apostolic writings are either spoken of Christ by the saints or are used by Christ about Himself, and applies some to a man considered by himself, apart from the Word, and others, because they befit God, solely to the Word who is from God the Father, let him be anathema."* [11] As can easily be deduced from these texts, the *communicatio idiomatum* is applied in both senses: the human is predicated of God and the divine of man. Already the New Testament affirms that Jesus is Lord,[12] and that all things are created through him.[13] In Christian terminology, it is possible to say that Jesus is God, who is creator and omnipotent. The Council of Ephesus sanctioned the use of calling Mary Mother of God. It is therefore incorrect to maintain that "the unlimited divine" is not predicated of Jesus. Sobrino's affirmation to the contrary is understandable only within the context of a *homo assumptus* Christology in which the unity of the person of Jesus is not clear, and therefore it would be impossible to predicate divine attributes of a human person. However, this Christology is in no way compatible with the teaching of the Councils of Ephesus and Chalcedon on the unity of the person in two natures. Thus, the understanding of the *communicatio idiomatum* which the Author presents reveals an erroneous conception of the mystery of the Incarnation and of the unity of the person of Jesus Christ.

## IV. Jesus Christ and the Kingdom of God

7. Father Sobrino advances a peculiar view of the relationship between Jesus and the Kingdom of God. This is a point of special interest in his works. According to the Author, the person of Jesus as mediator cannot be absolutized, but must be contemplated in his relatedness to the Kingdom of God, which is apparently considered to be something distinct from Jesus himself:

*"I shall analyze this historical relatedness in detail later, but I want to say here that this reminder is important because of the consequences [ . . . ] when Christ the mediator is made absolute and there is no sense of his constitutive relatedness to what is mediated, the Kingdom of God"* (Jesus the Liberator, 16).

*"We must first distinguish between the mediator and the mediation of God. The Kingdom of God, formally speaking, is nothing other than the accomplishment of God's will for this world, which we call mediation. This mediation [ . . . ] is associated with a person (or group) who proclaims it and initiates it: this we call the mediator. In this sense we can and must say, according to faith, that the definitive, ultimate, and eschatological mediator of the Kingdom of God has already appeared: Jesus. [ . . . ] From this standpoint, we can also appreciate Origen's fine definition of Christ as the autobasileia of God, the Kingdom of God in person: important words that well describe the finality of the personal mediator of the Kingdom, but dangerous if they equate Christ with the reality of the Kingdom"* (Jesus the Liberator, 108).

*"Mediation and mediator are, then, essentially related, but they are not the same thing. There is always a Moses and a promised land, and Archbishop Romero and a dream of justice. Both things, together, express the whole of the will of God, while remaining two distinct things"* (Ibidem).

On the other hand, Jesus' condition as mediator comes solely from the fact of his humanity: *"Christ does not, then, derive his possibility of being mediator from anything added to his humanity; it belongs to him by his practice of being human"* (Christ the Liberator, 135).

The Author certainly affirms a special relationship between Jesus (mediator) and the Kingdom of God (that which is mediated), in as far as Jesus is the definitive, ultimate, and eschatological mediator of the Kingdom. But, in these cited passages, Jesus and the Kingdom are distinguished in a way that the link between them is deprived of its unique and particular content. It does not correctly explain the essential nexus that exists between *mediator* and *mediation*, to use his words. In addition, by affirming that the possibility of being mediator belongs to Christ from the exercise of his humanity, he excludes the fact that his condition as Son of God has relevance for Jesus' mediatory mission.

It is insufficient to speak of an intimate connection, or of a constitutive relatedness between Jesus and the Kingdom, or of the finality of the mediator [ultimidad del mediador], if this suggests something that is distinct from Jesus himself. In a certain sense, Jesus Christ and the Kingdom are identified: in the person of Jesus the Kingdom has already been made present. This identity has been placed in relief since the patristic period.[14] In his encyclical *Redemptoris Missio*, Pope John Paul II affirms: "*The preaching of the early Church was centered on the proclamation of Jesus Christ, with whom the kingdom was identified.*"[15] "*Christ not only proclaimed the kingdom, but in him the kingdom itself became present and was fulfilled.*"[16] "*The kingdom of God is not a concept, a doctrine, or a program [ . . . ], but it is before all else a person with the face and name of Jesus of Nazareth, the image of the invisible God. If the kingdom is separated from Jesus, it is no longer the kingdom of God which he revealed.*"[17]

On the other hand, the singularity and the unicity of the mediation of Christ has always been affirmed by the Church. On account of his condition as the "only begotten Son of God," Jesus is the "definitive self-revelation of God."[18] For that reason, his mediation is unique, singular, universal, and insuperable: "*. . . one can and must say that Jesus Christ has a significance and a value for the human race and its history, which are unique and singular, proper to him alone, exclusive, universal, and absolute. Jesus is, in fact, the Word of God made man for the salvation of all.*"[19]

## V. The Self-consciousness of Jesus

8. Citing Leonardo Boff, Father Sobrino affirms that "*Jesus was an extraordinary believer and had faith. Faith was Jesus' mode of being*" (*Jesus the Liberator*, 154). And for his own part he adds: "*This faith describes the totality of the life of Jesus*" (*Ibidem*, 157). The Author justifies his position citing the text of Hebrews 12:2: "*Tersely and with a clarity unparalleled in the New Testament, the letter says that Jesus was related to the mystery of God in faith. Jesus is the one who has first and most fully lived faith (12:2)*" (*Christ the Liberator*, 136-137). He further adds: "*With regard to faith, Jesus in his life is presented as a believer like ourselves, our brother in relation to God, since he was not spared having to pass through faith. But he is also presented as an elder brother because he lived faith as its 'pioneer and perfecter' (12:2). He is the model, the one on whom we have to keep our eyes fixed in order to live out our own faith*" (*Ibidem*, 138).

These citations do not clearly show the unique singularity of the filial relationship of Jesus with the Father; indeed they tend to exclude it. Considering the whole of the New Testament it is not possible to sustain that Jesus was "a believer like ourselves." The Gospel of John speaks of Jesus' "vision" of the Father: "*Not that anyone has seen the Father except the one who is from God; he has seen the Father.*"[20] This unique and singular intimacy between Jesus and the Father is equally evident in the Synoptic Gospels.[21]

The filial and messianic consciousness of Jesus is the direct consequence of his ontology as Son of God made man. If Jesus were a believer like ourselves, albeit in an exemplary manner, he would not be able to be the true Revealer showing us the face of the Father. This point has an evident connection both with what is said above in number IV concerning the relationship between Jesus and the Kingdom, and what will be said in VI below concerning the salvific value that Jesus attributed to his death. For Father Sobrino, in fact, the unique character of the mediation and revelation of Jesus disappears: he is thus reduced to the condition of "revealer" that we can attribute to the prophets and mystics.

Jesus, the Incarnate Son of God, enjoys an intimate and immediate knowledge of his Father, a "vision" that certainly goes beyond the vision of faith. The hypostatic union and Jesus' mission of revelation and redemption require the vision of the Father and the knowledge of his plan of salvation. This is what is indicated in the Gospel texts cited above.

Various recent magisterial texts have expressed this doctrine: *"But the knowledge and love of our Divine Redeemer, of which we were the object from the first moment of His Incarnation, exceed all that the human intellect can hope to grasp. For hardly was He conceived in the womb of the Mother of God when He began to enjoy the Beatific Vision."*[22]

Though in somewhat different terminology, Pope John Paul II insists on this vision of the Father: *"His [Jesus'] eyes remain fixed on the Father. Precisely because of the knowledge and experience of the Father which he alone has, even at this moment of darkness he sees clearly the gravity of sin and suffers because of it. He alone, who sees the Father and rejoices fully in him, can understand completely what it means to resist the Father's love by sin."*[23]

Likewise, the *Catechism of the Catholic Church* speaks of the immediate knowledge which Jesus has of the Father: *"Such is first of all the case with the intimate and immediate knowledge that the Son of God made man has of his Father."*[24] *"By its union to the divine wisdom in the person of the Word incarnate, Christ enjoyed in his human knowledge the fullness of understanding of the eternal plans he had come to reveal."*[25]

The relationship between Jesus and God is not correctly expressed by saying Jesus was a believer like us. On the contrary, it is precisely the intimacy and the direct and immediate knowledge which he has of the Father that allows Jesus to reveal to men the mystery of divine love. Only in this way can Jesus bring us into divine love.

## VI. The Salvific Value of the Death of Jesus

9. In some texts some assertions of Father Sobrino make one think that, for him, Jesus did not attribute a salvific value to his own death: *"Let it be said from the start that the historical Jesus did not interpret his death in terms of salvation, in terms of soteriological models later developed by the New Testament, such as*

*expiatory sacrifice or vicarious satisfaction [ . . . ]. In other words, there are no grounds for thinking that Jesus attributed an absolute transcendent meaning to his own death, as the New Testament did later"* (*Jesus the Liberator,* 201). *"In the Gospel texts it is impossible to find an unequivocal statement of the meaning Jesus attached to his own death"* (*Ibidem,* 202). *". . . Jesus went to his death with confidence and saw it as a final act of service, more in the manner of an effective example that would motivate others than as a mechanism of salvation for others. To be faithful to the end is what it means to be human"* (*Ibidem,* 204).

This affirmation of Father Sobrino seems, at first glance, limited to the idea that Jesus did not attribute a salvific value to his death using the categories that the New Testament later employed. But later he affirms that there is in fact no data to suggest that Jesus granted an absolute transcendent sense to his own death. The Author maintains only that Jesus went to his death confidently, and attributed to it an exemplary value for others. In this way, the numerous passages in the New Testament which speak of the salvific value of the death of Christ are deprived of any reference to the consciousness of Christ during his earthly life.[26] Gospel passages in which Jesus attributes to his death a significance for salvation are not adequately taken into account; in particular, Mark 10:45,[27] *"the Son of Man did not come to be served but to serve, and to give his life as a ransom for many"*; and the words of the institution of the Eucharist: *"This is my blood of the covenant, which is poured out for many."*[28] Here again, the difficulty about Father Sobrino's use of the New Testament appears. In his writing, the New Testament data gives way to a hypothetical historical reconstruction that is erroneous.

10. The problem, however, is not simply confined to Jesus' consciousness about his death or the significance he gave to it. Father Sobrino also advances his point of view about the soteriological significance that should be attributed to the death of Christ: *"[I]ts importance for salvation consists in the fact that what God wants human beings to be has appeared on earth [ . . . ]. The Jesus who is faithful even to the cross is salvation, then, at least in this sense: he is the revelation of the homo verus, the true and complete human being, not only of the vere homo, that is of a human being in whom, as a matter of fact, all the characteristics of a true human nature are present [ . . . ]. The very fact that true humanity has been revealed, contrary to all expectations, is in itself good news and therefore is already in itself salvation [ . . . ]. On this principle, Jesus' cross as the culmination of his whole life can be understood as bringing salvation. This saving efficacy is shown more in the form of an exemplary cause than of an efficient cause. But this does not mean that it is not effective [ . . . ]. It is not efficient causality, but symbolic causality"* [*causalidad ejemplar*] (*Jesus the Liberator,* 229-230).

Of course there is great value in the efficacious example of Christ, as is mentioned explicitly in the New Testament.[29] This is a dimension of soteriology which should not be forgotten. At the same time, however, it is not possible to reduce the efficacy of the death of Jesus to that of an example or, in the words of the Author, to the appearance of the *homo verus*, faithful to God even unto the cross. In the cited text, Father Sobrino uses phrases such as "at least in this sense" and "is shown more in the form," which seem to leave the door open to other considerations. However, in the end this door is closed with an explicit negation: "it is not efficient causality but symbolic causality" [*causalidad ejemplar*]. Redemption thus seems reduced to the appearance of the *homo verus*, manifested in fidelity unto death. The death of Christ is *exemplum* and not *sacramentum* (gift). This reduces redemption to moralism. The Christological difficulties already noted in the discussion of the mystery of the Incarnation and the relationship with the Kingdom appear here anew. Only Jesus' humanity comes into play, not the Son of God made man for us and for our salvation. The affirmations of the New Testament, Tradition, and the Magisterium of the Church concerning the efficacy of the redemption and salvation brought about by Christ cannot be reduced to the good example that Jesus gives us. The mystery of the Incarnation, Death and Resurrection of Jesus, the Son of God become man, is the unique and inexhaustible font of the redemption of humanity, made efficacious in the Church through the sacraments.

The Council of Trent, in its Decree on Justification, states: "*When the blessed 'fullness of time' had come (Eph 1:10; Gal 4:4), the heavenly Father, 'the Father of all mercies and the God of all comfort' (2 Cor 1:3), sent his own Son Jesus Christ to mankind . . . to redeem the Jews, who are under the Law, and the Gentiles 'who were not pursuing righteousness' (Rom 9:30), that all 'might receive adoption as sons' (Gal 4:5). God has 'put Him forward as an expiation by His Blood, to be received by faith' (Rom 3:25), for our sins and 'not for our sins only, but also for the sins of the whole world' (1 Jn 2:2).*"[30]

This same decree affirms that the meritorious cause of justification is Jesus, the only Son of God, "*who, 'while we were still sinners' (Rom 5:10), 'out of the great love with which He loved us' (Eph 2:4) merited for us justification by His most holy passion and the wood of the cross, and made satisfaction for us to God the Father.*"[31]

The Second Vatican Council teaches: "*In the human nature united to Himself the Son of God, by overcoming death through His own death and resurrection, redeemed man and re-molded him into a new creation (cf. Gal 6:15; 2 Cor 5:17). By communicating His Spirit, Christ made His brothers, called together from all nations, mystically the components of His own Body. In that Body the life of Christ is poured into the believers who, through the sacraments, are united in a hidden and real way to Christ who suffered and was glorified.*"[32]

On this point, the *Catechism of the Catholic Church* says: "*The Scriptures had foretold this divine plan of salvation through the putting to death of 'the righteous one, my Servant' as a mystery of universal redemption, that is, as the ransom that would free men from the slavery of sin. Citing a confession of faith that he himself had 'received', St. Paul professes that 'Christ died for our sins in accordance with the scriptures' (1 Cor 15:3). In particular Jesus' redemptive death ful-*

*fils Isaiah's prophecy of the suffering Servant. Indeed Jesus himself explained the meaning of his life and death in the light of God's suffering Servant."*[33]

## Conclusion

11. Theology arises from obedience to the impulse of truth which seeks to be communicated, and from the love that desires to know ever better the One who loves—God himself—whose goodness we have recognized in the act of faith.[34] For this reason, theological reflection cannot have a foundation other than the faith of the Church. Only starting from ecclesial faith, in communion with the Magisterium, can the theologian acquire a deeper understanding of the Word of God contained in Scripture and transmitted by the living Tradition of the Church.[35]

Thus the truth revealed by God himself in Jesus Christ, and transmitted by the Church, constitutes the ultimate normative principle of theology.[36] Nothing else may surpass it. In its constant reference to this perennial spring, theology is a font of authentic newness and light for people of good will.

Theological investigation will bear ever more abundant fruit for the good of the whole People of God and all humanity, the more it draws from the living stream which—thanks to the action of the Holy Spirit—proceeds from the Apostles and has been enriched by the faithful reflection of past generations. It is the Holy Spirit who leads the Church into the fullness of truth,[37] and it is only through docility to this "gift from above" that theology is truly ecclesial and in service to the truth.

The purpose of this *Notification* is precisely to make known to all the faithful the fruitfulness of theological reflection that does not fear being developed from within the living stream of ecclesial Tradition.

*The Supreme Pontiff Benedict XVI, at the Audience granted to the undersigned Cardinal Prefect on October 13, 2006, approved this* Notification, *adopted in the Ordinary Session of this Congregation, and ordered it to be published.*

*Rome, from the Offices of the Congregation for the Doctrine of the Faith, November 26, 2006, the Feast of Christ, King of the Universe.*

**William Cardinal Levada**
*Prefect*

**Angelo Amato, S.D.B.**
Titular Archbishop of Sila
Secretary

## Notes

[1] The English translation of *Jesucristo liberador* is: *Jesus the Liberator: A Historical-Theological View* (Orbis Books, New York, 1993, 2003). All citations will be taken from the English version.

[2] The English translation of *La fe en Jesucristo* is: *Christ the Liberator: A View from the Victims* (Orbis Books, New York, 2001). All citations will be taken from the English version.

[3] Cf., for example, *infra* n. 6.

[4] Cf. Second Vatican Council Decree *Optatam Totius*, 16; John Paul II, Encyclical Letter *Fides et Ratio*, 65: AAS 91 (1999), 5-88.

[5] Cf. 1 Thes 1:10; Phil 2:5-11; 1 Cor 12:3; Rom 1:3-4, 10:9; Col 2:9, etc.

[6] Cf. Councils of Nicea, DH 125; Constantinople, DH 150; Ephesus, DH 250-263; Chalcedon, DH 301-302.

[7] Cf. DH 252-263.

[8] Chalcedon, *Symbolum Chalcedonense*, DH 301.

[9] Pius XII, Encyclical Letter *Sempiternus Rex*: AAS 43 (1951), 638; DH 3905.

[10] Council of Ephesus, *Anathematismi Cyrilli Alex.*, DH 252.

[11] *Ibidem*, DH 255.

[12] Cf. 1 Cor 12:3; Phil 2:11.

[13] Cf. 1 Cor 8:6.

[14] Cf. Origen, *In Mt. Hom.*, 14:7; Tertulian, *Adv. Marcionem*, IV 8; Hilary of Poitiers, *Com. in Mt.* 12:17.

[15] John Paul II, Encyclical Letter *Redemptoris Missio*, 16: AAS 83 (1991), 249-340.

[16] *Ibidem*, 18.

[17] *Ibidem*.

[18] *Ibidem*, 5.

[19] Congregation for the Doctrine of the Faith, Declaration *Dominus Iesus*, 15: AAS 92 (2000), 742-765.

[20] Jn 6:46; Cf. also Jn 1:18.

[21] Cf. Mt 11:25-27; Lk 10:21-22.

[22] Pius XII, Encyclical Letter *Mystici Corporis*, 75: AAS (1943) 230; DH 3812.

[23] John Paul II, Apostolic Letter *Novo Millennio Ineunte*, 26: AAS 93 (2001), 266-309.

[24] *Catechism of the Catholic Church*, 473.

[25] *Catechism of the Catholic Church*, 474.

[26] Cf., for example, Rom 3:25; 2 Cor 5:21; 1 Jn 2:2, etc.

[27] Cf. also Mt 20:28.

[28] Mk 14:24; cf. Mt 26:28; Lk 22:20.

[29] Cf. Jn 13:15; 1 Pt 2:21.

[30] Council of Trent, Decree *De justificatione*, DH 1522.

[31] *Ibidem*, DH1529; cf. DH 1560.

[32] Second Vatican Council, Dogmatic Constitution *Lumen Gentium*, 7.

[33] *Catechism of the Catholic Church*, 601.

[34] Cf. Congregation for the Doctrine of the Faith, Instruction *Donum Veritatis*, 7: AAS 82 (1990), 1550-1570.

[35] *Ibidem*, 6.

[36] *Ibidem*, 10.

[37] Cf. Jn 16:13.

# Appendix 2

*EXPLANATORY NOTE*
*on the NOTIFICATION*
*on the Works of Father Jon SOBRINO, SJ*

## 1. The Concern of the Church for the Poor

The proper function of the Congregation for the Doctrine of the Faith is the promotion and defense of doctrine on faith and morals for the whole of the Catholic world.[1] In this way, the Congregation seeks to be of service to the people of God, and particularly to the simple and poorest members of the Church. From the beginning, this preoccupation for the poor has been one of the characteristics of the Church's mission. If it is true, as the Holy Father has indicated, that "the first poverty among people is not to know Christ,"[2] then all people have the right to know the Lord Jesus, who is "the hope of the nations and the salvation of the peoples." What is more, each Christian has the right to know in an adequate, authentic, and integral manner the truth which the Church professes and expresses about Christ. This right is the foundation of the corresponding obligation of the ecclesial magisterium to intervene whenever this truth is placed in danger or negated.

It is because of this right of the faithful to the truth of Christ that this Congregation has seen the need to publish the attached *Notification* concerning some of the works of Father Jon Sobrino, SJ. These works contain propositions which are either erroneous or dangerous and may cause harm to the faithful. Father Sobrino manifests a preoccupation for the poor and oppressed, particularly in Latin America. This preoccupation certainly is shared by the whole Church. The Congregation for the Doctrine of the Faith, in its Instruction on Christian liberty and liberation *Libertatis conscientia*, indicated that "human misery [ . . . ] drew the compassion of Christ the Savior to take it upon himself and to be identified with the least of his brethren (cf. Mt 25:40, 45)" and that "The preferential option for the poor, far from being a sign of particularism or sectarianism, manifests the universality of the Church's being and mission. This option excludes no one. This is the reason why the Church cannot express this option by means of reductive sociological and ideological categories which would make this preference a partisan choice and a source of conflict." [3] Previously, this same Congregation in its Instruction on some aspects of liberation theology, *Libertatis nuntius*, observed that the warnings about this theological trend contained in that document were not able to be interpreted as a reproach to those who wish to be faithful to a "preferential option for the poor," nor could they be an excuse for those who remain indifferent to the grave problems of human misery and injustice.[4]

The citations clearly show the position of the Church with regard to this complex problem: "The evil inequities and oppression of every kind which afflict millions of men and women today openly contradict Christ's Gospel and cannot leave the conscience of any Christian indifferent. The Church, in her docility to the Spirit, goes forward faithfully along the paths to authentic liberation. Her members are aware of their failings and their delays in this quest. But a vast number of Christians, from the time of the Apostles onwards, have committed their powers and their lives to liberation from every form of oppression and to the promotion of human dignity. The experience of the saints and the example of so many works of service to one's neighbor are an incentive and a beacon for the liberating undertakings that are needed today."[5]

## 2. Procedure for Examining Doctrinal Teachings

This Notification comes as a result of a careful study of the writings of Father Sobrino according to the procedure established for the examination of doctrinal teachings. It may be helpful to explain briefly the way in which the Congregation for the Doctrine of the Faith proceeds towards a judgment on writings that appear to be problematic. When considering whether the writings of a certain Author present doctrinal difficulties or might damage the faith of the people of God, the Congregation initiates a procedure regulated by the *Agendi ratio in doctrinarum examine,* whose latest edition was approved by Pope John Paul II on 29 June 1997.[6]

The *ordinary process* entails sending the material in question to several experts for their review and opinion. The results of this, containing all the documentation required for the study of the case, is placed before the *Consulta,* a standing committee of the Congregation comprised of experts from various theological disciplines. The entire file, including the minutes of the discussion and the written opinions and evaluations of the Consulters regarding the existence of doctrinal errors or dangerous opinions in the writings, is then submitted to the *Ordinary Session* of the Congregation. This *Ordinary Session,* comprised of the Cardinals and Bishops who are members of the Congregation, undertakes a detailed examination of the entire question and decides whether or not to notify the author about the problems encountered. The decision of the *Ordinary Session* is then submitted for the approval of the *Supreme Pontiff.* Once approved, a list of erroneous propositions or dangerous opinions is sent to the Author through the Bishop or Religious Superior. The Author then has a period of three months in which to offer a reply. If the *Ordinary*

*Session* considers this reply to be sufficient, no further action is taken. If it is judged insufficient, then it must be decided what measures to adopt. One such measure would be the publication of a *Notification* which details the erroneous propositions or dangerous assertions of the Author.

When the writings of an Author are judged to be clearly in error and, at the same time, when their diffusion could present a danger or has already proven to be of grave damage to the faithful,[7] the process can be abbreviated. A *Commission* of experts is assembled and given the task of determining the erroneous propositions. The findings of this *Commission* are submitted to the *Ordinary Session* of the Congregation. In cases where the propositions are judged to be in fact erroneous and dangerous, the Congregation, after the approval of the *Holy Father*, transmits a list of these propositions through the Ordinary to the Author. The Author is then given two months in which to offer a correction or response. This response is examined by the *Ordinary Session* and the appropriate measures are taken.

## 3. The Particular Case of Father Sobrino

In the case before us now, the *Notification* itself indicates the steps that were taken according to this abbreviated *urgent examination*. This procedure was judged necessary given the wide diffusion of Father Sobrino's works, particularly in Latin America. In these works, one encounters grave deficiencies both in terms of methodology and content. Without repeating here what is treated in detail in the *Notification*, we note that among the primary methodological deficiencies of Father Sobrino is the affirmation that the "Church of the poor" is *the* ecclesial "setting" of Christology and offers it its fundamental orientation. This disregards the fact that it is only the *apostolic faith* which the Church has transmitted through all generations that constitutes the ecclesial setting of Christology and of theology in general. Father Sobrino tends to diminish the normative value of the affirmations of the New Testament as well as those of the great Councils of the early Church. These methodological errors give rise to conclusions which do not conform to the doctrine of the Church in certain key areas: the divinity of Jesus Christ, the Incarnation of the Son of God, the relationship of Jesus with the Kingdom of God, Jesus' self-consciousness, and the salvific value of Jesus' death.

In this regard, the Congregation for the Doctrine of the Faith wrote: "a theological reflection developed from a particular experience can constitute a very positive contribution, inasmuch as it makes possible a highlighting of aspects of the Word of God, the richness of which had not yet been fully grasped. But in order that this reflection may be truly a reading of the Scripture and not a projection on to the Word of God of a meaning which it does not contain, the theologian will be careful to interpret the experience from which he begins in the light of the experience of the Church herself. This experience of the Church shines with a singular brightness and in all its purity in the lives of the saints. It pertains to the pastors of the Church, in communion with the Successor of Peter, to discern its authenticity."[8]

It is hoped that this *Notification* will offer to both the pastors and to the faithful of the Church a secure basis, founded upon the doctrine of the Church, upon which to judge these questions, which are relevant both for theology and pastoral practice.

## Notes

[1] Cf. John Paul II, Apostolic Constitution *Pastor Bonus*, 48: AAS 80 (1988), 841-934.

[2] Benedict XVI, *Lenten Message 2006*.

[3] Congregation for the Doctrine of the Faith, Instruction *Libertatis conscientia*, 68: *AAS* 79 (1987), 554-599.

[4] Congregation for the Doctrine of the Faith, Instruction *Libertatis nuntius, Proemio:AAS* 76 (1984), 876-909.

[5] Congregation for the Doctrine of the Faith, Instruction *Libertatis conscientia*, 57.

[6] Congregation for the Doctrine of the Faith, *Agendi ratio in doctrinarum examine:* AAS 89 (1997), 830-835.

[7] Cf. *Ibidem*, 23.

[8] Congregation for the Doctrine of the Faith, Instruction *Libertatis conscientia*, 70.

# Contributors

**J. Matthew Ashley** is associate professor of systematic theology at the University of Notre Dame. He received his Ph.D. in theology from the University of Chicago Divinity School. He has written *Interruptions: Mysticism, Politics and Theology in the Work of Johann Baptist Metz* (Notre Dame, Ind.: University of Notre Dame Press, 1998); "The Turn to Apocalyptic and the Option for the Poor in Christian Theology: A Response to David Tracy," in *The Option for the Poor in Christian Theology,* ed. Daniel Groody, C.S.C. (Notre Dame, Ind.: University of Notre Dame Press, 2007); and "Religion, Spirituality and Church: The Case of Oscar Romero," *The Way* 44, no. 2 (April 2005): 113-33.

**Dean Brackley, S.J.,** is a professor of theology at the Universidad Centroamericana (UCA) in El Salvador, Central America. He received his Ph.D. from the University of Chicago. His published works include *Divine Revolution: Salvation and Liberation in Catholic Thought* (Maryknoll, N.Y.: Orbis Books, 1996); and *The Call to Discernment in Troubled Times: New Perspectives on the Transformative Wisdom of Ignatius Loyola* (New York: Crossroad, 2004).

**James T. Bretzke, S.J.,** is professor in the Department of Theology and Religious Studies at the University of San Francisco, where he teaches moral theology. He is the author of *A Morally Complex World: Engaging Contemporary Moral Theology* (Collegeville, Minn.: Liturgical Press, 2004).

**Lisa Sowle Cahill** is the J. Donald Monan Professor of Theology at Boston College. She received her Ph.D. from the University of Chicago. She has served as president of the Catholic Theological Society of America and the Society of Christian Ethics. She addressed the political implications of Christology in "The Atonement Paradigm," *Theological Studies* 68, no. 2 (2007). Her most recent book is *Theological Bioethics* (Washington, D.C.: Georgetown University Press, 2005).

**Jorge Costadoat, S.J.,** is the director of the Centro Teológico Manuel Larraín (2005-2007), professor of theology at the Catholic University of Chile, and coordinator of the Theological Commission of the Society of Jesus in Latin America. His publications include "La hermenéutica en las teologías contextuales de la liberación," *Teología y Vida* 46 (2005); "Pietas et eruditio en Alberto Hurtado

271

S.J.," *Teología y vida* 46 (2005); and "Centro Teológico Manuel Larraín: Interpretación teológica del presente," *Teología y Vida* 46 (2005): 503-9.

**Paul G. Crowley, S.J.**, is professor of theology and chair of the Religious Studies Department at Santa Clara University. He holds a Ph.D. from the Graduate Theological Union, Berkeley. His publications include *In Ten Thousand Places: Dogma in a Pluralistic Church* (New York: Crossroad/Herder, 1997); *Unwanted Wisdom: Suffering, the Cross and Hope* (New York: Continuum, 2005); and *Rahner beyond Rahner: A Twentieth Century Theological Giant Meets the Pacific Rim* (Lanham, Md.: Rowman & Littlefield/Sheed & Ward, 2005).

**Joseph Curran** is assistant professor and chair of the Department of Religious Studies at Misericordia University in Dallas, Pennsylvania. He received his Ph.D. in theological ethics from Boston College. His research interests include Catholic social teaching and Catholicism in American political life.

**Roberto S. Goizueta** is professor of theology at Boston College. He earned his Ph.D. from Marquette University. He is a past president of the Catholic Theological Society of America and the Academy of Catholic Hispanic Theologians of the United States. His book *Caminemos con Jesús: Toward a Hispanic/Latino Theology of Accompaniment* won a Catholic Press Association Book Award. He co-edited, with Justo L. Gonzales and Eldin Villafane, *Hispanic Christian Thought at the Dawn of the 21st Century: Apuntes in Honor of Justo L. Gonzalez* (Nashville: Abingdon, 2005). The *National Catholic Reporter* has named him one of the ten most influential Hispanic American educators, pastors, and theologians.

**Daniel J. Harrington, S.J.**, is professor of New Testament at the Boston College School of Theology and Ministry and is the editor of *New Testament Abstracts*. His recent books include *What Are We Hoping For? New Testament Images* (Collegeville, Minn: Liturgical Press, 2006); and *Jesus: A Historical Portrait* (Cincinnati: St. Anthony Messenger, 2007).

**Kenneth R. Himes, O.F.M.**, currently serves as chairman of the theology department at Boston College. He received his Ph.D. in religion and public policy from Duke University. He is a past president of the Catholic Theological Society of America and was chief editor of *Modern Catholic Social Teaching: Commentaries and Interpretations* (Washington, D.C.: Georgetown University Press, 2005). He is the author of *Responses to 101 Questions on Catholic Social Teaching* (Mahwah, N.J.: Paulist Press, 2001); and co-author (with Michael J. Himes) of *Fullness of Faith: The Public Significance of Theology* (Mahwah, N.J.: Paulist Press, 1991).

**James F. Keenan, S.J.**, is professor of theological ethics at Boston College. He received a doctorate from the Gregorian University. He edited *Practice What You Preach: Virtues, Ethics and Power in the Lives of Pastoral Ministers and Their Congregations* (Lanham, Md.: Sheed & Ward, 2000), which won the Catholic Press Award for best work in pastoral theology, and his edited volume *Catholic Ethicists on HIV/AIDS Prevention* (New York: Continuum, 2000) won the best work in ethics from the Jesuit Honor Society, Alpha Sigma Nu (2003). His most recent book is *The Works of Mercy: The Heart of Catholicism*, 2d ed. (Lanham, Md.: Sheed & Ward, 2007).

**Thomas M. Kelly** is associate professor of theology at Creighton University in Omaha, Nebraska. He received his Ph.D. from Boston College. He is the author of *Theology at the Void: The Retrieval of Experience* (Notre Dame, Ind.: University of Notre Dame Press, 2002); and "Sacramentality and Social Mission: A New Way to Imagine Marriage," in *Marriage in the Catholic Tradition*, ed. Todd A. Salzman, Thomas M. Kelly, and John J. O'Keefe (New York: Crossroad Publishing, 2004), 144-53.

**William Loewe** is an associate professor of theology at the Catholic University of America, where he teaches Christology and soteriology. He earned a doctorate in systematic theology from Marquette University. He is the author of *The College Student's Introduction to Christology* (Wilmington, Del.: Michael Glazier, 1996); co-editor of *Jesus Crucified and Risen: Essays in Honor of Dom Sebastian Moore* (Collegeville, Minn.: Liturgical Press, 1998); and, with Carol Dempsey, *Theology and Sacred Scripture* (Maryknoll, N.Y.: Orbis Books, 2002).

**Rafael Luciani** is associate professor of the faculty of theology at the Jesuit Universidad Católica Andrés Bello of Caracas, where he teaches Christology, the mystery of God, and theological method. He received his doctorate at the Gregorian University. His publications include *Despertar a la abundancia de la vida* (Caracas: Ediciones Paulinas, 2000), *El misterio de la diferencia: La analogía como estructura originaria de la realidad en Tomás de Aquino, Erich Przywara y Hans Urs von Baltasar y su uso en teología trinitaria* (Rome: Analecta Gregoriana, Pontificia Universitas Gregoriana, 2002); "El Jesús histórico como norma hermenéutica para la teología y criterio para ser testigos en el seguimiento," *ITER Teología* 37 (2005); and "Seguidores y Discípulos del Reino en la praxis fraterna del Jesús Histórico. Un Maestro y muchos hermanos," *ITER Teología* 43 (2007).

**William O'Neill, S.J.**, is associate professor of social ethics at the Jesuit School of Theology at Berkeley and the Graduate Theological Union. He received a doctorate from Yale University. He is author of *The Ethics of Our Climate:*

*Hermeneutics and Ethical Theory* (Washington, D.C.: Georgetown University Press, 1994). Recent publications include "Rights of Passage: The Ethics of Forced Displacement," *Journal of the Society of Christian Ethics* (2007); "Neither Thick Nor Thin: Politics and Polity in the Ethics of Margaret A. Farley," in *A Just and True Love*, ed. Maura Ryan and Brian Linnane, S.J. (Notre Dame, Ind.: University of Notre Dame Press, 2007); and, with Aquiline Tarimo, S.J., "What San Salvador Says to Nairobi: The Liberation Ethics of Ignacio Ellacuría," in *Love That Produces Hope*, ed. Kevin Burke and Robert Lassalle-Klein (Collegeville, Minn.: Liturgical Press, 2006).

**Félix Palazzi** is professor of the faculty of theology at the Jesuit Universidad Católica Andrés Bello of Caracas, where he teaches theological anthropology, the theology of grace, eschatology, and Mariology. His publications include *La Tierra en el cielo* (Caracas: Ediciones Paulinas—Publicaciones Universidad Católica Andrés Bello, 2007); and "El laico como signo del Misterio en el mundo y en la Iglesia," *ITER Teología* 40 (2006): 145-54.

**Margaret R. Pfeil** is an assistant professor of moral theology at the University of Notre Dame. She earned a Ph.D. from Notre Dame. Her publications include "Whose Justice? Which Relationality?" in *Just Policing, Not War: An Alternative Response to World Violence*, ed. Gerald W. Schlabach (Collegeville, Minn.: Liturgical Press, 2007), 111-29; "Liturgy and Ethics: The Liturgical Asceticism of Energy Conservation," *Journal of the Society of Christian Ethics* 27, no. 2 (Fall/Winter 2007); and "True Peace: The Power of Solidarity," *New Theology Review* (February 2007): 61-70.

**Stephen J. Pope** is professor of theology at Boston College, where he teaches Christian ethics. He received his Ph.D. from the University of Chicago. He is the author of *The Evolution of Altruism and the Ordering of Love* (Washington, D.C.: Georgetown University Press, 1994); and *Human Evolution and Christian Ethics* (Cambridge: Cambridge University Press, 2007); and the editor of *The Ethics of Aquinas* (Washington, D.C.: Georgetown University Press, 2003).

# Index